Computing Fundamentals
with C#

Martin Stepp
University of Washington, Tacoma

Rick Mercer
University of Arizona

Franklin, Beedle & Associates, Inc.
8536 SW St. Helens Drive, Suite D
Wilsonville, Oregon 97070
503-682-7668
www.fbeedle.com

*To my parents, Vicki and Larry Stepp, for teaching by
example; my love and respect to you always.*

—*M.S.*

*To my family, for understanding:
Diane, Chelsea, Austen, and Kieran.*

—*R.M.*

President and Publisher	Jim Leisy (jimleisy@fbeedle.com)
Production	Tom Sumner
	Jeni Lee
	Dean Lake

Printed in the U.S.A.

Rights and Permissions
Franklin, Beedle & Associates, Incorporated
8536 SW St. Helens Drive, Suite D
Wilsonville, Oregon 97070

Library of Congress Cataloging-in-Publication Data

Stepp, Martin.
  Computing fundamentals with C# / Martin Stepp, Rick Mercer.
    p. cm.
  Includes index.
  ISBN 1-887902-52-X
1. C# (Computer program language) I. Mercer, Rick II. Title.
  QA76.73.C154S74 2004
  005.13'3--dc22

                              2004023340

Contents

Preface

This textbook was written for a university-level CS1 introductory computer science course. It is appropriate for students with little or no programming background. Students with programming experience in other languages could also use this textbook to learn C#. It was developed for courses where students had a wide variety of programming experiences, from zero to many years in other programming languages.

After completing the first seven chapters, you should be comfortable with traditional programming concepts such as problem solving, control structures (selection and repetition), methods (functions), parameters, and arrays. You will also have learned the main concepts of object-oriented programming, such as partitioning systems into objects, message passing, and building classes. You will be able to write programs that use existing C# classes from the .NET Framework and classes you write on your own for a particular application. Design issues are interwoven in the form of algorithmic patterns and object-oriented design guidelines.

This textbook recognizes the relevance and validity of object-oriented programming and design, but not at the expense of traditional computing fundamentals. Many of the projects in this textbook involve creating and using objects, but objects and classes are not created on a whim or without good reason. The authors feel that—like many things in computer science—objects appear useful and clear to most students only if they are used in relevant and illustrative examples. The focus of the material in this text is on sound algorithmic and programming practice, encouraging critical thinking and reasoning to solve useful problems; it is not on detailed design of classes simply for the sake of doing so. The carefully maintained balance between object methodology and traditional programming used in this book highlights that objects are a vehicle for solving problems and are not themselves the answer.

Chapters 8 and above provide additional optional material sometimes presented in a first programming course. Chapter 8, "File Input/Output (I/O) and Exceptions," explains how to enhance programs' usefulness and interactivity by enabling them to manipulate files on the local machine. Chapter 8 also introduces the basics of C#'s exception handling mechanism for dealing with unexpected failures in file processing and other tasks. Chapter 9, "Recursion," introduces the concept of recursion and shows how recursive functions are used in programming.

Chapter 10, "Graphical User Interfaces," introduces techniques and classes in the .NET Framework that can be used to present rich graphical interfaces to the user. This chapter also shows the development of a relatively complex object-oriented system built upon material presented in previous chapters. This extended study provides the opportunity for understanding object-oriented programming in C# on a larger scale. The bank teller system directly uses many standard C# classes plus several classes written specifically for this application.

This textbook builds on over twenty years of the authors' combined experience in computer science education. Its style and approach are the result of the courses taught, conferences attended, instructors and educators consulted, textbooks and learning materials examined, and reasoning performed about how best to design the first course in the computer science curriculum. The book blends the critical need to teach sound fundamental programming and algorithmic skills with a solid integration of modern conventions such as object-oriented programming and design.

Features

○ **Focus on Traditional Topics.** This textbook recognizes the relevance and validity of object-oriented programming but does not sacrifice traditional topics such as problem solving, design, control structures, and arrays. The authors believe that the current trend of object-oriented programming has at times reduced the focus on key topics such as these in modern computer science texts. One of the foremost goals of this book is to cover object-oriented programming and concepts in the context of solving interesting problems, while not allowing objects to detract from the core task of doing useful computation.

○ **Flexible Objects-Early Approach.** The first three chapters of this textbook present the basics of programming and how to use several C# objects. This approach benefits from C#'s largely consistent object model, which treats primitive data similar to complex objects. Chapter 4 shows how classes are built; this allows selection and repetition to be studied in the context of methods in classes that are part of a larger system. This approach covers traditional topics such as methods, parameters, selection, loops, and arrays as would be expected in books that are not object-oriented. Along the way, students are introduced some useful implementation of object-oriented programming: to partition systems intelligently into objects and to encapsulate behavior and state, for example. This objects-early approach lets readers become comfortable using classes and later implementing small systems of two or three classes, building up to the bank teller case study at the end of the text, which uses over 20 different types of objects. In this way, students can more easily see the big picture, and why it is beneficial to use and create rich objects and classes. However, in consideration for instructors who wish to avoid teaching objects early, Chapter 4, "Classes," has been kept independent from the chapters after it as much as possible, and indeed may be covered after completing Chapter 5, "Selection," Chapter 6, "Repetition," and much of Chapter 7, "Arrays," if so desired.

○ **Carefully Chosen Subset of C# and .NET Framework.** Because students might have little or no programming experience, this textbook concentrates on a small subset of C#'s feature-rich language and platform. In particular, since the .NET Framework contains thousands of classes, an examination of more than a small fraction of them would be overwhelming to an introductory student. Therefore, the exercises in this textbook concentrate on gaining a deep understanding of a carefully selected few classes from the .NET Framework particularly suited to the tasks at hand. A half dozen C# classes that manage text strings, numbers, calendar dates, and interacting with files provide glimpses into the power of having a large, readily available standard library of classes. In later chapters, a mere eight C# classes and events provide a base for event-driven programming with graphical user interfaces.

○ **Algorithmic Patterns.** Algorithmic patterns help beginning programmers design algorithms around a set of common algorithm ideas. The first algorithmic pattern, Input/Process/Output, is introduced in Chapter 1 and reused in subsequent chapters. The Input/Process/Output pattern is especially useful for readers with no programming experience and to lab assistants who may be helping them. Other algorithmic patterns include the Guarded Action pattern in Chapter 5, "Selection," and the Indeterminate Loop pattern in Chapter 6, "Repetition." The patterns are revisited as needed, such as in Chapter 10, "Graphical User Interfaces," when it is shown that a graphical interface performs the Input/Process/Output pattern in a very similar way to the console.

○ **Event-Driven Programming the C# Way.** Chapter 10 presents the C# event model using delegates. The small subset of graphical components (`Button`, `Label`, `TextBox`, `Frame`, etc.), along with the `EventHandler` delegate, allow students to build some small modern day programs. Instructors can also use these as a base to add other events and controls. This textbook shows how C# does event-driven programming. Despite the inherent complexity of graphical programming, the authors have found that students often enjoy overcoming its challenges, even at an early point in their programming education. Also, most students have no more trouble creating graphical controls and C#'s event model than they do with other traditional topics. Because there is a small subset of graphical components and only one event handler, after two or three tries students understand the C# event model in a focused way that can be used repeatedly as a pattern for building event-driven programs with a graphical user interface. This textbook does not attempt to hide the C# event model with reliance on a particular development environment or on author-provided non-standard classes. C# consistently uses the same design to handle many other events such as mouse clicks and menu selections. Once one event handler is mastered, others are more easily understood. Since some instructors do not wish to introduce graphical interfaces to their students, this optional chapter appears late in the textbook, and only the graphical bank teller implementation depends on it.

❍ **Environment-Agnostic.** This textbook does not embrace or require any particular editing environment or platform. The authors are aware that Microsoft's own Visual Studio .NET is likely to be the most common editor used. However, in the educational environment, funding and laboratory software constraints are sometimes hard to predict. We felt that allowing for any editor or operating system would give the textbook maximum flexibility and compatibility with a variety of teaching styles and environments.

❍ **Adaptation from Java Textbook and Experience.** This book started as an adaptation of Rick Mercer's *Computing Fundamentals with Java*. The Java textbook was used in 11 courses at Penn State University and the University of Arizona from the summer of 1998 through the fall of 2001, being used by more than 1400 students. The extensive development and revision of the Java book provided a solid base for this C# textbook. However, naturally this book took on a life of its own, and is not by any means a duplication of the Java text. The authors have made extensive effort to incorporate the useful new features and libraries of C#, which has benefited the book's educational philosophy.

Pedagogy

This textbook has many pedagogical features that have made this introduction to programming, design, and object technology accessible to students.

❍ **Self-Check Questions.** These short questions allow students to evaluate whether or not they understand the details and terms presented in the reading. The answers to all self-check questions are located at the end of the book.

❍ **Exercises.** These transitional problems examine the major concepts presented in the chapter. Answers to all exercises are in the instructor's manual.

○ **General Forms.** The authors firmly believe that students learn very little by memorizing incantations and specific examples. To further aid student understanding of which parts of a program must be written as-is and which are free to be modified, all major topics and C# constructs are introduced through General Forms such as this one:

General Form 4.2: Field

private *type field-name;*

-or-

private *type field-name* = *initial-value;*

Examples:

```
private string name;
private double balance = 0.00;
```

○ **Programming Tips.** Each set of chapter programming projects is preceded by a set of programming tips intended to help students complete programs, warn of potential pitfalls, and promote good programming habits.

○ **Patterns.** At appropriate points in each chapter, algorithmic or design patterns are introduced to give the students sound fundamentals about how to decompose a problem and implement an intelligent solution to it. This is done on several levels— from smart algorithm design and good practices within a particular function to class and object-oriented design—to create well-encapsulated and intelligent objects. The following is an example algorithmic pattern:

Algorithmic Pattern 1.1

Pattern: Input/Process/Output (IPO)

Problem: The program requires input from the user in order to compute and display the desired information.

Outline: 1. Obtain the input data.
            2. Process the data in some meaningful way.
            3. Output the results.

○ **Programming Projects.** Many relatively small-scale problems have been extensively lab tested to ensure that projects can be assigned and completed with little or no instructor intervention. Chapter 1 has analysis and design projects that can be completed without a computer. Every other chapter has a set of programming projects representing a wide range of difficulty. Students typically complete from one to four programming projects per week in an acceptable amount of time. Homework assignments can be built from individual or multiple programming projects, easing classroom administration. Virtually all of the programming projects were assigned and successfully completed by students over the past 12 years.

Chapter Outlines

Chapter 1: Program Development is intended for students who have never written a computer program. However, students with some experience might appreciate the introduction to algorithmic patterns presented here. The Input/Process/Output pattern presented applies to simple text-based programs. Input/Process/Output also applies to event-driven programs with graphical user interfaces presented in Chapter 10. This chapter does not try to present the history of computers, binary number representation, definitions of the Web, networking, operating systems, and so on. While many introductory CS1 books do such an introduction, the authors have instead chosen to begin by concentrating on the process of writing computer programs while suggesting useful steps of problem analysis and design that can be done before going to the computer.

Chapter 2: An Introduction to C# introduces the low-level programming constructs such as primitive types, tokens, variables, expressions and statements, numerical computation and conversion, and console input and output. Students are also introduced to basic errors their programs can produce and ways to detect and correct them.

Chapter 3: Using Objects shows how to use objects of existing classes and presents the notion of objects and how to interact with them. The first class introduced is the author-supplied class `BankAccount`. Subsequently, several classes from the .NET Framework are introduced: `string`, `Random`, and `DateTime`. As is done throughout this textbook, students are encouraged to view object-oriented programs as a collection of objects that send messages to each other. By introducing a few interesting and easy-to-use C# classes, the first signs of something bigger arise.

Chapter 4: Classes shows how to implement C# classes. Fields, properties, constructors, and methods are introduced in the context of building a class. At the end of this chapter most students should see that object-oriented programs are about more than one object interacting with others—one program is more than just one class. Since this chapter is the first example of implementing new classes of one's own, this is where principles of object-oriented design are introduced. As in all chapters, programming projects offer the opportunity to implement and test one class, or to build a project using more than one class. In most cases, students are also using one or more existing .NET Framework classes.

Chapter 5: Selection is a traditional introduction to selection patterns and the C# constructs that provide solutions to problems where choices have to be made. Boolean logic is introduced and used to provide guarded action, if/else selection, and multiple selection using nested if/else statements.

Chapter 6: Repetition introduces repetition patterns and the C# constructs that provide the solutions to problems requiring repetition. This is a traditional chapter on repetitive control structures.

Chapter 7: Arrays introduces single-dimension array objects. This is a traditional chapter on arrays. Also introduced is a collection class that reinforces the use of an array instance variable.

Chapter 8: File Input/Output (I/O) and Exceptions provides an introduction to some of the C# stream classes for disk input and output. The second section presents exception handling in C#, which is often important when doing I/O to handle unexpected errors. The material in this chapter is also useful for the bank teller case study because it includes a section on object serialization, which can be used to make the objects in the bank teller system persistent.

Chapter 9: Recursion introduces the concept of recursion, recursive solutions that also have iterative solutions, and examples of backtracking. This chapter can be presented any time after the Arrays chapter.

Chapter 10: Graphical User Interfaces introduces event-driven programming with a graphical user interface. Because of the large scope of graphical programming, only a few important controls such as Button and TextBox are shown. The basics of creating a window and controls—and positioning those controls in the window—are shown with examples and illustrations. This chapter also introduces delegates and events so that the graphical programs the students create can respond to user actions.

Concept Summary by Chapter

Chapter Dependencies

This book can certainly be read linearly start to finish, and it is quite effective when used this way. However, there are several acceptable ways to order the topics and chapters other than covering the chapters in their original order. The dependencies between the chapters are summarized by the following chart and details below:

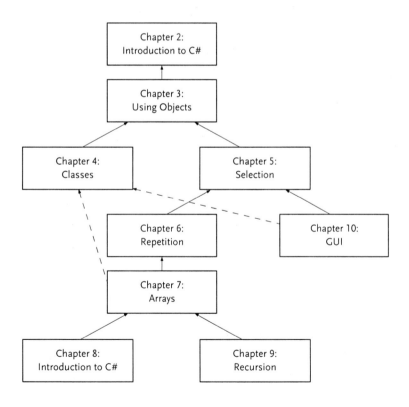

Here are some observations about the above chart:

❍ Chapters 2–7 present the core of the material of the textbook, with Chapters 8–10 providing advanced topics such as file I/O, recursion, and graphical interfaces.

❍ For instructors who prefer a more traditional topic order and want to avoid introducing objects early, Chapter 4, "Classes," may be pushed back until after Chapters 5, "Selection," and 6, "Repetition." (It may still be useful to cover Section 4.6 on writing static methods, as these are used in later chapters such as Chapter 7, "Arrays.")

❍ Instructors who wish to teach graphical interfaces and events may choose to do so as early as after Chapter 5, "Selection," or not at all.

❍ Chapters 8, "File Input / Output (I/O)," 9, "Recursion," and 10, "Graphical User Interfaces," may be presented in any order after the core chapters 2–7 have been completed.

Source Code

All C# source code from the textbook can be downloaded from the following URL: **www.fbeedle.com/csharp/code.exe**. When you execute this file, the code extracts into into a folder for each chapter. Some of these chapter folders hold files that will help to complete programming assignments. The root folder on the disk has the files common to many programming projects, such as `BankAccount.cs`.

Instructor's Manual

The instructor's manual is available as a CD to teachers who adopt this textbook. The CD includes the following items:

❍ Solutions to all programming projects.

❍ Answers to the all exercises.

❍ Teaching Suggestions for each chapter.

❍ Multiple versions of exams as used at the University of Arizona.

❍ Lecture notes for each chapter as Microsoft PowerPoint slides.

To obtain a copy of the CD, contact the publisher, Franklin, Beedle and Associates, at this Web site:

http://www.fbeedle.com

Acknowledgments

Critical feedback from students, teaching assistants, and other interested people is essential. Since moving to Arizona from Penn State in the fall of 1998, the authors have had the pleasure of working with many bright and highly motivated undergraduate section leaders and assistants. The section leader program at the University of Arizona has undergraduates leading recitation sections and helping to teach large classes. We would like to acknowledge and thank the students and the section leaders who have provided feedback for CSC courses 127A, 127B, 227, and 335 at the University of Arizona from Fall 1998 through Fall 2004.

The team at Franklin, Beedle & Associates gave a great deal of enthusiasm and energy in the development of this textbook. The authors thank the folks at FBA for their support and expertise in making this all possible: Jim Leisy, Tom Sumner, Dean Lake, Chris Collier, and Krista Brown.

In our teaching ventures, we have been fortunate to encounter many excellent educators from academia and industry who care about the same issues and think about them carefully. The debates and new ideas generated in discussions, both live and by e-mail, have allowed for the plethora of informed decisions necessary for producing a high-quality textbook. The authors wish to acknowledge the following people (listed in reverse alphabetical order) for their dedication, insights, and willingness to make things better: Suzanne Westbrook, Gene Wallingford, Dave West, Stuart Reges, Rich Pattis, Jim Leisy, Adele Goldberg, Mike Feldman, Ed Epp, Jutta Eckstein, Dwight Duego, Robert Duvall, Alistair Cockburn, Mike Clancy, Alyce Brady, Robert Biddle, Joe Bergin, Owen Astrachan, and Erzebet Angster.

We would also like to acknowledge the many authors and presenters who have influenced us with their opinions, creativity, and technical accuracy during our combined 22 years of computer science education experience.

Reviewers spend countless hours poring over material with critical eyes and useful comments. Because of the high quality of their work, criticisms and recommendations were always considered seriously.

<table>
<tr><td>Martin Stepp</td><td>Rick Mercer</td></tr>
<tr><td>Tacoma, Washington</td><td>Tucson, Arizona</td></tr>
<tr><td>stepp@u.washington.edu</td><td>mercer@cs.arizona.edu</td></tr>
</table>

Program Development

Coming Up

First, there is a need for a computer-based solution to a problem. The need may be expressed in a few sentences as a *problem specification*. The progression from understanding a problem specification to achieving a working computer-based solution is known as "program development." After studying this chapter, you will be able to:

- ○ apply a program development strategy to create complete programs.
- ○ understand the characteristics of a good *algorithm* (steps to solve a problem).
- ○ understand how algorithmic patterns can help in program design.
- ○ provide a deliverable from the analysis phase of program development.
- ○ provide a deliverable from the design phase of program development.

1

1.1   Program Development

A *program* is a set of instructions for a computer to perform. The goal of this textbook is to teach you techniques and fundamentals for writing programs. The practice of creating programs, from the initial idea to the final product, is called *program development*.

There are many approaches to program development. This chapter begins by examining a strategy with these three steps: analysis, design, and implementation.

Phase of Program	Development Activity
Analysis	Understand the problem.
Design	Develop a solution.
Implementation	Make the solution run on a computer.

Our study of computing fundamentals begins with an example of this particular approach to program development. Each of these three phases will be exemplified with a simple case study—one particular problem. Emphasis is placed on the *deliverables*—the tangible results—of each phase.

Here is a preview of the deliverables for each of the three stages:

Phase	Deliverable
Analysis	A document that lists the data that store relevant information.
Design	An algorithm that outlines a solution.
Implementation	A program ready to be used by the customer (or to be graded!).

Self-Check

1-1   What deliverable can you expect at the end of a successfully completed college career?

Analysis

Synonyms for analysis: inquiry, examination, study

Program development begins with a study, or *analysis*, of a problem. Obviously, to determine what a program is to do, you must first understand the problem. If the problem is written down, you can begin the analysis phase by simply reading the problem.

While analyzing the problem, you will find it helpful to name the data that represent the information. For example, you might be asked to compute the maximum weight allowed for successful liftoff of a particular airplane from a given runway under certain thrust-affecting weather conditions, such as temperature and wind direction. While analyzing the problem specification, you might name the desired information `maximumWeight`. The data required to compute that information could have names such as `temperature` and `windDirection`.

Although such data do not represent the entire solution, they do represent an important piece of the puzzle. The data names are symbols for what the program will need and what it will compute. One value needed to compute `maximumWeight` might be 19.0 for temperature.

Such data values must often be manipulated—or processed—in a variety of ways to produce the desired result. Some values must be obtained from the user, other values must be multiplied or added, and still other values must be displayed on the screen.

At some point, these data values will be stored in computer memory. Each value stays in the same memory location and can change while the program is running. The values also have a type, such as integers or numbers with decimal points (these different types of values are stored differently in memory). These named pieces of memory that store a specific type of value, which can change while a program is running, are known as *variables*.

You will see that there also are operations for manipulating those values in meaningful ways. It helps to distinguish data that it displays *output* from the data required to compute that result—*input*. The variables (the named places of memory) store values as the program carries out its operations.

Input and Output

Output	Information the computer must display.
Input	Information a user must supply to solve a problem.

To understand a problem, you must answer this question: What should be the output, given certain input? To figure out the answer, it is a good idea to plan out the problem with pencil and paper.

Here are two problems with variable names selected to accurately describe the stored values:

Problem 1: Analysis Deliverable			
Problem	**Data Name**	**Input or Output**	**Example**
Compute a	amount	Input	12500.00
monthly loan	rate	Input	0.08
payment	months	Input	48
	payment	Output	303.14

Problem 2: Analysis Deliverable			
Problem	**Data Name**	**Input or Output**	**Example**
Count how often	aBardsWork	Input	Much Ado About Nothing
Shakespeare wrote	theWord	Input	the
a particular word	howOften	Output	220
in a particular play			

In summary, you analyze a problem by doing these things:

1. Read and understand the problem specification.
2. Decide what data represent the answer—the output.
3. Decide what data the user must enter to get the answer—the input.
4. Create a document (like those above) that summarizes the analysis. This document is the input for the next phase of program development—design.

In textbook problems, the variable names and type of values that must be input and output (such as integers or numbers with a decimal point) are sometimes provided. If not, they are relatively easy to recognize. In real-world problems of significant scale, a great deal of effort is expended during the analysis phase. The next subsection provides an analysis of a small problem.

Self-Check

1-2   Given the problem of converting British pounds to U.S. dollars, name a value that must be input by the user, and a value that must be output.

1-3   Given the problem of selecting one CD from a 200-compact-disc player, what name might represent all of the CDs? What name might be appropriate to represent one particular CD selected by the user?

Example of Analysis

Problem: Using the following grade assessment scale:

Grade	Percentage of Final Grade
Test 1	25%
Test 2	25%
Final Exam	50%

Compute a course grade as a weighted average of two tests and one final exam. The dialogue must look exactly like this for the given input of 74.0, 79.0, and 84.0:

```
Enter first test: 74.0
Enter second test: 79.0
Enter final exam: 84.0
Course Grade: 80.25%
```

Start your analysis by reading the problem specification. Then, decide on the desired output, and the required input, to solve the problem. Determining and naming the output is a good place to start. The output stores the answer to the problem. It provides insight into what the program must do. After you have determined the need for a data value, and have given it a meaningful name, you can focus on what you need to do. For this problem, the desired output is the course grade (80.25% above). You might use the name courseGrade for the information to be output.

A complete analysis might answer other questions, such as:

○ What happens when the user enters non-numeric data?
○ Is it okay to enter 74 instead of 74.0?
○ Is 74.5 okay as input? What about 74.6?

To keep this example short, those issues will not be dealt with here.

This program must be able to calculate a final grade for one student, based on two tests and one final exam, each with a particular weight. But it is best if a program can be generalized to handle other circumstances. That way, it could be used later to compute course grades for many students with any set of grades.

Let's decide on, and create names for, the values that must be input. To determine courseGrade, three values are required: test1, test2, and finalExam.

The first three analysis activities are now complete. We understand:

1. The problem itself.
2. The information to be output: courseGrade.
3. The data to be input: test1, test2, and finalExam.

However, we do not have a sample problem yet. Many problem specifications in this textbook provide a sample dialogue that summarizes the input given by the user and the output that the user will see. User input will appear in boldface italic (74.0, for example). Everything else is program output.

Sample dialogues provide another important benefit. They show an answer (such as 80.25%) for one particular set of inputs. The early part of this book includes sample dialogues, to help introduce new concepts. When a problem does not have a sample dialogue, you should supply additional sample problems—at least one or two. If there is no dialogue, you should write down something similar—a combination of the input data and the output that is expected from it.

To create this courseGrade problem, you must understand the difference between a simple average and a weighted average. Because the three input items count for different amounts of the final grade (either 25% or 50%), you will need to compute a weighted average. If each test is weighted equally, the simple average of the set consisting of 74.0, 79.0, and 84.0 is 79.0. However, the weighted average computes differently. Recall that test1 and test2 are each worth 25%, and finalExam weighs in at 50%. When test1 is 74.0, test2 is 79.0, and finalExam is 84.0, the weighted average computes to 80.25, as shown below:

```
(0.25 x test1) + (0.25 x test2) + (0.50 x finalExam)
(0.25 x 74.0)  +  (0.25 x 79.0) +   (0.50 x 84.0)
   18.50       +     19.75      +      42.00
                  = 80.25
```

With the same exact grades, the weighted average of 80.25 is different from the simple average (79.0). If the program does not follow the problem specification, students may receive grades lower, or higher, than they actually deserve.

We have now analyzed the program, have named the input and output, and understand what the computer-based solution must do. We have also seen one sample problem. The following deliverable from the analysis phase summarizes these activities:

	Course-Grade Problem Analysis Deliverable		
Problem	Data Name	Input or Output	Sample
Compute a course grade	test1	Input	74.0
	test2	Input	79.0
	finalExam	Input	84.0
	courseGrade	Output	80.25

This is the first deliverable. The next section presents a method for designing a solution. During the design phase, we will concentrate on placing the appropriate activities in the proper order to solve the problem.

Self-Check

1-4   Complete an analysis deliverable for the following problem:

Problem: Compute the distance traveled for any moving vehicle. Allow the user to choose the unit of measurement (meters per second, miles per hour, or kilometers per hour, for example).

1-5   Complete an analysis deliverable for the following problem. You will need a calculator to determine the output.

Problem: Show the future value of an investment, given its present value, the number of periods (years, perhaps), and the interest rate. Be consistent with the interest rate and the number of periods. If the periods are in years, the annual interest rate must be supplied (0.085 for 8.5%, for example). If the period is in months, the monthly interest rate must be supplied (0.0075 per month for 9% per year, for example). The formula to compute the future value of money is:

$$\text{future value} = \text{present value} * (1 + \text{rate})^{\text{periods}}$$

1.2 Design

Synonyms of design: model, think, plan, devise, pattern, outline
Design refers to the set of activities that includes (1) defining an architecture for the program that satisfies the requirements and (2) specifying an algorithm for each program component in the architecture.

In later chapters, you will see the basic building blocks of programs. The design activity that follows focuses on the steps to solve the problem without concern for the actual details of how it will be executed by the computer. Such a step-by-step procedure for solving a problem or accomplishing some end, especially by a computer, is called an *algorithm*. A good algorithm must:

   ❍   List the activities that need to be carried out.
   ❍   List those activities in the proper order.

Consider an algorithm to bake a cake:
   1.   Preheat the oven.
   2.   Grease the pan.
   3.   Mix the ingredients.
   4.   Pour the ingredients into the pan.
   5.   Place the cake pan in the oven.
   6.   Remove the cake pan from the oven after 35 minutes.

If you change the order of the steps, you might end up with a very hot cake pan with raw cake batter in it, instead of a cake. If you omit a step, you probably won't get a baked cake—or there might be a fire. An experienced cook may not need such an algorithm. However, cake-mix marketers must be careful. They cannot, and do not, assume that their customers have this experience. Good algorithms list the proper steps in the proper order and are detailed enough to accomplish the task.

Self-Check

1-6   Cake recipes typically omit a very important activity. Describe an activity that is missing.

An algorithm often contains a step without much detail. For example, step 3, "Mix the ingredients," is not very specific. What are the ingredients? If the problem is to write a recipe algorithm that humans can understand, step 3 should be refined a bit to say how to mix the ingredients. The *refinement* (a more detailed and specific description of the activity) to step 3 could be something like this:

   3.   Empty the cake mix into the bowl and mix in the milk until smooth.

or for scratch bakers:
   3a.   Place the liquid ingredients in the bowl.
   3b.   Sift the dry ingredients.
   3c.   Add the dry ingredients one quarter-cup at a time, whipping until smooth.

Algorithms are often expressed in *pseudocode*—instructions written in a language that even nonprogrammers can understand. Pseudocode algorithms are an aid to program design. Pseudocode can be very expressive. One pseudocode instruction may represent many computer instructions. Pseudocode algorithms are not concerned about issues such as misplaced punctuation marks, or the details of a particular computer system. Pseudocode solutions make design easier by letting you defer details, so that you can concentrate on planning the algorithm. Program developers often design with pencil and paper, and sometimes design only in their heads.

Algorithmic Patterns

Problems often require input from the user in order to compute and display the desired information. This particular flow of three activities—input/process/output—occurs so often that it can be viewed as a pattern. It is one of several algorithmic patterns discussed in this textbook. These patterns will help you design programs.

A *pattern* is anything shaped or designed to serve as a model or a guide in making something else. An *algorithmic pattern* serves as a guide to develop programs. For instance, the following *Input/Process/Output (IPO) pattern* can be used to design your first programs. This pattern will provide a guideline for many programs in this textbook.

Algorithmic Pattern: Input/Process/Output (IPO)

Problem: The program requires input from the user in order to compute and display the desired information.

Outline:
1. Obtain the input data.
2. Process the data in some meaningful way.
3. Output the results.

This algorithmic pattern is the first of several. In subsequent chapters, you'll see other algorithmic patterns, such as Guarded Action, Alternative Action, and Multiple Selection.

To use an algorithmic pattern effectively, you should first become familiar with it. Try applying the Input/Process/Output algorithmic pattern while you develop programs in the first few chapters. This will help you design your first programs. For example, if you see that you have no meaningful values for the input data, it may be because you have placed the process step *before* the input step. Or, you may have skipped the input step altogether.

Patterns help solve other kinds of problems. Consider this quote from Christopher Alexander:[1]

> Each pattern describes a problem which occurs over and over again in our environment, and then describes the core of the solution to that problem, in such a way that you can use this solution a million times over, without ever doing it the same way twice.

Alexander is describing patterns in the design of furniture, gardens, buildings, and towns. However, his description of a pattern has been also applied to program development. The IPO pattern occurs frequently during program design. It guides the solution to many problems— especially in the first several chapters of this textbook.

An Example of Algorithm Design

The deliverable from the design phase is an algorithm that solves the problem. The Input/Process/Output pattern guides the design of the algorithm that relates to our `courseGrade` problem.

Three-Step Pattern	Pattern Applied to a Specific Algorithm
1. Input	1. Obtain `test1`, `test2`, and `finalExam`.
2. Process	2. Compute `courseGrade`.
3. Output	3. Display `courseGrade`.

---

[1] *A Pattern Language*, Christopher Alexander

Although algorithm development is usually an iterative process, using a pattern will help you quickly provide an outline of the activities needed to solve the courseGrade problem.

Self-Check

1-7   Read the three activities of the algorithm above. Do you see a missing activity?

1-8   Read the three activities of the algorithm above. Do you see any activity out of order?

1-9   Would this algorithm work if the first two activities were switched?

1-10   Is there enough detail in this algorithm to correctly compute courseGrade?

As shown above, the process step of the courseGrade problem does not have enough detail. The algorithm needs further refinement. Specifically, exactly how should the input data be processed to compute the course grade? The algorithm omits the weighted scale given in the problem specification. The process step also needs to be refined because the pseudocode algorithm does not describe how courseGrade will be computed.

The refinement of this algorithm (below) shows a more detailed process step. The step "Compute courseGrade" has been replaced with a refinement —a more detailed and specific activity. The input and output steps have also been refined. This is the design phase deliverable— an algorithm with enough detail to pass on as the input into the next phase, implementation.

Refinement of a Specific Input/Process/Output (IPO) Algorithm

1. Obtain test1, test2, and finalExam from the user.
2. Compute courseGrade = (25% of test1) + (25% of test2) + (50% of finalExam).
3. Display the value of courseGrade.

Try to think of program development in terms of the deliverables. This provides a checklist. What deliverables exist so far?

1. From the analysis phase, there is a document with a list of data (variables), and a sample problem.
2. From the design phase, there is an algorithm.

Algorithm Walkthrough

You can develop programs more quickly, and with fewer errors, by reviewing the algorithms before you move on to the implementation phase. Are the activities in the proper order? Are all the necessary activities present? To carry out this review, you should use an *algorithm walkthrough.* This simulates what a computer would do by stepping through the instructions of the algorithm.

As you know, a computer is a programmable electronic device that can store, retrieve, and process data. In an algorithm walkthrough, you simulate the electronic version of an algorithm by following that algorithm as if you were a computer. To do this, you manually perform the activities of storing, retrieving, and processing data using pencil and paper. The following algorithm walkthrough is a human (non-electronic) execution of the algorithm:

1. Retrieve some example values from the user and store them as shown:

```
test1: 80
test2: 90
finalExam: 100
```

2. Retrieve the values and compute courseGrade as follows:

```
courseGrade = (0.25 * test1)  + (0.25 * test2) +(0.50*finalExam)
              (0.25 * 80.0)   + (0.25 * 90.0)  +(0.50*100.0)
                   20.0        +      22.5      +    50.0
courseGrade = 92.5
```

3. Show the course grade to the user by retrieving the data stored in courseGrade to show 92.5%.

It has been said that good artists know when to put down the brushes. Deciding when a painting is done is critical for its success. By analogy, as a designer, you must decide when to stop designing. This is a good time to move on to the third phase of program development. In summary, here is what we have accomplished so far. We have:

○ understood the problem.
○ identified and named the data (variables).
○ identified the output for two sample problems (80.25% and now 92.5%).
○ developed an algorithm.
○ walked through the algorithm and simulated computer activities.

Self-Check

1-11 Walk through the previous algorithm when test1 is input as 0.0, test2 is input as 50.0, and finalExam is input as 100.0. What value is stored in courseGrade?

1.3 Implementation

Synonyms for implementation: accomplishment, fulfilling, making good, execution
You can do analysis and design of simple problems with pencil and paper. The implementation

phase of program development requires both software and hardware to obtain the deliverable. The deliverable of the implementation phase is a program that runs correctly on a computer. *Implementation* is the collection of activities required to complete the program so someone else can use it. The main tool you will use for implementation in this textbook is a ***programming language***, which is a set of rules for describing instructions to a computer using written words and symbols.

Here are some implementation phase activities and associated deliverables:

Activity	Deliverable
Translate an algorithm into a programming language.	Source code
Compile source code into an executable format.	Executable code
Run the program.	A running program
Verify that the program does what it is supposed to do.	A grade

Our view of the computer in the implementation phase will be at the programming language level. There are many programming languages that could be used. In this textbook, you will be using a language named C#, which is pronounced "C sharp." C# is the tool you will learn to use to control what happens at the computer.

The design phase provided a solution in the form of a pseudocode algorithm. The implementation phase requires nitty-gritty details. You must write the actual program in a precise manner, following the syntax rules of that programming language. You will need to pay attention to small details, such as the placement of semicolons, commas, and periods.

For example, take this algorithmic statement:

3.   Display the value of courseGrade.

It could be translated into C# source code that might look like this:

```
Console.WriteLine("Course Grade: {0}%", courseGrade);
```

This step generates screen output that might look like this (assuming that the value of courseGrade is 92.5):

```
Course Grade: 92.5%
```

After you have translated the program's needs into pseudocode, and then into a programming language, you need to use software that translates your language instructions into the binary computer code that the computer understands. Fortunately, there is a tool for performing these translations. Programmers use a tool called a ***compiler*** to translate the programming language source code—such as C#—into a language that is understood by the computer. In this way, the C# program can work on a variety of very different platforms, such as Windows or Linux.

Finally, to verify that the program works, you need to see how it actually behaves. Look at the output that results from the input. Did you get what you expected? If so, the program works—at least for one particular set of input data. You will still need to test the program by entering other sets of input. This will help you build confidence that the program works, as defined by the problem specification.

An Example of Implementation

The following program—a complete translation of the algorithm written in C#—previews many programming language details. You do not need to understand this C# code. The details are presented later. For now, just look at the code as an implementation of the pseudocode algorithm.

The names test1, test2, and finalExam represent user input. The output variable is named courseGrade. User input is done through an entity named Console. These C# language constructs are discussed in the next chapter.

Code Sample: Class TestCourseGrade

```
1  // This program computes and displays a final course grade as a
2  // weighted average after the user enters the appropriate input.
3  using System;
4
5  class TestCourseGrade
6  {
7    static void Main()
8    {
9      // Declare the input and output variables
10     double test1, test2, finalExam, courseGrade;
11
12
13     Console.WriteLine("This program computes a course grade when");
14     Console.WriteLine("you have entered three requested values.");
15     Console.WriteLine();
16
17     // I)nput test1, test2, and finalExam
18     Console.Write("Enter first test: ");
19     test1 = double.Parse(Console.ReadLine());
20
21     Console.Write("Enter second test: ");
22     test2 = double.Parse(Console.ReadLine());
23
24     Console.Write("Enter final exam: ");
25     finalExam = double.Parse(Console.ReadLine());
```

```
26
27      // P)rocess
28      courseGrade = (0.25 * test1) + (0.25 * test2) + (0.50 * finalExam);
28
30      // O)utput the results
31      Console.WriteLine("Course Grade: {0}%", courseGrade);
32
33   } // End of the Main method
34
35 } // End class TestCourseGrade
36
```

Dialogue

```
This program computes a course grade when
you have entered three requested values.

Enter first test: 80.0
Enter second test: 90.0
Enter final exam: 100.0
Course Grade: 92.5%
```

At the end of most programs in this textbook, you will see a section titled either "Dialogue" or "Output." A "Dialogue" section shows the program output, along with user input (shown in boldface italic). If there is no user input, the section will simply be titled "Output." These dialogues help show how programs execute, so that you can more easily learn how to read C# code. And it is important to read before you write.

Testing

Although this "Testing" section appears at the end of our first example of program development, do not assume that testing always comes after implementation. The important process of *testing* may, can, and should, occur at any phase of program development. The actual work is minimal, and it's worth the effort. However, you may not agree until you have felt the pain of *not* testing.

Testing During All Phases of Program Development

○ During analysis, create sample problems to confirm your understanding of the problem.

○ During design, walk through the algorithm to ensure that it has the proper steps in the proper order.

○ During testing, run the program several times with different sets of input data. Confirm that the results are correct.

○ Review the problem specification. Does the running program do what was requested?

You should have a sample problem before you write the program—not after. However, if you do decide to wait, it is still better late than never. Work out a sample program now. If nothing else, at least look at the input and the result of one program run, and convince yourself that the output is correct.

After you write a C# program and see its output, compare the output to the predicted results. If they do not match, you'll need to make adjustments. It means that the problem example, the program output, or perhaps both, are incorrect. By using problem examples, you can avoid the misconception that a program is correct just because it runs successfully and generates output. The output could be wrong! Simply executing does not make a program right. Even exhaustive testing does not prove that a program is correct. E. W. Dijkstra has argued that testing only reveals the presence of errors, not the absence of errors. Even with correct program output, the program is not always proven correct. But testing can increase your confidence that the algorithm, now implemented as a program, at least appears to be reliable.

Self-Check

1-12   If the programmer predicts that courseGrade should be 100.0 when all three inputs are 100.0, but the program displays courseGrade as 75.0, what is wrong: the prediction, the program, or both?

1-13   If the programmer predicts that courseGrade should be 90.0 when test1 is 80, test2 is 90.0, and finalExam is 100.0, but the program outputs courseGrade as 92.5, what is wrong: the prediction, the program, or both?

1-14   If the programmer predicts that courseGrade should be 92.5 when test1 is 80, test2 is 90.0, and finalExam is 100.0, but the program outputs courseGrade as 90.0, what is wrong: the prediction, the program, or both?

Chapter Summary

This chapter presented a three-step program development strategy of analysis, design, and implementation. The table below shows some of the activities performed during each of these three phases. The maintenance phase has been added to show how the three steps fit into the complete program life cycle. The maintenance phase requires the majority of the time, energy, and money of the program's life cycle.

Phase	Activities You Might Perform
Analysis	Read and understand the problem specification.
	Determine the input and output.
	Solve a few sample problems.
Design	Look for patterns to guide algorithm development.
	Write an algorithm—the steps needed to solve the problem.
	Refine the steps in the algorithm and walk through it.
Implementation	Translate the design into a programming language.
	Fix errors.
	Create an executable program.
	Test the program.
Maintenance	Update the program to keep up with a changing world.
	Enhance the program.
	Correct bugs (errors) as they are found.

Each phase of program development can be viewed in terms of the deliverables. This chapter introduced some useful analysis and design tools:

1. Naming the variables that help solve a problem.
2. Developing algorithms.
3. Refining one or more steps of an algorithm.
4. Using the Input/Process/Output algorithmic pattern.

Key Terms

algorithm	implementation	program
algorithm walkthrough	input	programming language
algorithmic pattern	Input/Process/Output (IPO)	pseudocode
analysis	pattern	refinement
computer	output	testing
deliverable	pattern	variable
design	problem specification	

Exercises

1. What is the difference between variables that store output values and variables that store values input by the user?
2. What activities do you need to perform when you design programs?
3. Describe the deliverable of the design phase of program development.
4. Describe the deliverable from the implementation phase of program development.
5. What are the characteristics of a good algorithm?
6. Does a running program always work correctly? Explain your answer.
7. Explain the importance of testing a program before a user gets it.
8. Write an algorithm for finding any phone number in the phone book. Will the search always be successful?
9. Write an algorithm that for directing someone from your classroom to the nearest grocery store.
10. Write an algorithm for arranging a collection of CDs (or tapes or record albums) in alphabetical order.

To prepare for the programming exercises at the end of Chapter 2, you need to have access to a C# development environment. If you are using your school computer lab, C# may already be set up, and your instructor should direct you how to use it.

Analysis/Design Projects

The following projects do not require a computer. Use a table like this to complete the analysis deliverable for each of the following analysis and design projects:

Problem	Data Name	Input or Output	Sample

1A   Simple Arithmetic

Problem: For any two numbers a and b, compute the product $(a * b)$ and the sum $(a + b)$. Also, display the difference between the product and the sum. The difference may be positive or negative, depending on the input values for a and b.

1. Complete an analysis deliverable (like the table above), with at least one sample problem.
2. Complete a design deliverable by writing an algorithm that solves the simple arithmetic problem. Include the arithmetic expressions.

1B   Simple Average

Problem: Find the average of three tests of equal weight.

1. Complete an analysis deliverable (like the table above), with at least one sample problem.
2. Complete a design deliverable by writing an algorithm (with the formula) that solves the simple average problem.

1C   Weighted Average

Problem: Determine a course grade using this grade assessment scale:

Quiz average	20%
Midterm	20%
Lab grade	35%
Final exam	25%

1. Complete an analysis deliverable (like the table above), with at least two sample problems.
2. Complete a design deliverable by writing an algorithm (with the formula) that solves the weighted average problem.

1D   Wholesale Cost

Problem: You know that a store has a 25% markup on compact-disc players. If the retail price of a CD player (what you pay) is $189.98, how much did the store pay for that item (the wholesale price)? In general, what is the wholesale price for any item, given its retail price and markup? Analyze the problem and design an algorithm that computes the wholesale price for *any* given retail price and *any* given markup. *Clue:* If you can't determine the equation, use this formula and a little algebra to solve for wholesale price:

retail price = wholesale price * (1 + markup)

1. Complete an analysis deliverable (like the table above), with at least two sample problems.
2. Complete a design deliverable by writing an algorithm (with the formula) that solves the wholesale cost problem.

1E   Grade Point Average

Problem: Compute a student's cumulative grade point average (GPA) for three courses. Credits range from 0.5 to 15.0. Grades can be 0.0, 1.0, 2.0, 3.0, or 4.0.

1. Complete an analysis deliverable (like the table above), with at least one sample problem that has courses with different credits.
2. Complete a design deliverable by writing an algorithm that solves this problem.

1F   Fahrenheit to Celsius

Problem: Use the following formula to convert Fahrenheit (F) temperatures to Celsius (C):

$$F = (9 / 5) * C + 32$$

1. Complete an analysis deliverable (like the table above), with at least one sample problem.
2. Complete a design deliverable by writing an algorithm (with the formula) that solves the F to C problem.

1G   Celsius to Fahrenheit

Problem: Use algebra and the formula of the preceding exercise to convert Celsius (C) temperatures to Fahrenheit (F).

1. Complete an analysis deliverable (like the table above), with at least one sample problem.
2. Complete a design deliverable by writing an algorithm (with the formula) that solves the C to F problem.

1H   Seconds

Problem: Determine the number of hours, minutes, and seconds represented by a total number of seconds. For example, 3,661 seconds is 1 hour, 1 minute, and 1 second.

1. Complete an analysis deliverable (like the table above), with at least one sample problem.
2. Complete a design deliverable by writing an algorithm (with the formula) that solves the seconds problem.

1I   U.S. Minimum Coins

Problem: Determine the number of each denomination of coins required to make change for cents in the range of 0 through 99. The number of coins should be the lowest possible. The available coins are half dollars (50 cents), quarters (25 cents), dimes (10 cents), nickels (five cents), and pennies (one cent). For example, if there is 91 cents change, you will have one of each coin.

1. Complete an analysis deliverable (like the table above), with at least one sample problem other than 91 cents.
2. Complete a design deliverable by writing an algorithm (with the formula) that solves the U.S. minimum coins problem.

1J   U.K. Minimum Coins

Problem: Determine the coins required to make change for any number of pence from 0 to 199. The number of coins should be the lowest possible. The available coins are 1p (p represents pence), 2p, 5p, 10p, 20p, 50p, and 100p (the one-pound coin). For example, if there are 188 pence, you will have one of each coin.

1. Complete an analysis deliverable (like the table above), with at least one sample problem other than 188 pence.
2. Complete a design deliverable by writing an algorithm (with the formula) that solves the U.K. minimum coins problem.

An Introduction to C#

Summing Up

The first chapter introduced a program development strategy summarized as three steps: analysis, design, and implementation. You are encouraged to do some analysis and design before writing code. The problems encountered in the early chapters of this book will not require much effort to produce analysis and design deliverables. Your analysis phase may simply be reduced to reading the problem. The design phase might end up as being able to say that you can picture the solution in your head.

Coming Up

This chapter presents the fundamentals of C# that will allow you to successfully translate algorithms into working C# programs. This requires an understanding of the smallest pieces of a program, and of how to put them together correctly. This chapter also shows how to input numeric data, process it, and display output on the screen.

After studying this chapter, you will be able to:

- ○ use numeric types (`int` and `double`) for mathematical calculations.
- ○ perform complex mathematical operations on numeric data.
- ○ use the `Console` and `Math` types from the .NET Framework.
- ○ obtain data from the keyboard and display information on the screen.
- ○ solve problems using the Input/Process/Output (IPO) pattern.
- ○ identify and correct several types of errors that occur while programming.

2.1   The C# Programming Language—A Start

A C# source code file is a sequence of text characters stored as a file, with a name that ends with
.cs. For a C# source code file to be an executable program, it must follow a certain structure and
must contain certain elements. One such element is a *class heading*, which gives the program a
name. Usually, the name matches the name of the source code file: if the program is named
GuessingGame, the source code file is usually named GuessingGame.cs.

Another required element is the **Main *method***. This is where you write code to represent the
functionality of a program. When a C# program is compiled and executed, the lines of C# code
in the Main method execute in sequence (one after another). Any class with an appropriate Main
method can be run as a program.

Here is a general form for a C# program:

General Form: A Simple C# Program

```
// Comments (optional)
using namespace-name;


class class-name
{
   static void Main()
   {
   C# code, which can include the following:
     variable declarations and initializations,
     operations such as arithmetic and variable assignments,
     method calls,
     object creations,
     sending messages to objects, ...
   }

}
```

A *general form* describes the *syntax*—the correct language—necessary to write programs. This
general form, like all others in this textbook, uses the following conventions:

- ○ Boldface elements must be written exactly as shown. This includes words such as
  static void Main and symbols such as [,], (, and).
- ○ Italic elements vary; often they are supplied by the programmer or elsewhere in the
  program. This includes phrases above like *class-name* (which the programmer selects).

The Major Elements of a C# Program

In this section, we will analyze an example C# program piece by piece to help understand its syntax and structure. The following program is presented in Code Sample format, which lists the program with each line preceded by a number on the left. The line numbers are for your reference and are not part of the actual program.

Code Sample: An Example C# Program

```
 1  // This program reads a number from the user,  1
 2  // then writes out that number squared.
 3
 4  using System;  2
 5
 6  class SquareIt  3
 7  {
 8      // This Main method runs my program.
 9      static void Main()  4
10      {
11          // I)nput   - get the number from the user
12          Console.Write("Enter a number: ");
13          double number = double.Parse(Console.ReadLine());
14                                                              5
15          // P)rocess -- make calculations based on the input
16          double result = number * number;
17
18          // O)utput  - display the results on the screen
19          Console.WriteLine("{0} squared = {1}", number, result);
20      }
21  }
```

Dialogue (user input in bold italic)

```
Enter a number: -12
-12.0 squared = 144
```

The numbered sections of the program represent the following:

1. Comment:

All lines that start with // are comments. *Comments* are like notes that the programmer writes to help make the code more understandable. They exist to serve as notes and reminders to the programmer, and to describe pieces of the program. This can help you and others understand the code. Comments are not part of the code of the program; when the code runs, the comments are ignored. A more detailed explanation of the syntax and use of comments appears later in this chapter.

2. *Using namespace directive:*

Lines that contain the word **using** allow programs to refer to external resources. Resources in C# are organized into collective units called ***namespaces***. C#'s standard namespace of typical resources is named System. Almost every C# program has the directive using System; at the top, because without it, the program cannot easily use C#'s most common types of data. By including using System;, the program can refer to and use these resources, such as the Console and the double data type. System, other namespaces, and data types will be explored in subsequent chapters.

3. *Class heading:*

Every C# program must belong to a unit called a ***class***, which can be thought of as a piece of a program. C# programs must contain a line that tells what class they belong to; this line is called a **class heading**. A simple program consists of just one class, but a more complex program could have several classes that combine their functionality. Classes are discussed in detail later in this chapter, as well as in Chapter 4, "Writing Classes."

From a syntax standpoint, a C# class is a collection of code enclosed within a set of braces { and }. More generally, a pair of braces encloses the beginning and ending of a section of a program (also called a **scope**). A class's name can be any valid C# identifier (identifiers are discussed in more detail later in the chapter). Generally, for clarity, the class name is the same as the file name prefix—the part before the .cs in the file name. For example, the code for the class named SquareIt should go in a file named SquareIt.cs (however, this is not required).

4. *Main method heading:*

The executable code for any C# program appears in a sub-region inside its class, with the following header:

```
static void Main()
```

This header signifies the beginning of a ***method***, which is a part of a class that contains code that can be executed. Methods group code together and allow programs to see and execute each other's code. In this particular case, the method Main is a special method that represents the entry point to start executing the program's code. When a C# program is run, the code in its Main method is executed sequentially from top to bottom.

5. Code statements:

After the `Main` method heading, there is a pair of braces representing the method's body. Enclosed within these braces is a series of statements. A *statement* is the fundamental unit of execution in a computer program. A statement can be one of many things: a mathematical calculation, a request to allocate some of the computer's memory, a command to write data to a file on a disk, a message to display text on the screen, and so on. In C#, all such statements end with a semicolon `;`.

A C# program begins by executing the first statement in `Main`. Each statement executes in sequence, from top to bottom. The `Main` method above contains statements that perform actions, like variable declarations, variable initializations, and calls to methods, all of which are described later in this chapter.

The Compiler

This C# source code is a file that will be given as input to a C# compiler. A *compiler* is a program that translates the source code of your program into a portable executable format. This format, called *intermediate language (IL)*, is not plain text like your source code, but is instead a binary (zeros and ones) format that is closer to the language understood at the level of the computer hardware.

To run your program, you must first *compile* it. The compiler translates your source code into intermediate code. If your program is syntactically correct, that is, if it is written correctly by the rules of what is allowed in the C# language, the compiler will turn your source code into an executable file; on Windows systems, this file will have an .EXE suffix. For example, if your program is named `BankSystem.cs`, the compiled IL file will be named `BankSystem.exe` by default. See Appendix B for a more detailed explanation about how to compile and run C# programs.

However, if your program violates any one of the many syntax rules, the compiler will generate error messages to the screen, instead of compiling it. You must then fix the source and compile it again before it can be executed. The time at which your program is given to the compiler is often called *compile-time*. If your program contains invalid commands or incorrect syntax, you will receive compile-time errors from the C# compiler. These compile-time errors are discussed in more detail later in this chapter.

After successfully compiling your C# program, you can run, or *execute*, it. To do this, you find the executable file created for your program (in our example, `BankSystem.exe`), and double-click it. When an IL EXE file is executed, it is first run through another translator named the *.NET virtual machine*, which converts the IL code into native instructions for your type of machine. For example, if you run Windows on an Intel Pentium system, the .NET virtual machine will translate the IL EXE file into Intel X86 instructions. The time at which your program is executed by the *virtual machine* is often called *runtime*; if your program contains faulty logic, you may receive run-time errors; these are also discussed in more detail later in this chapter.

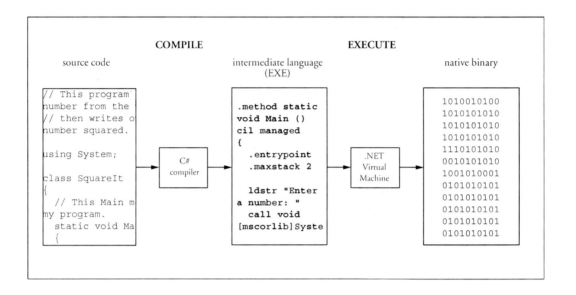

Figure 2.1: Compiling and Running a C# Program

In summary, three "translations" are needed to implement an algorithm using C# and make it execute on almost any computer.

1. The programmer translates algorithms into C# source code.
2. The compiler translates the source code into intermediate level (IL) code, which is a machine-independent format that can run on different platforms. This IL code file is usually stored as an EXE file, with the same name as the source file.
3. When the intermediate language EXE file is run, its IL code is translated into the instructions understood by the computer's operating system (for example, Windows or Linux).

Tokens—The Smallest Pieces of a Program

As the C# compiler reads the source code, it identifies individual *tokens*, which are the smallest recognizable components of a program. Tokens fall into four categories:

Type of Token	Examples
Special symbols	`; () , . { }`
Identifiers	`Main args credits courseGrade string`
Reserved identifiers	`static void class double int`
Literals	`"Hello World!" 7 -2.1 'C' null true`

These tokens are used to make up larger things. Knowing the types of tokens that make up C# programs should help you to:

○ code syntactically correct programs more easily.

○ understand better how to fix syntax errors detected by the compiler.

○ understand general forms.

Special Symbols

A *special symbol* is a sequence of one or two characters with one, or possibly many, specific meanings. Some special symbols separate other tokens; {, ;, and ,, for example. Other special symbols represent operators in expressions; +, -, and /, for example. An *operator* is a special symbol that performs an action on some number of other tokens, which are called *operands*. Operators are commonly used in expressions such as `0.25 * test1`.

Here is a partial list of single-character and double-character special symbols frequently seen in C# programs (their meanings and usage will be explained later):

```
( )    .    +    -    /    *    <=    >=    //    { }    ==    ;
```

Identifiers

A C# *identifier* is a token that represents a name for some entity in a program. For example, `string` is an identifier for a type of data that stores a collection of characters. Here are some other identifiers that C# has already given meaning to:

```
Console  string  null  WriteLine  System  Equals  int  double
```

Programmers must often create their own identifiers for each new class, method, variable, or other entity in a program. Each needs a name; this name is an identifier. For example, `ComputeResult`, `finalExam`, `Main`, and `courseGrade` are identifiers that can be defined by programmers.

All programs must follow these rules for creating C# identifiers:

○ The first character in an identifier must be an uppercase or lowercase letter (a through z, or A through Z), or the underscore character _.

○ Subsequent characters in an identifier may be uppercase and lowercase letters, digits (0 through 9), or underscore characters.

○ Identifiers are case sensitive. For example, Ident, ident, and iDENT would be three unique identifiers in a C# program.

Valid Identifiers

Main	account	incomeTax	MAX_SIZE	Money
Maine	URL	employeeName	all_4_one	_balance
miSpel	A1	world_in_motion	my_balance	_A_B_C_D_

Invalid Identifiers	Reasons
1A	It begins with a digit.
miles/Hour	The / is unacceptable.
first Name	The blank space is unacceptable.
pre-shrunk	The - is unacceptable (- means subtraction!).
double	It is a C# keyword (see below).

C# is case-sensitive. For example, the method that runs the program must be named Main. MAIN or main won't do. Also, note that several conventions may be used for upper- and lowercase letters. Some programmers prefer to avoid uppercase letters; others prefer to use uppercase letters for each new word in a multi-word identifier.

The conventions used in this textbook are based on what Microsoft has chosen. Variables begin with lowercase letters. Method names such as Main, and class names such as Console, begin with an uppercase letter. If an identifier has two or more words, each subsequent word begins with an uppercase letter. For example, a variable to represent a letter grade for a course would be named letterGrade rather than lettergrade, LetterGrade, or letter_grade. The .NET Framework uses the convention of beginning class and method names with an uppercase letter, such as the classes ArrayList, DateTime, and BankAccount and the methods WriteLine and Round.

Keywords (reserved identifiers)

A *keyword* is an identifier that has been set aside for a specific purpose. Keywords are reserved identifiers whose meanings are fixed by the standard language definition. They follow the same naming rules as identifiers.

Keywords have predefined meanings and purposes. A keyword cannot be used for any other purpose, such as naming a variable or method. Keywords are very important; they help give a programming language a vocabulary of recognized entities and operations. Here is a list of all keywords in C# (notice that C# keywords are written with all lowercase letters).

C# Keywords, the complete list

abstract	delegate	internal	readonly	try
as	do	is	ref	typeof
base	double	lock	return	uint
bool	else	long	sbyte	ulong
break	enum	namespace	sealed	unchecked
byte	event	new	short	unsafe
case	explicit	null	sizeof	ushort
catch	extern	object	stackalloc	using
char	false	operator	static	virtual
checked	finally	out	string	void
class	float	override	struct	volatile
const	for	params	switch	while
continue	if	private	this	
decimal	implicit	protected	throw	
default	int	public	true	

Literals (constants)

A *literal* (also known as a constant) represents a value in your source code. In C#, there are six types of literals. Integer literals are whole numbers without decimal points. They may be written in decimal (base 10), octal (base 8), or hexadecimal (base 16). *Floating-point* literals are real numbers with decimal points, or with numbers in exponential notation. Character literals are one written character enclosed within single quote marks (apostrophes). *String* literals are multi-character phrases enclosed within double quote marks. There are also two literal values for Boolean logic (`true` and `false`) and a literal for uninitialized objects (`null`).

Here are some examples of C# literal values:

C# Literals

integer	floating-point	character	string
-2147483648	-1.0	'a'	"A"
1E2A	10.5	'0'	"Hello World"
0	39.95	'?'	"This is a string"
1	1.234e02	' '	"$1.23 total"
2147483647	-1e6	'X'	"The answer is: "

	Boolean	uninitialized object	
	true	null	
	false		

Literals are important because they provide basic types of data that may be represented in a programming language. In later sections of this chapter, you will see how literals are an important part of mathematical calculations and the processing of textual data.

Comments

Comments are portions of text that annotate a program. Comments can be used as headers at the start of programs to give information about the program as a whole, such as the programmer's name, the date the code was written, and the goal of the program. Comments provide internal documentation to help one programmer read another's program. They are also used on a more fine-grained scale to explain individual lines or sections of code. Comments may be added anywhere throughout a program.

Using comments helps clarify and document the purpose of the source code. The goal is to make the program more understandable, easier to debug (correct errors), and easier to maintain (change when necessary). Comments are also used as "notes to self," reminders of decisions made in the past, or things to do in the future. They can help the programmer understand old code that may have been written days, weeks, months, years, or even decades ago.

There are several legal styles of writing comments in C#; one is the ***multi-line comment*** (also sometimes called the "C-style comment," because of its origins in the C language). Multi-line comments begin with the two-character special symbol /* and end with the corresponding symbol */. Any text between these "slash-star" and "star-slash" symbols is interpreted as comments and not as executable code. Multi-line comments get their name from the fact that the /* and */ symbols may appear many lines apart, so a comment may span multiple lines of a program.

Here are some examples of multi-line comments:

```
/*
   C SC 101A
   Spring 2005 Semester

   This is my program. It adds two numbers and then writes the answer.
*/

/* This piece of code averages the input data. */

/*****************************************************
 * I can draw boxes around my comments as long as    *
 * I don't write a star-slash symbol until the end!  *
 *****************************************************/
```

A second form of comments in C# is the *single-line comment.* Single-line comments begin with // and extend to the end of a line. Single-line comments do not need a special termination symbol like */ for multi-line comments; they end implicitly when the line they appear on ends. A single-line comment may appear on a line by itself, or at the end of a line, with code preceding it. The // comment causes the rest of its line to be interpreted as a comment, and not as code to execute; however, anything written before the // on the same line is still considered to be program code, as in the static void Main() header line below.

Code Sample: Class DoNothing

```
 1  // A complete C# program
 2  using System;
 3
 4  class DoNothing
 5  {
 6    static void Main()    // A comment after some code
 7    {
 8      // This program does nothing
 9    }
10  }
```

Because it makes the syntax less cluttered, most of the comments in the programs in this textbook will be written as single-line comments with //, rather than as multi-line comments with /* and */.

Be careful when writing multi-line comments. It can be easy to forget the closing */ to end a multi-line comment. If you do so, a large portion of your program could accidentally be interpreted as a comment, and not be executed! Using only one-line comments can make it easier to avoid accidentally "commenting out" large sections of code. Your mileage may vary.

C# has a third style of comments, known as *XML comments.* These XML comments begin with /// (note the third slash) and may contain documentation and special tags that allow you to convert your source code into Web pages, so that other programmers can see information about the code you have written. We will not discuss the details of the syntax of writing XML comments, since they are generally written on more complex programs and classes.

Fortunately, all of the code in C#'s class framework was written with XML comments. This means that you can view Web documentation for any part of C# to see how to use it. This will be useful later when writing more complex programs that take advantage of the features available in C#. A detailed discussion of XML comments is outside the scope of this textbook. Therefore, XML comments are not discussed further.

Self-Check

2-1 How many tokens are there in the first program of section 2.1 (`SquareIt`)? *Note:* `Console.WriteLine` has three tokens: one period, which is a special symbol, and two identifiers. Do not count comments.

2-2 Identify if each of the following is a valid identifier; if not, explain why it is not valid:

(a) `abc`   (l) `H.P.`
(b) `123`   (m) `Money$Money$Money`
(c) `ABC`   (n) `55_mph`
(d) `.`   (o) `sales Tax`
(e) `my Age`   (p) `Main`
(f) `k/s`   (q) `a`
(g) `Abc!`   (r) `_`
(h) `identifier`   (s) `_____`
(i) `(identifier)`   (t) `Mile/Hour`
(j) `Double`   (u) `student name`
(k) `mispellted`   (v) `Console`

2-3 List two special symbols that are one character long.

2-4 List two special symbols that are two characters long.

2-5 List two identifiers that have already been defined by C#.

2-6 Create two programmer-defined identifiers.

2-7 Which of the tokens shown below are valid:
(a) string literals?
(b) integer literals?
(c) real number literals?
(d) character literals?

2-8 Which of the following are valid and complete C# comments?
(a) `//  Is this a comment?`
(b) `/ / Is this a comment?`
(c) `/* Is this a comment?`
(d) `/* Is this a comment? */`
(e) `/// Is this a comment?`

2.2 Types and Variables

Computer programs store and manipulate data. The nature of the data and the operations that can be performed on the data is called the *type*. C# provides types to store integers, real numbers (also called floating-point numbers), and string data. Other types allow programmers to store a collection of data such as a list, perform calendar date arithmetic, display windows with buttons and menus, and for read Web pages from the Internet. Programmers also often create their own types for the application they are working on, such as a type to store all data needed to manage an account at a bank.

Data is "remembered" by a running program by having values stored in the computer's memory. The locations in memory for storing data are called *memory addresses*. However, it would be tedious for programmers to keep track of the memory addresses of every piece of data to store and retrieve it. Instead, modern programming languages allow the programmer to use identifiers to access places in memory by name. These named identifiers are called *variables*. Think of a variable as a storage bin that holds information that can be accessed or modified.

Variables in C# (and many other languages) are distinguished by the nature of the stored data. C# has two major classifications of data types: *value types* and *reference types*. The value types store a value in a fixed amount of computer memory. C# has thirteen predefined value types called the *simple types*, which are listed in the table below. Variables of these thirteen simple types store values such as numbers and single written characters. The identifiers for these simple types include int, double, and char. The simple types are also sometimes called *primitive types*.

The simple types are closely tied to computer hardware. For example, an int value is a positive or negative integer value stored in 32 binary digits or bits (4 bytes) of memory. These simple types are part of C# because of their simplicity and efficiency—their use helps make programs run faster. C#'s simple types stand out from other data types because their type names are lowercase, such as int or double, while most other types have uppercase names like DateTime and ArrayList.

There are also more complex value types, called structured types or *structs*. A struct variable stores more than one value. Structs can be thought of as combinations of several types of values working together to represent a combined entity. For example, a structured type Point could be written to hold an integer (that is, an int) for its x-coordinate and another int for its y-coordinate. Structs can also have special defined behavior and special operators. In general, a struct can be treated like any other value type (see the DateTime type in Chapter 3).

A *reference type* is a more complex and powerful entity. The most fundamental reference type in C# is a *class type*, which is described later in this chapter. A class type has a collection of related data and behavior that typically provide richer functionality than value types. The values of a class type can be quite complex; they may be composed of many other values and reference variables. A variable of a reference type is often called a *reference variable*. Class types are very similar to structured types, but there are differences in their behavior and usage, which will be discussed later.

In this chapter, the focus will be on the simple numeric types and the operations that can be performed on their values. You will also see differences between the way that value types and reference types behave, as well as different ways to handle them.

Here is summary of all types in C#:

C# Value Types (also known as the Simple Types)

Type	Size (bits)	Value Range
Integers		
sbyte	8	-128 to 127
byte	8	0 to 255
short	16	-32768 to 32767
ushort	16	0 to 65535
int	32	-2,147,483,648 to -2,147,483,647
uint	32	0 to 4,294,967,295
long	64	$-9,223,372,036,854,775,808$ to $9,223,372,036,854,775,807$
ulong	64	0 to 18,446,744,073,709,551,615
Real Numbers		
float	32	1.5×10^{-45} to 3.4×10^{38} accurate to 7 digits
double	64	5.0×10^{-324} to 1.7×10^{308} accurate to 15 digits
decimal	128	1.0×10^{-28} to 7.9×10^{28} with 28-29 significant digits
Other		
char	16	Unicode character set
bool	n/a	true or false

Other C# Value Types

struct (Chapter 3)
enum (Chapter 8)

C# Reference Types

class (Chapter 4)
array (Chapter 7)
delegate (Chapter 10)
interface (not covered in this textbook)

Do not be alarmed by how many types there are. The types have a large amount of overlap with each other, and only a few will be used in this textbook. The differences between the seemingly redundant simple types are their size in memory. The size determines what range of values they can store. Types that take more bits in memory can store numbers that are larger and more accurate. Some types are not signed and store only positive numbers. You do not need to understand every simple type in C# to write useful and complex programs.

However, two of C#'s simple types for storing numbers—int and double—are used frequently. The *int* type stores integers (whole numbers), and the *double* type[1] stores real numbers, which are numbers with a decimal point (a fractional component). There is also a *char* type that stores character literals, which are individual text characters surrounded by apostrophes (single quote marks), such as 'Q' and '!'. The char type is not as useful as int or double for now, but it used later in the textbook.

We will use the three types to learn how to do the following:
- ○ Create new variables and give starting values to them (declaration and initialization).
- ○ Change the value of a variable (assignment).
- ○ Use variables to make calculations and solve problems (expressions).
- ○ Display the value of a variable on the screen (output).
- ○ Enter numeric values with the keyboard and store them into variables (input).

Variable Declaration and Initialization

A variable *declaration* brings into a program a named data value that can change while the program is running. An *initialization* lets you set the initial value of the variable. These variable names are used later when you are interested in the current value of the variable or need to change that value.

Here are the general forms for declaring and initializing variables:

General Form: Declaration (making new variables without initial values)

```
// Declare a variable with no value stored in it
variable-type variable-name;


// Declare many variables, all of the same type,
// with no value (uninitialized)
variable-type variable-name1, variable-name2, ... , variable-name-N;
```

---

[1] The name of double for a floating point number comes from the number of bits used to store the number. A double variable uses twice, or *double*, the memory of a float. Although float is a more meaningful name, C# uses double most because the extra memory can more accurately represent the number.

Examples:

```
int total;
double midTerm, finalExam;
char letter;
```

General Form: Declaration and Initialization (variables with initial values)

```
// Declare variable variable-name and
// stores initial-value into it
variable-type variable-name = initial-value;

// Declare many variables, all of the given type, with given values
variable-type variable-name1 = initial-value1, ...,
         variable-name-N = initial-value-N;
```

Examples:

```
int total = 37;
double midterm = 86.5, finalExam = 82.0;
```

The *variable-type* may be any of C#'s simple types, and the *variable-name* can be any valid identifier. The following C# program declares several int, double and char primitive variables:

Code Sample: Class ShowSomeSimpleTypes

```
 1  //Initializes some numeric variables.
 2  using System;
 3
 4  class ShowSomeSimpleTypes
 5  {
 6    static void Main()
 7    {
 8      int credits = 22;
 9      double qualityPoints;
10      double GPA = 3.14;
11      char exclamation = '!';
12
13      int studentID = 6789, pinNumber = 1470;
14      double balance, tuition = 2500.00;
```

```
15        char letterGrade = 'A', exitCommand = 'x';
16    }
17 }
```

The primitive ***numeric types*** int, double, and char can be initialized with = followed by the initial value. This satisfies all three qualities of a variable:

1. The name, as specified by the identifier.
2. The available operations, as specified by the type.
3. The initial value, as specified by the value given after =.

The following figure summarizes the state of these variables. For variables of the simple types, it helps to think of the variable as a "box" into which a value can be stored. The boxes below with a question mark (?) inside represent uninitialized variables with no value.

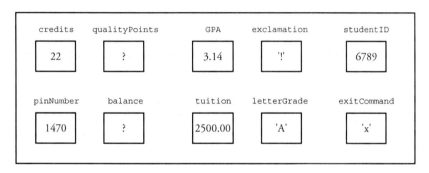

Figure 2.2: Variable Names and Values from the Preceding Program

Assignment

An ***assignment*** supplies a value to, and/or modifies the value of, a variable.

General Form: Assignment

variable-name = value;

Examples:

```
total = 76;
finalExam = 1.1 * finalExam; // A 10% bonus
letterGrade = 'B';
```

An assignment looks similar to an initialization, except that the variable's type is not written, only the variable name.

In an assignment, the *value* to the right of = replaces whatever value was previously in the variable to the left of =. The *value* must be a value that can legally be stored by the given variable. For example, a floating-point value can be stored into a double variable, and an integer can be stored in an int variable.

Here are some sample assignments, using variables from the previous example:

```
credits = 15;
qualityPoints = 45.67;
exitCommand = 'Q';
```

After the two assignments execute, the value of each variable is modified, and the values can be shown like this:

Variable	Value
credits	15
qualityPoints	45.67
exitCommand	'Q'

Assignments are subject to compatibility rules. For example, a string value cannot be assigned to a numeric type variable such as int or double, nor to a char variable. Similarly, a real number value cannot be assigned to an int variable, even if that number is equivalent to some integer, such as 2.0. The compiler will report an error at the attempted assignment.

```
qualityPoints = "a string"; // ERROR-Cannot store string in double
credits = 16.5;             // ERROR-Cannot store real number in int
letterGrade = 5.7;          // ERROR-Cannot store real number in char
```

However, there are a few special cases where assignment between different types is legal. For example, trying to store a value of type int into a variable of type double is legal, because an integer is also a real number. Strangely, it is also legal to store a char value into a variable of type int. This is because characters are represented internally in the computer as numbers (but this is not relevant to the examples in this chapter). When a value is converted automatically from one type to another in this way, it is called an ***implicit conversion***.

The following table lists all of the legal implicit conversions between simple types in C#.

Legal C# Implicit Conversions

From:	*To:*
sbyte	short, int, long, float, double, or decimal
byte	short, ushort, int, uint, long, ulong, float, double, or decimal
short	int, long, float, double, or decimal
ushort	int, uint, long, ulong, float, double, or decimal
int	long, float, double, or decimal
uint	long, ulong, float, double, or decimal
long	float, double, or decimal
char	ushort, int, uint, long, ulong, float, double, or decimal
float	double
ulong	float, double, or decimal

The following program uses C# assignment statements to give specific values to variables that were initially only declared, but not initialized.

Code Sample: Class <code>ShowAssignment</code>

```
1  // A few assignment statements
2  using System;
3
4  class ShowAssignment
5  {
6    static void Main()
7    {
8      int credits;
9      double qualityPoints, GPA;        // A list of variables
10     char letterGrade;
11
12     credits = 16;                     // Assignment
13     qualityPoints = 49.5;             // Assignment
14     GPA = qualityPoints / credits;    // Divide and assign
15     letterGrade = 'A';                // Assignment
16   }
17 }
```

It is important to understand the meaning of assignments between variables. For value types, when one variable is assigned to another, the value is copied between the two variables. For example, the code below assigns variable x to have y's value. Then y is assigned a new value. The accompanying pictures show the values of the two variables through each line of code.

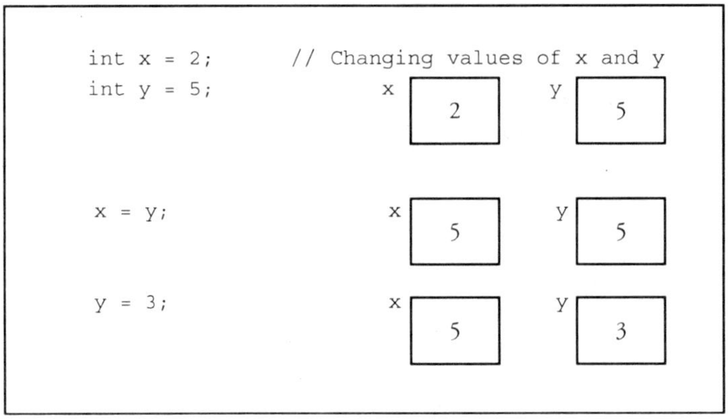

```
int x = 2;        // Changing values of x and y
int y = 5;            x  [        ]   y  [        ]
                         [   2    ]      [   5    ]


x = y;               x  [        ]   y  [        ]
                         [   5    ]      [   5    ]


y = 3;               x  [        ]   y  [        ]
                         [   5    ]      [   3    ]
```

Figure 2.3: Value-type Variable Assignment Behavior

When one value type variable is assigned to another, the value is copied. The variables themselves remain independent, and a subsequent change to one (such as the later assignment `y = 3;`) does not affect the other variable (in this case, x). You will see later that assignment to reference variables has a different behavior.

A variable cannot be used until it has been initialized. A compiler error results if the program attempts to use a variable prior to assigning it a value.

```
int x;
int y = x + 2;  // Error: Use of unassigned local variable 'x'
```

In summary, to use variables properly in a program, must do three things:
1. Give it a name in a declaration or initialization.
2. Declare it with a specific type.
3. Give it a meaningful value through initialization, assignment, input, or some other means.

Swapping Variables' Values

Consider the task of swapping the values that are stored in two variables.

```
int x = 2;
int y = 3;
```

The incorrect way to do so is to assign each to the other.

```
x = y;
y = x;          // This code does not work
```

The problem is that when the first line x = y; executes, it stores y's value of 3 into x. This causes x's old value of 2 to be lost. Now when the second statement y = x; is executed, it takes x's new value of 3 and stores it into y, which already stored 3. Therefore, at the end of the two statements, both variables have the value 3, not 3 and 2 as desired.

The problem with the above solution is that x's value is lost in the process. The solution is to introduce a third temporary variable to store x's value for safekeeping, so that it can be put into y.

```
int temp;     // This swapping code does work!
temp = x;
x = y;
y = temp;
```

Self-Check

2-9   Write code to initialize two primitive numeric variables with an initial value of -1.0. Use any variable names you want.

2-10   Which of the following are valid attempts at assignment, given the two following variable declarations?

```
double aDouble = 0.0;
int anInt = 0;
```

```
(a)      anInt = 1;
(b)      anInt = 1.5;
(c)      anInt = "1.5";
(d)      aDouble = 1;
(e)      aDouble = 1.5;
(f)      aDouble = "1.5";
```

2.3 Expressions

Many of the problems in this textbook require you to perform numerical calculations. To do this, you must be able to perform operations on numeric values and variables. A written operation on one or more values is called an *expression*. The simplest expression is a literal value or a variable that stores a value. Alternatively, an expression can be the result of an operator, a method call (discussed later), or a combination of other expressions.

Arithmetic Expressions

An expression involving numbers is called an *arithmetic expression*. Arithmetic expressions have two components: *operators* and *operands*. An arithmetic operator is one of the C# special symbols such as +, -, /, *, or %. The operands of an arithmetic expression may be numeric variable names such as studentGPA, numeric literals such as 5 and 0.25, or results of expressions such as 0.25 * finalExam. There are also other expressions, such as results of method calls, which will be discussed later in this chapter.

Assuming that aDouble is a variable of type double, the following expression has operands of aDouble and 4.5. The operator is +.

```
aDouble + 4.5
```

Together, the operator and operands determine the value of the arithmetic expression. The following table lists several common types of numeric expressions that will be necessary to solve the problems in this chapter.

Common Arithmetic Expressions (partial list)

Expression Form	Meaning	Example	Result
numeric variable	that variable's value	aDouble	aDouble's value
numeric literal	that literal's value	99.5	99.5
expr1 + *expr2*	add the expressions	4.1 + 2.0	6.1
expr1 - *expr2*	subtract	aDouble - 2.0	aDouble's value minus 2.0
expr1 * *expr2*	multiply	16 * 4.5	72.0
expr1 / *expr2*	divide	297.0 / 3.0	99.0
expr1 % *expr2*	modulus (remainder)	66 % 5	1
(*expr*)	parenthesize	(aDouble + 1)	aDouble's value plus 1
-*expr*	negation	-3	negates value of *expr*

Notice that many of the expressions listed above are based on other expressions; this means that a simpler expression, such as a numeric literal, can be used in a larger expression, perhaps with several operators or parentheses.

The +, -, *, and / operators do what you probably expect: they represent addition, subtraction, multiplication, and division, respectively. The % operator is probably new to you, however. It represents the *modulus*, or remainder, operator. The expression x % y returns the remainder when x is divided by y. For example, 44 % 7 evaluates to 2, because 44 / 7 is 5 with a remainder of 2. Be careful, though; when working with negative numbers, % can produce mathematically incorrect results (for example, -6 % 5 evaluates to -1) and probably should not be used.

Compound Expressions and Precedence

The previous definition of expression suggests that more complex arithmetic expressions are possible. Such expressions are often called *compound expressions*, since they combine the functionality of many operators (or of one operator used multiple times).

Here is an example of a compound expression:

```
1.5 * ((aDouble - 99.5) * 1.0 / aDouble)
```

Since arithmetic expressions may be written with many literals, numeric variable names, and operators, C# has rules to allow a consistent evaluation of compound expressions. The following table lists some C# arithmetic operators, and the order in which they are applied to numeric values in compound expressions. The order in which an operator is evaluated relative to other operators is called the *precedence* of the operator. Appendix A includes a table that lists the precedence of all C# operators.

Order of Evaluation (Precedence) of Common Arithmetic Operators

* / %	Evaluate in left to right order, before + and -
+ -	Evaluate in left to right order

When there are no parentheses, the multiplication, division, and modulus operators are evaluated before the addition and subtraction operators. In other words, *, /, and % have precedence over + and -. This means that in a compound expression, all of the *, /, and % operators will be evaluated left-to-right before any of the + or - operators are evaluated. The remaining + and - operators will also be evaluated left-to-right. This is consistent with general mathematical precedence rules you may have seen elsewhere, such as on calculators. Parentheses may be used to override these precedence rules.

The operators of the following expression are applied to the operands in this order: /, +, and lastly -.

```
2.0 + 5.0 - 8.0 / 4.0        // Evaluates to 5.0
```

Parentheses may alter the order in which arithmetic operators are applied to their operands.

```
(2.0 + 5.0 - 8.0) / 4.0      // Evaluates to -0.25
```

Because of the parentheses, the / operator evaluates last, rather than first. Because of this, the same set of operators and operands used in the previous example has a different result (-0.25 rather than 5.0).

These precedence rules apply to binary operators only. A ***binary operator*** is one that requires one operand to the left and one operand to the right. A ***unary operator*** only requires one operand. Consider this expression, which has the binary operator * and the unary minus operator -.

```
3.5 * -2.0                      // Evaluates to -7.0
```

Note that since whitespace (spaces and tabs) is generally not significant in C#, the following expressions would also be legal:

```
2.0+5.0-8.0/4.0                 // Evaluates to 5.0 as well
(2.0+5.0-8.0)/4.0               // Evaluates to -0.25 as well
3.5*-2.0                        // Evaluates to -7.0 as well
```

The unary negation operator - evaluates before the binary * operator: 3.5 times negative 2.0 results in negative 7.0. It may seem confusing to see the negative sign referred to as an operator, but it makes sense in light of the way expressions are defined. The negative sign performs an operation on the number (or more accurately, the expression) next to it: it negates its value. Since the - operator has two different meanings, the C# compiler relies on context to decide whether it is being used for subtraction (as a binary operator) or negation (as a unary operator).

Arithmetic expressions usually have variable names as operands. When C# evaluates an expression with variables, the variable name is replaced by its value. Consider the following code:

```
double numOne = 1.0;
double numTwo = 2.0;
double numThree = 3.0;
double answer = numOne + numTwo * numThree / 4.0;
```

The following simulation evaluates this arithmetic expression by first substituting the value for all variables, and then evaluating each subexpression, using the C# precedence rules:

```
answer = numOne + numTwo * numThree / 4.0;
       =   1.0 + 2.0 * 3.0 / 4.0      // Substitute values
       =   1.0 + 6.0 / 4.0            // * has precedence over +
       =   1.0 + 1.5                  // / has precedence over +
       =   2.5
```

Self-Check

2-11   Evaluate the following arithmetic expressions:

```
double x = 2.5;
double y = 3.0;
```

```
(a)   x * y + 3.0          (d)   1.5 * (x - y)
(b)   0.5 + x / 2.0        (e)   y + -x
(c)   1.0 + x * 3.0 / y    (f)   (x - 2.0) * (y - 1.0)
(c)   0.5 + y + 0.5        (g)   x / 2
```

Increment and Assignment Operators

Assignment operations alter computer memory even when the variable on the left of = is also involved in the expression to the right of =. For example, the variable int j is incremented by 1 with the following assignment operation. The expression j + 1 on the right is evaluated first, then this value is set to be the new value for j:

```
j = j + 1;
```

Programmers often need to add one to an integer variable. C# offers operators with this express purpose. The unary ++ and -- operators *increment* and *decrement* a variable by 1, respectively. For example, the expression j++ adds 1 to the value of j, and the expression x-- reduces x by 1. The ++ and -- unary operators alter the numeric variable that they follow (see the table below).

Statement	Value of j
int j = 0;	0
j++;	1
j++;	2
j--;	1

These new assignment operators are shown because they provide a convenient way to increment and decrement a variable with less typing and redundancy. You will see them often. In fact, the C++ programming language got its name from the ++ increment operator; C++ was one increment above C, if you will.

The ++ and -- operators can be placed after the variable, as shown in the preceding examples, or before it, as in ++j. The behavior is the same, except for one small distinction: the ++ and -- operators can be treated as expressions. So, for example, the following code is legal in C#:

```
int a = 5;
int b = a++;     // using a++ as an expression
```

Strangely, b will be assigned the value 5, not 6 as you might expect. An expression of the form *variable++* has *variable's* original value when used as an expression, then afterward it will increment *variable* as expected. So at the end of the second line above, the value of a will be 6 and the value of b will be 5. However, if the code is written as follows, the result will be different.

```
int a = 5;
int b = ++a;      // using ++a this time, instead of a++
```

When the ++ operator precedes (comes before) the variable, it will increment the variable before the variable is used in the expression. This means that after both lines of code have executed, both a and b will have the value 6. Because of this distinction, the ++ and -- operators are sometimes called pre-increment and pre-decrement when placed before the variable and post-increment and post-decrement when placed after it.

Again, when the *variable*++ is not used as an expression, it does not matter which side the ++ operator is on; in this case, it is usually preferred to use post-increment and post-decrement, putting the ++ or -- on the right side.

Sometimes it is more useful to increment or decrement a variable by a value other than one. To make this easier, C# has several modify-and-assign operators that can be used to add, subtract, multiply, and divide a variable by a value, and then store the result. For example, the two binary operators += and -= add and subtract a value on the right from the variable to the left, respectively.

Expression	Equivalent Meaning
var += *expr*	Increment variable *var* by the value of expression *expr*.
var -= *expr*	Decrement *var* by the value of *expr*.
var *= *expr*	Multiply *var* by the value of *expr*, and store the result in *var*.
var /= *expr*	Divide *var* by the value of *expr*, and store the result in *var*.

Generally the right-side expression *expr* is just a number or variable, but *expr* could be any arbitrarily complex C# expression. These new operators alter the numeric variable that they follow.

Statement	Value of j
int j = 0;	0
j += 3;	3
j += 4;	7
j -= 2;	5
j *= 3;	15
j -= j / 5;	12

Integer Arithmetic with the `int` Type

A variable declared as type `int` can store a limited range of whole numbers—numbers with no fractional component. C# int variables store integers in the range of -2,147,483,648 through 2,147,483,647 inclusive.

Since the double type stores real numbers, and real numbers are a superset of integers, it might seem better to always use the double type to represent numbers in C# programs. However, there are times when int is the better type to use, instead of double. Variables of type int take less memory to store than double variables, and arithmetic operations on them are faster. Also, double variables can store slightly incorrect answers because of approximations in the way they are stored. For these reasons, it is preferred to use int unless the computation specifically needs to use real numbers instead of integers.

All int variables can be used in arithmetic expressions with the operators presented so far, such as +, *, -, and =; using such expressions is called *integer arithmetic.*

Some differences exist in the way int variables behave in expressions. For example, it is illegal syntax to assign a floating-point literal value or a double variable to an int variable. The compiler complains with an error:

```
double aDouble = 2.0
int anInt = 1.999;         // ERROR
int anotherInt = 0.0;      // ERROR
int aThirdInt = aDouble;   // ERROR
```

Notice that the code produces an error even if the floating-point number used is equivalent to some integer; the third example shows that it is not legal to assign 0.0 into an int variable, even though to humans, the number 0.0 is identical to the integer 0.

The main difference between integer arithmetic and real number arithmetic lies in **integer division**. The / operator has different behavior when used on int operands versus double operands. Two integer operands divided with the / operator produce an integer result—not a floating-point result. If the dividend is divisible by the divisor (there is no remainder), this is not an issue; the expression 16 / 8 correctly produces the result 2. However, if the numbers don't divide evenly (if there's a remainder), the result will be different than what might be expected. Integer division produces the *whole number* quotient, without the remainder or fractional component. For example, the quotient obtained from dividing 7 by 4 with integer arithmetic is 1 (not 1.75 as might be expected), because 4 fits into 7 one time with a remainder of 3.

This peculiarity of integer division helps to show why the modulus operator % exists. Binary expressions using % produce the integer remainder from the division of the two numbers. For example, the result of 22 divided by 4 is 5 with a remainder of 2; therefore the C# binary expressions 22 / 4 and 22 % 4 result in 5 and 2, respectively. Numbers that divide evenly will have a remainder (sometimes called a "mod" for short) of 0. For example, 20 / 5 equals 4 and 20 % 5 equals 0.

Integer division is illustrated in the following code, which shows % and / operating on integer expressions and / operating on floating-point operands. In this example, the integer results describe whole hours and whole minutes, rather than the fractional equivalent.

```
// Show minutes in two different ways
int totalMinutes = 254;
int hours, minutes;
double fractionalHours;

fractionalHours = totalMinutes / 60.0;
hours = totalMinutes / 60;
minutes = totalMinutes % 60;
```

At the end of the execution of the preceding code, the variables have the following values:

```
totalMinutes      254
fractionalHours   4.233333333
hours             4
minutes           14
```

The preceding code shows that even though int and double are similar types, there are times when double is the more appropriate type than int, and vice versa. The double type should be specified when you need a numeric variable with a fractional component. Use the int type when you need whole numbers or need the quotient and remainder as whole numbers.

Self-Check

2-12   What value is stored in nickel?

```
int change = 97;
int nickel = 0;
nickel = change % 25 % 10 / 5;
```

2-13   What value is stored in nickel when change is initialized to each of the following?

(a) **4**   (d) **15**

(b) **5**   (e) **49**

(c) **10**   (f) **0**

Type Promotion: Mixing Integer and Floating-Point Operands

Whenever integer and floating-point values are used together in an expression, the integer operand is converted to its floating-point equivalent (3 becomes 3.0, for example). Clearly, this is a transformation that will always be successful; every integer has an equivalent floating-point number, because the set of real numbers contains all integers, and more. The automatic conversion is called a *type promotion*. The expression results in a floating-point number. The same rule applies when one operand is an `int` variable and the other a `double` variable. Consider the following variable declarations:

```
int nine = 9;
double three = 3.0;
```

Given the preceding variables, the expressions below would result in the following values:

Expression	Result	Types of operands
nine / 2	4	(int / int)
nine / 2.0	4.5	(int / double)
nine / three	3.0	(int / double)
nine + three	12.0	(int + double)
2 * nine	18	(int * int)
2.0 * nine	18.0	(double * int)
nine * nine + three	84.0	(int * int + double)
nine / 2 * three	12.0	(int / int * double)
three = nine;	9.0	(double = int)

Expressions with more than two operands will evaluate to floating-point values if one of the operands is floating-point—for example, (8.8 / 4 + 3) = (2.2 + 3) = 5.2. Operator precedence rules also come into play—for example, (3 / 4 + 8.8) = (0 + 8.8) = 8.8.

Self-Check

2-14   Evaluate the following numeric expressions:

(a) 5 / 9

(b) 5.0 / 9

(c) 5 / 9.0

(d) 2 + 4 * 6 / 3

(e) (2 + 4) * 6 / 3

(f) 5 / 2

(g) 7 / 2.5 * 3 / 4

(h) 1 / 2.0 * 3

(i) 5 / 9 * (50.0 - 32.0)

(j) 5 / 9.0 * (50 - 32)

Whitespace

Whitespace is a general programming term (not unique to C#) to describe blank space in a program, such as space characters, tabs, new line characters, etc. Whitespace separates statements, operators, identifiers, and tokens from each other.

In many cases, whitespace is optional. Blank spaces between tokens are ignored by the compiler and do not affect the way a program compiles or executes. You can use this to make your programs more readable. Putting spaces between operators and their operands, putting blank lines between sections of code, and putting comments on complex lines all help to improve the readability of a program.

There are some cases where whitespace does affect a program. For example, inside strings: `"hellothere"` is not the same string as `"hello  there"`. Also, spaces in the middle of an identifier will split it into two smaller identifiers. Trying to access a variable named `studentID` will not succeed if you accidentally type `student ID`.

The following two code fragments demonstrate the power of whitespace to improve the readability of a program. The fragment on the left is shorter (it even has two statements packed onto one line), but it is more difficult to read and interpret what it does. The fragment on the right is formatted more pleasantly, with spacing between operators like = and /, and it also has a comment above it, explaining what is going on.

Poor use of whitespace
```
double credits=42.0,points=117.0;
double GPA=points/credits;
```

Good use of whitespace
```
// calculates a student's grade
// point average (GPA)
double credits = 42.0;
double points = 117.0;

double GPA = points / credits;
```

2.4   Input and Output with the `Console`

Most programs are driven by interaction between the computer and the user. When a program receives data, such as from the user typing on the keyboard, it is called *input*. When the program presents information to the user, such as by writing text onto the screen, it is called *output*. Many programs interact with their users through keyboard input and screen output. This two-way communication using screen and keyboard is a critical component of many programs. In this case, the screen is a black text box called a *console*.

Output with `Console.WriteLine`

C# has an entity named `Console` that can handle interaction with the user. The C# `Console` can be asked to write any type of data onto the screen. A statement named `Console.WriteLine` makes this possible. This statement is followed by parentheses, with a value or expression between the parentheses. The value, or the result of the expression, will be written to the screen. The value may be a `string`, `int`, `char`, or any other expression.

General Form: Output to the Screen with the `Console.WriteLine` Statement

`Console.WriteLine(`*expression*`);`

Examples:

```
Console.WriteLine("Hello");         // output: Hello
Console.WriteLine(2 + 17 * -4);     // output: -66
```

The way to use the `Console` is to type `Console.WriteLine` and then an expression between parentheses. The expression can be a literal value such as `14`, `99.5`, or `"Hello!"`, or it can be the name of a variable that you have declared previously in your program, such as `employeeSalary` or `studentName`. When you put the name of a variable in the parentheses, its value is written on the screen, not its name. The value passed to `WriteLine` can even be the result of a complex expression, such as `5.0 * mySalary / 12`, in which case the expression's result will be displayed.

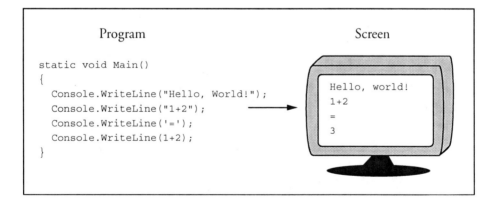

Figure 2.4: Output to the Screen with Console.WriteLine

It is also legal to use the `Console.WriteLine` statement with nothing between the parentheses. This causes a blank line to be written to the screen. The following example illustrates this. In the examples in the rest of the book, when `Console.WriteLine` statements appear in programs, the output they produce to the screen will be shown under the source code with a label of "Output."

```
Console.WriteLine("Line 1");
Console.WriteLine();                    // blank line
Console.WriteLine("Line 2");
```

Output

```
Line 1

Line 2
```

The `Console.Write` Statement

In addition to `Console.WriteLine`, there is also a similar `Console.Write` statement. Both `Console.Write` and `Console.WriteLine` display text to the screen. The difference between them is that while `Console.WriteLine` moves to the cursor to next line when it is finished, `Console.Write` remains on the same line after it is done writing the output. This provides a way to write multiple values on the same line, if so desired.

General Form: Output to the Screen with the `Console.Write` Statement

```
Console.Write(expression);
```

Examples:
```
Console.Write("Please type your name: ");  // A prompt
Console.Write(ID);                          // value of ID
Console.Write((myNumber + 7) * 6);          // expr. result
```

The onscreen result of `Console.Write` statements is illustrated by the following figure.

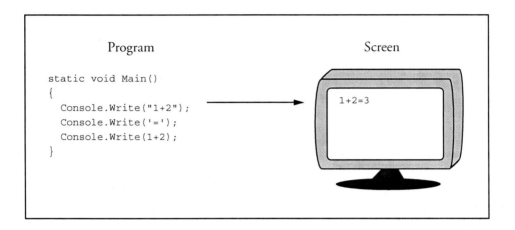

Figure 2.5: Output to the Screen with Console.Write

The following C# program presents an example of using Console.Write together with Console.WriteLine to display output to the screen:

Code Sample: Class WriteSomeConsoleOutput

```
1  // Display some output using the Console class
2  using System;
3
4  class WriteSomeConsoleOutput
5  {
6    static void Main()
7    {
8      int ID = 5678;
9      double salary = 8.50;
10
11     Console.WriteLine("Welcome to my program!");
12
13     Console.Write(2.5);
14     Console.Write(42);
15     Console.Write("ID");
16     Console.WriteLine("all on one line.");
17
18     Console.Write("Your ID is ");
19     Console.Write(ID);
20     Console.Write(" and your salary is ");
```

```
21      Console.WriteLine(salary);
22  }
23 }
```

Output

```
Welcome to my program!
2.542IDall on one line.
Your ID is 5678 and your salary is 8.5
```

There are several things to notice. First, in line 15, `Console.Write("ID");` wrote the letters `ID` on the screen, and then, in line 19, the `Console.Write(ID);` statement wrote the number `5678`. This is because the first statement asks the console to literally write the `string` of letters `"ID"` on the screen, while the second contains simply the name of a variable. In this case it is the variable `ID`, which caused the `Console` to write the variable's value of `5678`.

Second, the `2.5`, `42`, `"ID"`, and `"all on one line."` were all written together on the same line because the program used `Console.Write`, which puts the output on the same line, with no space or line break in between. If you want to write the values each on their own line, change the `Console.Write` statements to `Console.WriteLine`. This might make the program's output easier to read.

Third, notice that even though the salary variable was initialized to `8.50` in line 9, when written to the screen, it shows up as `8.5`. This is because the console by default only writes exactly enough decimal places to represent the given number. To force the console to write the salary in a better format, such as `$8.50`, we will need more advanced output techniques, described in a later section of this chapter.

Fourth, notice the way several `Console.Write` statements can be used to produce a more complex line of output—in this case, the line that displays the ID and salary. However, it is tedious to require four lines of code to make one line of output on the screen. Next, a better technique for complex output will be introduced.

Self-Check

2-15   What output will be written to the screen by the following `Console.Write` and `Console.WriteLine` statements?

```
int number = 24;
double gravity = 9.8;
```

```
Console.Write("number");
Console.Write(number);
Console.WriteLine();
Console.Write(gravity + 1);
Console.Write("gravity + number");
Console.WriteLine(gravity + number);
```

2-16   Write the overall entire output from the code in the previous question.

2-17   Write a complete C# program that displays your name on the screen.

Complex Output with Format Strings

The `WriteSomeConsoleOutput` program from the last section ran into trouble when more complex output was needed. It was difficult to write a long message that included a value from a variable. The workaround used was to write several `Console.Write` statements which, taken together, could show a complicated message. However, there is a better way; `Console.Write` and `Console.WriteLine` have another more advanced syntax, which is described below:

General Form: Output to the Console with Format Strings

Console.Write (*format-string, value0, value1, ..., value-N*);
Console.WriteLine (*format-string, value0, value1, ..., value-N*);

Example:
```
// Display the values of two variables and their sum.
// Output: 2 + 3 = 5
int a = 2,  b = 3;
Console.WriteLine("{0} + {1} = {2}", a, b, a+b);
```

The *format-string* is a string literal (a group of characters surrounded by " marks) that represents the message to write. The string is written in a special format that allows values to be placed inside it. This type of string is called a *format string*. In the example just shown, the format string is `"{0} + {1} = {2}"`.

The *value0* through *value-N* are typically names of variables to be inserted into the format string. They could also be expressions that evaluate to produce some value. In the example just shown, *value0* is the value of variable a (which is 2), *value1* is the value of variable b (which is 3), and *value2* is the value of the expression a+b (which is 5).

To write the value of variables or expressions inside the format string, you specify one or more *argument specifiers* in the format string. The specifiers consist of braces surrounding a positive integer, starting from 0, which is called the *argument*. For example, {0} and {3} are valid specifiers. The specifiers represent the numbers of the values that should be inserted into the output. Putting {0} into the format string, for instance, means to insert *value0* into the format string there.

The following example demonstrates this:

```
int ID = 5678;
double salary = 8.5;
Console.WriteLine("ID is {0} and salary is {1}", ID, salary);
Console.WriteLine("{0}: salary of {1} and ID of {0}", ID, salary);
```

Output

```
ID is 5678 and salary is 8.5
5678: salary of 8.5 and ID of 5678
```

In the above code, the variable ID can be thought of as *value0,* and the variable salary can be thought of as *value1.* When writing the message to the screen, the Console sees the argument specifiers in the format string and inserts the appropriate variable values at those points in the string. Notice how an argument specifier may be used multiple times to insert a variable's value at multiple places in the output, such as the {0} in the second statement.

Also notice that the argument specifiers begin their numbering at 0, not 1. {0} is the first argument specifier and refers to *value0,* the first argument after the format string; {1} is the second and refers to *value1,* the second argument after the string; and so on. This practice of counting starting at 0 is referred to as *zero-based indexing.*

In a group of items that uses zero-based indexing, the items are still numbered in increasing order, but the numbers are off by 1 from what might be expected. This means that element 0 is the first, element 1 is the second, and so on. A list of five values might be referred to as follows:

value 0   value 1   value 2   value 3   value 4

Zero-based indexing is a very important concept that will appear many times throughout the rest of this textbook. Many topics that require understanding of zero-based counting will be introduced later, such as indexing characters in a string (Chapter 3) and indexing elements in an array (Chapter 7). For now, it is important to understand the basic idea, because zero-based indexing is used in the numbering of the format specifiers in format strings.

Self-Check

2-18   What is the output from the following statements?

```
int x = 10,   y = 20;
Console.WriteLine("x is {0} and y is {1}", x, y);
Console.WriteLine("9 {0} 11", x);
Console.WriteLine("{0} days have September", x + y);
Console.WriteLine("{1} / {0} = {2}", x, y, y / x);
```

2-19   Write C# code that will produce the following output, using the definitions of x and y
from the previous question. Use format strings and the values of x and y wherever you
see their values in the output.

```
x10y20
20 10 20 10


In the year 2020, 20% were poor.
```

Advanced Format Specifiers

Argument specifiers can give additional information about the format in which the corresponding value should be written. Here is the general form of the information that can be part of an
argument specifier:

General Form: Argument Specifier

{*number, width : formatCode*}

Examples:

`{0}`	(writes *value0*, in its natural format)
`{2,3}`	(writes *value2*, at a size of 3 spaces wide)
`{1,5:C}`	(writes *value1*, at a size of 5 spaces wide, as a currency amount)

Notes:
The *number* is required and represents a zero-based integer index indicating which value to
format. The *width* is an optional integer width to indicate the number of spaces wide that the
formatted value should fill. The *formatCode* is an optional formatting string to explain what
kind of value is being written (such as a currency, date, real number, etc.).

If the actual length of the string representation of the value is less than *width*, the output is padded with spaces. If *width* is positive, the value is right-justified. If *width* is negative, the formatted value is left-justified. If *width* is not specified, it is assumed to be zero (and therefore the width of the argument is not modified). This type of **width specifier** is useful for aligning text horizontally on the screen.

```
Console.WriteLine("123456789");
Console.WriteLine("{0,9} right-justified", 1234);
Console.WriteLine("{0,-9} left-justified", 1234);
```

Output
```
123456789
     1234 right-justified
1234      left-justified
```

The *formatCode* is an optional string of formatting codes. A **format code** generally consists of one letter, optionally followed by a number. Format specifiers written inside argument specifiers cause the console to write the output differently for that argument. For example, {1:C} means to write *value1* as though it represents the currency of the country in which the program is run. The format specifier {2:F4} means to write *value2* as a floating-point number (real number) with 4 decimal places. Not all types of objects support formatting codes. If *formatCode* is not specified, the argument is formatted in its default format.

```
int ID1 = 5678,  ID2 = 97426;
double payRate1 = 8.5,  payRate2 = 13.79;
Console.WriteLine("ID1: {0,8} payRate1: {1:C}", ID1, payRate1);
Console.WriteLine("ID2: {0,8} payRate2: {1:F0}  {1:F1}  {1:F2}",
                  ID2, payRate2);
Console.WriteLine();
Console.WriteLine("ID1: {0,-8} payRate1: {1,7:C}", ID1, payRate1);
Console.WriteLine("ID2: {0,-8} payRate2: {1,7:C}", ID2, payRate2);
```

Output (when run in United States, where local currency is the dollar)
```
ID1:     5678 payRate1: $8.50
ID2:    97426 payRate2: 14  13.8  13.79

ID1: 5678     payRate1:    $8.50
ID2: 97426    payRate2:   $13.79
```

There is a large set of legal format codes that can be used to format numeric data in a variety of ways. The following is a partial list of some useful formats that can be given to numeric data. You do not need to learn them all or memorize them, but keep the following table handy as a reference when writing future programs that need complex output. The most useful format codes are shown in bold.

Numeric Format Codes

Code	Format	Numeric Argument	Example	Output
c, C	**currency**		**"{0:C}", 123**	**$123.00**
d, D	decimal	# of digits	"{0:D8}", 123	00000123
e, E	exponential	# of decimal places	"{0:E2}", 45.67	4.57E+001
f, F	**fixed precision**	**# of decimal places**	**"{0:F3}", 45.67**	**45.670**
g, G	general	# of significant digits	"{0:G2}", 45.67	46
n, N	numeric	# of decimal places	"{0:N4}", 45.67	45.6700
p, P	percentage	# of decimal places	"{0:P1}", 0.03	3.0 %
x, X	hexadecimal	minimum # of digits	"{0:X}", 100	64

The D and X format specifiers only work on integers, not on real numbers like double values. In all cases, the numbers after D and X are optional, and defaults will be used if no numeric argument is specified (such as a default of 2 decimal places on a percentage).

The rich set of formatting options available in C# output makes it easy to write numbers on the screen exactly the way you want them, whether your program is used for financial, scientific, or computational purposes.

The following program demonstrates some of these format specifiers in action:

Code Sample: Class `DemonstrateFormatting`

```
1  // Demonstrate formatted strings with format specifiers.
2  using System;
3
4  class DemonstrateFormatting
5  {
6    static void Main()
7    {
8      double d = 1472.59;
9      int n = 676685;
10
11      Console.WriteLine("The many formats of {0} and {1}:", d, n);
12      Console.WriteLine("-----------------------------------");
13
14      Console.WriteLine("{0:C}    {0:E2}    {0:F3}", d);
15      Console.WriteLine("{0:G4}    {0:N}    {0:P0}", d);
16      Console.WriteLine("{0:D}    {0:N}    {0:X8}", n);
17    }
18  }
```

Output

```
The many formats of 1472.59 and 676685:
----------------------------------------
$1,472.59    1.47E+003    1472.590
1473    1,472.59    147,259 %
676685    676,685.00    000A534D
```

Self-Check

2-20   What kind of format will be given to a numeric argument if its argument specifier is {0,10:C}?

2-21   Given the following variable declarations:
```
int bigNumber = 1234567;
double biggerNumber = 1230000000.0;
```

Write the Console.WriteLine statements with appropriate argument specifiers to produce the following output:
```
1,234,567.00
1.23E+009
```

Input of Numeric Data with Console.ReadLine

We have just explored output to the screen using the Console. Console is also useful for obtaining input from the screen, such as having the user type values into a program. To make programs more general—for example, to find the GPA for any student—variables are often assigned values by keyboard input. This allows the user to enter any data desired.

Similar to the Console.WriteLine statement for output, there is a Console.ReadLine statement for input. Console.ReadLine reads an entire line of text from the keyboard and returns it as a string value. While the Console.Write and Console.WriteLine statements required you to write a value in parentheses (specifying the value to write), the Console.ReadLine statement just has parentheses with nothing between them. When a Console.ReadLine statement is executed, the program waits for the user to type a value and press Enter. Once the value is typed, the program continues executing. The Console.ReadLine statement can be treated as an expression whose value is equal to the value that the user types on the keyboard.

The `Console.ReadLine` statement is useful; however, by default it produces text data (as a string), not numbers like `int` or `double`. For example, if the user types `3.1415` on the screen, `Console.ReadLine` produces a string with the value `"3.1415"`. It would be more useful to be able to use this value as a `double` with the value `3.1415`.

If the user types a string of letters/numbers that represents a number, it can be converted from a string into a numeric type. This is done with a statement named *type*.`Parse`, where *type* represents the type that you wish to convert into (in this case, `int` or `double`).

The *type*.`Parse` statement, like the `Console.WriteLine` statement, is followed by parentheses with the value to convert between them. In our case, the value to convert is the value that the user types in at the keyboard, so `Console.ReadLine()` (notice the empty parentheses) is written in the parentheses for *type*.`Parse`. The combined expression `int.Parse(Console.ReadLine())` reads a value from the keyboard and converts it into an integer. Similarly, the combined expression `double.Parse(Console.ReadLine())` reads a value from the keyboard and converts it into a real number.

Admittedly, this syntax can be somewhat confusing for a new programmer. However, being able to read numbers from the keyboard is a very important ability, so it is worthwhile to learn the way to do so.

The following is the general form of how the programs in this textbook will gather integer and real number input from the keyboard.

General Form: Reading and Storing Numeric Input from the Console

int-variable = `int.Parse(Console.ReadLine());`
double-variable = `double.Parse(Console.ReadLine());`
Examples:
```
int accountNumber = int.Parse(Console.ReadLine());
double finalExam = double.Parse(Console.ReadLine());
```

Reading input from the console can be thought of as taking numeric data from the keyboard and inserting it into your C# program. When a variable is assigned a value from `Console.ReadLine`, that value is fetched from the keyboard using the console, and the value is stored into the variable.

Normally, when code samples are shown in this textbook, their output is listed at the bottom. However, if a program accepts input from the user with `Console.ReadLine`, the program's output likely depends on what values the user types—for this reason, the output is instead called the *dialogue* for clarity. The idea is that the program and the user are communicating and having a "dialogue" with each other.

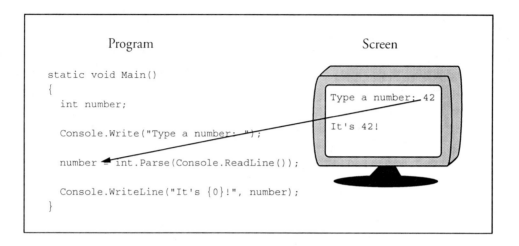

Figure 2.6: Input from the Console with Console.ReadLine

The following code uses the Console.Write statement to prompt the user to enter a number. The Console.ReadLine statement then pauses until the user types the number and presses the Enter key. At that point, int.Parse converts the text typed by the user into a real number. That real number is then assigned to the variable named qualityPoints.

```
double qualityPoints;
Console.Write("Enter quality points: ");          // Prompt the user
qualityPoints = double.Parse(Console.ReadLine()); // Convert / assign
```

Technically, the double.Parse and Console.ReadLine statements could be separated, if so desired. To do this, the program would have to store the result of Console.ReadLine into a string variable, and then write this variable's name in the parentheses for double.Parse. The code would look like this:

```
double qualityPoints;
Console.Write("Enter quality points: ");   // Prompt the user
string input = Console.ReadLine();         // Store input as a string
qualityPoints = double.Parse(input);       // Convert string and assign
```

However, for brevity's sake, the more compact combined style will be used in the rest of the book.

The following program uses numeric input to compute the GPA of a student:

Code Sample: Class NumericInput

```
1  // Reads an int and a double from the keyboard.
2  using System;
3
4  class NumericInput
5  {
6    static void Main()
7    {
8      int credits;
9      double qualityPoints;
10
11     // User inputs an integer, which gets stored in credits
12     Console.Write("Enter credits: ");
13     credits = int.Parse(Console.ReadLine());
14
15     // User inputs a double, which gets stored in qualityPoints
16     Console.Write("Enter quality points: ");
17     qualityPoints = double.Parse(Console.ReadLine());
18
19     // Calculate GPA and write results on screen
20     double GPA = qualityPoints / credits;
21     Console.WriteLine("Credits completed: {0} total", credits);
22     Console.WriteLine("You have {0} quality points",
23                              qualityPoints);
24     Console.WriteLine("GPA is {0}", GPA);
25   }
26 }
```

Dialogue (user input is shown in bold italic)

```
Enter credits: 15
Enter quality points: 48.0
Credits completed: 15
You have 48.0 quality points
GPA is 3.2
```

Prompt and Input Pattern

The output and input operations are often used together to obtain values from the user. The program tells the user what must be entered with an output message and then reads the input to get values for the variables. This happens so often that this activity can be considered to be a programming *pattern* (a solution to a problem that is used so frequently that it is given a nick-name). The ***Prompt and Input pattern*** has two activities:

1. Ask the user to enter a value (prompt).
2. Obtain the value for the variable (input).

Algorithmic Pattern: Prompt and Input

Problem: The user must enter something.

Outline: 1. Prompt the user for input.
                2. Input the data.

Example:
```
Console.Write("Enter credits: ");
int credits = int.Parse(Console.ReadLine());
```

Strange things may happen if the prompt is left out. The user will not know what to enter. Whenever you require user input, make sure you prompt for it first. Write the code that tells the user precisely what you want. First output the prompt, and then obtain the user input.

Here is another instance of the Prompt and Input pattern:

```
Console.Write("Enter test #1: ");

// Initialize test1 with user input
double test1 = double.Parse(Console.ReadLine());
Console.WriteLine("You entered {0}", test1);
```

Dialogue

```
Enter test #1: 97.5
You entered 97.5
```

In general, tell the user what value is needed, then input a value into that variable with a statement such as double.Parse(Console.ReadLine());.

General Form: Prompt and Input of Numeric Data

```
Console.Write("some string that prompts user to type a value");
double-variable = double.Parse(Console.ReadLine());
```
 or
```
int-variable = int.Parse(Console.ReadLine());
```

Example:

```
Console.Write("Enter final exam score: ");
double finalExam = double.Parse(Console.ReadLine());
```

Self-Check

2-22 Write the value for GPA given each of the dialogues shown below:

```
using System;
class SomeArithmetic
{
  static void Main()
  { // Declare several numeric variables
    double c1, c2, g1, g2, GPA;

    // I)nput
    Console.Write("Credits for course 1: ");
    c1 = double.Parse(Console.ReadLine());
    Console.Write("Grade for course 1: ");
    g1 = double.Parse(Console.ReadLine());
    Console.Write("Credits for course 2: ");
    c2 = double.Parse(Console.ReadLine());
    Console.Write("Grade for course 2: ");
    g2 = double.Parse(Console.ReadLine());

    // P)rocess
    GPA = ((c1 * g1) + (c2 * g2)) / (c1 + c2);

    // O)utput
    Console.WriteLine("GPA: {0}", GPA);
  }
}
```

Dialogue 1

```
Credits for course 1: 2.0
Grade for course 1: 2.0
Credits for course 2: 3.0
Grade for course 2: 4.0
```
(a)   GPA: _____

Dialogue 2

```
Credits for course 1: 1.5
Grade for course 1: 4.0
Credits for course 2: 3.0
Grade for course 2: 3.0
```
(b)   GPA: _____

Dialogue 3

```
Credits for course 1: 0.5
Grade for course 1: 4.0
Credits for course 2: 3.0
Grade for course 2: 0.0
```
(c)   GPA: _____

2.5   Calling Static Methods, in Brief

You have now seen interaction with the Console with the Console.Write, Console.WriteLine, and Console.ReadLine statements. This section explains more of the terminology and syntax behind these statements and others like them.

Technically, the Console is an example of a C# entity called a *class*. A class is a named piece of code that, among other things, can declare behaviors to be performed in a program. The predefined *Console class* can perform behavior to do input and output in your C# programs. You have used three of its behaviors: Write, WriteLine, and Read.

These behaviors that can be performed by a class are called *methods*. A method is an executable unit of code that is grouped together and given a name. Think of methods as off-the-shelf tools that your program can access to do useful work.

You can execute methods to use their functionality in your program. This is referred to as *calling a method*. Calling a method causes the program to execute the method's code. Once the statements in the method finish executing, the program returns to the point in the code just after the method call, then it resumes where it left off.

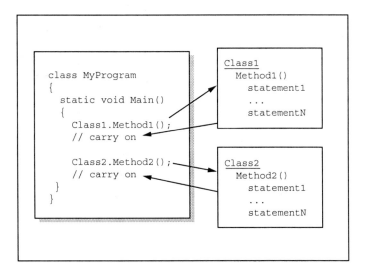

Figure 2.7: Calling Methods

The static void Main in your own code is an example of a method—a special method that must be written in any executable program. When your program is executed, it begins by executing the statements in the Main method. (You can also write additional methods in your own code to enhance the power and readability of your programs; this will be discussed in later chapters.)

There are thousands of prewritten methods available to use in your C# programs. These methods are part of the provided programming support tool known as the **.NET Framework** (pronounced "dot-net"). Some sets of methods relate to mathematics, some to processing strings, others to graphical user interfaces, and still others to transferring information over networks. Some examples of methods in the .NET Framework are Console.WriteLine, int.Parse, and Math.Sin. (The Math class will be covered later in this chapter.)

These types of methods that belong to a class are called *static methods*. Your own Main method is also an example of a static method; note the word static in its declaration. (There are other kinds of methods that will be presented later.) Since it is so powerful to be able to call these methods and use their behavior, let's take a look at the general syntax for static method calls

Syntax for Calling Static Methods

The general form of calling a static method involves stating the class name, then a period, then the method name followed by a list of **arguments**—the values needed by the method—in parentheses. These arguments optionally provide additional information to the method to help it do its work. For example, when you call the `WriteLine` method in the `Console` class (which writes a value onto the screen as text), it needs to know what text should be written. Therefore, a value is written between the parentheses as an argument whenever `WriteLine` is called. To call a method that does not require any arguments, simply write empty parentheses `()` after its name.

General Form: Calling a Static Method

class-name . method-name (*argument0, argument1, ..., argument-N*)

Examples:
```
Console.WriteLine("Hello, world!");
double nineSquared = Math.Pow(9.0, 2);
string input = Console.ReadLine();
int difference = Math.Abs(x - y);
int smallest = Math.Min(x, Math.Min(y, z));
```

Some methods produce a result that is given back to your program. One such method is the `Round` method of the `Math` class. It takes a number, rounds it, and gives back the answer. This is called the **return value** from a method. The entire method call and all of its arguments can be thought of as an expression that evaluates to produce the return value. This means that the result from a method call can be assigned to variables or used in expressions. In fact, the result of one method call can be used as an argument to another method call. This is called a **nested call**. You used a nested method call when you read numeric data, such as `int.Parse(Console` `.ReadLine())`. The return value from the `Console.ReadLine` call was given as an argument to the `int.Parse` method.

Consider the following figure that uses the `Abs` method in the `Math` class. `Abs` accepts an integer argument as an `int` and returns the absolute value as its return value. The expression `Math.Abs(-2)` has a return value of 2. This expression can be used in a larger compound expression, passed as an argument to another method, or assigned into a variable to make the variable's value become the same as the result of the expression.

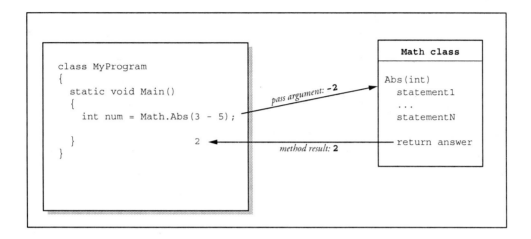

Figure 2.8: Static Method Call with Argument and Return Value

The statements in the Abs method in the Math class examine the number passed to them as their argument and return an appropriate answer that represents the number's absolute value. When the program is run and the method call is evaluated, the statement:

```
int num = Math.Abs(3 - 5);
```

is replaced by the result of the method call, which is essentially the same as:

```
int num = 2;
```

The Math class will now be introduced in more detail.

2.6 Mathematical Operations with the Math Class

C# has a **Math** *class* with methods that help solve mathematical and scientific problems. Here are some examples of methods found in Math:

```
Math.Sqrt(number)    // Return the square root of number
Math.Pow(x, y)       // Return x^y; x to the yth power
Math.Sin(angle)      // Return the sine of angle in radians
```

As with all static methods, these `Math` methods are called by specifying the class name `Math`, followed by a dot, followed by the name of the method, followed by the appropriate number and type of arguments, within parentheses. The `Math` methods are for processing numeric types.

`Math` methods typically require one or more arguments and return a number. Here is one general form to call `Math` methods.

General Form: Calling a Static Method of the Math Class

Math. *method-name(argument(s))*

Examples:
```
Math.Sqrt(4.0)
Math.Round(123.4)
```

The *method-name* is a previously declared identifier representing an operation that belongs to the `Math` class. The arguments represent a set of zero or more expressions separated by commas. In the following method call, the method name is `Sqrt` (square root) and the argument is `81.0`:

```
Math.Sqrt(81.0)   // Example method call whose result is 9.0
```

Although most `Math` methods require exactly one argument, the `Pow` method requires two. In the following message, the method name is `Pow` (for power), the arguments are `number` and `power`, and the method call `Pow(number, power)` calculates $number^{power}$, which in this case is `8.0`:

```
double number = 2.0;
double power = 3.0;
Console.WriteLine(Math.Pow(number, power));   // Output: 8.0
```

Any argument used in a method call must be an expression from an acceptable type. For example, the method call `Math.Sqrt("Bobbie")` results in an error because the argument is a `string`, not a number.

Here are some mathematical and trigonometric methods available to you. An example program that calls several of these methods follows.

Method	Argument	Returns	Value Returned	Example	Result
Math.Abs(x)	double	double	Absolute value of x	Math.Abs(-1.5)	1.5
Math.Abs(i)	int	int	Absolute value of i	Math.Abs(-345)	345

Math.Cos(x)	double	double	Cosine of x radians	Math.Cos(1.0)	0.5403
Math.Pow(x,y)	double	double	x to the yth: x^y	Math.Pow(2, 4)	16.0
Math.Round(x)	double	long[3]	Nearest integer	Math.Round(4.6)	5
Math.Sin(x)	double	double	Sine of x radians	Math.Sin(1.0)	0.842
Math.Sqrt(x)	double	double	Square root of x	Math.Sqrt(4.0)	2.0

Code Sample: Class ShowMathMethods

```
1  // Show the return value from calling Math methods.
2  // The Math class is in the System namespace.
3  using System;
4
5  class ShowMathMethods
6  {
7    static void Main()
8    {
9      double x = -2.1;
10
11     Console.WriteLine("x: {0}", x);
12     Console.WriteLine("Abs(x): {0}", Math.Abs(x));
13     Console.WriteLine("Abs(10-27): {0}", Math.Abs(10 - 27));
14     Console.WriteLine("Pow(x, 2.0): {0}", Math.Pow(x, 2.0));
15     Console.WriteLine("Round(x): {0}", Math.Round(x));
16     Console.WriteLine("Round(3.5): {0}", Math.Round(3.5));
17     Console.WriteLine("Round(9.9): {0}", Math.Round(9.9));
18    }
19 }
```

Output

```
x: -2.1
Abs(x): 2.1
Abs(10-27): 17
Pow(x, 2.0): 4.41
Round(x): -2
Round(3.5): 4
Round(9.9): 10
```

Integer expressions may also be used as arguments to Math methods, even though they are looking for a double argument. As with assignment, the integer value will be promoted to a double. So Math.Sqrt(4) returns the same result as Math.Sqrt(4.0) without error.

Self-Check

2-23   Evaluate `Math.Pow(4.0, 3.0)`.

2-24   Evaluate `Math.Round(3.49999)`.

2-25   Evaluate `Math.Abs(123 - 125)`.

2-26   Evaluate `Math.Abs(123.0 - 125.0)`.

2.7   Errors

Several types of errors can occur when you write a program:

- *Syntax errors*—errors that occur when compiling source code into intermediate language.
- *Intent errors*—the program does what you wrote, not what you intended (also known as "logic errors").
- *Exceptions*—errors that occur while the program is executing (also known as "runtime errors").

Errors may occur when you are compiling your source code, or when the program is running. The easiest errors to detect and fix are those generated by the compiler. These are syntax errors that occur at compile time.

Syntax Errors Detected at Compile Time

A programming language requires strict adherence to its own set of formal syntax rules. Unfortunately, it is easy to violate these syntax rules while translating algorithms into their programming language equivalents. All it takes is a missing { or ; to really foul things up.

As you are writing your source code, you will often use the compiler to check the syntax of the code you wrote (see Figure 2.1). As the C# compiler translates source code into intermediate language so it can run on a computer, it also locates and reports as many errors as possible. If you have any syntax errors, the intermediate language will not be generated. The program will not run. To get a running program, you need to fix all of your syntax errors.

A syntax error occurs when the compiler recognizes the violation of a syntax rule. The intermediate language cannot be created until all syntax errors have been removed from the program. The compiler can generate many strange-looking error messages as it reads your source code. Unfortunately, deciphering syntax errors takes practice, patience, and a complete knowledge of the language. Of course, you will have to decipher these errors before you have a complete knowledge of the language.

So, to improve this situation, here are some examples of common syntax errors and how they are corrected. *Note:* Your C# compiler will generate different error messages.

Compile-time Error	Incorrect Code	Corrected Code
Splitting an identifier	`int my Weight = 0;`	`int myWeight = 0;`
Misspelling a keyword	`integer sum = 0;`	`int sum = 0;`
Leaving off a semicolon	`double x = 0.0`	`double x = 0.0;`
Not closing a string literal	`.Write("Hi);`	`.Write("Hi");`
Failing to declare a variable	`testScore = 97.5;`	`double testScore;`
		`testScore = 97.5;`
Ignoring case sensitivity	`double x;`	`double x;`
	`X = 5.0;`	`x = 5.0;`
Forgetting parentheses	`Console.ReadLine;`	`Console.ReadLine();`

Compilers generate many error messages. However, your source code is the source of these errors. You are the one that wrote the source code. Whenever your compiler appears to be nagging you, remember that the compiler is trying to help you correct as many errors as possible.

The following program attempts to show several errors that the compiler should eventually detect and report. Because the error messages generated by compilers vary among systems, the reasons for the errors below are indexed with numbers to the explanations that follow. Your system may generate different error messages.

```
                      Code Sample: Class CompiletimeErrors (with errors)
 1  using System;
 2
 3  class Compile timeErrors 1
 4  {
 5    static void Main()
 6    {
 7      int pounds = 0;
 8
 9      Console.WriteLine 2 "Enter weight in pounds: " 3
10      pounds = int.Parse(Console.ReadLine 4 ;
11      Console.WriteLine("In the U.K. you weigh {0 5 stone, {1}",
12                        6 Pounds / 14; 7 pounds % 14);
13    }
14  }
```

There are seven errors in the above code; a compiler would catch the five syntax errors, but not the two intent errors.

1. syntax error: Class name cannot contain a blank space

2. intent error: Programmer used `Console.WriteLine` instead of `Console.Write`

3. syntax error: A semicolon (;) is missing

4. syntax error: Missing parentheses after `Console.ReadLine`

5. intent error: A closing brace (}) is missing from the argument specifier

6. syntax error: `pounds` was written as `Pounds`

7. syntax error: The list of values should be separated by commas, not semicolons

Syntax errors take some time to get used to, so try to be patient and find where the error occurred. The error is usually near the line where it was detected, although you may have to fix preceding lines. Always remember to fix the first error first. An error that was reported on line 10 might be the result of a semicolon that was forgotten on line 5. The corrected source code is given next, followed by an interactive dialogue:

Code Sample: Class `CompiletimeErrors` (without errors)

```
 1  // There are no syntax errors here
 2  class CompiletimeErrors
 3  {
 4    static void Main()
 5    {
 6      int pounds = 0;
 7
 8      Console.Write("Enter weight in pounds: ");
 9      pounds = int.Parse(Console.ReadLine());
10      Console.WriteLine("In the U.K. you weigh {0} stone, {1}",
11                        pounds / 14, pounds % 14);
12    }
13  }
```

Dialogue

```
Enter weight in pounds: 146
In the U.K. you weigh 10 stone, 6
```

Exceptions

After your program compiles with no syntax errors, you will have a program containing the intermediate code that can be run on certain computers. However, when programs run, errors still may occur. Perhaps the user enters a string that is supposed to be a number. Or perhaps an arithmetic expression results in division by zero, the result of which is mathematically undefined. Or perhaps the program tries to read a file from a disk, but there is no disk in the drive. All of these errors will cause a program to crash and halt its execution. Such errors that occur while a program is running are known as *exceptions*. Exceptions take their name from the fact that they should only occur rarely in well-written code; they should be the exception, rather than the norm.

Exceptions bring a program to a crashing stop. Whenever possible, code should be written to ensure that it does not generate exceptions. This means that you must carefully inspect mathematical operations to ensure that they do not produce undefined results, check values input by the user for validity, and so on. There are other cases where exceptions are out of the programmer's control, such as when there is no disk available for writing. In these cases, the exceptions should be handled using special code discussed in Chapter 8. For now, the key is exception avoidance—preventing exceptions from occurring in programs in the first place.

The output for the following program shows that C# does not allow integer division by zero. The compiler does a lot, but it does not check the values of variables. Therefore, if at runtime a denominator in a division happens to be 0, a `DivideByZeroException` occurs.

Code Sample: Class `ExceptionExample`

```
1  using System;
2
3  class ExceptionExample
4  {
5    static void Main()
6    {
7      // Integer division by zero causes a DivideByZeroException
8      int numerator = 5;
9      int denominator = 0;
10     int quotient = numerator / denominator;   // A runtime error
11     Console.WriteLine("This message will not be reached");
12   }
13 }
```

Output

```
Unhandled Exception: System.DivideByZeroException:
Attempted to divide by zero.
   at ExceptionExample.Main() in c:\ch02\ExceptionExample.cs:line 10
```

When you encounter one of these exceptions, look at the file name
(ExceptionExample.cs) and the line number (10) where the error occurred. The reason for the
exception (Attempted to divide by zero) and the name of the exception
(DivideByZeroException) are two other clues to help you figure out what went wrong.

Intent Errors (Logic Errors)

Even when no syntax errors are found and no runtime errors occur, the program still may not
execute properly. A program may run and terminate normally, but it may not be correct. Consider the following program:

Code Sample: Class IntentError

```
 1 using System;
 2
 3 // Find the average given the sum and the size of a set of numbers
 4 class IntentError
 5 {
 6   static void Main()
 7   {
 8     double sum = 0.0;
 9     double average = 0.0;
10     int number = 0;
11
12     // Input:
13     Console.Write("Enter sum: ");
14     sum = double.Parse(Console.ReadLine());
15     Console.Write("Enter number: ");
16     number = int.Parse(Console.ReadLine());
17
18     // Process
19     average = number / sum;
20
21     // Output
22     Console.WriteLine("Average: {0}", average);
23   }
24 }
```

Dialogue (may look like this:)

```
Enter sum: 291
Enter number: 3
Average: 0.0103092783505155
```

Such intent errors occur when the program does what you wrote, not what you intended. The compiler cannot detect such intent errors. The expression `number / sum` is syntactically correct—the compiler just has no way of knowing that this programmer intended to write `sum / number` instead.

Intent errors, also known as logic errors, are the most insidious, and usually the most difficult to correct. They may also be difficult to detect in the first place. The user, tester, or programmer may not even know they exist.

Intent errors have caused some disastrous consequences in the past. Consider the program controlling the Therac 3 cancer radiation therapy machine. Patients received massive overdoses of radiation resulting in serious injuries and death, while the indicator displayed everything as normal. Another infamous intent error involved a program controlling a probe that was supposed to go to Venus. Because a comma was missing in the source code (which was written in the Fortran language), an American Viking Venus probe burned up in the sun. Both programs had compiled successfully and were running at the time of the accidents. However, they did what the programmers had written—not what they intended.

Detecting and correcting intent errors can be a difficult process. Perhaps the best way to detect and correct intent errors is to observe mistakes in the execution of a program. Looking at the output from the averaging program above, it is clear that something is wrong with the calculations. By looking backward, you can find the inverted division. Also, a way to prevent intent errors in large programs is to code incrementally, by adding a small portion of the code and then testing its correctness. Testing code's correctness is often as simple as writing the values of some variables onto the screen with `Console.WriteLine`. Performing incremental tests like this provide a sanity check to help prevent larger errors later.

Self-Check

2-27   Assume that a program is supposed to find an average, given the sum and the size of a set of numbers, and that the following dialogue is generated. What clue reveals the presence of an intent error?

```
Enter sum: 100
Enter number: 4
Average: 0.04
```

2-28   Assuming that the following code was used to generate the dialogue above, how can you correct the intent error?

```
Console.Write("Enter sum: ");
number = int.Parse(Console.ReadLine());
Console.Write("Enter number: ");
sum = double.Parse(Console.ReadLine());
average = sum / number;
```

When the Software Does Not Match the Specification

Even when a process has been automated and delivered to the customer in working order as per the perceptions of the developers, there may still be errors. There have been many instances of software working, but not doing what it was supposed to do. This occurs when software developers do not understand the customer's problem specification. Something could have been missed. Something could have been misinterpreted. The customer may not have expressed what was wanted.

A related error occurs when the customer specifies the problem incorrectly. This could be the case when the customer is not sure what she or he wants. A trivial or critical omission in specification may occur, or the request may not be written clearly. In addition, the customer may change her or his mind after program development has begun.

For the most part, the programming exercises in this textbook simply ask you to fulfill the problem specification. If there is something you do not understand, don't hesitate to ask your instructor questions. It is better to understand the problem and know what it is that you are trying to solve before getting to the design and implementation phases of program development. The problem may have been incorrectly specified, or it may have been incompletely specified. Both happen in the real world.

Chapter Summary

  ○ The smallest pieces of a program (tokens) can help you understand general forms and fix syntax errors. C# tokens include special symbols, identifiers, keywords (reserved identifiers), and literals.

  ○ Arithmetic expressions are made up of operators, such as +, -, * (multiplication), / (division) and % (modulus or remainder). A binary arithmetic operator requires two operands, which may be numeric literals (1 or 2.3), numeric variables, or another arithmetic expression.

○ When / has two integer operands, the result is an integer. So `5/2` is `2`.

○ When / has one floating-point operand, the result is floating point: `5/2.0` is `2.5`.

○ The `%` operator returns the integer remainder of one integer operand divided by another. So `5 % 2` is `1`.

○ Be careful in choosing `int` and `double`. Use `double` if there could be a decimal or fractional component to the value, and `int` if you are sure that the value will only need to be an integer. For example, `credits` should be declared as a `double` since it is possible to have `0.5` credits in a course, but `numStudents` would be an `int` because you can't have half a student. (At least, not without an expensive lawsuit!)

○ Write text to the screen using the `Console.Write` and `Console.WriteLine` static methods. Read numeric data using the `int.Parse(Console.ReadLine())` and `double.Parse(Console.ReadLine())` nested method calls.

○ C# provides a mechanism to format data in as wide variety of ways.

○ C# uses zero-based indexing, which means that the first element of a list (such as a format string's argument specifier list) is referred to as number 0, not 1.

○ Methods are collections of related code statements. Classes are groups of related methods and data.

○ Methods of a class are called static methods. The .NET Framework contains many classes with useful static methods.

○ Calling a static method of a class requires writing the class name, then a period, then the method name, followed by parentheses that contain any arguments needed by the method. Example: `double fourSquared = Math.Pow(4, 2);`

○ Instances of the Prompt and Input pattern will occur in this textbook's early programming exercises. Use it whenever a program needs to get some input from the user.

○ The `Math` class contains useful static methods like `Pow`, `Round`, and `Abs` to perform numeric manipulations and calculations.

○ Errors may be present in a program because the problem statement was incorrect or incomplete.

○ Intent errors can be the most difficult to fix—they are often difficult even to detect. Nothing is perfect, including programs that you pay for. They are often released with known errors (called "bugs" or "issues" in an effort to pretend they are not errors).

○ Testing is important, but it does not prove the absence of errors. Testing can only detect errors. But testing can build confidence that a program appears to work.

Key Terms

Abs

argument

argument specifier

assignment

binary operator

char

class

class heading

comment

compile

compiler

compile-time

compound expression

Console class

declaration

decrement

dialogue

double

exception

expression

floating-point

format code

format string

general form

identifier

implicit conversion

increment

initialization

input

integer arithmetic

intent error

int

keyword

literal

Main method

Math class

method

modulus

.NET virtual machine

numeric type

operand

operator

output

namespace

precedence

Prompt and Input pattern

Read

ReadLine

reference variable

Round

runtime

simple type

special symbol

Sqrt

static method

string

syntax

syntax error

token

type

type promotion

unary operator

using

variable

.NET virtual machine

width specifier

Write

WriteLine

XML comments

zero-based indexing

Exercises

1. List three operators that may be applied to a double.
2. List three operators that may be applied to an int.
3. Give one reason why a program should have comments.
4. Describe how programs change the value of a variable.
5. List four types of C# tokens, and give two examples of each.

6. Which of the following are valid identifiers?

    a. `a-one`   g. `1_2_3`

    b. `R2D2`   h. `A_B_C`

    c. `registered_voter`   i. `all right`

    d. `BEGIN`   j. `"doubleVariable"`

    e. `1Header`   k. `{Right}`

    f. `$$$$`   l. `Mispelt`

7. Declare `totalPoints` as a variable to store a floating-point number.

8. Write code that sets the value of `totalPoints` to 100.0.

9. Write the entire dialogue generated by the following program when `5.2` and `6.3` are entered at the prompt. Make sure you write the user-supplied input, as well as all program output, including the prompt.

```
using System;
class Exercise9
{
   static void Main()
   {
      double number = 0.0;
      double y = 0.0;
      double answer = 0.0;

      // 1. Input
      Console.Write("Enter a number: ");
      number = double.Parse(Console.ReadLine());

      Console.Write("Enter another number: ");
      y = double.Parse(Console.ReadLine());

      // 2. Process
      answer = number * (1.0 + y);

      // 3. Output
      Console.WriteLine("Answer: {0}", answer);
   }
}
```

10. Write a message that displays the value of a numeric variable `total`.

11. Given the following two variable initializations, either write the value that is stored in each variable, or report the attempt as an error.

```
int anInt = 0;
double aNumber = 0.0;
```

a. anInt = 4;

b. anInt = 4.5;

c. anInt = "4.5";

d. aNumber = 8;

e. aNumber = 8.9;

f. aNumber = "8.9";

12. With paper and pencil, write a complete C# program that prompts for a number from 0.0 to 1.0 and stores this input value into the numeric variable named relativeError. Echo the input (output the input). The dialogue generated by your program should look like this:

```
Enter relativeError [0.0 through 1.0]: 0.341
You entered: 0.341
```

13. A WriteLine message generates a new line on the screen. However, if you use Write instead, the output appears on the same line. Write the output generated by the following code:

```
// a.
Console.Write("+--+");
Console.Write("+--+");
Console.Write("+--+");
```

```
// c.
Console.Write(1);
Console.Write(2);
Console.Write(3);
```

```
// b.
Console.WriteLine("+--+");
Console.WriteLine("+--+");
Console.WriteLine("+--+");
```

```
// d.
Console.WriteLine(1);
Console.WriteLine(2);
Console.WriteLine(3);
```

14. Assuming that x is 5.0 and y is 7.0, evaluate the following expressions:

a. x / y

b. y / y

c. Math.Pow(2.0, 4.0)

d. Math.Sqrt(x - 1.0)

e. Math.Round(-0.7)

f. 2.0 - x * y

g. (x * y) / (x + y)

h. Math.Round(y + 0.3 - x)

i. Math.Abs(-23.4)

j. Math.Round(0.6)

15. Write the output generated by the following program:
```
using System;
class Exercise15
{
  static void Main()
  {
    double x = 1.2;
    double y = 3.4;

    Console.WriteLine(x + y);
    Console.WriteLine(x - y);
    Console.WriteLine(x * y);
    Console.WriteLine(x / y);
  }
}
```

16. Write the output generated by the following program:
```
using System;
class DoubleArithmetic
{
  static void Main()
  {
    double x = 0.5;
    double y = 2.3;

    Console.WriteLine(x * (1 + y));
    Console.WriteLine(x / (1 + y));
    Console.WriteLine(x / y);
  }
}
```

17. Write the complete dialogue (program output and user input) generated by the following program when the user enters each of the following input values for sale:

    a. **10.00**   b. **12.34**   c. **100.00**

```
using System;
class Exercise17
{
  static void Main()
  {
    double sale = 0.0;
    double tax = 0.0;
    double total = 0.0;
    double TAX_RATE = 0.07;
```

```
            // I)nput
            Console.Write("Enter sale: ");
            sale = double.Parse(Console.ReadLine());

            // P)rocess
            tax = sale * TAX_RATE;
            total = sale + tax;

            // O)utput
            Console.WriteLine("Sale: {0}", sale);
            Console.WriteLine("Tax: {0}", tax);
            Console.WriteLine("Total: {0}", total);
        }
    }
```

18. Explain how to fix the syntax error in each of these lines:

a. `Console.WriteLine("Hello world")`

b. `Console WriteLine("Hello world");`

c. `Console.WriteLine("Hello world);`

d. `Console.WriteLine "Hello world";`

19. Explain the error in this program:

```
using System;
class HasError
{
    static void Main()
    {
        int anInt = 0;

        Console.WriteLine("Enter an integer");
        anInt = double.Parse(Console.ReadLine());
    }
}
```

20. Define the phrase *intent error.*

21. Does the following code always correctly assign the average of x, y, and z to average?

```
        double average = x + y + z / 3.0;   // Compute average
```

22. What value is stored in average after this expression executes?

```
        double average = (81 + 90 + 83) / 3;
```

23. Compute the value stored in slope given this assignment for the slope of a line:
```
slope = (y2 - y1) / (x2 - x1);
```

```
x1      y1      x2      y2      slope
0.0     0.0     1.0     1.0
0.0     0.0    -1.0     1.0
6.0     5.2     6.0    -14.0
```

Programming Tips

1. Use this outline for writing simple classes for your first projects.

   This outline shows the minimal code needed for a C# program (in boldface). The comments are provided to suggest that the projects in this chapter can be solved using the Input/Process/Output pattern.

   ```
   // First-name last-name.
   // Comments describing what this program does.
   using System;

   class FileName
   {
     static void Main()
     {
       // Write code here.
         // Declare any variables needed
         // Obtain input
         // Process data
         // Display output
     }
   }
   ```

2. Name the file the same as your class name.

   The class name and the first part of the file name (before .cs) do not have to match exactly for the program to work, but it makes it easier to find your program later. Consider the following class (program) that has the name FileNameDoesNotMatch stored in a file named NotHere.cs.

```
// File name: NotHere.cs
using System;
class FileNameDoesNotMatch
{
  static void Main()
  {
    Console.WriteLine("Hello");
  }
}
```

This code compiles and runs, but if you have many programs or files, it may be hard to remember what this program does later.

3. Semicolons terminate statements. They do not belong at the end of every line. Make sure you terminate declarations, assignments, and messages with ;. However, do not place a semicolon after static void Main().

4. Fix the first error first.
    When you compile, you may get dozens of errors. Do not panic. Try to fix the very first error first. That may actually fix some of your other errors. Also, note that sometimes fixing one error causes new errors. Do not be too surprised to find out that after fixing an error, the compiler generates errors that were previously undetected. It usually takes many tries to remove all errors.

5. Use intention-revealing names.
    Although you may be tempted to use cryptic identifiers, such as x for credits, go ahead and make the extra keystrokes. Use a name that documents itself. All names should describe what they are intended for. This makes programs more readable to others. Perhaps even more importantly, this makes the program more readable to you. It will help you fix intent errors.

6. Give meaningful values to your variables.
    Although it is not always necessary to initialize ints and doubles at first, attempts to use uninitialized variables later without a value will result in errors. Consider declaring variables when they are needed.
    Instead of this:
    ```
    double credits, qualityPoints, GPA;
    GPA = qualityPoints / credits;
    ```

which results in two C# syntax errors:

```
Variable qualityPoints may not have been initialized.
GPA = qualityPoints / credits;
              ^

Variable credits may not have been initialized.
GPA = qualityPoints / credits;
        ^
```

Declare the variables when they are needed (instead of at the top of the method), like this:

```
double credits = double.Parse(Console.ReadLine());
// Prompt or whatever
double qualityPoints = double.Parse(Console.ReadLine());
// Prompt or whatever
double GPA = qualityPoints / credits;
```

7. Integer arithmetic in C# is different than on calculators.
   Integer division results in an integer. Therefore 5 / 2 is 2, not the 2.5 that your brain and calculator feel are so right.

8. The % arithmetic operator causes confusion.
   The expression a % b is the integer remainder after dividing a by b. Try these now:

   ```
   99 % 50 = ____           101 % 2 = ____
   99 % 50 % 25 = ____      102 % 2 = ____
   4 % 99 = ____            103 % 2 = ____
   ```

9. Have sample problems before you code.
   Know the output with several inputs before you write the program. This helps you understand the problem up front. You should also have some known results for testing your program. Make sure the expected results match the actual output. If they do not match, determine which is wrong.

10. Do more than is required.
    Consider doing more of the programming exercises than you are assigned. Experience makes you a better programmer.

11. The compiler is your friend.
    The compiler may seem like an annoyance, pointing out errors in your program before allowing it to compile. However, this is a very useful thing, because it helps make sure your program is as correct as possible before it runs.

Programming Projects

Each project in this textbook has the following elements:

○ A project number (2A, for example) and a title ("Simple Arithmetic," for example).

○ A problem specification (written paragraphs explaining what the program does).

○ Possibly sample dialogues, asking you to reproduce the dialogue.

2A   Simple Arithmetic

Implement and test a C# program that solves the problem specified in Exercise 1A, "Simple Arithmetic." The problem: For any two numeric inputs a and b, compute the product (a * b) and the sum (a + b). Then display the difference between the product and the sum. The difference should always be positive (*Hint:* use the absolute value). Your dialogue must look like this (except your input will not be in boldface italic):

```
Enter a number: 5.0
Enter a number: 10.0
Product = 50.0
Sum = 15.0
Product - sum = 35.0
```

2B   Simple Average

Implement and test a C# program that solves the problem specified in analysis/design exercise 1B, "Simple Average." The problem: Find the average of three tests of equal weight. One dialogue must look like this (except your input will not be in boldface italic):

```
Enter test 1: 90.0
Enter test 2: 80.0
Enter test 3: 70.0
Average = 80.0
```

2C   Weighted Average

Implement and test a C# program that solves the problem specified in analysis/design exercise 1C, "Weighted Average." The problem: Determine a course grade using this weighted scale:

Quiz average	20%
Midterm	20%
Lab grade	35%
Final exam	25%

One dialogue must look like this (except your input will not be in boldface italic):

```
Enter Quiz Average: 90.0
Enter Midterm: 80.0
Enter Lab Grade: 100.0
Enter Final Exam: 70.0
Course Average = 86.5
```

2D   Wholesale Cost

Implement and test a C# program that solves the problem specified in analysis/design exercise 1D, "Wholesale Cost." The problem: You happen to know that a store has a 25% markup on compact-disc (CD) players. If the retail price (what you pay) of a CD player is $189.98, how much did the store pay for that item (the wholesale price)? In general, what is the wholesale price for any item, given its retail price and markup? Analyze the problem and design an algorithm that computes the wholesale price for any given retail price and any given markup. *Clue:* If you can't determine the equation, use this formula and some algebra to solve for wholesale price:

```
retail price = wholesale price * (1 + markup)
```

Your dialogues must look like this (except your input will not be in boldface italic):

```
Enter the retail price: 255.00
Enter the markup percentage: 50
Wholesale price = 170.0

Enter the retail price: 200.00
Enter the markup percentage: 100
Wholesale price = 100.0
```

2E   Grade Point Average

Implement and test a C# program that solves the problem specified in analysis/design exercise 1E, "Grade Point Average." The problem: Compute a student's cumulative grade point average (GPA) for three courses. Credits range from 0.5 to 15.0. Grades can be 0.0, 1.0, 2.0, 3.0, or 4.0. One dialogue must look like this (except your input will not be in boldface italic):

```
Credits for course 1: 2.0
  Grade for course 1: 2.0
Credits for course 2: 3.0
  Grade for course 2: 4.0
Credits for course 3: 3.0
  Grade for course 3: 4.0
GPA: 3.5
```

2F   Fahrenheit to Celsius

Use the following formula, which converts Fahrenheit (F) temperatures to Celsius (C):

$$C = 5/9(F-32)$$

to write a C# program that inputs a Fahrenheit temperature and outputs the Celsius equivalent. Your dialogues must look like these two when 212.0 and 98.6 are entered for F (except your input will not be in boldface italic):

```
Enter Fahrenheit temperature: 212.0
212.0 Fahrenheit is 100.0 Celsius

Enter Fahrenheit temperature: 98.6
98.6 Fahrenheit is 37.0 Celsius
```

2G   Celsius to Fahrenheit

Use algebra and the formula of the preceding programming exercise to convert degrees Celsius (C) to degrees Fahrenheit (F). Write a C# program that inputs any Celsius temperature and displays the Fahrenheit equivalent. Your dialogues must look like these two when the user enters -40 and 37 for C (except your input will not be in boldface italic):

```
Enter C: -40.0
-40.0 C is -40.0 F

Enter C: 37.0
37.0 C is 98.6 F
```

2H   Seconds

Write a program that reads a value in seconds and displays the number of hours, minutes, and seconds represented by the input. Your dialogues must look like these two (except your input will not be in boldface italic):

```
Enter seconds: 32123
8:55:23

Enter seconds: 61
0:1:1
```

2I   U.S. Minimum Coins

Write a C# program that prompts for an integer that represents the amount of change (in cents) to be handed back to a customer in the United States. Display the minimum number of half dollars, quarters, dimes, nickels, and pennies that make the correct change. *Hint:* With increasingly longer expressions, you could use / and % to evaluate the amount of each coin. Or you could calculate the total number of coins with / and the remaining change with %. Verify that your program works correctly by running it with a variety of input. Your dialogues must look like these (except your input will not be in boldface italic):

```
Enter change [0..99]: 83
Half(ves) : 1
Quarter(s): 1
Dime(s)   : 0
Nickel(s) : 1
Penny(ies): 3

Enter change [0..99]: 14
Half(ves) : 0
Quarter(s): 0
Dime(s)   : 1
Nickel(s) : 0
Penny(ies): 4
```

2J   U.K. Minimum Coins

Write a C# program that prompts for an integer that represents the amount of change in pence to be handed back to a customer in the United Kingdom. Display the minimum number of coins that make the correct change. The available coins are (p represents pence) 1p, 2p, 5p, 10p, 20p, 50p, and 100p (the one-pound coin). Verify that your program works correctly by running it with a variety of input. Your dialogues must look like these (except your input will not be in boldface italic):

```
Enter change: 298
100p: 2
 50p: 1
 20p: 2
 10p: 0
  5p: 1
  2p: 1
  1p: 1

Enter change: 93
100p: 0
 50p: 1
 20p: 2
 10p: 0
  5p: 0
  2p: 1
  1p: 1
```

2K   Circle

Write a C# program that reads a value for the radius of a circle and then outputs the diameter, circumference, and area of the circle. Use the Math.Pow method to compute the area.

- ◯ Diameter = 2 * radius
- ◯ Circumference = pi * diameter
- ◯ Area = pi * radius^2

Note: Use the variable Math.PI, which is as close to pi as your computer allows. For example, this message generates the output shown in the comment:

```
Console.WriteLine(Math.PI);   // 3.141592653589793
```

Run your program with radius = 1.0. Verify that your values for circumference and area match the preceding dialogue. After this, run your program with the input radii of 2.0 and 2.5 and verify that the output is what you expect. Your program must generate a dialogue that looks like this when the input is 1.0 (except your input will not be in boldface italic):

```
Enter Radius: 1.0
Diameter: 2.0
Circumference:  6.283185307179586
Area:  3.141592653589793
```

2L   Range

Write a program that determines the range of a projectile using this formula:

range = sin(2 * *angle*) * *velocity*^{2} / *gravity*

where *angle* is the angle of the projectile's path (in radians), *velocity* is the initial velocity of the projectile (in meters per second), and *gravity* is the acceleration at 9.8 meters per second per second (a constant).

The take-off angle must be input in degrees. Therefore, you must convert this angle to its radian equivalent. This is necessary because the trigonometric method Math.Sin assumes that the argument is an angle expressed in radians. An angle in degrees can be converted to radians by multiplying the number of degrees by pi/180 where pi = 3.14159. For example, 45° = 45 * 3.14159 / 180, or 0.7853975 radians. In this problem, use the constant in the Math class named Math.PI for the value of pi. Math.PI is the closest value to pi that your computer can support.

Your program must generate a dialogue that looks like this when the input is 45.0 degrees and the initial velocity is 100 meters per second (except your input will not be in boldface italic). Round your answer to two decimal places.

```
Takeoff Angle (in degrees): 45.0
Initial Velocity (meters per second): 100.0
Range = 1020.41 meters
```

2M   Departure Times

Write a C# program that reads in two different train departure times (where 0 is midnight, 0700 is 7:00 a.m., 1314 is 14 minutes past 1:00 p.m., and 2200 is 10 p.m.) and displays the difference between the two times in hours and minutes. The program should work even if the first departure time input is later in the day than the second departure time. Assume that both times are on the same date, and that both times are valid. For example, 1099 is not a valid time because the last two digits are minutes, which should be in the range of 00 through 59. Similarly, 2401 is not valid because the hours (the first two digits) must be in the range of 0 through 23. Verify that your program works correctly by running it with a variety of valid input. Here are three sample dialogues with the correct results:

```
Train A departs at: 1255
Train B departs at: 1305
0 hours and 10 minutes

Train A departs at: 2350
Train B departs at: 0055
22 hours and 55 minutes

Train A departs at: 0730
Train B departs at: 0845
1 hours and 15 minutes
```

Using Objects

Summing Up

The previous chapter presented some details about writing simple C# programs that follow the input/process/output pattern. You saw frequently used primitive types such as `int`, `double`, and `char`. You also saw some classes (`Console` and `Math`) and learned how to call static methods such as `ReadLine`, `Write`, and `WriteLine`, which perform well-defined functions that can be used by any program you write.

Coming Up

This chapter is mostly about using objects and getting comfortable with sending messages to objects. A variety of C# types are introduced to show just a little bit of C#'s extensive library of classes. The types will be used in several places throughout this textbook. You will begin to see that programs have many types. After studying this chapter, you will be able to:

- ○ create objects of several different existing types.
- ○ send messages to those objects.
- ○ understand the relationship between classes, types, and objects.
- ○ use C# objects for creating strings, generating random numbers, and storing dates.
- ○ appreciate why programmers partition software into classes, which are collections of methods combined with related data.

3.1 Getting Started with Objects

The previous chapter showed how to call static methods in existing C# classes. You wrote programs with one programmer-defined class and one static method: `Main`. A typical program will use a mix of value types such as `int` and `double`, reference types such as `string`, and programmer-defined types built for the particular system being written. The final program will have many different types from many different sources. Each type is a cohesive unit that provides a set of related methods and data.

Data types in C# fall into two categories: value types and reference types. Value types represent basic values such as the three presented in the previous chapter: `int`, `double`, and `char`. Reference types are typically more complex, in that they can store many values and can store several values of different types. There are four reference types in C#: interface, array, delegate, and the class type. This chapter presents the class type.

The *class* reference type acts as a blueprint for building objects. An *object* is an entity in memory that stores a set of related values and methods of the class. This chapter shows how to build and use objects to help write meaningful programs.

For example, you will see how to use the author-provided type *BankAccount*. `BankAccount` objects store three pieces of data: an account balance as a `double`, a `string` to represent an ID and another optional `string` for its Personal Identification Number, or PIN. A `BankAccount` object can also perform services such as withdrawals and deposits.

Additionally, C# provides many useful class types that you can use in your programs. For example, the `string` type allows `string` objects to store a collection of characters that can represent words, phrases, names, and addresses in any alphabet from around the world. Other types represent time and calendar dates. Others create window, button, and input area objects for graphical user interfaces. Still other C# types allow objects to access databases over networks.

The .NET Framework provides a large number of types. However, it does not supply every type that a programmer could need. You will need to write your own types to model things that are appropriate for your applications. You do this by writing classes, as shown in Chapter 4. For now, a type named `BankAccount` will be introduced that represents account information for users of a banking system.

BankAccount Objects

A banking system program needs to keep track of different customers' account data. You could create several variables to represent each bank account: for example, a `string` for an account ID, a `double` for the account balance, and optionally another `string` for its PIN. However, it would be tedious to create many accounts, and it would be easy to mix up data from different accounts. It seems more natural to think of a bank account as its own entity. If you could declare

BankAccount variables, each one could hold all of the information for one account. If you wanted three accounts, you could just create three BankAccount variables.

There is no BankAccount type in C#. However, C# makes it easy to create your own types. Writing a class creates a new type. You can design the class to have methods and data that let it act as a template of what each object of its type should know, and how it should behave (see Chapter 4).

The authors have written a BankAccount class in a file named BankAccount.cs. If you copy BankAccount.cs from the downloadable source code at **www.fbeedle.com/csharp/code.exe** into the same folder as the C# program that uses it, you can create variables of the BankAccount type in your own code. If you are using an integrated development environment such as Visual Studio .NET, add BankAccount.cs to your project. If you are compiling using the free csc command-line compiler, include BankAccount.cs as an argument during compilation:

```
csc AccountTest.cs BankAccount.cs
```

Other than BankAccount, you will not need to make any special accommodations for the types of objects presented in this chapter. That is because unlike BankAccount, the others are part of C#'s provided libraries. The BankAccount class is supplied to show how existing types can be used. It has been kept simple for ease of study. The available methods on a BankAccount object include Withdraw, Deposit, and ToString.

Constructing Objects

To bring a bank account into a program, declare a variable of type BankAccount and give it a name. This is the same as declaring any other type of variable. The difference comes when initializing the variable to hold a value. Your code must ask for a new object—a new instance of the class. A new object is built by calling a *constructor*. This is a special method in a class, designed for building objects. The name of the constructor is the same as the name of the type. Unlike other methods, constructors must be preceded by the keyword **new** to indicate that a new object is being constructed.

Like all methods, calls to constructor methods are followed by parentheses. The parentheses may contain one or more arguments. Generally, an *argument* is a value that is needed to initialize the *state* of each object (the values the object will store). For example, in the case of a BankAccount, you need to specify the account's ID and the account's initial balance (since the PIN is optional, it need not be specified). This means that BankAccount objects are constructed with two arguments to help initialize them:

1. A sequence of characters (a string) to represent the account holder's name / ID.
2. A number (stored as a double) to represent the initial account balance.

The `BankAccount` object is given a default empty PIN unless it is changed later. Here is one example of how to construct a `BankAccount` object that will have the ID `"Chris"` and an account balance of `125.50`.

```
BankAccount anAccount = new BankAccount("Chris", 125.50);
```

General Form: Constructing an Object and Storing Its Reference

type variable-name **= new** *type(argument(s))*;

Examples:
```
Random generator = new Random(999);
string name = "Devon";
BankAccount anotherAccount = new BankAccount(name, 4065.12);
```

Notes:
The *type* is any valid object type.
The *argument(s)*, if any, help to initialize the object.

Writing `new` followed by a type name constructs and returns a reference to an object of that type. The reference is stored into the variable named *variable-name*. In the line of code above, the `BankAccount` object is stored in memory. The reference used to find it is assigned to `anAccount`, a class-type variable.

In the following figure, the right side shows the new `BankAccount` object in memory. On the left is the reference variable named `anAccount` that stores the information necessary (shown as an arrow) for finding the object in memory. Arrows represent reference values.

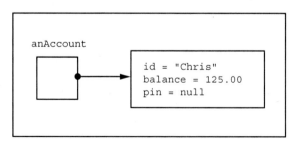

Figure 3.1: A C# Reference Variable and Object

Characteristics of an Object

Every object has the following characteristics:

- ❍ **state:** the values that the object remembers.
- ❍ **behavior:** the set of messages/methods that the object understands.

Given the following construction,

```
BankAccount anotherAccount = new BankAccount("Justin", 60.00);
```

one can derive this information about it:

- ❍ **state:** an account ID of "Justin" and a balance of 60.00.
- ❍ **behavior:** anotherAccount has methods Withdraw, Deposit, and ToString.

Other BankAccount objects have their own separate state. Here is another BankAccount object with its values:

```
BankAccount theNewAccount = new BankAccount("Kim", 1000.00);
```

- ❍ **state:** an account ID of "Kim" and a balance of 1000.00.
- ❍ **behavior:** theNewAccount has methods Withdraw, Deposit, and ToString.

Both BankAccount objects have the same set of methods. The BankAccount class used to build these objects has several methods, including these three:

- ❍ Withdraw (reduce the balance).
- ❍ Deposit (increase the balance).
- ❍ ToString (return a textual representation of a BankAccount object).

The characteristics of an object are shown in the following figure. The class diagram on the left represents the class used as the overall template for each BankAccount object. A class diagram lists the class name in the topmost compartment. The values stored by each object of the class appear in the next compartment. The bottom compartment lists the *messages* that each object will understand (here, it also includes the Balance and PIN properties: see the next section). The three instance diagrams on the right represent three instances of the BankAccount type that were previously constructed. These diagrams describe the current state of three different BankAccount objects. From these diagrams, you can see that one type can have many objects, each with its own separate state.

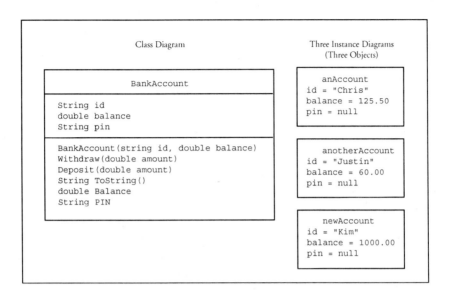

Class Diagram

Three Instance Diagrams
(Three Objects)

```
                BankAccount

String id
double balance
String pin

BankAccount(string id, double balance)
Withdraw(double amount)
Deposit(double amount)
String ToString()
double Balance
String PIN
```

```
       anAccount
id = "Chris"
balance = 125.50
pin = null
```

```
     anotherAccount
id = "Justin"
balance = 60.00
pin = null
```

```
       newAccount
id = "Kim"
balance = 1000.00
pin = null
```

Figure 3.2: BankAccount Class and Instance Diagrams

Different types of objects are constructed differently, depending on what values are needed to let the objects have a meaningful state. Here are a few example object constructions that preview some C# types presented in this chapter:

1. `Random rand = new Random();`
2. `string message = "You have new mail!";`
3. `DateTime newYear = new DateTime(2004, 1, 31);`

These objects work as follows:

1. The `rand` variable refers to a Random object, which can generate random numbers for any program that needs them.
2. A `string` object represents written characters. String objects are special in that they do not need the `new` keyword (discussed later).
3. The `newYear` variable refers to an object that represents the exact date of 31-January-2004.

Self-Check

3-1   What are the two characteristics of every object?

3-2   Consider the following object:

```
BankAccount account22 = new BankAccount("Sally", 75.00);
```

Given the two characteristics you listed in Question 3-1, what are the values of those characteristics for this object?

3.2   Interacting with Objects

After an object is constructed, your code can interact with it. There are two main ways to interact with objects in C#:

1.   Getting or setting values of an object (the properties).
2.   Sending messages to an object (calling an object's methods).

Accessing and Modifying Objects' State: Object Properties

Properties represent the state of an object. In the case of a `BankAccount`, the properties of a `BankAccount` object include its ID string, its PIN number, and its cash balance. Properties are named identifiers inside of an object. They can be thought of as variables inside an object. Properties have names and types, and they represent state values. The values can be optionally accessible and/or modifiable from within the program. `BankAccount` has properties named `ID` (a `string`), `PIN` (stored here as a `string`) and `Balance` (a `double`). By convention, the first letter of a property name is capitalized.

You can access the properties of an object by typing the name of the object, a period, then the name of the property. Stating the name of an object's property can be thought of as an expression that results in the value of that property. You can modify some properties by assigning a value to them. This can be thought of as assigning a value to a variable, where the variable is the object name followed by a dot and the property name.

General Form: Accessing and Modifying State with Properties

```
// an expression used to access property's value
object-name . property-name
```

```
// assigns property to have value of value (set)
```

object-name . property-name = value;

Examples:

```
int numLetters = aString.Length;   // access string's Length
anAccount.PIN = "0291";            // modify account's PIN
```

Notes:

Some properties, such as the Length of a string, cannot be modified.

Here are some examples of accessing the Balance, PIN, and ID properties of a BankAccount. This example also shows that PIN is a modifiable property. This program shows property access or modification in bold:

Code Sample: Class AccountPropertyTest

```
1  // Accesses and sets the properties of a BankAccount object.
2  using System;
3
4  class AccountPropertyTest
5  {
6    static void Main()
7    {
8      BankAccount ba = new BankAccount("Chris", 150.00);
9
10     // PIN is null until the property is set
11     Console.WriteLine("ID {0}, PIN '{1}', Balance {2}",
12                       ba.ID, ba.PIN,    ba.Balance);
13
14     // Set the PIN property
15     ba.PIN = "0123";
16     Console.WriteLine("ID {0}, PIN '{1}', Balance {2}",
17                       ba.ID, ba.PIN,    ba.Balance);
18   }
19 }
```

Output

```
ID Chris, PIN '', Balance 150
ID Chris, PIN '0123', Balance 150
```

Notice that no attempt is made to set the `Balance` property. This property can only be accessed, not modified. A program that tries to modify the Balance property will not compile. This is because the `BankAccount` class was designed with `Balance` as a **read-only property**. This means that code can directly access its value, but not change it. By contrast, `PIN` has a **read-and-write property**. You can set it to have a new value if you so desire (you can change the PIN of a bank account). If you want to change the balance of a `BankAccount` object, you must send a message to the object. The balance of any `BankAccount` object can be modified, but not through a property. The balance can only be changed with the `Withdraw` and `Deposit` methods.

Sending Messages to Objects: Calling an Object's Methods

While properties allow access to some of an object's state, **methods** are often used to perform some task and/or access information about an object. These methods perform some actions. When a method is called on an instance of a class, it is known as *sending a message*. An object-oriented program is one where objects send messages to each other to accomplish the required tasks. For example, any `BankAccount` object has a ***ToString*** method to return information about the account. A `ToString` message to a `BankAccount` object returns a string that is a textual representation of the account. `Withdraw` and `Deposit` messages perform the actions on the account that are represented by their names.

A message is coded by writing the object, followed by a period, the name of the method, and a pair of parentheses that contain any arguments required by the method. This is identical to the syntax for calling a static method, except that instead of preceding the method's name by the name of the class, you precede it with a reference to the object.

General Form: Sending a Message to an Object

object . method-name(argument0, argument1, ..., argumentN)

Example:
```
anAccount.Withdraw(60.00);
string currentState = myObject.ToString();
```

Notes:
The *object* must be of a type that has a method named *method-name*, or the code will not compile.

When a message is sent to an object, the argument list contains zero or more expressions. These are the values required by the method to fulfill its responsibility. For example, `Withdraw` needs to know how much money to withdraw. On the other hand, `ToString` doesn't need any arguments to return the current textual representation of a `BankAccount` object.

Here are some sample messages sent to several different types of C# objects. Note that different messages have zero, one, or two arguments.

Example Messages to Various C# Objects

```
anAccount.Deposit(237.42)      // Credit balance
anAccount.Withdraw(50.00)      // Debit anAccount's balance
anAccount.ToString()           // Get text representation of anAccount
aString.ToUpper()              // Get aString in all uppercase letters
aString.IndexOf(",")           // Find where "," is in aString
aString.Substring(2, 10)       // retrieve characters at index 2 to 12
aRandom.Next(1, 100)           // Get a random number from 1 to 100
```

The following messages result in syntax errors at compile time. Your compiler will generate different error messages than those shown here.

Syntactically Incorrect Messages (compile time errrors)

```
theAccount.Deposit()           // Missing argument (how much to deposit)
Deposit(100.0)                 // Missing an object name and a period
BankAccount.Deposit(100.0)     // Deposit is not a static method
someAccount.Deposit            // Missing parentheses and argument
anAccount.Withdraw("10")       // Wrong type of argument—needs a number
myAccount.Withdrawl(10.00)     // Withdraw is misspelled
```

Fortunately, a failure to supply the object name, the dot, or the method name in the proper order usually generates an error message or warning. In addition, as with any other method, the compiler complains if the code does not supply the required number and type of arguments. Sometimes, you can modify the state of an object by sending messages to that object. For example, calling the `Withdraw` and `Deposit` methods on a `BankAccount` indirectly changes the value of the account's `Balance` property. A deposit increases the balance, and a withdrawal decreases the balance. This change will be reflected the next time the program asks for the value of the `Balance` property. It will contain the new value, plus or minus the amount of the any deposits or withdrawals that have occurred.

This shows why the `Balance` property is read-only. If it could be changed by anything other than a withdrawal or deposit, it would be easy for a program to set the account balance to any amount! Think of the financial consequences this could have. With `Balance` as a read-only property, `BankAccount` objects have control over the balance. This protects against accidental modification of the balance. Also, withdrawals that exceed the account balance can be disallowed, and attempts to withdraw negative amounts of money can be avoided.

In addition to `Deposit` and `Withdraw`, `BankAccount` objects also have a `ToString` method for returning a textual version of their state. The following program constructs two `BankAccount` objects and sends messages to both objects. Those method calls result in the following actions:

○ $133.33 is deposited to the account referred to by `anAcct`.

○ $250.00 is withdrawn from the account referred to by `anotherAcct`.

○ The names and modified balances of both objects are displayed.

Code Sample: Class AccountMethodTest

```
 1  // Send messages to two BankAccount objects.
 2  using System;
 3
 4  class AccountMethodTest
 5  {
 6    static void Main()
 7    {
 8      // Construct two BankAccount objects and store them
 9      BankAccount anAcct = new BankAccount("Hall", 100.00);
10      BankAccount anotherAcct = new BankAccount("Fuller", 987.65);
11
12      // Modify the state of both objects
13      anAcct.Deposit(133.33);
14      anotherAcct.Withdraw(250.00);
15
16      // View the state of both objects
17      Console.WriteLine("ID of anAcct: {0}", anAcct.ID);
18      Console.WriteLine("Balance of anAcct: {0}", anAcct.Balance);
19      Console.WriteLine("anotherAcct: {0}",
20                        anotherAcct.ToString());
21    }
22  }
```

Output:

```
ID of anAcct: Hall
Balance of anAcct: 233.33
anotherAccount: Fuller $737.65
```

Instance vs. Class Methods (object dot or class name dot?)

You have now seen messages that begin with the object reference name. These are known as *instance methods*. In Chapter 2, you saw methods that begin with the class name. Those `static` methods are also known as *class methods*. Class methods, (declared as `static` methods) do not require an instance of the class (an object). There are no values for them to remember; there is no state. For example, the `Math` class uses only static methods because it performs stateless mathematical operations that can only be done one way. There is only one way to calculate the cosine of an angle, or to round a number. It would be useless to be able to use many different `Math` objects. The functionality of the `Math` class is global and unwavering; it does not store values that can change. Therefore, `Math`'s methods are static, meaning they are called using the `Math` class name. Any data that is needed is passed as an argument.

```
double two = Math.Sqrt(4.0);        // correct
```

It is incorrect syntax to try to create `Math` objects and call methods on them. Math is an abstract thing, a concept or idea, not a class for which there are many instances. Therefore, the following code does not make sense (and, indeed, will not compile):

```
Math mymath = new Math();           // incorrect
double two = mymath.Sqrt(4.0);      // this code does not work!
```

On the other hand, rather than class names, instance methods require object reference names. The individual objects have their own state, which may change while the program executes. For example, a `Withdraw` or `Deposit` message to a `BankAccount` changes the account balance. Because each account has its own balance, there may be thousands of `BankAccount` objects. Therefore, the message starts with a reference to the object, to specify which account is to be modified. This is how C# knows which balance to change.

```
BankAccount ba1 = new BankAccount("Chris", 150.00);
BankAccount ba2 = new BankAccount("Kim", 3256.78);
BankAccount ba3 = new BankAccount("Devon", 740.00);
ba1.Withdraw(100.00);   // Chris has 50.00
ba2.Withdraw(56.78);    // Kim has 3200.00
ba3.Withdraw(40.00);    // Devon 700.00
```

When you forget whether a certain method is static, use the same logic as above. Most static methods are associated with a class of things, or a general entity or idea. These include the static methods in the `Math` and `Console` classes. There is really only one math, and most computers only have one console. By contrast, instance methods need a context, or identity, to use them. For example, the Deposit method in the BankAccount class needs to know which bank account should receive the deposit. It would not make sense if the Deposit method were a static method. That would make it very hard for the BankAccount class to know whose account should receive the money.

Furthermore, if the methods in the BankAccount class were designed as class (static) methods, it would be impossible to create multiple accounts! Obviously, this would not be very useful. Having the ability to make many accounts and manipulate them individually is the reason the BankAccount class uses instance methods (non-static).

Self-Check

3-3   Write the output generated by the following code:

```
BankAccount b1 = new BankAccount("B. Linn", 0.00);
BankAccount b2 = new BankAccount("N. Li", 500.00);
b1.Deposit(222.22);
b1.Withdraw(20.00);
b2.Deposit(55.55);
b2.Withdraw(10.00);
Console.WriteLine("{0}: {1}", b1.ID, b1.Balance);
Console.WriteLine("{0}: {1}", b2.ID, b2.Balance);
```

3-4   Each of the lettered lines has an error. Explain why.

```
BankAccount b1 = new BankAccount("B. ");       // a.
BankAccount b2("The ID", 500.00);              // b.
BankAccount b3 = new Account("N. Li", 200.00); // c.
b1.Deposit();                                  // d.
b1.Deposit;                                    // e.
b1.Deposit("100.00");                          // f.
B1.Deposit(100.00);                            // g.
b1.deposit(100.00);                            // h.
Withdraw(100);                                 // i.
Console.WriteLine(b4.ID);                       // j.
Console.WriteLine(b1.ID());                     // k.
Console.WriteLine(b1.GetBalance);               // l.
```

3-5   Write a C# program that constructs one BankAccount object and then uses every possible method and property of that object.

Reading Method Headings and Property Headings

Before you can *send messages* to objects, you must know what the instance method does, what information it needs to accomplish its task, and what can go wrong if the method is used improperly. More specifically, you must know:

1. the method name (remember case sensitivity: ToString is not Tostring).
2. the proper type and number of arguments to pass to the method.
3. the result of the method (what it returns, if it returns something).

All of this information is specified in the *method heading*. A method heading is a declaration of a method's name, return type, and parameters. It may also begin with one or more *modifiers*. Modifiers are keywords such as public, private, and static. They specify the characteristics of the method, such as what other classes are able to see and use it. The examples shown will use public only. The public modifier allows messages to be sent from other objects and classes. You saw several method headings in the previous section on argument passing. Here is the general form for a method heading.

General Form: Method Heading

public *return-type method-name(type1 parameter-name1,*
type2 parameter-name2, ..., typeN parameter-nameN)

Examples:
```
public double Round(double numToRound, int decPlaces)
public int IndexOf(string substring)
```

The *method-name* can be any valid unused C# identifier. The *return-type* represents the type of value returned from the method. The return type may also be void. The **void** keyword indicates the absence of a type. A void method does not return any value (one example is the Console.WriteLine method). The *return-type* can be any primitive type, such as int or double. The return type could also be an object, such as string, DateTime, or BankAccount.

Here are a few syntactically correct method headings:

Method Heading	Found In Type:
public int CompareTo(Object anotherString)	string
public void Withdraw(double amount)	BankAccount
public string ToUpper()	string
public double NextDouble()	Random
public int LastIndexOf(string str)	string

Like methods, properties have headings that represent their type, name, and accessibility. Properties can be read-only, write-only, or read/write. A property heading also specifies whether `get` or `set` is legal for that property (as explained below).

General Form: Property Heading

public *type property-name* {get;}

public *type property-name* {set;}

public *type property-name* {get; set;}

Examples:
```
public int Length {get;}          // used by string class
public int Height {get; set;}     // used by Button class
public int Hour {get;}            // used by DateTime struct
public double PIN {get; set;}     // used by BankAccount class
public double Hours {set;}        // used by Employee class
```

If a property has `get;` in its heading, it is legal to access it (read). If it has `set;` in its heading, it is legal to modify it (write). If it has both `get;` and `set;` it is legal to both access and modify the property (read/write). It is important to understand the syntax of property headings so that you can read them and understand if a property is read, read/write, or write. Property headings like this are shown for the C# types in this chapter, and in the documentation for C#.

Passing Arguments in Messages

Since most methods need one or more pieces of information to get the job done, methods may declare *parameters*. Parameters (also known as formal parameters) are declarations that specify the number and type of arguments that must be used when calling that method. A parameter is an identifier declared between the method's parentheses. For example, this method heading from the `string` class has two different types of parameters:

```
// From the string class
// Return the index of the first value found beginning at startIndex
public int IndexOf(string value, int startIndex)
```

A parameter has a name and a type. For example, this `IndexOf` method has a parameter of type `string` that is named `value`. The second parameter is of type `int` and is named `startIndex`. When you design a method, you specify the number and type of parameters that the method will use. For example, the parameters `value` and `startIndex` will be used by the

IndexOf method to search for a matching character in a string, beginning at the position specified by startIndex.

A method may need zero, one, two, and occasionally even more parameters. These provide information such as "How much money do you want to withdraw from the BankAccount object?" "What is the index of the character you want?" "In what range do you want the random number to be?" "You want the square root of what number?" The parameters specify what values must be passed when a method is called, or a message is passed to it.

When you call a method or send a message to it, you must specify values that correspond to each parameter. These values are the *arguments* (also known as actual parameters). You have already passed arguments to several methods. By doing so, you were giving values to those methods' parameters so that the methods could perform their tasks.

Sending a Deposit message to a BankAccount object requires an argument to specify the amount of money to be deposited. According to the following method heading, this is a double. In the example below, the argument 253.59 is passed to the Deposit method. The value of the argument is assigned to amount inside the Deposit method.

```
// Credit this account by the
// argument associated with amount
public void Deposit(double amount)      // the method heading
                           ↑
        anAccount.Deposit(253.59);      // sending a message
```

The arrow indicates that the value of the argument is passed to the method. This is like an assignment. The value of the argument is assigned to the parameter. The usual rules for assigning values to variables apply.

Calling Math.Pow (a static method) requires two double arguments to be able to return a^b: the base a, and the power b.

```
// Returns the first argument raised to the
// power of the second argument
public static double Pow(double a, double b)     // the method heading
                          ↑          ↑
                 Math.Pow(2.547, 3.02)            // calling a method
```

Constructors also use arguments to correctly initialize an object. For example, to construct a BankAccount, you must supply a string argument (the account ID) followed by a double argument (the initial balance). The principle is the same: the constructor has parameters, which are assigned the values of the arguments.

```
     // The BankAccount constructor header
     public BankAccount(string init_ID, double init_Balance)
                                    ↑                    ↑
BankAccount anAcct = new BankAccount("Darryl", 1576.48);
```

The example above uses literals `"Darryl"` and `1576.48` as arguments. However, an argument may also be a variable, or any expression that evaluates to the parameter's declared type. The usual assignment compatibility rules apply; for example, an argument of type `int` may be passed to a `double` parameter in the method, but not vice versa.

Matching Arguments and Parameters

Arguments are assigned in order. When a method requires more than one argument, the first argument in the method call message is assigned to the first parameter; the second argument is assigned to the second parameter, and so on. Failure to supply the correct number and type of arguments in a method call or message results in a compile-time (syntax) error. `Math.pow(2.0)` is an example. Also, to get correct results, you must order the arguments correctly. For example, to get the value of x raised to the yth power, the method call should be `Math.Pow(x,y)`, not `Math.Pow(y,x)`, which would return to value of y raised to the xth power. Supplying the correct number and type of arguments in the wrong order is a logic error. Remember, the program does what you type, which is not necessarily what you intended.

By looking at the parameters in a method's heading, you can figure out the arguments that must be passed to it. You can also determine what (if anything) the method returns as its result. In short, you can learn how to use the method from its heading.

For example, look at the heading of the ***Substring*** method of C#'s string type (strings will be discussed in detail later in this chapter).

```
// Return a length-long portion of this string starting at startIndex
public string Substring(int startIndex, int length)
```

The method heading for `Substring` provides the following information:
- ❍ The method name: `Substring`.
- ❍ How many arguments are required: 2.
- ❍ What type of arguments are required: `int, int`.
- ❍ What kind of result the method returns: `string`.
- ❍ What the result represents: a part of the string of `length` characters, starting from the position given by `startIndex`.

Since `Substring` is an instance method of the `string` class, you call this method by writing a `string` literal or a `string` reference variable, then a dot, then the method name followed by its arguments in parentheses:

```
string str1 = "forever";
Console.WriteLine(str1.Substring(0, 3));       // for
Console.WriteLine(str1.Substring(3, 4));       // ever

string str2 = "small";
Console.WriteLine(str2.Substring(1, str2.Length - 1)); // mall
```

This following message asks the `string` object referenced by `fullName` to return its characters starting at `startIndex`, which is the character `'M'` (index 0), to length - 1, which is the character `'y'` (index 5).

```
string fullName = "Murphy, John";
string lastName = fullName.Substring(0, 6);
```

A `Substring` message requires two arguments, which specify the portion of the `string` to return. As shown in the method heading, these are `startIndex` and `length`. Both are type `int` because the parameters in the `Substring` method heading are declared as type `int`.

```
public string Substring(int startIndex, int length)
                              ↑              ↑
             fullName.Substring(0,         6);
```

In the example above, when this message is sent, the argument 0 is assigned to the first parameter, `startIndex`. The argument 6 is assigned to the second argument, `length`. The method then uses this information to produce the desired result. As an aside, you cannot see this code as part of the C# `string` class (for which you presumably do not have the source code).

Self-Check

3-6   Determine the following for the Insert method from the string class.

```
// Return a new string with value inserted into this
// string at the specified location startIndex
// An error occurs if startIndex is negative or
// greater than the length of this instance.
public string Insert(int startIndex, string value)
```

    (a) return type

    (b) method name

    (c) number of arguments

    (d) first argument type (if any)

    (e) second argument type (if any)

    (f) third argument type (if any)

3-7   Assuming that `string s = "abcd";`, write `"valid"` for each syntactically valid message, or explain why the message is invalid.

    (a) `s.Insert(1, "e")`

    (b) `s.Insert("e", 1)`

    (c) `s.Insert("X")`

    (d) `"abc".Insert(1, s)`

    (e) `s.Insert("ab", "bc")`

    (f) `s.Insert(6, s)`

3-8   What does this message return, assuming that `string s3 = "time";`?

    `s3.Insert(2, "P")`

3-9   What does this message return, assuming that `string s4 = "time";`?

    `s4.Insert(4, "less")`

3.3   Random Objects

The `BankAccount` class does not come as part of the .NET Framework. It was created by the authors. However, you can create any new type that you need for an application (see Chapter 4). But before seeing how to build your own types, it is important to learn how to use existing types which are included with C# and the .NET Framework.

To further increase your familiarity with using objects, the following predefined C# types will be discussed:

    ○ `Random`: a tool to generate random numbers

    ○ `string`: a sequence of characters

    ○ `DateTime`: a particular instant in time

There are times when you will want random numbers in your programs. For example, you might want to write a guessing game that asks the user to try to guess a random number. In times like these, objects of the **Random** type can prove useful. Random objects can give you random int or `double` values within a specified range. Think of a `Random` object as a way to tell your program, "Give me a number between 1 and 100," or something similar.

No arguments are necessary to construct a Random object:

```
// A new object to generate random numbers
Random rand = new Random();
```

At this point, the object referred to by `rand` can be asked to return a random integer, using its `Next` method. There are multiple versions of the `Next` method. There is also a `NextDouble` method that returns a real number between 0 and 1. If you want a number in a different range than from 0.0 to 1.0, you can multiply or add to scale the number.

The following list shows some of the methods that can be sent to `Random` objects. The methods are listed by their headings. As discussed previously, this should give you most of the information you will need about any particular method.

Random Object (Instance) Methods

```
public int Next()
```
Returns a random integer; the integer can be any legal int.

```
public int Next(int max)
```
Returns a random integer between 0 (inclusive) and max (exclusive).

```
public int Next(int min, int max)
```
Returns a random integer between min (inclusive) and max (exclusive).

```
public int NextDouble()
```
Returns a random real number between 0.0 (inclusive) and 1.0 (exclusive).

Some example uses of `Random`'s methods follow:

```
// get any random positive integer
int randomNumber = rand.Next();
Console.WriteLine("A random integer: {0}", randomNumber);

// get any random integer up to (but not including!) 100
int randomNumber2 = rand.Next(100);
Console.WriteLine("An integer between 0 and 99: {0}", randomNumber2);

// get any random integer between -10 and 10 (including 10 itself)
int randomNumber3 = rand.Next(-10, 11);
Console.WriteLine("An integer between -10 and 10: {0}", randomNumber3);
```

```
// get a random double between 0.0 and 1.0
double randomNumber4 = rand.NextDouble();
Console.WriteLine("A real number between 0.0 and 1.0: {0}",
                  randomNumber4);

// get a random double between 1.0 and 5.0
double randomNumber5 = rand.NextDouble() * 4.0 + 1.0;
Console.WriteLine("A real number between 1.0 and 5.0: {0}",
                  randomNumber5);
```

Possible Output (different each time program is run, because numbers are random)

```
A random integer: 3205981
An integer between 0 and 99: 42
An integer between -10 and 10: -3
A real number between 0.0 and 1.0: 0.6209872345894
A real number between 1.0 and 5.0: 3.5392532830775
```

One application where you could use Random objects is to write a guessing game. The computer would use a Random object to make a random number, and then the user would try to guess the number. An example of such a program appears below:

Code Sample: Class GuessingGame1

```
 1    // A guessing game written using the Random type.
 2    using System;
 3
 4    class GuessingGame1
 5    {
 6      static void Main()
 7      {
 8        // generate a random value between 1 and 100 (inclusive)
 9        int maximumValue = 100;
10        Random randGen = new Random();
11        int randomNumber = randGen.Next(1, maximumValue + 1);
12
13        // prompt the user to guess the random number
14        Console.Write("Enter a number between 1 and {0}: ",
15                      maximumValue);
16        int guess = int.Parse(Console.ReadLine());
17        Console.WriteLine("You guessed {0} and the right answer was {1}",
18                      guess, randomNumber);
19      }
20    }
```

Output

```
Enter a number between 1 and 100: 42
You guessed 42 and the right answer was 57
```

Of course, this game can be frustrating, because it only allows only one guess, and its behavior is the same whether the user guesses correctly or not! In the `GuessingGame` programming exercise in Chapter 6, you will write a better guessing game, which asks repeatedly until the guess is right. To do so, you need to use concepts discussed in the next three chapters.

Self-Check

3-10 Write the C# code to create a random `int` value between `1` and `9999` inclusive.

3-11 Write the C# code to create a random `double` value between `0.25` and `1.75`.

3-12 Write a complete C# program that flips a "coin" using a `Random` object that can only choose between the values 0 (heads) and 1 (tails); write the answer on the screen like this:

```
Coin Flip (0=heads, 1=tails): 1
```

3.4 **string** Objects

C# provides a `string` type that holds text as a *string*, or sequence of characters. Strings have many uses: a `string` object could represent an address, a name, identification (ID), or many other things.

You have already seen strings in many of the programs in this book. In C#, a `string` object is created by writing a string literal—a sequence of characters enclosed within " and ". Since `string` objects are so ubiquitous in programming, C# was designed so you do not need to call a constructor or use the `new` keyword to create a string. Instead, you simply declare a `string` variable and store a string literal in it.

General Form: Constructing and Assigning a String Object (no constructor)

string *variable-name* = "*some sequence of characters*";

Example:

```
string aString = "this is a string";
```

A `string` object can be thought of as a sequential list of characters. (Technically, each letter in a `string` is stored as type `char`; a `string` could be thought of as a group or collection of `char` characters.) The characters in a `string` are numbered from zero. This is an example of zero-based indexing, as discussed in Chapter 2. The zero-based indexes of the characters come into play when you call various methods on a `string` object, such as asking what character is at a particular position in the string, or asking for the position of the first occurrence of a particular character in the string.

The following figure represents the state of a variable initialized to refer to a `string` object:

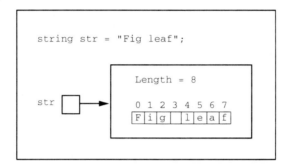

Figure 3.3: String Variable and Object

As with other types of variables, if a `string` variable is declared, but no value has been assigned to it, the variable cannot be used. In the following example, the variable `s1` is declared. Note that it is only initialized and does not refer to any `string` object yet. Until it has been assigned a reference to a string object, it cannot be used as an expression. This means that trying to use `s1` in the following `WriteLine` method call will generate a compile time error:

```
string s1;
Console.WriteLine("s1: {0}", s1);
```

The Compiletime Error from One Compiler

```
Teststring.cs:10: Use of unassigned local variable 's1'
```

A more correct usage of a `string` variable is to assign it a value before using it:

```
string s2 = "I am a string literal";
Console.WriteLine("s2: {0}", s2);
```

Output

s2: I am a string literal

It is also legal to create a `string` object with no characters in it, with the string literal `""`. Notice that the output begins with an empty blank line:

```
string myEmptyString = "";
Console.WriteLine(myEmptyString);
Console.WriteLine("Empty{0}Empty", myEmptyString);
```

Output

EmptyEmpty

Escape Sequences and Interpretation in Strings

Since strings are represented in C# as a sequence of characters between `"` quotation marks, it begs the question, how does one create a string with a `"` character inside it? Also, what about a string that represents two lines of text? How would the programmer put a new-line break or a tab into the string? Simply pressing Enter or Tab in the editor is the wrong solution; C# does not allow string literals to span more than one line and discourages tab characters in strings.

Instead, there are special sequences of characters that can be inserted into strings that represent control commands that would otherwise be impossible to specify. These special characters are called *escape sequences*. An escape sequence in C# consists of a backslash `\` followed by another character. The following abridged list shows some useful escape sequences in C#:

Escape Sequence	Meaning
\\"	quote character "
\\n	new line
\\t	tab
\\\\	backslash character \\

The `\\` escape sequence is needed, because using `\` as a special character removes its ability to be used as a normal character. Writing `\\` solves this; the two adjacent `\` marks combine to represent one backslash character in the string.

If you declare a `string` with escape sequences in it, when the string is printed, each escape sequence will cause a particular action. In the following example, the cursor moves to a new line when "\n" is encountered, and a tab character is printed when "\t" is encountered:

```
string s1 = "Painting \"Starry Night\"\n\tby Vincent Van Gogh";
string s2 = "C:\\Document\\MyFile.doc";
Console.WriteLine(s1);
Console.WriteLine(s2);
```

Output

```
Painting "Starry Night"
        by Vincent Van Gogh
C:\Document\MyFile.doc
```

An escape sequence can also be used in a `char` character literal, since technically the two characters really combine to represent one letter. There is an additional escape sequence \' used with type `char`, because it is needed to represent an apostrophe as a `char` value.

```
char ch1 = '\n';
char ch2 = '\'';
Console.Write(ch2);
Console.Write(ch1);
Console.Write('\t');
Console.Write(ch2);
```

Output

```
'

    '
```

Concatenating `string` Objects with the + Operator

By default, C#'s binary operators only work on specific types. For example, you cannot add two `Random` objects with the + operator; this would not make sense. However, some of the standard operators that you have already used with numeric data can also be used on `string` objects. But their meaning changes when they are used this way. Giving different meanings to operators when they are applied to different types is called *operator overloading*. An operator whose meaning has been specially defined for a particular type is called an overloaded operator.

One example of an overloaded operator for `string` objects is the + operator. With numeric data, + signifies addition. But when it is applied to one or two `string` operands, the result of the expression is a new string that contains the characters from the first string, followed by the characters of the second string:

Expression	Result
`"abc"` + `"123"`	`"abc123"`
`"123"` + `"abc"`	`"123abc"`
`"a"` + `"B"` + `"c"`	`"aBc"`
`"abc"` + `""`	`"abc"`
`""` + `"abc"`	`"abc"`
`"1"` + `"2"` + `"3"`	`"123"`

The + evaluates an expression with string operands through a process known as *concatenation*. Neither of the original strings is changed. Concatenation results in a new `string` that contains both string operands. Concatenating an empty string, `""`, has no effect. This means that `""` + any other string `string2` produces the same `string2`.

Note that concatenation of strings is not really addition in a mathematical sense, and therefore it is not commutative: `string1` + `string2` does not necessarily equal `string2` + `string1` (the results will only be equal if `string1` and `string2` are the same, or if at least one is the empty string `""`). Also note that concatenation of strings that look like numbers has nothing to do with actually adding the numbers. For example, `"1"` + `"2"` equals `"12"`, not `"3"`. The fact that the strings' contents happen to look like numbers does not mean that they will behave like numbers in an expression.

Concatenation can also occur with the + operator in an expression that has only one string operand. Consider the following examples. They result in a string, even though one of the operands is a char in one and an int in the other.

Expression	Result
`"abc"` + `'4'`	`"abc4"`
`'4'` + `"abc"`	`"4abc"`
`"abc"` + `123`	`"abc123"`
`123` + `"abc"`	`"123abc"`
`"1"` + `2` + `3`	`"123"`
`1` + `2` + `"3"`	`"33"`

The last two expressions in the preceding list are of special interest. Notice that, since the + operator evaluates in left-to-right order, performing `"1"` + `2` + `3` is the same as (`"1"` + `2`) + `3`, or `"12"` + `3`, or `"123"`. However, `1` + `2` + `"3"` is the same as (`1` + `2`) + `"3"`, or `3` + `"3"`, or `"33"`.

Just like with primitive types, the string + operator can be combined with the assignment operator = to do a concatenation and assignment:

```
string str = "hello ";
str += "there, ";          // now str is "hello there, "
str += 12345;              // now str is "hello there, 12345"
```

The overloaded + operator also can be used when printing strings to the console. Some instructors and textbooks write formatted output by chaining strings together with + rather than using the {0} format placeholders. Below is an example; the two WriteLine statements would have the same output:

```
// older-style formatting using +
Console.WriteLine("Acct " + acct.ID + " balance is " + acct.Balance);

// newer formatting with {0} and {1}
Console.WriteLine("Acct {0} balance is {1}", acct.ID, acct.Balance);
```

The latter {0} style is recommended, for several reasons. First, it is often cleaner and easier to read. Second, it allows fancier formatting, such as {0:C} for printing currency. Third, it is faster and more efficient for the computer to execute.

The other numeric operators, such as - and *, are not defined for the string type. In general, non-numeric types have few or no defined overloaded operators, because it would be unclear what the operator meant.

The following code demonstrates operators and their use on string objects:

Code Sample: Class StringPlusOperator

```
 1   // Demonstrates overloaded string operator +
 2  using System;
 3
 4  class StringPlusOperator
 5  {
 6    static void Main()
 7    {
 8      string one = "one";
 9      string two = "two";
10      string s_thirty = "30";
11      int i_thirty = 30;
12
13      Console.WriteLine("plus?        {0}", (one + two));
14      Console.WriteLine("plus i30?    {0}", (one + i_thirty));
15      Console.WriteLine("plus s30?    {0}", (one + s_thirty));
```

```
16        Console.WriteLine("i30 plus i30? {0}", (i_thirty + i_thirty));
17        Console.WriteLine("i30 plus s30? {0}", (i_thirty + s_thirty));
18        Console.WriteLine("sixty?        {0}",
19                        (i_thirty + i_thirty + one + two));
20        Console.WriteLine("all?          {0}",
21                        (i_thirty + one + two + s_thirty));
22   }
23 }
```

Output

```
plus?          onetwo
plus i30?      one30
plus s30?      one30
i30 plus i30? 60
i30 plus s30? 3030
sixty?         60onetwo
all?           30onetwo30
```

In the preceding program, notice that when an instance of int is combined with an instance of string using +, the result is a string. It is as though the int is converted into the equivalent string, such as the int literal 30 being converted to the string literal "30". This is another example of type promotion, similar to that seen in Chapter 2 when discussing mixed arithmetic between int and double values.

The following table illustrates forms of expressions that may be created using strings and the + operator:

string Operator +

Expression Form and Meaning	Result Type	Example Expressions and Results
string1 + *string2*	*string*	"yes" + "no" → "yesno"
value1 + *string1*		25 + "yes" → "25yes"
string1 + *value1*		"no" + 2.5 → "no2.5"

Concatenation between two strings, or between a string and some other value; the string representation of the left operand, plus the string representation of the right operand, is returned as the result

`string` Properties and Methods

In addition to their useful operators, objects of type `string` have many useful properties and methods. Here is a partial list:

string object (instance) properties

`public int Length {get;}`
The number of characters in this string. A read-only property.
Example: `"Hello, World!"`. Length has the value `13`.

string object (instance) methods

Methods for learning information about a string:

`public int IndexOf(string value)`
Returns the zero-based index in this string where the string given by value first occurs.
If `value` does not occur in this string, returns `-1`.
Example: `"Michael Pace".IndexOf("a")` returns `4`.

`public int LastIndexOf(string value)`
Returns the zero-based index in this string where the string given by `value` occurs last.
If `value` does not occur in this string, returns `-1`.
Example: `"Michael Pace".LastIndexOf("a")` returns `9`.

Methods for creating a different string from an existing string:
`public string Substring(int startIndex)`
Returns the characters in this string, from `startIndex` (inclusive) to the end of the string.
Example: `"abcdefghij".Substring(3)` returns `"defghij"`.

`public string Substring(int startIndex, int length)`
Returns the next length characters in this string, starting from startIndex (inclusive).
Example: `"abcdefghij".Substring(3, 4)` returns `"defg"`.

`public string ToLower()`
Returns a string that has the same characters as this string, but all uppercase letters are converted to lowercase.
Example: "Lecture Notes".ToLower() returns "lecture notes".

`public string ToUpper()`
Returns a string that has the same characters as this string, but all lowercase letters are converted to uppercase.
Example: "Lecture Notes".ToUpper() returns "LECTURE NOTES".

The rich set of available methods in string objects makes them powerful tools in your C# programs. With the above methods and the Length property, you can send a message to any string object to find out how many letters it has and what letters are in it, and to get a new string with different casing or extra characters. Notice that the indexes returned by methods such as IndexOf and LastIndexOf are zero-based.

The methods of string objects are illustrated in the following program:

```
                    Code Sample: Class DemonstrateSomeStringMethods
 1  // Shows a few string constructions and methods.
 2  using System;
 3
 4  class DemonstrateSomeStringMethods
 5  {
 6    static void Main()
 7    {
 8      string a = "Any old";
 9      string b = " string";
10      string astring = a + b;    // Concatenate a and b
11      // astring is now "Any old string"
12
13      // Show the string in all lowercase.
14      Console.WriteLine("ToLower: {0}", astring.ToLower());
15
16      // Show the string in all uppercase.
17      Console.WriteLine("ToUpper: {0}", astring.ToUpper());
18
19      // Show the number of characters in the string.
20      Console.WriteLine("Length: {0}", astring.Length);
21
22      // Show the position of "ring" in "Any old string".
23      Console.WriteLine("IndexOf: {0}", astring.IndexOf("ring"));
24
25      // Return the Substring, beginning at the first index 4,
26      // 5 characters in length.
27      Console.WriteLine("Substring 1: {0}",
28                          astring.Substring(4, 5));
29
30      // Return the Substring, beginning at the first
31      // argument (4), extending to the end of the string.
32      Console.WriteLine("Substring 2: {0}", astring.Substring(4));
33
34      // Write the original string again, just to prove a point
35      Console.WriteLine("astring: {0}", astring);
36    }
37  }
```

Output

```
ToLower: any old string
ToUpper: ANY OLD STRING
Length: 14
IndexOf: 10
Substring 1: old s
Substring 2: old string
astring: Any old string
```

Self-Check

3-13   What is the value of positionOfG?

```
string s1 = "abcdefghi";
int positionOfG = s1.IndexOf("g");
```

3-14   What is the value of s3?

```
string s2 = "abcdefghi";
string s3 = s2.Substring(4, 2);
```

3-15   What is the value of lastIndex?

```
string s4 = "abcdefghi";
int lastIndex = s4.Length - 1;
```

3-16   Write the value of the expression "Wheatley" + ", " + 123;.

3-17   For each of the following messages, if there is something wrong, write "error"; otherwise write the value of the expression.

```
string s = "Any string";
```

(a) Length(s)
(b) s.Length()
(c) s(Length)
(d) s.IndexOf(" ")
(e) s.Substring(2, 3)
(f) s.Substring("tri")

String Indexing

The Substring method allows access to parts of a string. However, for accessing individual characters from the string, the syntax of Substring is cumbersome.

```
// an example of why Substring is clumsy for individual letters
string str = "A string with many letters";
Console.WriteLine("The 11th letter is: {0}", str.Substring(10, 1));
```

Output

```
The 11th letter is: i
```

There is an easier way to access individual characters in a string, using what is called *string indexing*. To refer to an individual character in a string, write the name of the variable that refers to the string, followed by the index surrounded by square brackets [and]. As with the Substring method, the indexes are zero-based. For example, the seventh letter of a string referred to by a variable named myName is written as myName[6]. This special square-bracket notation to access information about a string object is called an *indexer*, which is a special kind of property.

String indexing provides an easier way to refer to individual letters than using Substring. The preceding code example could be rewritten using string indexing:

```
string str = "A string with many letters";
Console.WriteLine("The 11th letter is: {0}", str[10]);
```

Output

```
The 11th letter is: i
```

An expression using string indexing has type char. String indexing expressions can be used to concatenate strings, or in any place where a char literal value can be used.

Code Sample: Class TestStringIndexing

```
1  using System;
2
3  class TestStringIndexing
4  {
5     static void Main()
6     {
7        string str1 = "Index this string!";
8        string str2 = "Testing ";
9        Console.WriteLine(str2);
10
```

```
11      str2 = str2 + str1[8];    // the i in "this"
12      str2 += str2[3];          // the t in "Testing"
13
14      // string indexing produces a value of type char
15      char lastLetter = str1[17];  // the ! mark
16      str2 += lastLetter;
17
18      Console.WriteLine(str2);
19    }
20  }
```

Output

```
Testing
Testing it!
```

String indexing can only be used to retrieve the value of a given character from a string; it cannot be used to modify a character. In the above example, if you want to change the string str1 so that it has a capital "S" in the word "string" (the 12th letter of the string, therefore index 11), it might be tempting to try to assign a 'S' character into index 11 using the [] indexer; but this is illegal. The following code causes a compiler error:

```
str1[11] = 'S';
```

This is the compiler error message produced:

```
TestStringIndexing.cs(19,5): error CS0200: Property or indexer
'string.this[int]' cannot be assigned to — it is read only
```

As with Substring, using an index value that is outside the bounds of the string—that is, less than 0 or greater than or equal to the string's length—will cause an exception.

```
Console.WriteLine(str2[100]);
Console.WriteLine(str2[-3]);
```

This is the runtime exception produced:

```
Unhandled Exception: System.IndexOutOfRangeException: Index was outside the
bounds of the array.
    at TestStringIndexing.Main()
```

The following table shows the string indexer with some examples.

string Indexer [ ]

Expression Form and Meaning	Result Type	Example Expressions and Results		
string[integer]	char	"hello"[1]	→	'e'
Indexing on a string, which		"HaXoRz"[2]	→	'X'
retrieves an individual		"Plunk 192"[7]	→	'9'
character from that		"o u t e r"[3]	→	' '
string and returns it				
as a char				

Creating Formatted Strings with **string.Format**

In Chapter 2, you used format strings for console output with Console.Write and Console.WriteLine. You can use the same syntax to create specially formatted string values using the static method Format in the string class.

The string.Format method takes a format string and a list of values, and returns a formatted string to match. The syntax is identical to that used in Console.Write and Console.WriteLine, except that the resulting formatted string is not written on the screen, but is instead returned as the method's return value. This means that it can be stored in a variable, used in an expression, or used any other place you would use a string.

General Form: Generating a Format String with string.Format

string.Format(*formatString, value0, value1, ...*)

The following are some examples of string.Format:

```
int numStudents = 32767;
double averageGPA = 2.75;
double tuitionCost = 3950.0;

string stu = string.Format("{0:N0} students with an avg GPA of {1:F3}.",
                           numStudents, averageGPA);

string cost = string.Format("It costs {0:C} to go to college!",
                            tuitionCost);
```

After this code is run, the formatted strings have the following values:

```
stu    32,767 students with an avg GPA of 2.750.
cost   It costs $3,950.00 to go to college!
```

Using format strings with `string.Format` is useful because it lets you generate very complex strings, with precise formatting. This comes in handy when you need to produce complex strings to solve a problem or to write as output to the screen.

Self-Check

3-18   What is the output of the following code?

```
// index:        0123456789012345678901234567889
string mystr = "Four score and seven years ago";
string myst2 = "She sells seashells";
Console.WriteLine(mystr[14]);
Console.WriteLine(mystr[12]);
Console.WriteLine(myst2[7]);
Console.WriteLine(myst2 + mystr[4] + mystr[21] + mystr[29]);
```

3-19   Write the C# code to make an acronym from the following string variables. In other words, concatenate the first letter from each word, then print the result as a message.

```
string word1 = "Digital";
string word2 = "Millenium";
string word3 = "Copyright";
string word4 = "Act";
```

3-20   Write the output generated by the following code:

```
using System;

class StringFormatSelfCheck
{
  static void Main()
  {
    double avogadro = 6.022 * Math.Pow(10, 23);
    int numInches = 12;
    double inchToCM = 2.54;     // 12 * 2.54 = 30.48

    string inchStr = string.Format("{0} inches is {1:F3} cm",
                             numInches, numInches * inchToCM);

    string mole = string.Format("{0:E3} is a lot of atoms!",
                             avogadro);
```

```
        Console.WriteLine(inchStr);
        Console.WriteLine(mole);
    }
}
```

3-21 Write a C# program that constructs one BankAccount object and then, using a format string, builds the following string when the BankAccount's ID is "Chris" and its balance is 54.3:

```
Hello Chris, what a pity you only have $54.30 in your account!
```

String Immutability, Modification, and Reassignment

The string messages seen so far do not actually change the value of the string object. By itself, a ToUpper message to a string object never changes that object, even though names such as ToUpper, ToLower, and Insert sound as if they do. Instead, the methods above like ToUpper and Substring return a new string as their result. If you want to keep the upper case version of a string, you need to assign the return value into a reference to the string object that received the message. Failure to do so is analogous to performing arithmetic on a numeric variable but not storing the result.

Here are two examples showing that assignments are needed to modify both a string and int variable:

Coding Mistake: Modification without Reassignment

```
int x = 7;        string s = "hello there";
x + 10;           s.ToUpper();  // Return value ignored
```

Better: Modification and Reassignment

```
int x = 7;        string s = "hello there";
x = x + 10;       s = s.ToUpper();
```

In each of the examples above, the first line assigns values to x and to string, and the second line attempts to modify them. The "modification without reassignment" code on the left adds 10 to x, but unless the result of that expression is assigned back to x, (as in the "modification and reassignment" example), the value of x does not change. The same is true for the code on the right that uses the methods of string objects. The ToUpper method does not modify the string object itself. Instead, the message evaluates to a new string that is in uppercase. To alter the variable's original value, the new string must be reassigned to store the result of the expression (as in the "modification and reassignment" example). When that happens, the string object

"hello there" is no longer accessible. Instead "HELLO THERE" is an object in memory referenced by the string reference variable s.

The reason that these methods return a new string, instead of modifying the string that you
call them on, is that the string type in C# is *immutable*. The word "immutable" means "not
changeable" or "fixed." In the case of a C# object, "immutable" means that once the object is
created, its internal state cannot be modified. There is no way to change a string object's
internal state (the letters in the string) simply because C# does not provide any message that does
so. Instead, the way to "modify" a string object is to create a brand new string object based on
an existing string, but with the desired modification. This is why the various string methods
return new string objects.

Self-Check

3-22   What is the value of the string object referenced by str after this code executes?

```
string str = "abc123";
str.toUpper();
```

3-23   What is the value of the string object referenced by str after this code executes?

```
string str = "abc123";
str = str.ToUpper();
```

String Input with `Console.ReadLine`

The Console type uses its ReadLine method to read textual input from the keyboard. A
ReadLine message returns a reference to a string object that has from zero to many characters,
as typed by the user at the keyboard. When reading keyboard input using Console.ReadLine, a
reference to a string object is returned that contains all characters and whitespace typed, until the
user types a new line character (presses Enter on the keyboard). The string may contain blank
spaces and tabs, if the user enters these. A line of code can contain the special character \n to
represent the Enter key, but the new line marker is not included in the string returned by
ReadLine; it is discarded.

In the previous chapter, ReadLine was used in conjunction with Parse to produce numeric
input from the keyboard. Fortunately, it is easier to get text input as strings from the keyboard;
no nested calls are needed. To read a string from the user, call Console.ReadLine and store the
method's result into a string variable.

The following program demonstrates the use of ReadLine to gather string input:

Code Sample: Class ReadSomeLines

```
1  // Uses the Console class's ReadLine method to read strings.
2  using System;
3
4  class ReadSomeLines
5  {
6    static void Main()
7    {
8      string firstName, address;
9
10     Console.Write("Enter first name: ");
11     firstName = Console.ReadLine();
12
13     Console.Write("Enter address: ");
14     address = Console.ReadLine();
15
16     Console.WriteLine("Hello {0}, do you really live at {1}?",
17                       firstName, address);
18   }
19 }
```

Dialogue 1

```
Enter first name: John
Enter address: 1600 Pennsylvania Avenue
Hello John, do you really live at 1600 Pennsylvania Avenue?
```

But what if the user enters multiple input values on one line? When speaking about strings, a *word* is a sequence of printable characters separated from the next sequence by whitespace. As described in Chapter 2, whitespace is defined as blank spaces, tabs, or new line characters. Just as a program can contain whitespace, a string often contains whitespace separating words within the string. So, phrased differently, what if the user enters multiple words, and the programmer wants to read and process each word separately?

The Console class does not have a ReadWord or similar method. If you want to split a line of input into words, and the words are separated by spaces, you have to read the entire line, then look for the spaces that separate the words on the line (another method for this is shown in Chapter 8). The string type has the IndexOf method, which is helpful when breaking up long strings into words. If you search for the index of blank space(s) in a string, you will find the places where the words begin and end; you can then divide the string into its individual words using the Substring method.

The following program demonstrates this technique:

131

Code Sample: Class ReadSomeWords

```
1  // Uses the Console class to read multiple input words on one line
2  using System;
3
4  class ReadSomeWords
5  {
6    static void Main()
7    {
8      string name, firstName, lastName;
9
10     Console.Write("Enter your name: ");
12     name = Console.ReadLine();
13
14     // Break up the whole name into first and last name
15     int indexOfSpace = name.IndexOf(" ");
16     firstName = name.Substring(0, indexOfSpace);
17
18     // Store characters from indexOfSpace+1 to end of string
19     lastName = name.Substring(indexOfSpace + 1);
20
21     Console.WriteLine("Your name is: {0}", name);
22     Console.WriteLine("Your first name is: {0}", firstName);
23     Console.WriteLine("Your last name is: {0}", lastName);
24   }
25 }
```

Dialogue

```
Enter your name: Chris Linn
Your name is: Chris Linn
Your first name is: Chris
Your last name is: Linn
```

Self-Check

3-24   Write a line of code that reads one line of input from the keyboard and stores it as a
       `string`.

3-25   Write the C# code that reads a full name from the keyboard and inverts the name before
       writing it back to the screen. The output should be as follows (user input in bold italic):

```
Enter your name: Michael Pace
Alphabetized name: Pace, Michael
```

Converting Objects to Strings and Back: **ToString** and **Parse**

You have already seen that BankAccount objects have a method named ToString to return a textual representation of a bank account. It turns out that ToString is a special method that most data types implement to make it easy to write objects of those types to the screen. C# makes intelligent use of ToString: for any type that has a ToString method, if Console.WriteLine is called on an object of that type, the result of that object's ToString method is written to the screen.

Even better, when an object needs to be treated as a string, C# detects this and automatically converts the object into its string representation by sending a ToString message to it. This includes writing to the screen with Console.WriteLine, as well as concatenating strings and objects using the + operator. When this happens, ToString is called implicitly; when you specify ToString in a line of code, it is called explicitly.

Here is an example of ToString being called implicitly and explicitly to show a textual representation of a BankAccount:

```
BankAccount b1 = new BankAccount("Mary", 123.45);
Console.WriteLine(b1.ToString());
Console.WriteLine(b1);
```

Output
```
Mary $123.45
Mary $123.45
```

As stated previously, ToString is also called implicitly whenever an object is concatenated with a string:

```
BankAccount b1 = new BankAccount("Mary", 123.45);
string str1 = "Let's concatenate it: " + b1;
Console.WriteLine(str1);
```

Output

```
Let's concatenate it: Mary $123.45
```

The ToString method is very powerful because it is used automatically in many places, with no need to call it explicitly. This is helpful because if an object has a ToString method, you can easily have it converted into a string and written on the screen. In Chapter 4, when you learn to write your own classes, you will learn how to add a ToString method of your own.

`ToString` converts an object into an equivalent `string` representation. But it is sometimes also useful to do the opposite—convert a `string` back into the object that it represents. This is called *parsing*. In C#, some data types implement a static ***Parse*** method that takes a `string` argument and returns an object of the given type. This method is useful because it allows easy conversion from `strings` to objects of that data type. For example, the user could type in data at the keyboard, which is then converted to instances of some type by calling that type's `Parse` method.

You have already used the `Parse` method for two of C#'s data types: `int` and `double`. When you called `int.Parse(Console.ReadLine())`, you were taking a string (the result of `Console.ReadLine`) and passing it to the static `Parse` method of the int type, which takes a `string` argument and returns the equivalent `int`. Parsing is also included in many other C# types, such as the `DateTime` type.

3.5 `DateTime` Objects

C# has a `struct` type named *DateTime* for storing calendar dates, such as the current date set on the system clock. A `DateTime` object is constructed with the month, day, and year you want to represent (and optionally, the time of day as well). A `DateTime` object can also be constructed with 0 arguments. In this case, the state will represent the current date and time of the computer clock. For example, if you wish to create an object to represent the date of May 22, 2004, you can construct a `DateTime` object like this:

```
DateTime may22 = new DateTime(2004, 5, 22);
```

`DateTime` objects have a `ToString` method, so they can be written to the screen to see a textual representation of the date they represent. As always, you can do this implicitly by just writing the object itself to the screen:

```
Console.WriteLine(may22);
```

Output
```
5/22/2004 12:00:00 AM
```

`DateTime` Properties
There are many read-only properties in a `DateTime` object. The property names include `Day`, `Month`, and `Year`.

Code Sample: Class ShowDate

```
1  // Shows properties of a DateTime object.
2  using System;
3
4  class ShowDate
5  {
6    static void Main()
7    {
8      DateTime aDay = new DateTime(2004, 5, 22);
9
10     int year  = aDay.Year;
11     int month = aDay.Month;
12     int day   = aDay.Day;
13     Console.WriteLine("Day {0} of month {1} of the year {2}",
14                       day, month, year);
15   }
16 }
```

Output

```
Day 22 of month 5 of the year 2004
```

DateTime has a very useful read-only static property named Now. The Now property returns a DateTime object representing the date and time of the computer clock. It can be used to write programs that use or print the current date when they run. So for example, the following program shows the current date, no matter what day it runs.

Code Sample: Class ShowToday

```
1  // Uses the DateTime.Now property to display the current date.
2  using System;
3
4  class ShowToday
5  {
6    static void Main()
7    {
8      DateTime rightNow = DateTime.Now;     // current date and time
9
10     int year  = rightNow.Year;
11     int month = rightNow.Month;
12     int day   = rightNow.Day;
13     Console.WriteLine("Today is {0}/{1}/{2}", year, month, day);
```

```
14    }
15 }
```

Output (when run on the date of July 24, 2004)

```
Today is 2004/7/24
```

The following program examines `DateTime.Now`, to explore some of the many properties that can be accessed in any `DateTime` object:

Code Sample: Class DateTimeNowTest

```
1  // Explores the properties of a DateTime object.
2  using System;
3
4  class DateTimeNowTest
5  {
6     static void Main()
7     {
8        DateTime rightNow = DateTime.Now;
9        Console.WriteLine("Now = {0}", rightNow);
10       Console.WriteLine("Date = {0}", rightNow.Date);
11       Console.WriteLine("Month = {0}", rightNow.Month);
12       Console.WriteLine("Day = {0}", rightNow.Day);
13       Console.WriteLine("Year = {0}", rightNow.Year);
14       Console.WriteLine("Hour = {0}", rightNow.Hour);
15       Console.WriteLine("Minute = {0}", rightNow.Minute);
16       Console.WriteLine("Second = {0}", rightNow.Second);
17    }
18 }
```

Output (when run during the wee hours of July 25, 2004)

```
Now = 7/25/2004 1:15:17 AM
Date = 7/25/2004 12:00:00 AM
Month = 7
Day = 25
Year = 2004
Hour = 1
Minute = 15
Second = 17
```

The following is a partial list of the useful properties of DateTime objects, and of the DateTime class as a whole. Notice that you ask the DateTime class (using the static Now property)—not any particular DateTime object—for the current time:

DateTime class (static) properties

```
public static DateTime Now {get;}
```
Represents right now: the current date and time.

```
public static DateTime Today {get;}
```
Represents the current date, at time 12:00:00 AM. Equivalent to DateTime.Now.Date.

DateTime object (instance) properties

```
public DateTime Date {get;}
```
A new DateTime object with the same date (month, day, and year) as this DateTime, with a time of 12:00:00 AM.

```
public int Day {get;}
```
The day of the month.

```
public int DayOfYear {get;}
```
The day of the year, between 1 and 366.

```
public int Hour {get;}
```
The hour of the day, in 24-hour time format, between 0 and 23.

```
public int Minute {get;}
```
The minutes past the hour, between 0 and 59.

```
public int Month {get;}
```
The month of the year, between 1 and 12.

```
public int Second {get;}
```
The seconds past the minute, between 0 and 59.

```
public int Year {get;}
```
The year, between 1 and 9999.

`DateTime` Methods and Date/Time Arithmetic

`DateTime` objects have a large number of useful methods, mainly related to performing date and time arithmetic. Date/time arithmetic is useful to answer questions like: "What date is 90 days ahead of May 22, 2004?" Since months have different numbers of days, it can be nontrivial to figure out the answer to these kinds of questions. Luckily, `DateTime` objects have methods named `AddDays`, `AddMonths`, `AddHours`, etc. Each of these methods takes a numeric argument to generate a new `DateTime` relative to the object receiving the message. To move backward in time, the `Add___` methods can accept a negative argument.

Consider the following code that computes the date 90 days ahead of May 22, 2004. As it executes, the `AddDays` method keeps track of the varied days in a month, turnover into future years, and whether or not the year is a leap year, when February 29 would be a valid date. This method of `DateTime` hides many details and is much easier to use than performing date arithmetic yourself.

Code Sample: Class DateTimeArithmetic1

```
1  // Performs simple DateTime arithmetic.
2  using System;
3
4  class DateTimeArithmetic1
5  {
6    static void Main()
7    {
8      DateTime dateOfPurchase = new DateTime(2004, 5, 22);
9      // Move 90 days ahead
10     dateOfPurchase = dateOfPurchase.AddDays(90);
11
12     int year  = dateOfPurchase.Year;
13     int month = dateOfPurchase.Month;
14     int day   = dateOfPurchase.Day;
15     Console.WriteLine("Warranty expires on {0}/{1}/{2}",
16                                        year, month, day);
17   }
18 }
```

Output

```
Warranty expires on 2004/8/20
```

In line 10, notice that just calling AddDay on dateOfPurchase would not change the value stored in dateOfPurchase. This line is an example of needing to use an assignment statement to replace the old object referenced with the new object.

It is easy to accidentally write code that throws away the new value, like the following:

```
DateTime someDate = new DateTime(2004, 6, 17);
someDate.AddDays(45);
```

To avoid losing the new value, you must write code that saves it, like this:

```
DateTime someDate = new DateTime(2004, 6, 17);
someDate = someDate.AddDays(45);
```

In the discussion of string objects, you saw that many methods did not modify the string they were called upon, but rather returned a new string with the modified value. The same is true for the code above that uses the methods of DateTime objects: the methods do not modify the DateTime object itself, but rather evaluate like an expression that returns a new DateTime with the modified value. To save the new value, assign the new object to store the result of the expression.

The following is a partial list of the useful methods of the DateTime class, and of DateTime objects:

DateTime class (static) methods

```
public static int DaysInMonth(int year, int month)
```
Returns how many days the given month has in the given year.

```
public static DateTime Parse(string value)
```
Converts the given string into a DateTime, if possible.

DateTime object (instance) methods

```
public DateTime AddDays(double value)
```
Adds the given number of days to this DateTime and returns a new DateTime.

```
public DateTime AddHours(double value)
```
Adds the given number of hours to this DateTime and returns a new DateTime.

```
public DateTime AddMinutes(double value)
```
Adds the given number of minutes to this DateTime and returns a new DateTime.

```
public DateTime AddMonths(int months)
```

Adds the given number of months to this `DateTime` and returns a new `DateTime`.

```
public DateTime AddSeconds(double value)
```
Adds the given number of seconds to this `DateTime` and returns a new `DateTime`.

```
public DateTime AddYears(int value)
```
Adds the given number of years to this `DateTime` and returns a new `DateTime`.

```
public override string ToString()
```
Returns a textual representation of this `DateTime`.

```
public string ToShortDateString()
```
Returns month / day / year as a string (no time).

By making the argument negative, you can use the various Add___ methods to specify a date in the past. This is especially useful when used with the static `DateTime` properties like `Today` and `Now`:

```
DateTime halfHourAgo = DateTime.Now.AddMinutes(-30);
DateTime yesterday = DateTime.Today.AddDays(-1);
```

Self-Check

3-26   Write code that will put the following output on the screen, using a `DateTime` object:
```
10/8/2001 12:00:00 AM
```

3-27   Write code that writes the current date and time on the screen.

3-28   Write code that asks the user to type a year, then displays how many days February had in that year. The output should be as follows (user input in bold italic):

```
Enter a year: 1996
In 1996, February had 29 days.
```

Console Input of **DateTime** Objects with **DateTime.Parse**

A noteworthy method listed above is the `DateTime.Parse` method. This method provides an example of parsing, as discussed earlier in this chapter. The `Parse` method takes a `string` that represents a date and converts it into a `DateTime` object, which is returned as the result value. Generating `DateTime` objects with `Parse` is useful when grabbing input of dates and times from the keyboard.

The following time machine program shows how you can use date arithmetic with the `DateTime.Parse` method to manipulate dates that the user types in:

Code Sample: Class DateTimeArithmetic2

```
1  // Demonstrates more date arithmetic and DateTime.Parse method:
2  using System;
3
4  class DateTimeArithmetic2
5  {
6    static void Main()
7    {
8      int years, days;
9      string startDateStr;
10     DateTime date;
11
12     // prompt user to enter a date
13     Console.WriteLine("It's the amazing time machine!");
14     Console.Write("What date would you like to start from? ");
15
16     // read date and convert to a DateTime object
17     startDateStr = Console.ReadLine();
18     date = DateTime.Parse(startDateStr);
19
20     // prompt user for time to travel
21     Console.Write("How many years would you like to travel? ");
22     years = int.Parse(Console.ReadLine());
23
24     Console.Write("And how many days? ");
25     days = int.Parse(Console.ReadLine());
26
27     // perform some date arithmetic (modify and reassign)
28     date = date.AddYears(years);
29     date = date.AddDays(days);
30
31     Console.WriteLine();
32     Console.WriteLine("POOF! The date is now {0}", date);
33   }
34 }
```

Dialogue

```
It's the amazing time machine!
What date would you like to start from? 12/25/2000
How many years would you like to travel? 500
And how many days? 150

POOF! The date is now 5/24/2501 12:00:00 AM
```

Self-Check

3-29   Write C# code to calculate the date 120 days past February 1, 1992 and write it on the screen.

3-30   Write code that asks the user to type a month, then a day, then a year, then uses that information to create an appropriate `DateTime`. Then make a new `DateTime` that is 50 years backward from the original `DateTime`, and write it on the screen, as follows:

```
Enter a month: 9
Enter a day: 19
Enter a year: 1979
50 years before that was 9/19/1929 12:00:00 AM
```

3-31   Write the same code, except let the user enter the entire date on one line, as follows:

```
Enter a date: 9/19/1979
50 years before that was 9/19/1929 12:00:00 AM
```

DateTime in Format Strings

As mentioned earlier, `DateTime` objects can be written to the screen using `Console.WriteLine`. By default, a `DateTime` object is written out in a general format that displays its date and its time. However, there are times when it is more useful to write the `DateTime` in a different way. For example, perhaps only the date is of interest, or only the time is important. Sometimes, you may want additional details like the seconds or the day of the week, while at other times they just get in the way.

To get more flexibility and control over the way a `DateTime` is written to the screen, you can put a format specifier for a `DateTime` in a format string. The following table summarizes the legal format specifiers and their resulting output:

Specifier	Format	Example	Output
d	short date	{0:d}	4/10/2001
D	long date	{0:D}	Tuesday, April 10, 2001
f	short full date/time	{0:f}	Tuesday, April 10, 2001 3:51 PM
F	long full date/time	{0:F}	Tuesday, April 10, 2001 3:51:24 PM
g	short general date/time	{0:g}	4/10/2001 3:51 PM
G	long general date/time	{0:G}	4/10/2001 3:51:24 PM
m, M	month and day	{0:M}	April 10
t	short time	{0:t}	12:00 AM
T	long time	{0:T}	12:00:00 AM
y, Y	year and month	{0:Y}	April, 2001

The following program shows several DateTime format specifiers in action. Notice how the default format for the DateTime object is the long general form, identical to the G format specifier:

Code Sample: Class DateTimeFormats

```
1  // Demonstrates date/time format specifiers.
2  using System;
3
4  class DateTimeFormats
5  {
6    static void Main()
7    {
8      DateTime date = DateTime.Now;
9
10     Console.WriteLine("  = {0}", date);
11     Console.WriteLine("d = {0:d}", date);
12     Console.WriteLine("D = {0:D}", date);
13     Console.WriteLine("f = {0:f}", date);
14     Console.WriteLine("F = {0:F}", date);
15     Console.WriteLine("g = {0:g}", date);
16     Console.WriteLine("G = {0:G}", date);
17     Console.WriteLine("M = {0:M}", date);
18     Console.WriteLine("t = {0:t}", date);
19     Console.WriteLine("T = {0:T}", date);
20     Console.WriteLine("Y = {0:Y}", date);
21   }
22 }
```

Output (when run on July 28, 2004, at 4:41:06 PM)

```
  = 7/28/2004 4:41:06 PM
d = 7/28/2004
D = Sunday, July 28, 2004
f = Sunday, July 28, 2004 4:41 PM
F = Sunday, July 28, 2004 4:41:06 PM
g = 7/28/2004 4:41 PM
G = 7/28/2004 4:41:06 PM
M = July 28
t = 4:41 PM
T = 4:41:06 PM
Y = July, 2004
```

3.6   Reference Variable Semantics

Assignments to value type variables and to *reference variables* have different meanings. That is, assigning one *primitive variable*—such as int or double—to another differs from assigning one reference variable—an object such as string or BankAccount—to another. The following code behaves as you probably expect:

```
int num1 = 456;
int num2 = 789;
num2 = num1;
num1 = 123;
Console.WriteLine("num1 is {0}", num1);
Console.WriteLine("num2 is {0}", num2);
```

Output

```
num1 is 123
num2 is 456
```

Both of these variables—num1 and num2—store integer values. They are unique values. A change to one value type variable does not change the other. More specifically, when num1 becomes 123, num2 does not change. Remember that all of the "primitive" types like int, double, and char, and all struct types, such as DateTime (seen earlier in this chapter) are value types.

Assignment to a value type variable results in a copying operation that duplicates the value to the right of the = operator. In the case of a primitive value like an int, the int's value is copied from one variable to the other. Now, there are two copies of the value, and modifying one copy does not affect the other one. The same holds true for structures. Assigning one `struct` variable to another copies the structure's contents. After such a copy is made, modifying the copy does not affect the original, and vice versa. (One notable `struct` type we have seen so far is `DateTime`.)

The following diagram shows the state of the num1 and num2 variables after initialization and assignments:

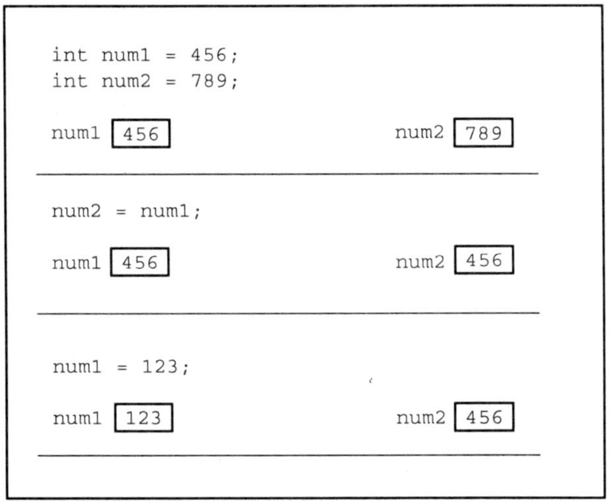

```
int num1 = 456;
int num2 = 789;

num1 456                    num2 789


num2 = num1;

num1 456                    num2 456


num1 = 123;

num1 123                    num2 456
```

Figure 3.4: Assignment to Primitive Variables

With reference types, things are entirely different. A reference variable stores the type and memory location of an object, not the object itself. By analogy, a reference variable is like the address of a friend. It may be a description of where your friend is located, but it is not your actual friend. You may have the addresses of many friends, but these addresses are not your actual friends.

When you create a reference type object with the `new` operator, the object is built somewhere in memory. The `new` operator also returns a reference to the location of that newly constructed object. The reference value is stored into the reference variable to the left of `=`. For example, the following line of code first constructs a `BankAccount` object with the values `"Chris"` and `567.89`. It then stores the reference to this new object into the reference variable named `chris`.

```
BankAccount chris = new BankAccount("Chris", 567.89);
```

You can now send messages to the object by way of the reference variable named chris. The memory that holds the actual state of the object is stored elsewhere. Because you will use the reference variable name for the object, it is intuitive to think of chris as being the object. However, chris is actually the *reference* to the object, which is located in some other place in the computer's memory.

Assigning one reference variable to another does not copy the object. Instead, it copies the *address* of the object. This means that two reference variables can refer to the same object. Any changes made to that object using one reference variable are also reflected in the other reference variable.

The following code mimics the same assignments that were made to the primitive variables above. The big difference is that the Deposit message sent to chris also modifies the object referenced by kim. This happens because after the assignment kim = chris is made, the reference variables chris and kim both refer to the same object in memory. In fact, the object originally referred to by the variable kim is lost forever. Once the memory used to store the state of an object no longer has any references, its memory is reclaimed so it can be reused to store other new objects. This allows your computer to recycle memory that is no longer needed.

```
BankAccount chris = new BankAccount("Chris", 0.00);
BankAccount kim = new BankAccount("Kim", 100.00);

// Assign one reference value to another
kim = chris;

// The values (state) of the object were not assigned.
// Rather, the reference to chris was assigned to kim.
// Now both reference variables refer to the same object.

Console.WriteLine("Why does a change to 'chris' change 'kim'?");
chris.Deposit(555.55);
Console.WriteLine("Kim's balance was 0.00, now it is {0}",
                  kim.Balance);
```

Output

```
Why does a change to 'chris' change 'kim'?
Kim's balance was 0.00, now it is 555.55
```

Assignment statements copy the values to the right of = into the variable to the left of =. When the variables are primitive number types like int and double, the copied values are numbers. However, when the variables are references to objects, the copied values are the locations in memory, not actual objects.

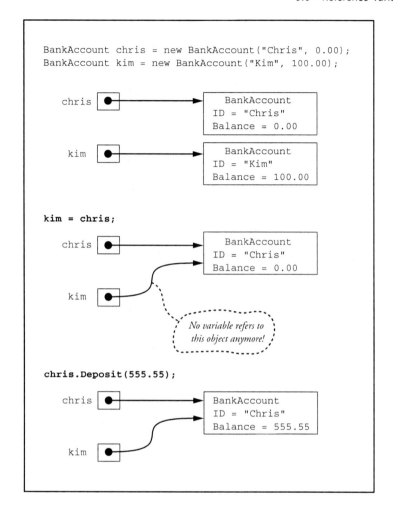

Figure 3.5: Assignment to Reference Variables

After the assignment `kim = chris`, `kim` and `chris` both refer to the same object in memory. Now a message to either reference variable (`chris` or `kim`) accesses or modifies the same object, which now has the values `"Chris"` and `555.55`.

The way to change a primitive variable is through assignment. However, assigning a reference value to another reference variable of the same type does not change the object itself; it changes what object the variable refers to. The state of an object can only be changed by setting its properties, or by sending messages to the object that modify its state.

Remember, when one reference variable is assigned to another, they both refer to the same object. This is why changes made to one variable also affect the other, as in the case of the bank accounts above.

Null References and the `null` Object Literal

It is possible to declare a variable but not store an object into it. C# has a special single object value that represents the *lack* of an object; this value is the uninitialized object literal *null*. A variable that stores null does not refer to any object, and is called a *null reference.* Any attempt to send a message to a null reference causes a program to crash at runtime. This type of error is called a *null reference exception.*

The following code initializes a variable to null and attempts to send a message to it. When run, a null reference exception occurs and halts execution of the program.

Code Sample: Class NullExample

```
1  // Attempts to send a message to a null reference variable.
2  using System;
3
4  class NullExample
5  {
6     static void Main()
7     {
8        BankAccount acct = null;
9
10       // the next line causes a null reference exception
11       double bal = acct.Balance;
12
13       Console.WriteLine(bal);
14    }
15 }
```

Output

```
Unhandled Exception: System.NullReferenceException:
  Object reference not set to an instance of an object.
    at NullExample.Main()
```

The following figure shows the state of the null and non-null variables:

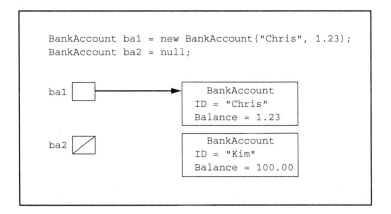

```
BankAccount ba1 = new BankAccount("Chris", 1.23);
BankAccount ba2 = null;
```

ba1 ☐ ———————→
```
   BankAccount
   ID = "Chris"
   Balance = 1.23
```

ba2 ▱
```
   BankAccount
   ID = "Kim"
   Balance = 100.00
```

Figure 3.6: Null and Non-null Reference Variables

The variable ba1 refers to a BankAccount object with an ID and balance stored in it. The ba2 variable was assigned to null, which means that it does not refer to any BankAccount object at all. Attempting to send a message to ba2 by calling a method on it or referring to its properties causes the program to terminate with a NullReferenceException. The variable does not refer to any object, so it is not possible to call methods like Deposit, ToString, etc. on it. Null references are often depicted by a box with a slash through it, to indicate that the reference variable does not refer to any object.

Just as sending a message to a null variable causes an exception, it is also usually a bad idea to pass null as an argument to a method that expects an object as its argument. The method will likely terminate with a null reference exception.

Self-Check

3-32   Consider the following code:

```
BankAccount b1 = new BankAccount("Jim", 100.00);
BankAccount b2 = new BankAccount("Sally", 150.00);
BankAccount b3 = b1,  b4 = b3,  b5 = b2;
b1.Deposit(25.00);
b4.Withdraw(75.00);
b5.Withdraw(130.00);
```

Answer the following questions:

(a) How many `BankAccount` variables are declared?

(b) How many `BankAccount` objects are created?

(c) For each of the variables, what is the ID of the account that the variable refers to? What is the balance?

3-33   Write code that initializes the two `BankAccount` reference variables `b1` and `b2`. Assign `b1` to `b2`. Send a deposit message to `b2`, then write the balance of `b1`.

3.7   Abstraction: Methods and Classes

By now you have seen several objects that can be used in C# programs. However, since objects are admittedly complex and challenging at first, it begs the question: What is the benefit of using so many objects and classes in modern computer programs? The answer is that objects provide a very useful level of abstraction to the programmer.

In programming, *abstraction* is the process of viewing a problem at a higher level, rather than focusing on every detail of solving it. Consider recipes for cooking. A typical recipe contains instructions in a brief and informal format, such as, "Heat oven to 300 degrees. Stir flour, milk, and eggs until smooth." If a recipe gave every detail of how to bake a cake, it would contain instructions such as "Walk to oven. Lift right arm. Grab oven temperature dial. Rotate dial to 300 degrees. Open flour package." This would be cumbersome and unnecessary. It would also be more prone to error, if the author were so unfortunate as to switch a few of the directions around!

Abstraction lets the programmer consider the relevant features of a complex system, while ignoring the many details. For example, abstraction allows us to use the computer at the programming-language level without full knowledge of the many complex details at lower levels. You can call the `Console.WriteLine` method to write to the screen without understanding the details of how it actually gets the text onto the monitor. Abstraction is a tool to avoid complexity.

Object-oriented programming (along with a good set of types to use) provides abstractions for many common programming tasks. For example, you can use methods such as a `BankAccount`'s `Deposit` method without knowing the details of how the methods work inside the computer. Abstraction lets you easily use primitive types, such as `int` or `double`, and more complex classes, such as `Random` and `string`. You can understand the characteristics of the int type (a specific range of integer values) and of int operations, such as addition, multiplication, assignment, input, and output, without knowing the details of those operations, how those values are stored, or how these operations are implemented in the hardware and software. Abstraction makes life easier and helps keep us sane.

You can also understand a type through the abstraction provided by its collection of methods and properties. For example, `string` objects have methods such as `ToUpper` and `IndexOf`, and properties such as `Length`. And `BankAccount` objects include the methods `Withdraw` and `Deposit`. You can understand how a `BankAccount` object works by concentrating on the messages that an instance of the type can understand.

Even though C# has a large collection of types, you will often need additional types for specific applications. New abstractions are built from existing objects, methods, and algorithms. As you begin to design and implement type abstractions, set a goal to build these abstractions so they are easy to use and perform a well-defined method. Even after you have long forgotten the details of implementation, you will still be able to use the abstraction, because you know what it does. You won't have to remember how it does it.

Although a method may consist of many lines of detailed code, once you have created it, you can execute it with one message. You can also send the same message repeatedly. So, when you have code that you need to use more than once in a program, implement it in a method that becomes one of the messages available to the objects of a type (see Chapter 4, "Writing Classes"). Remember, a message represents many hidden instructions and details. Once it is created, you do not need to see, nor understand, that implementation.

By partitioning low-level details into methods, you can write the implementation only once. You can then use the same method repeatedly, with a one-line message. Rather than having one huge `Main` method, this lets you build programs with many smaller and more understandable methods.

Here are some reasons why C# programmers use existing methods and objects to better manage the complexity of software development:

❍ To reuse existing code, rather than write it from scratch.
❍ To concentrate on the bigger issues at hand.
❍ To reduce errors by writing the method once, and testing it thoroughly.

In the early days of programming, programs were written as one big `Main` method. As programs became bigger, structured programming techniques became popular. One major feature of structured programming was to partition programs into methods for more manageable modules. Programmers found this helped them understand the program better. Object-oriented programming, as in C#, advances things even further.

The Early Days Unstructured	Structured Organized into Methods	Object-Oriented Organized into Classes
| ```
main()
{
 // 1
 ─────
 ─────
 ─────
 ─────
 ─────
 ─────
 ─────
 ─────
 ─────
 ─────
 ─────
// 500
 ─────
 ─────
 ─────
 ─────
 ─────
 ─────
 ─────
 ─────
 ─────
 ─────
// 1000
}
``` | ```
one()
{
 ─────
 ─────
}
 ─────
two()
{

//...

ninety9()
{
 ─────
}
 ─────
hundred()
{
 ─────
}

main()
{
 ─────
 ─────
 ─────
 ─────
}
``` | ```
class ONE
{
  one()
  two()
  // ...
  ten()
}

// ...

class NINE
{
  eighty1()
  eighty2()
  // ...
  ninety()
}

//...

class TEN
{
  ninety1()
  ninety2()
  //...
  hundred()
}

Main()
{

}
``` |

Figure 3.7: Historical Progression of How Programs Are Organized into Modules
```

It is easier to maintain programs that keep related details in various independent methods. It is easier to fix a 20-line method in a program with 100 methods than it is to fix an undivided 2,000-line program. Other reasons for dividing a program into smaller methods include the following:

- Putting details into methods makes the code easier to understand.
- Using methods makes it easy to perform the same actions more than once.
- Methods can be reused in other programs.

In the procedural programming of the 1970s and 1980s, data was passed around from one function to another. When data is available everywhere throughout a large program, it can become dangerously susceptible to unintentional changes. Using methods helps you avoid this problem.

Using object technology and methods lets data items be "encapsulated" with the method that uses them. This way, other parts of the program cannot touch that data. Developers, and you, don't have to throw data items around between functions, or leave them open for accidental change. Figure 3.7 shows an abstract representation of this progression in software development.

Self-Check

3-34   What are some good reasons for partitioning code into methods?

3-35   Give one non-programming example of how you use abstraction in your everyday life.

Chapter Summary

- An object is an instance of a type that has its own state, and a collection of messages. Each object stores its own data separately from other objects. This allows for thousands of unique `BankAccount` and `DateTime` objects, for example.
- A type specifies the set of methods and data for any variable of that type. This chapter introduced two types that are classes: `string` and `BankAccount`.
- Object-oriented programs have a collection of interacting objects. Some may be predefined by C#. Others types are written by programmers for a particular application.
- The `string` type has a number of methods for manipulating all or part of the characters in a `string`. These methods include `IndexOf`, `Substring`, `ToLower`, and `ToUpper`.

❍ Sending a message to an object requires the object name and a dot (.) before the method name and arguments. Use `aString.Substring(2,5)` rather than `Substring(aString, 2, 5)`.

❍ Almost all types in this textbook are part of the readily available C# and .NET libraries. The `BankAccount` class is supplied on the downloadable source code at **www. fbeedle.com/csharp/code.exe**. You should copy the required author-supplied files into the folder with the program that needs them.

❍ In the 1950s, programs were written as collections of statements. By the 1970s, programs were usually collections of statements called functions. In the 1990s, more and more programs were written as collections of interacting objects, where each object is an instance of a type that contains a collection of related data and methods. Each development allows more complex software to be more easily developed and more easily maintained.

❍ Abstraction means that a programmer can send a message to a method, without knowing the implementation details. The programmer does need to know the method name, the return type, and the number and type of arguments.

Key Terms

abstraction	method heading	`Random`
argument	modifier	read-only property
`BankAccount`	`new`	read-and-write property
class	`null`	reference variable
class method	null reference	send message
concatenation	null reference exception	state
constructor	object	string
`DateTime`	operator overloading	string indexing
escape sequence	parameter	`Substring`
immutable	`Parse`	`ToString`
indexer	parsing	`void`
instance method	primitive variable	word
message	property	write-only property
method		

Exercises

1. Choose the most appropriate types to do each of the following, from the set of types that have been discussed so far.
    a. Represent the number of students in a class
    b. Represent a student's grade point average
    c. Represent a student's name
    d. Represent the number of questions on a test
    e. Represent a person's checking account
    f. Get input from the user
    g. Send output to the screen
    h. Represent a day 90 days past the current date
2. What things need to be present in a message?
3. Write the output generated by the following program:
```
using System;
class TwoAccounts
{
  static void Main()
  {
    BankAccount b1 = new BankAccount("One", 100.11);
    BankAccount b2 = new BankAccount("Two", 200.22);

    b1.Deposit(50.00);
    b2.Deposit(30.00);
    b1.Withdraw(20.00);

    Console.WriteLine(b1.Balance);
    Console.WriteLine(b2.Balance);
  }
}
```

4. Write the complete dialogue (output and user input) of this program, when the user enters this input in the order requested (input is shown in boldface italic comments).
```
using System;

class WithdrawAndDeposit
{
  static void Main()
  {
    string name;
    double start, amount;
```

```
            // Read the initial state of a BankAccount
            Console.Write("First and last name (on one line): ");
            name = Console.ReadLine();              // Your Name

            Console.Write("initial balance: ");     // 111.11
            start = double.Parse(Console.ReadLine());

            // Construct the BankAccount
            BankAccount anAcct = new BankAccount(name, start);

            // Enter a deposit amount and a withdrawal amount
            Console.Write("deposit? ");             // 22.00
            amount = double.Parse(Console.ReadLine());
            anAcct.Deposit(amount);

            Console.Write("withdraw? ");            // 44.00
            amount = double.Parse(Console.ReadLine());
            anAcct.Withdraw(amount);

            Console.Write("Ending balance for account {0} is {1}",
                    anAcct.ID, anAcct.Balance);
        }
    }
```

5. Name two reasons why programmers use or implement methods.

6. Write the entire range of integers that could be returned by the following message.
```
Random randomNumberGenerator = new Random();
Console.WriteLine(randomNumberGenerator.Next(1,11));
```

7. Write the output of this code, assuming it is run in the year 2007.
```
DateTime today = DateTime.Now;
today.AddMonths(12);
Console.WriteLine(today.Year);
today = today.AddMonths(12);
Console.WriteLine(today.Year);
Console.ReadLine();
```

8. What is the value of position?
```
string s = "012345678";
// Initialize position to the first occurrence of "3" in s
int position = s.IndexOf("3");
```

9. What is the value of firstBlank?
```
string s = "Michael B. Pace";
int firstBlank = s.IndexOf(" ");
```

10. What is the value of s2?
```
string s1 = "abcdefghijklm";
string s2 = s1.Substring(3, 6);
```

11. What is the value of lengthOfstring?
```
string s3 = "012345678";
int lengthOfstring = s3.Length;
```

12. Write the output of this code.
```
string aString = "abc123";
aString.ToUpper();
Console.WriteLine(aString);
```

13. Write expressions to store the middle character of a string into a string object named mid. If there is an even number of characters, store the character to the right of the middle. For example, the middle character of "abcde" is "c" and of "Robert" is "e".

14. Finish the following assignment so it will store any person's first name into a string object named firstName. The first name is always preceded by ", ".

```
string name = "Deveraux, Hailey";

string firstName = _____

Console.WriteLine(firstName);    // Output: Hailey
```

15. Write the code necessary to store the current date as a string in the order of day, month, and year. If the computer's clock is set to May 26, 2004, the string should be 26/5/2004.

Programming Tips

1. You will need author-supplied types to complete certain programming exercises at the end of this chapter.

   Some of the following programming exercises require author-supplied types that are available on the downloadable source code at **www.fbeedle.com/csharp/code.exe**. For example, you will need the BankAccount type, from the file named BankAccount.cs, to complete Programming Exercises 3A and 3B. It is recommended that you copy the needed file(s) from the source code into the same folder where you plan to complete the programming exercises that need the file(s). If you are working in a lab setting, your instructor may have placed the .cs files where C# can find them. If so, you will not need to copy any files.

2. Even if no arguments are required, method-call messages need parentheses ().

You have now seen several method calls that require no arguments. If a method has no parameters, it requires no arguments. Do not forget parentheses in messages that do not require arguments. This differs from accessing properties, which do not use parentheses.

The following lines of code will not compile correctly:

```
int randomNumber = rand.Next;   // ERROR, missing () after Next
string up = myString.ToUpper;   // ERROR: missing () after ToUpper
```

Without the parentheses (and), there is no method call—even when the method requires no arguments. In addition, although there are many times when an object can be constructed without any arguments, the parentheses are still required.

This attempt to construct a Random object results in an error message:

```
Random rand = new Random;

MissingParentheses.cs:6: '(' expected.
```

3. C# begins string indexing at 0, not at 1.

The first character in a string is referred to with index 0, not 1. The third character is at index 2, not 3.

```
string s = "Boxing Day";
Console.WriteLine(s[0]);  // the first char, 'B'
Console.WriteLine(s[2]);  // the third char, 'x'
```

Don't try to index past the end of, a string, or before the start. In other words, do not try to reference a value that is not in the range of 0 to Length - 1. In general, do not reference characters in a string that do not exist, such as an index that starts at invalid number like -1:

```
string s = "This string has 29 characters";
Console.WriteLine(s[-1]);              // ERROR: -1 out of range
Console.WriteLine(s.Substring(30, 5)); // ERROR: 30 out of range
```

Assume that the above code is in `Main` in the `TestStringIndex` program, in a file named `TestStringIndex.cs`. When the second line with the message s[-1] executes, the program will terminate early, with the exception shown in the following message. Similar exceptions occur if you call the Substring method with invalid indexes.

```
Unhandled Exception: System.IndexOutOfRangeException: Index was out-
side the bounds of the array.
   at TestStringIndex.Main()
```

4. You don't need to write `ToString()` in a `Write` or `WriteLine` message.

    The `BankAccount` type used the ToString method like this to show a textual representation of the objects:

```
BankAccount anAccount = new BankAccount("Devon", 8765.15);

// Show a textual view of the objects
Console.WriteLine(anAccount.ToString());
```

    However, if you just use the object name and leave off `ToString()`, the result is the same.

```
Console.WriteLine(anAccount); // Automatically sends ToString messages
```

5. There is a difference between method calls and sending messages.

    Some classes have methods that can be called without constructing an object of that type. In fact, you are not allowed to create an instance some classes, such as `Math` and `Console`. To call methods such as `Sqrt`, `ReadLine` and `WriteLine`, start the call with the class name. Some classes allow multiple instances, each with their own unique state. To send messages to objects that have changing states, start the message with the name of the reference variable that refers to the object.

Programming Exercises

3A   Two Bank Accounts

Write a complete C# program that performs the following actions:

- ○ Initialize two different BankAccount objects, named one and theOther, both with an initial balance of 1000.00.
- ○ Make a deposit of 123.45 to one and a deposit of 50.00 to theOther.
- ○ Make a withdrawal of 20.00 from one and a withdrawal of 60.00 from theOther.
- ○ Show the names and balances of both objects (make sure you send messages to the objects to access the balance—do not maintain balances outside of the accounts).
- ○ Show the combined balances of both objects after the transactions (*Hint:* the combined balance that you must output should be 2093.45).

Construct your BankAccount objects exactly as shown here:

```
BankAccount one = new BankAccount("Mellisa", 1000.00);
BankAccount theOther = new BankAccount("Jutta", 1000.00);
```

Then your program must generate the following output. *Hint:* use the ToString method of BankAccount to display the final state of the objects, which is shown on lines 1 and 2 of the output.

```
Mellisa $1,103.45
Jutta $990.00
Combined: $2,093.45
```

3B   The Final Balance

Write a C# program that initializes a BankAccount object with an ID of "Mike" and an initial balance of 111.11. Then ask the user for an amount to deposit, and an amount to withdraw. Send the withdrawal and deposit messages to the BankAccount. Then show the final balance. Make sure you show the balance of the BankAccount. Do not maintain the balance separately as a double. Your program and input of 20.00 and 40.00 must generate a dialogue that looks like this (your currency may appear differently in locales outside the United States):

```
Mike's initial balance: 111.11
Enter amount to deposit: 20.00
Enter amount to withdraw: 40.00
The account: Mike $91.11
```

3C   IndexOf

Write a program that reads two strings from user input and shows the position of the first string as a substring in the second. Your program and the user input of another and the must generate a dialogue that looks exactly like this:

Dialogue 1

```
Enter string 1: another
Enter string 2: the
'the' is in 'another' at position 3
```

Dialogue 2

```
Enter string 1: one
Enter string 2: huh
'huh' is in 'one' at position -1
```

3D   Substring

Write a C# program that inputs a name in the form of the last name, a comma, a space, the first name, a space, an initial, and a period (as shown in the input below). Display the first name, a space, the initial, a period, a space, and the last name. Make sure the comma is after Jones on input, and that the comma is *not* in the rearranged name. If you enter *Jones, Kim R.* your program must generate a dialogue that looks exactly like this:

Dialogue

```
Enter name as Last, First I. Jones, Kim R.
'Jones, Kim R.' rearranged is: 'Kim R. Jones'
```

3E   A Little Cryptography (Indexing with [ ])

Write a C# program that hides a message in five words. Use one of the characters in the five input strings to spell out one new word. This code generates the output Secret message: ba.

```
string astring = "ab";
Console.WriteLine("Secret message: {0}{1}", astring[1], astring[0]);
```

Run your program with the following input and make up at least one other message:

```
Enter five words: cheap energy can cause problems
Enter five integers:
4
2
1
0
5
Secret message: peace
```

3F   Next 4 Fortnights

Write a C# program that displays the current date, followed by the calendar dates of the next four fortnights. A fortnight is a two-week period. If the program runs on November 30, 2004, the output should look like this (use DateTime's ToShortDateString method to get the format shown):

```
11/30/2004
12/14/2004
12/28/2004
1/11/2005
1/25/2005
```

3G   Pretend to Roll a Die Twice

Write a C# program that simulates two rolls of the same die that can have the values of 1 through 6 inclusive. The output should look like this, where the integers may change each time the program runs:

```
Roll 1: 3
Roll 2: 6
```

CHAPTER 4

Classes

Summing Up

The previous chapters introduced several classes. Some are part of C#'s library: `string`, `Random`, and `DateTime`. `BankAccount` is another C# class supplied by the authors. You now understand how to construct instances of existing classes and send messages to those objects.

Coming Up

This chapter introduces how to write C# classes of your own. You will learn to read and understand classes as blueprints for constructing many objects. You will learn to implement methods and the data that represents the state of an object. You will also see a few object-oriented design guidelines that help explain why classes are designed the way they are. After studying this chapter, you will be able to:

- ○ understand how to read existing C# classes
- ○ implement classes of your own
- ○ create your own methods, constructors, fields, and properties
- ○ write static methods, and implement other static class behavior
- ○ apply some object-oriented design guidelines to help implement better C# classes

4.1   The C# Class

Object-oriented programs have different types of objects. The objects are constructed from their respective classes. The class provides a blueprint for new objects. It describes the values that objects can store, the ways in which the values can be accessed, and the messages that the objects can understand.

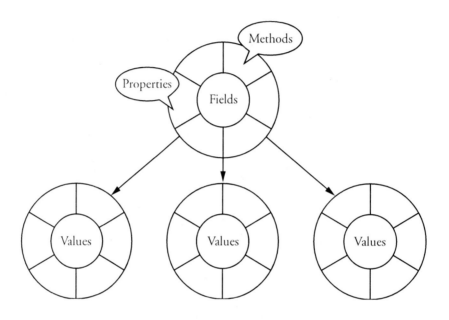

Figure 4.1: One Class Constructing Three Objects, Each with Its Own State

This section shows how to implement an entire class, which consists of methods, properties, and fields that are related to each other. Classes contain the following elements:

1. *fields* to store the internal state of each object of that class's type
2. *constructors* to create new objects and initialize their state
3. *properties* to view and/or modify the state of an object
4. *methods* to cause an object to perform a behavior

General Form: A C# Class

```
// Class heading
public class class-name
{
  // Fields:
  // Each object of this class will have its own copy of
  // these variables to store its state
  private type1 field-name1;
  private type2 field-name2;


  // Constructors:
  // A special method with the same name as the class, that
  // constructs objects and initializes their state
  public class-name(parameter(s))
  {
    constructor body
  }


  // Methods:
  // Bodies of code that cause an object to perform a behavior
  public return-type method-name(parameter(s))
  {
    method body
  }


  // Properties:
  // Identifiers inside each object that can be used to access
  // and/or modify the state of that object
  public property-type property-name
  {
    get  // optional; not all properties need to be 'gettable'
    {
      code that returns property's value
    }

    set  // optional; not all properties need to be 'settable'
```

```
    {
        code that sets the property's value
    }
  }
} // End of class-name
```

A class begins with a **class header**, which contains the text `public class` followed by the class name. After the class header comes a pair of braces. All the code for the class goes inside the braces. When a class represents a new type, the class's name represents the name of the new data type that is being created. Generally, the name should be meaningful and representative of the purpose of the new type.

Inside the class is a list of any **fields**, **properties**, **constructors**, and **methods** that each object of the class's type should have. The order in which these appear is not important, but generally it is best to follow a consistent order. This makes it easier to find things in a class that you write.

Here is a simplified version of the `BankAccount` class that was used in the preceding chapter. This preview will be discussed in detail in the next sections.

Code Sample: A Simplified Version of a `BankAccount` Class

```
 1 using System;
 2
 3 // This class models a minimal bank account.
 4 public class BankAccount
 5 {
 6    // Fields
 7    // Each BankAccount object will have its balance, ID, and PIN
 8    private double balance;
 9    private string id;
10    private string pin;
11
12    // Constructor
13    // Initializes the fields
14    public BankAccount(string init_id, double init_balance)
15    {
16       id = init_id;
17       balance = init_balance;
18       pin = null;
19    }
20
21    // Properties
22    // Allow access to an account's balance (gettable, not settable)
23    public double Balance
```

```
24    {
25       get { return Math.Round(balance, 2); }
26    }
27
28    // Provide access to an account's ID (gettable, not settable)
29    public string ID
30    {
31       get { return id; }
32    }
33
34    // Provide access to an account's PIN (gettable and settable)
35    public string PIN
36    {
37       get { return pin; }    // Provides the value of the field
38       set { pin = value; }   // changes the field
39    }
40
41    // Methods
42    // Add amount to this account's balance
43    public void Deposit(double amount)
44    {
45       // avoid negative deposits
46       double realAmount = Math.Max(0, amount);
47       balance = balance + realAmount;
48    }
49
50    // Subtract amount to this account's balance. The balance could go
51    // negative (see Chapter 5 to change this behavior)
52    public void Withdraw(double amount)
53    {
54       balance = balance - amount;
55    }
56 }  // End class BankAccount
```

4.2 Object State: Fields

The first things that appear inside the BankAccount class are declarations of *fields*. Fields store the state of objects. They are very similar to variables, and in fact they are often called instance variables. A field is declared with the keyword private, the variable's type, and its name. Here is the general form:

General Form: Field Declaration and Initialization

private *type field-name*;

-or-

private *type field-name* = *initial-value*;

Examples:

```
private string name;
private int numberSoFar;
private double average;
```

For example, the `BankAccount` class has the following header and fields:

```
public class BankAccount
{
    private double balance;
    private string id;
    private string pin;
```

This means that every `BankAccount` object will have its own `double` value named `balance`, its own `string` value named `id`, and its own `string` variable named `pin`. These three fields are directly accessible only within the class because they are declared as `private`. Properties and methods will access these variables directly. Each `BankAccount` object has its own `balance`, `id`, and `pin` values, which are separate from those of other `BankAccount` objects. This is a good thing. You would not want someone else's withdrawal to reduce the balance of your bank account!

Notice that the fields are not declared within a method. They are declared within the set of braces that bounds the class. This means that the fields are known throughout the class. Every other part of the class will have direct access to these fields. It turns out that most objects' methods will need access to these variables. If you look at the `BankAccount` class again, you will notice that every method references at least one field. The methods and data are strongly related. Because it has private fields, a `BankAccount` object's `balance` and its `id` and `pin` fields can only be seen by that `BankAccount` object; the advantage of this is that it protects the encapsulation of the object. *Encapsulation* is the ability of data to be accessible to the methods that need it, while being hidden—not visible or accessible—to other pieces of code. Encapsulation is an important programming concept because it maintains abstraction and separation of responsibilities in a program. Encapsulation with private fields means that the object can be sure that no outside entities can modify its internal state without permission. Encapsulation is one of the main characteristics of object-oriented programming.

Fields may be declared without a value. They may also be given initial values, like any other variable. Here are some examples:

```
public class BankAccount
{
  private double balance = 0.0;
  private string id = "no name";
  private string pin = "??";
```

Remember that `private` fields are not accessible or visible to any code except the actual object they belong to. This means that inside the methods in the `BankAccount` class, `balance`, `id`, and `pin` can be directly accessed and modified. Anywhere outside the `BankAccount` class, it is illegal to refer to `balance`, `id`, and `PIN` in that way. Code outside the `BankAccount` class that tries to access a `BankAccount`'s fields directly will not compile. For example:

```
BankAccount acct = new BankAccount("Thomas", 42.00);
acct.balance = 100.00;   // this line causes a compile-time error
```

A summary of the difference between `public` and `private` access follows:

Access Mode	Where the identifier can be accessed (*where is the identifier known?*)
public	In all other methods, constructors, and properties in the same class
	In any method or class where the object gets constructed
	In any method or class where the object gets used later
	Essentially everywhere; all code in all classes can see the identifier
private	Only in all methods, constructors, and properties in the same class

This represents a widely held principle of software development—data should be hidden. Making fields `private` is one step on the way to writing well-designed object-oriented classes and programs.

Self-Check

4-1   What might the declaration look like for a field of type `int` that represents an account's number of transactions?

4-2   Should most fields be made public or private?

4-3   Can other objects and classes see an object's private fields?

4.3   Initializing Objects: Constructors

The BankAccount class from the preceding code sample shows that all BankAccount method headings are public. Most have return types (including void to mean return nothing). Some have *parameters*. But there is something different about the method named BankAccount.

○   The method named BankAccount has no return type.
○   The method named BankAccount has the same name as the class.

This special method is called a ***constructor*** because it is called to construct (build) new objects. When a new object is created with the new keyword followed by the class name (and possibly some *arguments*), a constructor executes. A constructor helps to allocate memory for the objects. It also initializes the fields for the objects being built.

For example, creating a new BankAccount object causes the BankAccount constructor to be called:

```
BankAccount anAcct = new BankAccount("Kate", 10.00);
```

You have invoked constructors several times for a variety of existing C# types. However, to successfully write your own classes, you must first write one or more constructors to describe how your objects will be initialized.

A constructor is implemented by writing the public keyword, the class name, and a pair of parentheses, which usually contain parameters. This constructor method heading is followed by a constructor body, a set of matching curly braces that contain the code that will execute when the constructor is invoked. The body of a constructor typically initializes the fields for instances of the class. Here is the general form for a constructor.

General Form: Constructor

```
public  class-name(argument(s))
{
   code to initialize fields for the objects
}
```

Example

```
// A constructor to initialize LibraryBook objects
public LibraryBook(string initialCallNumber, string initTitle)
{
   callNumber = initialCallNumber;
   title = initTitle;
}
```

The following code implements the two-parameter `BankAccount` constructor introduced in Chapter 3. The fields are shown here to show that the constructor assigns values to the fields for this object, in addition to helping provide a place in memory for the objects to reside. The fields (declared within the class, not within a method body) are accessible to any method of a class, including the constructors.

```
class BankAccount
{
   private double balance;
   private string id;
   private string pin;

   public BankAccount(string ID, double startingBalance)
   {
      id = ID;
      balance = startingBalance;
      pin = null;  // pin is not set yet
   }
   // ...
}
```

This constructor executes the three assignments whenever a new `BankAccount` is created with two arguments (a `string` followed by a number). In the following code, the `ID` `"Stein"` is passed to the parameter `ID`, which in turn is assigned to the private field `id`. The starting balance of `250.55` is passed to the parameter named `startingBalance`, which in turn is assigned to the private field `balance`. By default, `pin` is set to `null` to indicate that the `BankAccount` object has no personal identification number (PIN) yet.

```
// Call the two-parameter constructor to initialize acct1
BankAccount acct1 = new BankAccount("Stein", 250.55);
Console.WriteLine(acct1.ID);
Console.WriteLine(acct1.Balance);
```

```
// The pin field is null; when written, no output occurs
Console.WriteLine("'{0}'", acct1.PIN);
```

Output

```
Stein
250.55
''
```

When writing a class, you get to decide what arguments the constructor will take. Choosing the right parameters is important when writing a class. If the constructor for BankAccount objects did not have a string and double argument, there would not be sufficient information to sensibly initialize new BankAccount objects. The pin field is considered optional in this type of BankAccount. In another situation, the programmer may decide that the constructor needs to take a third argument to initialize the PIN.

Sometimes, it is desirable to construct objects of a class in more than one way. To do this, you write multiple constructors for the same class. Each constructor must take a different number and/or type of arguments. For example, you could add a second constructor to the BankAccount class that took the string ID as its only argument. It could assume that the account's initial balance was $0.00.

```
// A second constructor method to initialize BankAccount objects
public BankAccount(string ID)
{
  id = ID;
  balance = 0.0;
  pin = null;
}
```

Having this second constructor would make it legal to create BankAccount objects in this additional way:

```
// Call the one-parameter constructor to initialize anotherAccount
BankAccount acct2 = new BankAccount("Stein");

Console.WriteLine(acct2.ID);
Console.WriteLine(acct2.Balance);
Console.WriteLine(acct2.PIN);
```

Output

```
Stein
0.0
```

A third constructor could also be added to initialize the PIN.

If a class is written without a constructor, it receives an implicit *default constructor* that requires no arguments and initializes all fields to their type's default value. That is, numeric fields are set to 0 or 0.0, reference object fields are set to null, and so on.

Self-Check

4-4   Write the output when class TestLibraryBook runs (*Note:* The boldface WriteLine in the LibraryBook constructor is for this question only—normally one would not have WriteLine calls in a constructor).

```csharp
using System;

class TestLibraryBook
{
  static void Main()
  {
    LibraryBook aBook = new LibraryBook("Early Bird", "Joist");
    LibraryBook anotherBook = new LibraryBook("Night Hawk",
                                              "Floris");
  }
}

//////////////////////////////////////////////////////////////////
// This LibraryBook is built in subsequent self check questions
public class LibraryBook
{
  private string title;
  private string author;
  private string borrower;

  public LibraryBook(string bookTitle, string bookAuthor)
  {
    title = bookTitle;
    author = bookAuthor;
    borrower = "--";
    Console.WriteLine("'{0}' by {1}",
                      title, author);
  }
}
```

4-5   Write a constructor for `BankAccount` that would initialize all three fields (including the personal identification number (PIN) to whatever the programmer desires. The following code would be legal with the new constructor:

```
BankAccount anAccount = new BankAccount("Kim", 123.45, "0157");
```

4.4   Accessing Object State: Properties

As emphasized earlier, it is best to declare `private` access for fields. The question then arises, if the fields are private, how will any code outside the `BankAccount` class learn about the state of a `BankAccount` object? The answer is through *properties*. These are publicly visible identifiers used to access and modify an object's state. You have used properties in the previous chapters, such as the `Length` property of a `string`, or the `Year` property of a `DateTime`. Properties can be thought of as fields that all code can see, but not necessarily access or modify.

Declaring a property requires writing a header with the keyword `public`, followed by the type of the property. The type should match the type of the field that you wish to provide access to. This is followed by the property's name. The property name can be the same as the field name; however, this is not necessary. After the header comes a pair of braces. Inside the braces goes the code to access (`get`) and modify (`set`) the property's value.

General Form: Property

```
public type property-name
{
   get          // (optional)
   {
      code to get property's value
   }

   set          // (optional)
   {
      code to set property's value
   }
}
```

For example, in the `BankAccount` class, the following three properties are defined:

```
// Allow access to an account's balance (can't be set!)
public double Balance
{
  get
  {
    return Math.Round(balance, 2);
  }
}

// Provide access to an account's ID (read only property)
public string ID
{
  get
  {
    return id;
  }
}

// Provide access to an account's PIN and allow a program
// to set the PIN (read and write property)
public string PIN
{
  get
  {
    return pin;
  }
  set
  {
    pin = value;
  }
}
```

To make it legal to access a property's value, you must write get (followed by a pair of braces) inside the braces for that property; this is called a **get** *clause*. The get clause contains the code that returns the value of the property with the C# return statement.

The C# **return** keyword allows a property or method to return a result value to the code that called it. The return keyword is followed by an expression that represents the value that the method or property returns as its result. The expression's type must match the type of the property or method (or must be implicitly convertible into that type, such as int to double). Any property or method with a return type other than void must return a value; otherwise, the code generates a compile-time error. A line of code that specifies the value to return from a method is called a **return** *statement*. Here is its general form:

General Form: Return Statement

return *expression*;

Example:
```
return balance;
```

Any property or method that is declared with a type other than `void` must return a value of that type. For example, a property declared with type `string` (as in a `BankAccount` object's `PIN` property) must return a reference to a `string`. A method declared to return a `double` (as in `Math.Pow`) must return a primitive `double` value. Fortunately, the compiler will generate an error if the return type is missing or incorrect.

Return statements are central to `get` clauses of properties. In the case of the `ID` property, `ID` represents the account's identification number, stored in its `id` field. The code needed in the `ID` property's `get` clause is simply a statement that returns the value of the `id` field. This is done with the following return statement:

```
get
{
   return id;
}
```

Any time a `BankAccount`'s `ID` is accessed, such as when it is used in an expression, written to the screen, or assigned to another variable, the `get` clause of the `ID` property is called. In the case of the `Balance` property, the `BankAccount` object rounds the balance to two decimal places before returning it:

```
get
{
   return Math.Round(balance, 2);
}
```

To be able to modify a property's value, the property must have a ***set clause***, which consists of the keyword `set` (followed by a pair of braces) inside the body of that property. The `set` clause contains a body of code that assigns the new value to the property. The code in the body of the `set` clause can refer to an implicit parameter named `value` that represents the value to be assigned to the property.

Consider this code:

```
pin = value;
```

It means to store the given value into the private pin field. After this is done, future calls to get the value of the PIN property will reflect this change, since the get clause returns the value of pin. Notice that a set clause does not need a return statement because the set clause does not return a value as its result.

If the set clause for the PIN property were excluded, the pin field would not be modifiable, and once a BankAccount object was constructed, its PIN would not be changeable. In fact, this is the case for the Balance property, which has a get clause but no set clause. The balance of a BankAccount object may be examined and accessed from anywhere. However, it cannot be directly modified from any code outside the BankAccount class. This makes Balance a *read-only property.*

Properties that allow both get and set are called *read-write properties.* It is also legal to have just a set clause and no get clause, which creates a *write-only property.* However, this is rare, because it is not often useful to change an object's state (set) without being able to see that state (get).

The power of using properties is that they allow controlled access to the state of objects. For example, the following code would not compile, because it tries to directly access a BankAccount's balance field from outside the BankAccount class:

```
BankAccount acct = new BankAccount("Thomas", 42.00);
double bal = acct.balance;   // can not access private field balance
```

However, this next piece of code would compile because it uses the Balance property, which is publicly visible, rather than the balance field, which is not.

```
BankAccount acct = new BankAccount("Thomas", 42.00);
double bal = acct.Balance;   // Can access public Balance property
```

Here, the field and property names only differ in the capitalization of the first letter. But it is not required for the names to be so similar. The field could have been named myBalance and the property could have been named AccountBalance. However, the convention is usually to name fields the same as their corresponding properties, but with a lowercase letter. The capitalization helps you differentiate whether code is referring to a field or a property.

Self-Check

4-6 Write the output from the Main method below (after two get properties have been added to the LibraryBook class).

```
using System;
```

```
class TestLibraryBook
{
  static void Main()
  {
    LibraryBook aBook = new LibraryBook("Early Bird", "Joist");

    Console.WriteLine("Main: Borrower is {0}", aBook.Borrower);
    aBook.Borrower = "Kim";
    Console.WriteLine("Main: Borrower is {0}", aBook.Borrower);
    aBook.Borrower = "--";
    Console.WriteLine("Main: Borrower is {0}", aBook.Borrower);   }
  }

public class LibraryBook
{
  private string title;
  private string author;
  private string borrower;

  public LibraryBook(string bookTitle, string bookAuthor)
  {
    title = bookTitle;
    author = bookAuthor;
    borrower = "--";
  }

  public string Borrower
  {
    get
    {
      Console.WriteLine("Getting borrower's value of {0}",
                         borrower);
      return borrower;
    }
    set
    {
      Console.WriteLine("Setting borrower to {0}", value);
      borrower = value;
    }
  }
}
```

4-7   Write the code to add properties named Title and Author of type string to the LibraryBook class above. Allow the properties to be accessed but not modified.

4.5 Methods

So far, fields, constructors, and properties have been introduced. With those three entities, objects can be created to hold a useful state. However, if this were all there were to objects, they would be of limited use; they would just serve as containers for the state stored in their fields. In fact, objects are much more powerful than this because they can be written to have behavior of their own, through constructs called *methods*.

Methods are generally used to provide interaction with objects that are too complex or powerful to be easily described by the get and set syntax of properties. Consider the BankAccount class; it already has a Balance property to view its current account balance. If the designer of the BankAccount class wanted to make it possible to perform transactions on the account, it might seem best to make Balance a read-write property with a set clause. While this would allow users to set their bank account balances, it would be too open and prone to mistakes. A preferred solution (the one you have already used) is to write Deposit and Withdraw methods to perform these operations on the account. These methods can perform the transaction. More importantly, they also ensure other important conditions, such as that the account has a legal balance above 0.00.

A C# class typically has many methods. These methods are the operations that can be performed on each object of that class. When writing a method of your own, you have a lot of freedom to create the method as you see fit. As long as you follow proper syntax rules, your method can be made to do whatever is possible. Of course, it is recommended that your method do what it says it does, no more, no less. The Deposit method of a BankAccount object probably should not also print out a bank statement (this could be accomplished by writing a PrintBankStatement method or something similar). A Deposit method certainly shouldn't withdraw money from the account.

Method Headings

Every method requires a *method heading* to describe itself. To write a method heading, answer the following questions:

- ❍ What should the method's name be?
- ❍ What parameters does the method need to do its work?
- ❍ What type should each parameter be?
- ❍ What type of result should the method return (if any)?
- ❍ What will the result represent?

For example, if you would like to add a method to apply interest to a BankAccount object, ask yourself the questions shown above:

❍ *What should the method's name be?*
Since the method applies interest to the account, `ApplyInterest` would be a suitable name.

❍ *What parameters does the method need to do its work?*
The method will need one parameter: the rate of interest to apply. A reasonable name for this parameter would be `interestRate`.

❍ *What type should each parameter be?*
The rate of interest can be a double that represents a percent of interest. For example, 0.15 would be 15% interest.

❍ *What type of result should the method return (if any)?*
The method does not need to return any information. It might seem like a good idea to return something, like the account's new balance after the interest was applied; but this is redundant. If the person calling the `ApplyInterest` method wants to know the new balance, he or she can consult the `Balance` property to find out.

❍ *What will the result represent?*
This is not applicable, since the method does not return a value.

Based on the above answers, you should be able to construct an appropriate heading for the `ApplyInterest` method. In the example below, the programmer decided that the method requires a `double` argument named `interestRate` and returns no value (`void`). This suggests the following method heading:

```
public void ApplyInterest(double interestRate)
```

Method Bodies

After writing a method's heading, the next step is to write its ***method body***. The body is the area of code inside a set of matching curly braces, which follows the method heading. The code in this body performs the actual work. Writing a method body can take a varying amount of time, depending on the complexity of the method. Some method bodies are very short—sometimes only one line of code. Other methods require many statements to accomplish their task, perhaps even by calling other methods in the process.

Combining the concept of writing a method heading and writing a method body, here is a general form for writing a method:

General Form: Method

```
public return-type method-name(argument(s))
{
code to implement the method's behavior
}
```

Example

```
public void PayMonthlyFee(double feePayment)
{
   balance = balance - feePayment;
}
```

To implement a method, decide the task that it must perform, and then write the C# code to perform the task. Continuing the `ApplyInterest` example above, the body of `ApplyInterest` should do what the method name and heading imply—it should take the given interest rate and apply it to the account. Applying the interest involves taking the account's current balance, multiplying it by the interest rate, and adding that amount to the previous balance.

Before writing the method, consider how it would be used. The following code shows that the balance should change and have 2.00 added to it.

```
BankAccount anAccount = new BankAccount("Kim", 100.00);
anAccount.ApplyInterest(0.02);
Console.WriteLine(anAccount.Balance);   // Output should be 102.0
```

Since the `ApplyInterest` method will be inside the `BankAccount` class, it has access to the account's private fields. Specifically, you can modify the value of the account's `balance` field within the `ApplyInterest` method.

Translating the algorithm for `ApplyInterest` into C# code, the method could look like this:

```
public void ApplyInterest(double interestRate)
{
  // calculate the amount of interest to apply
  double interest = balance * interestRate;

  // add the interest and store the new balance
  balance = balance + interest;
}
```

The `ApplyInterest` method is now complete. `ApplyInterest` is an example of a method that modifies the state of the object it is called on. After `ApplyInterest` has run, the account balance will change (assuming that the interest rate is not 0.0). As discussed in the following sections, methods can often be classified by whether they modify the object (*modifier methods*) or access some information from the object (*accessor methods*).

Implementing Method Behavior

Some methods might use fields or other values to do more complex processing. For example, an `Employee` object's `CalculateIncomeTax` method could be quite complex. This method would need to use the `Employee` object's fields, along with complex United States Internal Revenue Service tax tables, and evaluations of other methods, such as `CalculateGrossPay`. The methods that only access data, but do not change it, should be accessor methods. For example, your program might need to access the IRS tax tables, but it probably should not modify them.

Other methods need to modify the state of the objects, so they must be modifier methods. For example, consider `BankAccount`'s `Deposit` method, which modifies the private field `balance`.

```
// Credits this account by amount.
// If amount is negative, account's balance will not change.
public void Deposit(double amount)
{
  double realAmount = Math.Max(0, amount);
  balance = balance + realAmount;
}
```

The `Math.Max` method ensures that if `amount` is negative, the deposit will not reduce the balance. This is one way to ensure that negative deposits are not permitted. When the following `Deposit` message is sent, the argument (`157.42`) is assigned to the parameter `amount`:

```
anAccount.Deposit(157.42);
```

The code in the body of the method executes. In this case, the private field `balance` is increased by the value of the argument.

`BankAccount`'s `Withdraw` method is another method that modifies the state of a `BankAccount` object. Specifically, a `Withdraw` message debits `amount` from `balance`.

```
  // Debits this account by amount.
  // If amount is negative, has no effect on account's balance.
  // If amount is greater than account balance, withdraw
  // as much as possible.
```

```
public void Withdraw(double amount)
{
   balance = balance - amount;
}
```

The reason that Math.Max is not used here, as it was in Deposit, is that this way, the Withdraw method can allow for overdrafts. If an account has only $5.00, you can still withdraw $10.00. This avoids unexpected results, such as asking to withdraw $10.00, but having only $5.00 actually be withdrawn. Therefore, currently the account allows more to be withdrawn than the current balance. (This flaw will be revisited and corrected in Chapter 5.)

When the following Withdraw message is sent, the argument (50.00) is assigned to the parameter amount, which is then subtracted from anAccount's balance:

```
anAccount.Withdraw(50.00);
```

Notice that neither Deposit nor Withdraw returns a result value. Their function is not to return information to the caller, but instead to modify the object upon which they were called. If a method does not return a value, its return type is void.

Self-Check

4-8   Do you need to know the names of an object's methods to use the object?

4-9   Do you need to know how an object's method bodies are written to use the object?

4-10   Describe where the public methods in a class are known.

4-11   Describe where the private methods and fields of a class are known.

4-12   Write the output when class TestLibraryBook runs. Note: The WriteLines in the methods of LibraryBook are present for this question only. Also note that the Borrower property is now read-only because its modification is done through the BorrowBook and ReturnBook methods.

```
using System;

class TestLibraryBook
{
  static void Main()
  {
    LibraryBook aBook = new LibraryBook("Early Bird", "Joist");
```

```
    LibraryBook aBook2 = new LibraryBook("Night Hawk", "Flo");

    aBook.BorrowBook("Chris");
    aBook.ReturnBook();

    aBook2.BorrowBook("Kim");
    aBook2.ReturnBook();

    Console.ReadLine();
  }
}

// This LibraryBook will be built in subsequent self-checks
public class LibraryBook
{
  private string title;
  private string author;
  private string borrower;

  public LibraryBook(string bookTitle, string bookAuthor)
  {
    title = bookTitle;
    author = bookAuthor;
    borrower = "--";
  }

  public string Borrower
  {
    get { return borrower; }
  }

  public void BorrowBook(string borrowerName)
  {
    borrower = borrowerName;
    Console.WriteLine("{0} borrows '{1}'", borrower, title);
  }

  public void ReturnBook()
  {
    Console.WriteLine("{0} returns '{1}'", borrower, title);
    borrower = "--";
  }
}
```

Implementing the ToString Method

Most classes have a ToString method, which provides a textual representation of the state of the objects. You have seen ToString used to view the string representation of data in code like this:

```
BankAccount anAcct = new BankAccount("Jerri", 100);
Console.WriteLine("an account: {0}", anAcct.ToString());
```

Output
an account: Jerri $100.00

The designers of C# recommend that every class should have a ToString method. This allows full information about an object's state to be quickly and easily examined. ToString must take no arguments and must return a string. Because of this, when writing the method body for ToString, you must specify what value should be returned at the end of the method, using an appropriate return statement.

The method body of ToString should build and return a string that represents the current state of the object. Here is the ToString method for the BankAccount class:

```
public override string ToString()
{
  // build the string representation of this account
  string result = string.Format("{0} {1:C}", ID, Balance);

  // return the answer to the code that called this method
  return result;
}
```

The return value should represent the state of each BankAccount object. If ToString returned an uninformative string like, "This is a BankAccount!", it would not be as useful or informative.

Note the presence of the **override** keyword in the heading for ToString. The override keyword is not needed for most other methods. But it is required here because this ToString method overrides the default way in which an object is written on the screen. When you write a ToString method in a class, you must include the override keyword. If you do not override the default behavior, ToString will only return the class name.

The following table shows the different behavior of ToString when it is called before and after the default ToString is overridden:

ToString return values before and after ToString is overridden

Default ToString	*Overridden ToString*
BankAccount	Jerri $100.00

As discussed previously, recall that writing `.ToString()` after a variable in a `Console.WriteLine` statement is optional, so the `WriteLine` statement could have been written as:

```
Console.WriteLine("an account: {0}", anAcct);
```

Self-Check

4-13 Write the output from the `Main` method below.

```
using System;

class TestLibraryBook
{
  static void Main()
  {
    LibraryBook aBook = new LibraryBook("Early Bird", "Joist");

    Console.WriteLine(aBook);  // calls ToString
    aBook.BorrowBook("Kim");

    Console.WriteLine(aBook);  // calls ToString
    Console.ReadLine();
  }
}

// LibraryBook continues to grow in the self check questions
public class LibraryBook
{
  private string title;
  private string author;
  private string borrower;

  public LibraryBook(string bookTitle, string bookAuthor)
  {
    title = bookTitle;
    author = bookAuthor;
    borrower = "--";
  }
```

```
  public string Borrower
  {
    get { return borrower; }
  }

  public void BorrowBook(string borrowerName)
  {
    borrower = borrowerName;
  }

  public void ReturnBook()
  {
    borrower = "--";
  }

  public override string ToString()
  {
    return string.Format("'{0}', by {1}, borrowed by {2}",
                         title, author, borrower);
  }
}
```

4-14 Write class `PiggyBank` that can begin with any amount of money, such as 2.34. Messages include `AddPennies`, `AddNickels`, and `AddDimes` to increase the money total. (Assume that the argument passed to these methods is non-negative; you do not need to use `Math.Max`.) Include a property to get the total money. The property and methods you need to implement are shown in boldface. The following code should generate the output shown in the comments:

```
// The constructor takes the initial amount
PiggyBank curly = new PiggyBank(2.34);

// TotalMoney is a property
Console.WriteLine("Total {0:C}", curly.TotalMoney);
// Total $2.34
// Include three methods to add money to this U.S. Piggy Bank
curly.AddPennies(3);   // 1 cent
Console.WriteLine("Total {0:C}", curly.TotalMoney);
// Total $2.37
curly.AddNickels(4);   // One nickel is five cents
Console.WriteLine("Total {0:C}", curly.TotalMoney);
// Total $2.57
curly.AddDimes(5);     // One dime is 10 cents
```

```
Console.WriteLine("Total {0:C}", curly.TotalMoney);
// Total $3.07
```

4.6   Static Fields and Static Methods

Just as you can write variables, properties, and methods in your classes that act on individual objects of a type, you can also define the state and behavior of the type as a whole. Such behavior is called class or static behavior.

You have used static methods since Chapter 2, when you learned about methods like `Console.ReadLine`, `Math.Pow`, and others. In Chapter 3, you saw static properties like `DateTime.Now`. Generally, static behavior is used to represent qualities of a type as a whole and not of an individual object of that type.

Static behavior can be thought of as things that there is only one of, rather than a different one for each object of a type. For example, the concept of "now" is a distinct single date and time; there is only one "now." It makes sense that `Now` is found in the `DateTime` type, and it makes sense that `Now` is static, since each `DateTime` object does not have its own unique notion of `Now`; `Now` is absolute at any given instant. Similarly, there is only one screen console to which your program can write text, so it would not make sense to force the programmer to create a `new Console()` object to write lines to it. Situations like these are ideal for using static (class) behavior.

Static Fields

Sometimes there are individual values that are useful to every object of a particular type. A good way to implement such values is as static fields. *Static fields* are class variables that behave like object fields, except that there is only one of them for the entire type, rather than a unique copy for each object (as with object fields). All objects of the type can refer to the static field, but they all share the same copy of it; if one object modifies the field's value, it changes that value for all objects. Static fields are declared like regular object fields, but with the **static** modifier added.

General Form: Static Field

private static *type field-name*;
private static *type field-name* = *initial-value*;

Example:
```
private static int ourNumInstances = 0;
private string defaultName;
```

A good use of a static field would be to enhance `BankAccount` to keep track of the number of `BankAccount` objects that have been created. This way, each account could have a unique internal number, or tag number, for later verification. This could be done by adding a static field named `numInstances` to the `BankAccount` class, as well as adding a normal nonstatic field named `myNumber`. As each account was constructed, it would remember the number of its tag number by storing `numInstances`'s current value into that object's `myNumber` field. It would then increase this number by one, so that the next account created would get the next higher number as its tag.

Code Sample: Class UseStaticFields

```
 1  using System;
 2
 3  class UseStaticFields
 4  {
 5    static void Main()
 6    {
 7      BankAccount lucy = new BankAccount("Lucy", 34.50);
 8      BankAccount mike = new BankAccount("Michael", 99.99);
 9      BankAccount martha = new BankAccount("Martha", 1.0);
10
11      Console.WriteLine(lucy);
12      Console.WriteLine(mike);
13      Console.WriteLine(martha);
14    }
15  }
16
17  // This modified version of BankAccount has a static field.
18  public class BankAccount
19  {
20    // Static fields (all BankAccount objects share them)
21    private static int numInstances = 0;
22
23    // Fields (each BankAccount object will get its own set)
24    private double balance;
25    private string id;
26    private int tag;
27
28    // Constructor initializes fields with arguments
29    public BankAccount(string init_id, double init_balance)
30    {
31      id = init_id;
32      balance = init_balance;
33
```

```
34       tag = numInstances;
35       numInstances = numInstances + 1;
36     }
37
38     // Return a textual representation of the state of this object
39     public override string ToString()
40     {
41       return string.Format("Account {0}: {1} {2:C}",
42                 tag, id, balance);
43     }
44  } // End class BankAccount
```

Output

```
Account 0: Lucy $34.50
Account 1: Michael $99.99
Account 2: Martha $1.00
```

Class Constants

Static fields are often used to represent constant values related to a particular type. This kind of static field is called a *class constant*. Class constants are public static fields that everyone can access. They usually contain values that should not be changed, so they are normally declared with the **readonly** modifier. The readonly modifier specifies that a variable is actually a constant, so that once it is given a value, the value can never be changed. It can be viewed and accessed, but no new value can be assigned to it. Usually, public class constants are given upper-case names, since they are visible to the outside world.

General Form: Class Constant

public static readonly *type field-name = value*;

For example, you could add a class constant to the BankAccount class to represent the interest rate on accounts. This information would be visible to all BankAccounts (and to all other objects), but no rogue BankAccount object could accidentally change the rate.

Code Sample: Class UseClassConstant

```
 1  Using System;
 2
 3  // This modified version of BankAccount uses a class constant.
 4  public class BankAccount
 5  {
 6     // Class Constant:
 7     // All objects share one copy; none can modify its value
 8     public static readonly double InterestRate = 0.06;
 9
10     // Fields (each BankAccount object will get its own set)
11     private double balance;
12     private string id;
13
14     // Constructor initializes fields with arguments
15     public BankAccount(string init_id, double init_balance)
16     {
17        id = init_id;
18        balance = init_balance;
19     }
20
21     // Uses shared interest rate constant to increase balance.
22     public void ApplyInterest()
23     {
24        balance =  balance * (1.0 + InterestRate);
25     }
26  }
27
28  class UseClassConstant
29  {
30     static void Main()
31     {
32        Console.WriteLine("Interest rate is {0:P}",
33                          BankAccount.InterestRate);
34     }
35  }
```

Output

```
Interest rate is 6.00 %
```

Notice how the InterestRate field was visible from the outside in the UseClassConstant class. Because InterestRate was public, the UseClassConstant class was still able to see and use its value. Since `InterestRate` is in the `BankAccount` class, and not in the `UseClassConstant` class, its full name of `BankAccount.InterestRate` needed to be written. However, inside the `BankAccount` class (such as in the `ApplyInterest` method), only `InterestRate` needed to be written, since it was in the same class.

Static class constants are good ways to avoid the phenomenon sometimes known as magic numbers. A *magic number* is a constant value that is used in a program, often in many places, without good explanation of what the value represents. Having magic numbers in your programs is a bad thing because if you ever need to change the number, you have to hunt down all places the number is used in the program. It's easy to miss one, which makes for tough debugging later! Consolidating constant values into class constants is a great way to avoid these kinds of problems.

Self-Check

4-15   Write a class constant that represents the number of days in a leap year.

4-16   Write a class constant that represents the maximum GPA attainable at your favorite school or university.

4-17   In what classes might you find constants such as those you wrote in the last two questions?

4-18   Write a class constant named `NON_BORROWER_CODE` with the value of `"--"` that represents the borrower whenever a `LibraryBook` is available.

4-19   Which two `LibraryBook` methods (see Self-Check question 4-13) should be modified such that a change to the class constant would update every place where the value is used? For example, if `NON_BORROWER_CODE` is changed to "?", the code should use "?" everywhere; never "--".

Static Methods

A *static method* is a named group of statements that gives behavior to a class, much like an object method gives behavior to an object. You have been calling static methods since Chapter 2, when you learned methods like `Console.WriteLine` and `Math.Round`. In fact, one of the first things introduced in this textbook was a static method—`Main`! As shown below, writing a static method is similar to writing an object method, except with the `static` modifier added:

General Form: Static Method

public static *return-type method-name(argument(s))*

{

   code to implement the method's behavior

}

Static methods are useful for several reasons. First, they can be used to implement behavior that is specific to an entire type or class, not just to particular objects of that type. You saw this in methods like `string.Format`; making format strings was a responsibility of the `string` type. Static methods are good for separating code in your programs and for merging redundant code into a common location. Rather than having three nearly identical pieces of code in `Main`, it is often better to have a helping static method that `Main` calls three times.

Using static methods can reduce redundancy in a program's `Main` method. Consider the improvements made in the following code by adding a static method:

Code Sample: Class StaticMethods (Before Adding a Static Method)

```
1  using System;
2
3  class StaticMethods
4  {
5     static void Main()
6     {
7        string name;
8        double balance;
9
10       Console.Write("Name? ");
11       name = Console.ReadLine();
12
13       Console.Write("Balance? ");
14       balance = double.Parse(Console.ReadLine());
15
16       BankAccount b1 = new BankAccount(name, balance);
17
18       Console.Write("Name? ");
19       name = Console.ReadLine();
20
21       Console.Write("Balance? ");
22       balance = double.Parse(Console.ReadLine());
23
24       BankAccount b2 = new BankAccount(name, balance);
25
```

```
26        Console.WriteLine("Accounts: {0} {1}", b1, b2);
27    }
28  }
```

Code Sample: Class StaticMethods (After Adding a Static Method)

```
 1  using System;
 2
 3  class StaticMethods
 4  {
 5    static void Main()
 6    {
 7      // use helper method to make each account, and save the results
 8      BankAccount b1 = MakeAccount();
 9      BankAccount b2 = MakeAccount();
10      Console.WriteLine("Accounts: {0} {1}", b1, b2);
11    }
12
13    // A static "helper" method to make and return one account
14    public static BankAccount MakeAccount()
15    {
16      Console.Write("Name? ");
17      string name = Console.ReadLine();
18
19      Console.Write("Balance? ");
20      double balance = double.Parse(Console.ReadLine());
21
22      BankAccount acct = new BankAccount(name, balance);
23      return acct;
24    }
25  }
```

Adding the static MakeAccount method to the StaticMethods class has several benefits. First, it makes the program shorter. Second, it makes the Main method smaller, which makes it easier to tell what the program is doing as a whole. You can scan Main quickly and can easily see that it makes two accounts and writes their state to the screen. Third, it merges the logic of creating an account into one central place in the class, rather than having it redundantly placed twice in the class.

Combining commonly used code like this is good because it makes the code easier to debug, and it also makes it easier to change the code later. If you decided to change the first prompt to read "ID? " rather than "Name? ", you would only have to change the code in one place, rather than two or more.

Now think about uses of static methods that are related to the class's data type. A useful common application of static methods is to make it so your objects can be parsed from strings. You saw in Chapters 2 and 3 that it is possible to convert a `string` into an `int`, `double`, or even a `DateTime` object because each of those types defined a static `Parse` method. You could do the same for a class you write, which would allow your objects to be read in as strings.

How could you write a `Parse` method for the `BankAccount` class? If you know the format in which `BankAccount` objects are printed as strings, you can retrieve the necessary information from the string to reproduce the `BankAccount` object.

The `ToString` of a `BankAccount` comes out looking like this:

```
Lucy Jones $34.50
```

To correctly parse such a string to retrieve the original information, you need to split up the above string into the `ID` and the `balance`. The `IndexOf`, `LastIndexOf`, and `Substring` methods from the `string` object are helpful in doing this.

Here is a `Parse` method for `BankAccount` that does the job:

```
public static BankAccount Parse(string acctStr)
{
  // Strip leading and trailing blanks
  acctStr = acctStr.Trim();

  // Pull out the part of the string for the id
  int idLength = acctStr.LastIndexOf(" ");

  string id = acctStr.Substring(0, idLength);

  // pull out the part for the balance (assumes US $)
  int balStart = idLength + 2;
  int balLength = acctStr.Length - balStart;

  string balanceAsString = acctStr.Substring(balStart, balLength);
  double balance = double.Parse(balanceAsString);

  return new BankAccount(id, balance);
}
```

The `Parse` method could be used in code like this:

```
static void Main()
{
```

```
    Console.Write("Account? ");
    BankAccount ba = BankAccount.Parse(Console.ReadLine());
    Console.WriteLine("You made this account object: {0}",
                                        ba.ToString());
}
```

Output

```
Account? James Hale $444.56
You made this account object: James Hale $444.56
```

Note that the above `Parse` method is not as globalized as the rest of `BankAccount`. If the program is run in German, the currency will show as Deutsche marks, and the string indexing may not come out right. A better solution would take advantage of the `System.Globalization.NumberStyles` and other C# libraries to allow parsing of any currency, but that is a topic for another day.

Self-Check

4-20   Write a static method named `SumAll` that takes 3 `doubles` as arguments and returns their sum.

4-21   Write a static method named `Max3` that takes 3 `ints` as arguments and returns the biggest of the three. (*Hint:* Use `Math.Max` to help you.)

4.7   Scope and Context Within a Class

The *scope* of an identifier is the area of code where that identifier is known. Private fields have a different scope than the variables declared inside methods and the parameters declared inside method headings. Knowing the scope of identifiers will help you avoid errors. For example, a parameter or variable declared in a method is only known in that method; a field is known throughout its class; a public class is known throughout the program.

You have already seen that private fields cannot be accessed outside of their class. You have also seen that public class constants can be accessed from anywhere the class in known. However, it is easy to write code that violates these rules, either from careless mistakes or from misunderstandings about scope and access.

To help you avoid problems, this section presents a few errors that are commonly made when writing classes. The following code results in a compile-time error because there is an attempt to access a parameter that is declared in another block of code (the constructor).

Code Sample: Class SimpleClass1 (A common mistake)

```
1  using System;
2
3  public class SimpleClass1
4  {
5    private string id;
6
7    public SimpleClass1(string initialID)
8    {
9      id = initialID.Trim(); // Scope of initialID is the constructor
10   }
11
12   public string ID
13   {
14     get
15     {
16       return initialID.ToUpper();   // Should be id.ToUpper();
17     }
18   }
19 }
```

Compile-Time Error

```
SimpleClass1.cs(16): The type or namespace name 'initialID' could not be
found (are you missing a using directive or an assembly reference?)
```

This common mistake is caught by the compiler, which points out that the identifier `initialID` is not known. It is known inside the constructor, but not the `ID` property.

Another common mistake is to declare a local variable with the same name as a field. The `SimpleClass2` constructor initializes the local `id` to a trimmed (spaces removed from both ends) version of `initialID`. However, the field `id` has a default initial value of `null`. This code compiles, but it behaves incorrectly.

Code Sample: Class SimpleClass2 (Another common mistake)

```
1  using System;
2
3  public class SimpleClass2
4  {
5    static void Main()
6    {
7      SimpleClass2 sc = new SimpleClass2("an Id");
```

```
 8       Console.WriteLine(sc.ID);
 9     }
10
11    private string id;  // Default value of id is null
12
13    public SimpleClass2(string initialID)
14    {
15      // Do not do this!  Declare a new id that is local to this
16      // constructor. This leaves the field's value as null.
17      string id = initialID.Trim();
18    }
19
20    public string ID
21    {
22      get
23      {
24        return id.ToUpper();   // The field id is null
25      }
26    }
27 }
```

Run time Error

An unhandled exception of type 'System.NullReferenceException' occurred

---

A runtime error occurs when the main method asked for the value of the ID property. The ToUpper message is sent to an object reference that is null, the default value of fields.

Generally, the scope of a declared identifier (such as a variable) is the innermost set of braces in which it is declared. For example, fields are declared inside a class, so their scope is throughout that class. Local variables declared inside a method exist until the end of that method, and no further. Trying to refer to them from another method will result in a compiler error.

Summary of the Scope of Identifiers: From Where Can They Be Referred?

Local variables	only in the method where they are declared
Parameters	only in the method where they are declared
Private fields	from any method
Public classes, methods and constants (such as Math.PI)	from anywhere the class is accessible

Context and the Keyword `this`

Often when writing a class or program, it is natural to want to know something about a given point in the code. At some line X, what variables are visible and can be used? What method is this line a part of? What class is it in? This kind of information is called the *context* of a piece of code.

Inside the code for an object property, constructor, or method, all of the fields, methods (public and private), and other data in the class are visible. Think of it as if you were inside the body of an object method. You could see everything it sees. You could refer to fields of that object, call methods on that object, and so on. This context of being inside a particular object is called *object context*; all lines in object methods, properties, and constructors are in the context of their respective objects.

There is a special keyword *this* that represents the current object. Inside a block of code that has some object context, this is a reference to that object. Think of this as a variable that is wired to always refer to the current object. The this keyword can be used optionally on code that refers to methods, fields, or properties of the current object, or it may be omitted. For example, the constructor for BankAccount could have been written:

```
public BankAccount(string init_id, double init_balance)
{
   this.id = init_id;
   this.balance = init_balance;
}
```

The meaning here is the same as it was in the original constructor because referring to id is implicitly referring to the ID of the current BankAccount object whose context you are in, namely, this.id.

The this keyword is also useful when you need to pass the current object as an argument to a method. For example, if a BankAccount object wanted to write itself on the screen, the following code could be used:

```
public BankAccount(string init_id, double init_balance)
{
   id = init_id;
   balance = init_balance;

   Console.WriteLine("Here I am! {0}", this);
}
```

When inside a static method or property, the context rules are a bit different; such a context is called *static context*. There is no implied current object in a static context, so using the this keyword makes no sense. In fact, it is illegal syntax and generates a compiler error. It is also not legal to try to call object methods or access other object data directly from within a static method. Here is an example:

Code Sample: Class SimpleAccount

```
 1 using System;
 2
 3 class SimpleAccount
 4 {
 5    public void ObjectMethod()
 6    {
 7       Console.WriteLine("I'm in an object method!");
 8    }
 9
10    public static void StaticMethod()
11    {
12       // illegally try to call an object method
13       ObjectMethod();
14    }
15 }
```

Compiler Error

```
SimpleAccount.cs(13,5): error CS0120: An object reference is required
for the nonstatic field, method, or property 'SimpleAccount.ObjectMethod()'
```

It is, of course, legal for one static method to call other static methods, and also for a static method to call object methods on a specific object.

Self-Check

4-22   Given the following code, which of the following statements (a) through (j) are legal?

```
using System;
class Class1
{
  private int x;

  public void Method1()
  {
```

```
   x = 1;                       // (a)
   this.Method2();              // (b)
}

public void Method2()
{
   this.x = 2;                  // (c)
   Method1();                   // (d)
   Method3();                   // (e)
}

public static void Method3()
{
   x = 3;                       // (f)
   this.x = 4;                  // (g)
   Method1();                   // (h)
   Method2();                   // (i)
}

public static void Method4()
{
   Method3();                   // (j)
   this.Method3();
}
}
```

4.8 Object-Oriented Design Guidelines

As mentioned in Chapter 3, abstraction refers to the practice of using and understanding something without full knowledge of its implementation. Abstraction allows programmers to concentrate on the behavior of the messages that manipulate state. For example, a programmer using objects of the string type need not know the details of the internal data representation, or how its methods are implemented in the hardware and software. Programmers can concentrate on the set of allowable messages—the set of methods implemented within the class.

This chapter presented some implementation issues that so far have been hidden. The first part of this chapter presents the now familiar BankAccount class at the implementation level. However, before examining class design, first consider some of the logical design decisions that were made during the design of this textbook's BankAccount class.

The process of creating well-made classes and objects is called *object-oriented design*. An object-oriented *design guideline* is a rule intended to help produce good object-oriented software. The following sections introduce several such guidelines.

Choosing the Right Methods

All `BankAccount` objects have three methods: `Deposit`, `Withdraw`, and `ToString`. `BankAccount` objects also have three properties: `ID`, `Balance`, and `PIN`. There could have been more, or there could have been less. The methods and properties for `BankAccount` were chosen to keep the class simple and to provide a concise collection of methods for a first example of a complete class.

The `BankAccount` methods are only a subset of the methods named by a group of students who were asked this question: "What should we be able to do with bank accounts?" The properties and underlying fields are also a subset of the potential state named by students who were asked this question: "What should bank accounts know about themselves?"

When asked, students usually suggest many additional `BankAccount` methods, such as `Transfer`, `ApplyInterest`, and `PrintMonthlyStatement`; and many additional fields, such as type of account, record of transactions, address, social security number, and mother's maiden name. These are not included here.

The design of this class was guided by the intention of keeping it as simple as possible while retaining some realism. However, a group of object-oriented designers developing a large-scale application in the banking domain would likely use many of the methods and states suggested by the students. There is rarely one single design that is correct for all circumstances. Design decisions should be influenced by the desired outcomes. With `BankAccount`, the most important outcome was an easy-to-relate-to example, with easy-to-understand methods.

Designing anything requires making decisions to make that thing "good." "Good" might mean having a software component that is easily maintainable, having classes designed for reuse in other applications, or having a system that is very robust—one that can recover from almost any disastrous event. "Good" might mean a design that results in something that is easy to use, or that runs very fast, or that is prettier, and so on. There is rarely a single perfect design. There are usually tradeoffs. Design is an iterative process that evolves with time. Design is influenced by personal opinion, evolving research, the domain in which the code is used (banking, information systems, games, process control, or e-commerce, for example), and a variety of other influences.

Encapsulating Fields

One particular decision made while designing classes involves determining the level of access other objects have to fields and methods. More specifically, you must decide if fields should be declared `public` or `private`. The following design guideline suggests that it is good object-oriented design to protect the state of objects from accidental changes from the outside. This protection is called encapsulation, as mentioned earlier.

Object-Oriented Design Guideline 4.1:
All data should be hidden within its class.[1]

Although any field can be made `public`, the convention used in the classes shown so far—and in any good class—is this: "Hide the fields." C# fields are easily hidden when declared as `private` inside the class. This simplifies one design decision that you must make in any new classes that you develop. The state of all instances of the class is then protected from accidental and improper alteration. With fields declared `private`, the state of any object can be altered only through a message, or by setting a property.

For example, it becomes impossible to accidentally make a false debit like this:

```
// If balance were public, what would the balance be after this?
acctOne.balance = acctOne.balance - acctOne.balance;
// A compiletime error occurs at this attempt to modify private data
```

However, if `balance` had been declared as a `public` field, the compiler would not protest. The resulting program would allow you to destroy the state, without making necessary checks or triggering some transaction. By being hidden, `balance` can be modified only when the transaction is allowed according to some policy. What happens, for instance, if a `withdrawalAmount` exceeds the account balance in a `Withdraw` message? Some accounts allow this by transferring money from a savings account. Others may generate loans in increments of `100.00`, or some other amount.

With `balance` declared as `private`, it can only be debited by a `Withdraw` message. The code relies on the `BankAccount` to determine if the withdrawal is to be allowed. Perhaps the `BankAccount` object will ask some other object if the withdrawal is permitted. Perhaps it will delegate authority to an unseen `BankManager` object, for example. Or perhaps the `BankAccount` object itself will decide what to do. Although this textbook's implementation of `BankAccount` doesn't do much, real-world withdrawals certainly do.

When data and other details are hidden, credits and debits must "go through the proper channels." This might be quite complex. For example, each withdrawal or deposit may be recorded in a transaction file to help prepare monthly statements for each `BankAccount`. The `Withdraw` and `Deposit` methods may have additional processing to prevent unauthorized credits and debits. Part of the hidden red tape might include manual verification of a deposit, or a check-clearing method at the host bank. There may be some sort of human or computer intervention before any debit or credit is actually made. Such additional processing and protection within the deposit and withdrawal methods help give `BankAccount` a "safer" design. Because all hidden processing and protection is easily circumvented when fields are exposed

---

[1] Some design guidelines (including this one) are from the book *Object-Oriented Design Heuristics*, by Arthur J. Riel (Riel 1996), who cataloged and/or wrote 60 such guidelines.

through `public` access, you must enforce proper object use and protection by hiding the fields. It's easy; simply declare all fields `private`.

Cohesion

The set of methods specified in a class should be strongly related. The fields should also be strongly related. In fact, all elements of a class should have a close affiliation with each other. These ideas relate to the preference for high *cohesion* (which means solidarity, hanging together, adherence, or unity) within a class. For example, don't expect a `BankAccount` object to understand the message `Preheat`. This may be an appropriate message for an `Oven` object, but certainly not for a `BankAccount` object.

Here is one guideline related to the desirable attribute of cohesion.

Object-Oriented Design Guideline 4-2:
Keep related data and behavior in one place.

The `BankAccount` class should hide certain policies, such as handling withdrawal requests that are greater than the balance. The system's design improves when you combine behavior and data this way to accomplish the withdrawal algorithm. This makes for nice clean messages like this:

```
anAccount.Withdraw(withdrawalAmount);
```

This code relies on the `BankAccount` object to determine what should happen. The behavior should be built into the object that has the necessary data. As noted earlier, perhaps the algorithm allows a withdrawal amount greater than the balance, with the extra cash coming as a loan or as a transfer from a savings account. A bank account class might have many hidden actions that are triggered during every withdrawal message.

Self-Check

4-23   If the method name `Withdraw` were changed to `WithdrawThisAmount` after the class was already in use by dozens of programs, would these dozens of programs need to be changed?

4-24   Would it be sensible to add a method to `BankAccount` objects named `ApplyInterest`?

4-25   Would it be sensible to add a method to `BankAccount` objects named `ResizeWindow`?

Chapter Summary

This chapter showed a class as a collection of methods and properties that represent the messages that can be sent to any object of that class's type. Remember that:

- ○ Method headings with documentation provide the following information:
  - ○ whether or not the method is available to the outside world (public or private)
  - ○ the return type (the kind of value that a message will evaluate to)
  - ○ the method name that begins a valid method call
  - ○ the parameter list (the number and type of arguments required)
  - ○ documentation describing what the method does
- ○ The familiar assignment rules apply for assigning arguments to parameters.
- ○ A C# class contains:
  - ○ a class heading
  - ○ fields, known collectively as the state
  - ○ properties, which allow outside access to the state
  - ○ one or more constructors, to initialize the state
  - ○ method headings, with parameters and return types
  - ○ implementation of those methods in method bodies
- ○ Each object may store many values, which may be of different types. For example, each `BankAccount` object stores a `string` field for the `ID`, a `string` for the `PIN`, and a number for the balance. Other objects may have a state that is more complex.
- ○ Fields are accessed and modified through properties and modifier methods.
- ○ Constructors are called to build and initialize objects like this:
  `BankAccount anotherAccount = new BankAccount("Calissario", 4320.10);`
- ○ Some methods change the state of the object (for example, `Add`, `SetSize`, `Withdraw`, and `Move`).
- ○ Other methods provide access to the state of an object (for example, `ToString`).
- ○ Some methods ask other types and objects for help to fulfill their responsibility.
- ○ The ramifications of adhering to the guideline "All data should be hidden within its class" include the following:
  - ○ You cannot accidentally (or intentionally) mess up the object's state. The compiler will complain.
  - ○ You need to implement additional accessing methods and properties (like `Balance` or `ToString`, for example), but this is sound design.
- ○ The ramifications of adhering to the guideline "Keep related data and behavior in one place" include the following:
  - ○ A more intuitive design (things make more sense).

❍ Code is easier to maintain.
❍ Fields should be declared `private`.
❍ A class should be designed to exhibit high cohesion. This means:
  ❍ The data should be used by the methods.
  ❍ The methods and properties should have a meaningful relationship to each other.
❍ Most classes need public methods, private fields, and a constructor to initialize the state of an object.
❍ An object can send itself a message, or pass itself as an argument to a method, by using the `this` keyword.

Key Terms

accessor method
argument
class constant
class header
cohesion
constructor
context
default constructor
design guideline
encapsulation
field
get clause
magic number

method
method body
method heading
modifier
modifier method
object context
object-oriented design
override
parameter
private
property
public
readonly

read-only property
read-write property
return
return statement
scope
set clause
static
static context
static field
static method
this
write-only property

Exercises

Use the following class to do exercises 1 through 6:

```
using System;
public class SillyClass
{
   private double my_leftOperand;
   private double my_rightOperand;

   public SillyClass(double leftOperand, double rightOperand)
   { // Construct an object with two arguments
     my_leftOperand = leftOperand;
```

```
    my_rightOperand = rightOperand;
  }

  public double Sum
  {
    get { return my_leftOperand + my_rightOperand; }
  }

  public double Product
  {
    get { return my_leftOperand * my_rightOperand; }
  }

  public double Quotient
  {
    get { return my_leftOperand / my_rightOperand; }
  }
```

1. Name the fields in the `SillyClass` class.

2. Name the properties that each `SillyClass` object has.

3. How many arguments are required to construct an object of type `SillyClass`?

4. Using the method headings and documentation for the `SillyClass` class above, write the output generated by the following program:

```
using System;
class TestSilly
{
  static void Main()
  {
    // Reference variable names are kept short to fit on this page
    SillyClass a = new SillyClass(1.2, 2.0);
    SillyClass b = new SillyClass(6.0, -3.0);
        Console.WriteLine("a: {0} {1} {2}", a.Sum,
                    a.Product, a.Quotient);
    Console.WriteLine("b: {0} {1} {2}", b.Sum,
                    b.Product, b.Quotient);

  }
}
```

5. Add a property named `Difference` that returns the difference between the two operands of any `SillyClass` object. The return value can never be negative.

6. Send a `Difference` message to the `SillyClass` object named b.

7. Which of the following represent valid method headings?
   a. `public int Large(int a, int b)`
   b. `public double(double a, double b)`
   c. `public int F(int a; int b;)`
   d. `public int F(a, int b)`
   e. `public double F()`
   f. `public string C(string a)`

8. Given the `ClickCounter` class shown below, write the output generated by the following code:

```
static void Main()
{
   // aCounter only counts from 0 to 3
   ClickCounter aCounter = new ClickCounter(3);

   Console.WriteLine(aCounter.Count);
   aCounter.Click();
   Console.WriteLine(aCounter.Count);
   aCounter.Click();
   Console.WriteLine(aCounter.Count);
   aCounter.Click();
   Console.WriteLine(aCounter.Count);
   aCounter.Click();
   Console.WriteLine(aCounter.Count);
   aCounter.Click();
   Console.WriteLine(aCounter.Count);
}
```

ClickCounter
int START_COUNT
int count
int maxCount
int Count
Click()
Reset()

```
     public class ClickCounter
{
   public static readonly int START_COUNT = 0;
   private int count;
   private int maxCount;

   // Constructer
   public ClickCounter(int init_maxCount)
   {
      count = START_COUNT;
      maxCount = init_maxCount;
   }

   // Change the count of this clickCounter.
   // If at maximum, reset to 0, otherwise add 1
```

```
public void Click()
{
    count = (count + 1) % (maxCount + 1);
}

// Evaluate to this clickCounter's count
public int Count
{
    get
    { // Return the count of this ClickCounter
        return count;
    }
}
}
}
```

9. With paper and pencil, add a `Reset` method as if it were in the `ClickCounter` class. The method must always set `Count` to `0`.

10. Send a `Reset` message to the object constructed in the `Main` method above.

11. Write the output when the `Mystery` class shown here is run with the following `Main` method.

```
using System;
static void Main()
{
    Mystery aMystery = new Mystery(93);
    Console.WriteLine(aMystery);
    Mystery anotherMystery = new Mystery(-123);
    Console.WriteLine(anotherMystery);
}


class Mystery
{
    private int my_value;

    public Mystery(int v)
    {
        my_value = v;
    }

    public override string ToString()
    {
        string result = string.Format("[{0}]", my_value);
```

```
            return result;
        }
    }
```

12. Using the `Car` and `Mystery2` classes shown here, write the output generated by the
    `Main` method in the `CarAndMystery2` class.

```
using System;
class CarAndMystery2
{
    static void Main()
    {
        Car c1 = new Car(0.0, 0.0);
        Car c2 = new Car(72.0, 3.0);

        c1.Measure(100.0, 5.0);
        Console.WriteLine("a) {0}", c1.MilesPerGallon);
        Console.WriteLine("b) {0}", c2.MilesPerGallon);

        Mystery2 m = new Mystery2();
        c1.Measure(230.0, 10.0);
        Console.WriteLine("c) {0}", c1.MilesPerGallon);
        m.Huh(c1);
        m.Huh(c2);
        Console.WriteLine("d) {0}", m.HuhTwo());

        Car c3 = new Car(128.0, 4.0);
        m.Huh(c3);
        Console.WriteLine("e) {0}", m.HuhTwo());
    }
}

public class Car
{
    private double my_miles;
    private double my_gallons;

    public Car(double miles, double gallons)
    {
        my_miles = miles;
        my_gallons = gallons;
    }

    public void Measure(double miles, double gallons)
    {
        my_miles = my_miles + miles;
        my_gallons = my_gallons + gallons;
    }
```

```
      public double MilesPerGallon
      {
        get
        {
          return my_miles / my_gallons;
        }
      }
    }

    public class Mystery2
    {
      private double my_value;
      private int n;

      public Mystery2()
      {
        my_value = 0.0;
        n = 0;
      }

      public void Huh(Car aCar)
      {
        my_value = my_value + aCar.MilesPerGallon;
        n = n + 1;
      }

      public double HuhTwo()
      {
        return my_value / n;
      }
    }
```

Programming Tips

1. Make all fields private.

This protects the state of objects, while hiding implementation details. Other programmers can use your class by looking at your documentation. Documented method headings provide information about how to use instances of the class.

2. Some programming exercises require some author-supplied files.

These files are downloadable at **www.fbeedle.com/csharp/code.exe**. To find any file in this textbook, remember that each public class is stored in a file that has the following name:

```
ClassName.cs
```

Therefore, the `BankAccount` class, which begins like this:

```
public class BankAccount
```

is stored in a file named `BankAccount.cs`. Remember that C# is case-sensitive. Errors occur when the file name and the class name differ in case.

3. Working with two or more files is more difficult than working with one.
Some programming exercises require that you work with more than one file. This takes a little patience as you grow accustomed to working with multiple files. You will sometimes have a class in a file that will be used by another class in another file.

4. Classes are designed with values in mind.
When using someone else's class, remember that the design was influenced by what was important at the time to that particular programmer. This sometimes makes it more difficult to agree with the particular methods and properties that were selected. When you become more familiar with the class, or become aware of the values that influenced the design, the decisions may seem more logical.

5. Avoid magic numbers.
Whenever you need a numeric value in several places, consider writing it as a class constant that has a meaningful name.

Programming Exercises

4A   Person

Write a `Person` class so the test code below generates the output shown. A `Person` object stores a person's name and age. The `Person` class must have the following methods and properties:

- ⭕ `Person(string name, int currentAge)`
  A `Person` object constructed with data to set the name and the age.
- ⭕ `public string Name`
  A property to return the person's name.
- ⭕ `public int YearsTo(int newAge)`
  A method to return how many years it takes to turn the age that is passed as an argument. The result may be negative.

○ `public void AgeBy(int years)`

A method that increases the persons's age by the value of the argument. The argument could be negative, to make the person younger.

○ `public override string ToString()`

A method to return the name and age of any person as a string (see the output below).

The following testing class shows the behavior of a few `Person` objects:

```
using System;
class TestPerson
{
  static void Main()
  { // Test drive Person
    Person one = new Person("Kim", 19);
    Person two = new Person("Devon", 21);
    Person tre = new Person("Chris", 79);

    Console.WriteLine(one.ToString());
    Console.WriteLine(two.ToString());
    Console.WriteLine(tre.ToString());
    Console.WriteLine();
    Console.WriteLine("{0} turns 21 in {1} years",
                      one.Name, one.YearsTo(21));

    Console.WriteLine("{0} turns 40 in {1} years",
                      two.Name, two.YearsTo(40));

    Console.WriteLine("{0} turns 65 in {1} years",
                      tre.Name, tre.YearsTo(65));

    one.AgeBy(5);
    Console.WriteLine("AgeBy(5): {0}", one.ToString());
  }
}
```

Output

```
Kim is 19 years old
Devon is 21 years old
Chris is 79 years old

Kim turns 21 in 2 years
Devon turns 40 in 19 years
Chris turns 65 in -14 years

AgeBy(5): Kim is 24 years old
```

4B   `SalariedEmployee`

Write a `SalariedEmployee` class so that the test code below generates the output shown. Each `SalariedEmployee` object must know the employee's name (a `string`) and annual salary (a `double`). The `SalariedEmployee` class must have the following methods and properties:

- ○ `public SalariedEmployee(string name, double annualSalary)`
  A constructor that takes the employee's name (a string) and annual salary (a double) to initialize fields.
- ○ `public double AnnualSalary`
  A property for getting the annual salary of an employee.
- ○ `public double MonthlySalary`
  A property for getting the monthly salary of an employee.
- ○ `public void GiveRaise(double percentage)`
  Raise the annual salary by this percentage.
- ○ `public string override ToString()`
  Provides a textual representation of the object—the name and annual salary (see the output below). Make sure the salary has two decimal places and is preceded by $, or whatever your currency symbol is.

Run the following test code and verify that you have all the methods and properties specified. You must generate the output exactly as shown:

```
using System;
class TestSalariedEmployee
{
  static void Main()
  {
    SalariedEmployee empOne = new SalariedEmployee("Jack", 52000.00);
    SalariedEmployee empTwo = new SalariedEmployee("Jill", 53000.00);

    Console.WriteLine("{0} annual {1:C}", empTwo.Name,
                      empTwo.AnnualSalary);
    Console.WriteLine("{0} monthly {1:C}", empTwo.Name,
                      empTwo.MonthlySalary);

    Console.WriteLine("{0} annual {1:C}", empOne.Name,
                      empOne.AnnualSalary);
    Console.WriteLine("{0} monthly {1:C}", empOne.Name,
                      empOne.MonthlySalary);

    empTwo.GiveRaise(0.05);
    empOne.GiveRaise(0.10);
```

```
    Console.WriteLine(empTwo);
    Console.WriteLine(empOne);
  }
}
```

Output

```
Jill annual $53,000.00
Jill monthly $4,416.67
Jack annual $52,000.00
Jack monthly $4,333.33
Jill makes $55,650.00 per year
Jack makes $57,200.00 per year
```

4C   Course and Student

Implement two classes named Course and Student so that they work together to maintain a student's grade point average (GPA). All Student objects must be able to compute their own GPA, which is:

```
    GPA = total quality points / total units
where
    qualityPoints = units * numeric grade
```

This means that the RecordCourse methods must increment the total units and quality points represented by the Course arguments. A student's total credits should also be incremented. The methods and properties are given for both classes.

In addition to all methods and properties specified, add a ToString method for each class, and add another class that tests your Course and Student in its Main method.

Methods and properties to be written in the Course class are:

○ public Course(double credits, double numericGrade)
    A constructor that initializes Course objects.
○ public string CourseNumber
    A property to return the course number.
○ public double Grade
    A property to return the numeric grade for this course.
○ public double Units
    A property to return the number of units of this course.

    ❍ `public override string ToString()`
      A method to return a textual representation of this `Course` object.

Methods and properties to be written in the `Student` class are:
    ❍ `public Student(string name)`
      A constructor to set the student's name.
    ❍ `public string Name`
      A property to return the student's name.
    ❍ `public double GPA`
      A property to return the student's current GPA.
    ❍ `public override string ToString()`
      A method to return a textual representation of this `Course` object.
    ❍ `public void RecordCourse(Course aCourse)`
      A method that adjusts the state with a newly completed course.

The test class below sends messages to all of the new methods. It, along with its output, is intended to help you understand the behavior of the objects. When you complete both classes, the test class must generate the output exactly as shown.

    In addition to the methods specified in the interfaces above, remember to add a `ToString` method to both classes. Use the test class output shown below to determine how you should implement `ToString`. Run this test class to test your two new classes: `Course` and `Student`.

```
using System;
class TestStudentAndCourse
{
  // This is a test class for Course and Student;
  // Constructs one Student object and try every method and property.
  static void Main()
  {
    // Test Student
    Student s1 = new Student("Devon"); // No courses yet
    Console.WriteLine(s1.ToString());
    Console.WriteLine("Name: {0}", s1.Name);
    Console.WriteLine(" GPA: {0}", s1.GPA);

    // Test Course
    Console.WriteLine();
    Course CS1 = new Course("CSc127A-042002", 3.0, 4.0);  // 3-unit A
    Console.WriteLine(CS1.ToString());
    Console.WriteLine("units: {0}", CS1.Units);
    Console.WriteLine("grade: {0}", CS1.Grade);
```

```
    Course CS2 = new Course("CSc127A-012004", 4.0, 3.0); // 4-unit B
    Course PE101 = new Course("PE101-022004", 1.0, 2.0); // 1-unit C

    // Test the relationship between Student and Course
    s1.RecordCourse(CS1);
    s1.RecordCourse(CS2);
    s1.RecordCourse(PE101);

    Console.WriteLine();
    Console.WriteLine(s1);
  }
}
```

Output

```
Devon's GPA is 0.0
Name: Devon
 GPA: 0.0

CSc127A-042002 3.0 units with grade 4.0
units: 3.0
grade: 4.0

Devon's GPA is 3.25
```

4D WeeklyEmployee

Completely implement a class named `WeeklyEmployee` that is intended to be part of a payroll system. Each instance of `WeeklyEmployee` must keep track of an employee's name, number (an `int`), hourly rate of pay, and number of hours worked during the current week. Each instance of `WeeklyEmployee` must be able to compute its own:

1. Gross pay, which is defined as (hours worked * hourly rate of pay)
2. Social security tax, which is defined as 6.2 percent of gross pay
3. Medicare tax, which is defined as 1.45 percent of gross pay

There is no overtime pay. A programmer using this class must be able to set the hours worked each week, since this changes from week to week. Because the time clock measures hours worked in tenths of an hour, hours worked must have a fractional part (you could make this a double). In addition, a programmer using this class must be able to give any `WeeklyEmployee` object a raise in pay, such as 0.03 for 3%.

1. Determine what each WeeklyEmployee must be able to do.

On paper, write a method heading for each responsibility with a comment indicating what the method/property does.

2. Determine what each WeeklyEmployee must know.

Provide a name for each value, and also the type (such as int, double, or string). Use meaningful identifiers that accurately describe what the variables will store.

Type of Value   Variable Name

3. Write the class.

Using the previous documents as guidelines, complete the WeeklyEmployee class as C# source code. Remember to include all of these elements:

- ○ class heading
- ○ public class constants for 0.062 and 0.0145
- ○ fields
- ○ constructor to initialize the fields
- ○ properties
- ○ methods

4. Test the class.

Add a second class with a Main method to test your WeeklyEmployee class. At a minimum, it should construct two instances of WeeklyEmployee and send every possible message to both objects. Keep modifying and fixing WeeklyEmployee as you test your class. Generate output that verifies that your objects are behaving correctly.

CHAPTER **5**

Selection

Summing Up

You have learned how to use objects, and most recently, how to implement classes of objects of your own. This provides the basis for powerful object-oriented programming. However, so far the programs in this textbook have executed all statements in sequential fashion—in order, from the first statement to the last. When a message was sent, the statements in methods were also executed in sequential fashion. This has limited the power of the programs you were able to write.

Coming Up

A well-written program needs to be able to execute certain actions only under specific circumstances. It must be able to choose among many alternative courses of action. This chapter presents statements that allow such selections. After studying this chapter, you will be able to:

- ○ use the `bool` data type to generate logical expressions that are true or false
- ○ solve problems using the Guarded Action pattern with the `if` statement
- ○ create and evaluate Boolean expressions with the Boolean operators `!`, `||`, `&&`
- ○ solve problems using the Alternative Action pattern with the `if/else` statement
- ○ solve problems using the Multiple Selection pattern with nested `if/else` statements and the `switch` statement

5.1   Selective Control

Programs must often behave differently depending on the situation. For example, an automated teller machine (ATM) must serve valid bank customers, but it must also reject invalid access attempts. Once validated, a customer may wish to perform a balance query, a cash withdrawal, or a deposit. The code that controls an ATM must permit these different requests. Clearly, the code for such an ATM must be able to behave differently based on various conditions. Without *selective control* —the ability for the program to adjust its behavior based on conditions—all bank customers could only perform one particular transaction or action. Worse, invalid PINs could not be rejected!

Before any ATM becomes operational, programmers must implement code that anticipates all possible transactions. The code must turn away customers with invalid PINs. It must prevent invalid transactions, such as cash withdrawals that are not in the proper increment (of $5.00, $10.00, or $20.00, for example). It must also be able to deal with customers who attempt to withdraw more than they have.

To accomplish these tasks, a new form of control is needed—a way to permit or prevent execution of certain statements, depending on the current state of the program. Making use of this kind of control is called *selection*. Code using selection will need to be able to evaluate logical expressions that can be true or false, and to instruct the program to behave differently depending on whether the statement is true or false. The following sections explain how to construct logical expressions to be used in programs that need selective control.

Logical Expressions with the bool Type

C# has a *bool type* that stores either of the two Boolean logic literals: true or false. The bool type is used to represent logical statements of truth or falsehood. Logical statements are important in programs because they allow the program to test various conditions to see whether they are true or false, and to then take some action based on that information.

Whereas arithmetic expressions evaluate to a number, *Boolean expressions*, such as credits > 60, always evaluate to one of the two bool values of true or false. A Boolean expression often contains one or more *relational operators*, which compare how values are related to each other. Examples of relational operators are < (less than) or == (equal to).

When an expression contains both arithmetic and relational operators, such as < and >=, the relational operators evaluate after the arithmetic operators. For example, the expression 3 < 1 + 4 is true since the addition operator evaluates first, making the expression 3 < 5.

The following table shows some common Boolean expressions. More operators for working with bool values will be introduced later in this chapter.

Common Boolean Expressions

Expression Form	Meaning	Example	Result
`bool` variable	that variable's value	`amFinished`	`amFinished's value`
`bool` literal	that literal's value	`false`	`false`
expr1 < *expr2*	less than	`1.1 < 2.0`	`true`
expr1 > *expr2*	greater than	`1.1 > 2.0`	`false`
expr1 <= *expr2*	less than or equal to	`4 <= 4`	`true`
expr1 >= *expr2*	greater than or equal to	`1.1 >= 4 / 2`	`false`
expr1 == *expr2*	equal to	`16 == 4 * 4`	`true`
expr1 != *expr2*	not equal to	`1 + 1 != 2`	`false`
(*expr*)	parenthesize	`(1 == 1) == true`	`true`
!*expr*	logical negation	`!false`	`true`

The values that are compared by a relational operator are its operands. When a relational operator is applied to two operands, the result is one of two values: `true` or `false`. The next table shows some more examples of simple Boolean expressions and their resulting values.

Boolean Expression	Result
`true`	`true`
`false`	`false`
`true == true`	`true`
`true == false`	`false`
`false == false`	`true`
`3.1 < 5.0`	`true`
`1.4 > 5.0`	`false`
`int x = 2.6;`	
`x <= 5.0`	`true`
`5.0 == x`	`false`
`x != 5.0`	`true`
`x == 2.6`	`true`
`x >= 2.6`	`true`
`x <= 2.6`	`true`
`x > 1 + 2 * 3`	`false`
`x - 2 < 1.0`	`true`

Like numeric variables, `bool` variables can be declared, initialized, and assigned a value. The assigned expression should be a Boolean expression—one that evaluates to `true` or `false`. This is shown in the initializations and assignments of three `bool` variables in the following code:

```
// Initialize three bool variables to false
bool ready = false;
bool willing = false;
bool able = false;
double credits = 28.5;
double hours = 9.5;

// Assign true or false to all three bool variables
ready = hours >= 8.0;
willing = credits > 20.0;
able = credits <= 32.0;
```

When written to the screen, a true Boolean value writes the word `true` on the screen and a false value writes `false`, just as you might expect.

```
bool myBoolValue = 1 >= 2;
Console.WriteLine(true);
Console.WriteLine(false);
Console.WriteLine(myBoolValue);
```

Output

```
true
false
false
```

Many objects have methods that deal with Boolean (`bool`) values. The `string` and `DateTime` types introduced in the previous section, for example, have some methods that return `bool` values based on whether certain conditions are true. There are methods to learn if a string has a certain prefix (beginning) or suffix (ending) of characters, and a static method to learn whether a certain year was a leap year.

`string` object (Instance) Methods with `bool` Return Type

`public bool StartsWith(string value)`
Returns whether or not this string starts with the characters in value.
Example:
`"Colleen Linn".StartsWith("Col")` returns true.

`public bool EndsWith(string value)`
Returns whether or not this string ends with the characters in value.
Example:
`"Colleen Linn".EndsWith("inn")` returns true.

DateTime Class (Static) Methods with bool Return Type

```
public static bool IsLeapYear(int year)
```
Returns whether the specified year is a leap year.

Example:

`DateTime.IsLeapYear(2008)` returns true.

Self-Check

5-1   In the preceding code with the three Boolean variables ready, willing, and able, what are the values of the following expressions:

(a) `hours >= 8.0`
(b) `credits > 20.0`
(c) `credits <= 32.0`
(d) `(ready == willing == able)`

5-2   Which expressions evaluate to true, assuming that j and k are initialized like this:

```
int j = 4;
int k = 8;
```

(a) `(j + 4) == k`
(b) `0 == j`
(c) `j >= k`
(d) `j != k`
(e) `j < k`
(f) `4 == j`
(g) `j == (j + k - j)`
(h) `(k - 2) == (j + 2)`

Comparing string Objects with ==, != Operators

Just as you previously saw that the string type has an overloaded + operator to concatenate strings, there are also two other operators that the string type overloads for equality comparisons. The first is the equality operator ==. This operator tests whether two string objects are equal to each other. More specifically, when comparing with ==, the two strings are compared character-by-character to see if they contain the exact same characters, in the same order. If so, the expression evaluates to true; otherwise, the expression evaluates to false.

```
"abc" == "abc"   // True
"abc" == "123"   // False
```

The second is the inequality operator !=. An expression with != evaluates to true if the strings differ in any way. The same expression would evaluate to false if the strings contain the same exact sequence of characters:

```
"abc" != "abc"   // False
"abc" != "123"   // True
```

As with most string operations, these operators are case-sensitive, if the letters are the same, except that one is uppercase and one is lowercase, they are considered to be different.

```
"abc" == "aBc"   // False
"abc" != "aBc"   // True
```

If a string is built using concatenation with +, it will compare as equal to the entire combined string. For example:

```
"abc" + "123" == "abc123"   // True
"abc" + '4' == "abc4"       // True
```

Other relational operators such as < and >= are not defined for the string type. There are other ways to compare strings, without using overloaded operators, that will be discussed later in this chapter. The lack of more overloaded operators is largely because it is considered confusing when classes have too many overloaded operators without clear meanings.

The following code demonstrates the relational operators and their use on string objects. Note that writing a Boolean expression to the console does not write the expression itself, but its result. Therefore, Console.WriteLine(str1 == "hen"); writes neither str1's value nor the word hen on the screen, but instead writes true or false, depending on whether they are equal.

Code Sample: Class StringRelationalOperators

```
1 // Demonstrates overloaded string operators ==, !=
2 using System;
3
4 class StringRelationalOperators
5 {
6    static void Main()
7    {
```

```
 8        string str1 = "hen";
 9        string str2 = "house";
10        string str3 = "1234";
11        string str4 = "henhouse";
12
13        Console.WriteLine(str1 == "hen");
14        Console.WriteLine(str1 != "HEN");
15        Console.WriteLine(str1 + str2 == "HenHouse");
16        Console.WriteLine(str4 == str1 + str2);
17        Console.WriteLine(str4 == str2 + str1);
18        Console.WriteLine(str4.Substring(0, 3) == str1);
18        Console.WriteLine(1 + 23 + "4" == str3);
20    }
21 }
```

Output

```
True
True
False
True
False
True
False
```

The following table summarizes the general forms of relational expressions that may be created using strings and their operators:

string Operators ==, !=

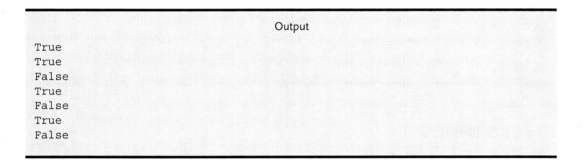

Expression Form and Meaning	Result Type	Example Expressions and Results
string1 == *string2* Equality test between two strings; checks characters of each to decide equality (case-sensitive)	bool	"yes" == "yes" ⇨ true "yes" == "no" ⇨ false "yes" == "YES" ⇨ false
string1 != *string2* Inequality test between two strings; checks characters to decide inequality (case-sensitive)	bool	"yes" != "YES" ⇨ true "yes" != "yes" ⇨ false "yes" != "" ⇨ true

The Guarded Action Pattern

Programs often need actions that do not always execute. At one moment, a particular action must occur. At some other time—the next day, or the next millisecond, perhaps—the same action must be skipped. For example, one student may make the dean's list because the student's grade point average (GPA) is 3.5 or higher. The next student may have a GPA lower than 3.5 and should not become part of the dean's list. The action—adding a student to the dean's list—is guarded.

Algorithmic Pattern: Guarded Action

Problem: Do something only if a certain condition is true.

Outline: if (Boolean condition is true)
                 execute these statements

Example:
```
if (student.GPA() >= 3.5)
    Console.WriteLine("{0} made the dean's list", student);
```

The `if` Statement

This *Guarded Action pattern* is often implemented with the *if* statement. The if statement specifies a Boolean condition, followed by code that will be executed only if that condition's Boolean value is true. The code to execute may be a single statement, or a block of many statements, surrounded by braces.

General Form: if Statement

if (*Boolean expression*)
{
  statement(s);
}
Notes:
The braces are optional if only one statement is used.
Examples:
```
if (hoursWorked > 40.0)
{
    regularHours = 40.0;
```

```
    overtimeHours = hoursWorked - 40.0;
}


if (studyTime <= 5)
    Console.WriteLine("You are not ready for the test");
```

When an `if` statement is encountered, the Boolean expression is evaluated to determine its result of `true` or `false`. The *statement* that follows `if` executes only if the Boolean expression evaluates to `true`. Therefore, in the example above, the output `"You are not ready for the test"` appears only if the value of `studyTime` is less than or equal to 5. When the input is more than 5, the condition is false and the *statement* is skipped—the action is guarded.

Here is a flowchart view of the Guarded Action pattern:

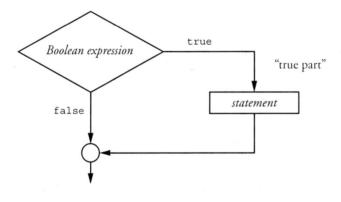

Figure 5.1: Flowchart View of the Guarded Action Pattern

The `ToString` method of class `CD` below illustrates how selection alters the flow of control. Each of the sample dialogues below illustrates code that performs different actions according to a variety of conditions. More specifically, depending on the current state of any `CD` object, the `ToString` method returns a different `string` that reflects the object's state.

Code Sample: Class CD

```
1 // Instances of the CD class maintain the number of units sold
2 // and can describe something about its music certification:
3 //      1. No music certification
4 //      2. Gold
5 //      3. Platinum
```

```
 6 //   Show that the same code can return three different results.
 7 //   ToString has three examples of the Guarded Action pattern.
 8 using System;
 9
10 class CD
11 {
12   private string artist;
13   private string title;
14   private int sales;
15
16   // Construct a CD with the given title
17   // The default state is that this CD has 0 copies sold.
18   public CD(string initArtist, string initTitle)
19   {
20     artist = initArtist;
21     title = initTitle;
22     sales = 0;
23   }
24
25   // Update the state of this CD so it knows about any new sales.
26   // unitsSold: CDs sold not already added to total record sales.
27   public void RecordNewSales(int unitsSold)
28   {
29     sales += unitsSold;
30   }
31
32   // Provide access to the state of this CD to show
33   // unit sales and current music certification.
34   // Returns the title, the sales, and a message.
35   public override string ToString()
36   {
37     // Put a new line in each result with "\n"
38     string result = string.Format("{0} by {1}; sales are {2}\n",
39                                   title, artist, sales);
40
41     if (sales < 500000)
42       result += " --No certification yet. Try more concerts.\n";
43
44     if (sales >= 500000)
45       result += " --Congrats, your music is certified gold.\n";
46
47     if (sales >= 1000000)
48       result += " --It's also gone platinum!";
49
50     return result;
51   }
52 } // end class CD
```

The following `Main` method and output show how the same method can return different results based on the values of a field:

Code Sample: Class TestCD

```
1  // Show the CD class and its varying versions of
2  // ToString results based on the number of units sold.
3  using System;
4
5  public class TestCD
6  {
7    static void Main()
8    {
9        // Construct two instances of CD and view state with ToString
10       CD album1 = new CD("20-Cent", "Shout First");
11       CD album2 = new CD("Bungles", "Green Album");
12
13       Console.WriteLine(album1);
14       album1.RecordNewSales(250000);
15       Console.WriteLine(album1);
16       album1.RecordNewSales(300000);
17       Console.WriteLine(album1);
18       album1.RecordNewSales(600000);
19       Console.WriteLine(album1);
20
21       // Another CD Object
22       Console.WriteLine();
23       album2.RecordNewSales(501342);
24       Console.WriteLine(album2);
25    }
26  } // end class TestCD
```

Output

```
Shout First by 20-Cent; sales are 0
 --No certification yet. Try more concerts.

Shout First by 20-Cent; sales are 250000
 --No certification yet. Try more concerts.

Shout First by 20-Cent; sales are 550000
 --Congrats, your music is certified gold.

Shout First by 20-Cent; sales are 1150000
 --Congrats, your music is certified gold.
```

```
--It's also gone platinum!

Green Album by Bungles; sales are 501342
 --Congrats, your music is certified gold.
```

As shown above, through the power of the `if` statement, the same exact code executes differently for different conditions. The `if` statement controls execution because the true part executes only when the Boolean expression is `true`. The `if` statement also controls statement execution by disregarding statements when the Boolean expression is `false`. For example, the platinum message is disregarded when the value of `sales` is less than one million.

Self-Check

5-3   What is the output from the following code?

```
double num1 = 2.5;
int num2 = 2;

if (num1 + 2 >= 5)
   Console.WriteLine("Greater");
if (num1 < 10)
{
   Console.WriteLine("Less");
   num1 = 2.0;
}

if (num1 == num2)
   Console.WriteLine("Same");
```

5-4   Write the output generated by the following code samples:

(a)

```
int grade = 45;
if (grade >= 70)
   Console.WriteLine("passing");
if (grade < 70)
   Console.WriteLine("dubious");
if (grade < 60)
   Console.WriteLine("failing");
```

(b)

```
grade = 65;
if (grade >= 70)
   Console.WriteLine("passing");
if (grade < 70)
```

```
    Console.WriteLine("dubious");
if (grade < 60)
    Console.WriteLine("failing");
```

5-5   Write if statements to display your name if the int variable option has the value 1
        and to display your school if option has the value 0.

5-6   How could the CD class above be modified to only record the sales if the argument value
        is non-negative? This would be good to add, to avoid accidentally entering negative sales
        for the CD.

5.2 Alternative Action: `if/else`

The if statements in the previous section showed the power that selection gives to programs.
However, these statements only specified what to do if the if statements were true. Sometimes,
programs must also specify what to do if an if statement is false. For example, say that one
student passes with a final grade that is ≥ 60.0. The next student fails with a final grade that is <
60.0. We want to specify what to do in both cases. This example uses the Alternative Action
algorithmic pattern. The program must choose one course of action or another.

	Algorithmic Pattern: Alternative Action
Problem:	Need to choose one action from two alternatives.

Outline:	if (Boolean condition is true)
	    execute action-1
	else
	    execute action-2

Example:	`if (finalGrade >= 60.0)`
	   `Console.WriteLine("passing");`
	`else`
	   `Console.WriteLine("failing");`

The `if`/`else` Statement

The *Alternative Action pattern* can be implemented with C#'s ***if/else*** statement. This control structure can be used to choose between two different courses of action (and, as shown later, to choose between more than two alternatives).

General Form: if/else Statement

```
if (Boolean-expression)
{
  statement(s);        // true part
}
else
{
  statement(s);        // false part
}
```

Note:

The braces are optional if only one statement is used.

Examples:

```
// Assume sales is the amount to withdraw
if (withdrawalAmount <= myAccount.Balance)
{
   myAccount.WithDraw(withdrawalAmount);
   Console.WriteLine("Current balance: {0}", myAccount.Balance);
}
else
{
   Console.WriteLine("Insufficient funds");
   double thisMuch = withdrawalAmount - myAccount.Balance;
   Console.WriteLine("You lack {0}", thisMuch);
}


// Assume sales is initialized as a total monthly sales
if (sales <= 20000.00)
   Console.WriteLine("No bonus");
else
   Console.WriteLine("Bonus coming");
```

When an if/else statement is encountered, the Boolean expression evaluates to either false or true. When true, the true part executes—the false part does not. When the Boolean expression evaluates to false, the false part executes—the true part does not.

When aNumber has a value greater than or equal to zero, the output is "Non negative." When aNumber is less than zero, the false part executes and "Negative" is the output.

```
Console.Write("Enter a number: ");
double aNumber = double.Parse(Console.ReadLine());

if (aNumber >= 0.0)
   Console.WriteLine("Non negative");
else
   Console.WriteLine("Negative");
```

Here is one dialog when a user enters a negative number.

```
Enter a number: -2.3
Negative
```

The output is different when the user enters a non-negative number.

```
Enter a number: 0
Non negative
```

The following flowchart shows the flow of control of an if/else statement. Notice that whether the condition is true or false, execution continues at the same place after the if/else statement.

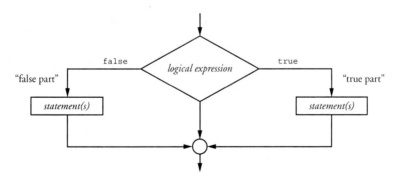

Figure 5.2: A Flowchart View of the Alternative Action Pattern

Here is another example of if/else that uses alternative action. This one depends on the value of the Boolean expression (miles > 24000.0). When miles is greater than 24,000, the true part executes; when miles is less than or equal to than 24,000, the false part executes.

```
Console.WriteLine("Enter miles: ");
double miles = double.Parse(Console.ReadLine());

if (miles > 24000.0)
  Console.WriteLine("Tune-up {0} miles overdue", (miles - 24000.0));
else
  Console.WriteLine("Tune-up due in {0} miles", (24000.0 - miles));
```

When 30123.0 is input for miles, the output is Tune-up 6123 miles overdue. When 23500.0 is input for miles, the false part executes and the output is Tune-up due in 500 miles.

Self-Check

5-7   What output is generated when miles is input as 24000.0?

The ability to choose is a powerful feature of any programming language. The if/else statement lets programmers make a program general enough to generate useful information appropriate to a variety of data. For example, if an employee's hours are less than or equal to 40, that person's gross pay may be calculated as the number of hours multiplied by the hourly rate. However, some employers must pay time-and-a-half to employees who work more than 40 hours per week. Gross pay with overtime must be computed differently than when there is no overtime.

By providing alternative actions, a program can correctly compute the gross pay for a variety of values, including when hours worked are less than 40, equal to 40, and more than 40. The following program uses the Alternative Action pattern to correctly calculate gross pay in all these cases.

Code Sample: Class GrossPay

```
1  using System;
2
3  class GrossPay
4  {
5    static void Main()
6    {
7      double pay, hoursWorked, hourlyRate, OTPay;
```

```
 8
 9        Console.Write("Enter hours worked: ");
10        hoursWorked = double.Parse(Console.ReadLine());
11        Console.Write("Enter hourly rate: ");
12        hourlyRate = double.Parse(Console.ReadLine());
13
14        if (hoursWorked <= 40.0)
15          pay = hoursWorked * hourlyRate;
16        else
17        {
18          OTPay = (hoursWorked - 40) * 1.5 * hourlyRate;
19          pay = (40 * hourlyRate) + OTPay;
20        }
21
22        Console.WriteLine("Gross pay: {0}", pay);
23      }
24  }
```

Dialogue 1

```
Enter hours worked: 32.0
Enter hourly rate: 10.0
Gross pay: 320
```

Dialogue 2

```
Enter hours worked: 50.0
Enter hourly rate: 10.0
Gross pay: 550.0
```

Dialogue 3

```
Enter hours worked: 40.0
Enter hourly rate: 10.0
Gross pay: 400.0
```

Self-Check

5-8   Given the `if` statement below, what is the final value of hours when the initial value of hours is each of the following?

(a) 38
(b) 40
(c) 42.0
(d) 43.0

```
if (hours >= 40.0)
   hours = 40 + 1.5 * (hours - 40);
```

5-9   Write the output generated, given these initializations of `j` and `x`:

```
int j = 8;
double x = -1.5;
```

(a)

```
if (x < -1.0)
   Console.WriteLine("true");
else
   Console.WriteLine("false");
Console.WriteLine("after if/else");
```

(b)

```
if (j >= 0)
   Console.WriteLine("zero or pos");
else
   Console.WriteLine("neg");
```

(c)

```
if (x >= j)
   Console.WriteLine("x is high");
else
   Console.WriteLine("x is low");
```

Using Blocks of Statements with Selection

C# uses the special symbols { and } to specify that the statements and variable declarations that they enclose are to be treated as one statement for the body of a method. These two special symbols delimit (mark the boundaries of) a block. The block groups together many actions, which can then be treated as one.

Blocks are also useful for combining more than one action as the true or false part of an `if/else` statement. Here is an example:

Code Sample: Class GPA

```
1  using System;
2
3  class GPA
4  {
5    static void Main()
6    {
7      Console.Write("Enter GPA: ");
8      double GPA = double.Parse(Console.ReadLine());
9
10     if (GPA >= 3.5)
11     { // True part contains more than one statement in this block
12       Console.WriteLine("Congrats, you are on the dean's list.");
13       double margin = GPA - 3.5;
14       Console.WriteLine("You made it by {0} points.", margin);
15     }
16     else
17     { // False part contains more than one statement in this block
18       Console.WriteLine("Sorry, you are not on the dean's list.");
19       double margin = 3.5 - GPA;
20       Console.WriteLine("You missed it by {0} points.", margin);
21     }
22   }
23 }
```

The block makes it possible to group many statements together. When GPA is input as 3.7, the Boolean expression (GPA >= 3.5) is true and the following output is generated:

Dialogue

```
Enter GPA: 3.7
Congrats, you are on the dean's list.
You made it by 0.2 points.
```

When GPA is 2.9, the Boolean expression (GPA >= 3.5) is false and this output occurs:

Dialogue

```
Enter GPA: 2.9
Sorry, you are not on the dean's list.
You missed it by 0.6 points.
```

This alternative execution is provided by the two possible evaluations of the Boolean expression GPA >= 3.5. If it evaluates to true, the true part executes; if it evaluates to false, the false part executes.

Common Pitfalls When Using Selection

There are several mistakes that are easy to make when you write selection code. This section attempts to address what they are and how to handle them.

A first common pitfall when using if/else is to use multiple if statements and omit the else. Seemingly innocent code can then have unexpected behavior because more than one of the multiple if statements executes.

For example, the following code is intended to write a student's grade on the screen, with different output for students who got A's or B's. However, it is incorrect:

```
if (grade >= 90)
   Console.WriteLine("You got an A!");
if (grade >= 80)
   Console.WriteLine("You got a B.");
```

If a student scored 80 or above, but less than 90, the code executes correctly. The second if statement is true, but the first one is not. However, if a student scored 90 or above, both if statements are true. In that case, the following output is produced:

```
You got an A!
You got a B.
```

Another common pitfall when programming using selection is accidentally placing a semicolon after the parenthesized Boolean expression. The if statement should not have a semicolon after the Boolean expression; if one is there, it will change the meaning of the code in a way that is likely not intended. The C# compiler will assume that the "true part" of the if statement is the semicolon itself—an empty statement! This means that if the Boolean condition is true, nothing will happen. The line following the if statement will no longer be regarded as being part of the if statement—it will always be executed, regardless of whether the condition is true or not.

For example, the following code will always use the overtime pay formula, no matter how many hours the employee works:

```
if (hoursWorked > 40.0);   // This semicolon shouldn't be here!
   hoursWorked = hoursWorked + 1.5 * (hoursWorked - 40);
pay = (hoursWorked * hourlyRate);
```

Although this code compiles and is correct when hours > 40.0, those who work 40 hours or less would lose money:

```
Enter hours worked: 20
Enter hourly rate: 10
Gross pay: -100.0
```

This is a common mistake. As noted earlier, the true part of the `if` statement is empty, so nothing happens. Now, what follows is *not* part of the `if` statement. The assignment to hoursWorked always occurs. In the case shown above, the hoursWorked is less than earned, and the gross pay is calculated as negative.

A third selection pitfall is letting indentation trick your eyes into assuming that a statement is part of a block in an `if/else` statement, when really it isn't. Neglecting to use proper block form with `if/else` statements can cause a variety of errors.

For example, here is a modified version of the earlier GPA example. It shows what can go wrong if you intend for more than one statement to be executed as the result of an `if`, but the statements are not blocked together:

```
if (GPA >= 3.5)
  margin = GPA - 3.5;
  Console.WriteLine("Congrats, you are on the dean's list.");
  Console.WriteLine("You made it by {0} points.", margin);
else  // <- ERROR: Unexpected else
```

Without the { and } there is no block. Although the margin = GPA - 3.5; statement belongs to the preceding `if/else`, the bolded statements do not, even though the indentation might make it appear that they do. As far as the compiler is concerned, the two WriteLine messages are not part of the `if`. So when it reaches the else, it complains because there is no statement in C# that begins with an else. Fortunately, the compiler will catch this error and issue an error message.

Here is another example of what can go wrong when a block is omitted. This time, { and } are omitted after else.

```
if (GPA >= 3.5)
  margin = GPA - 3.5;
else
  margin = 3.5 - GPA;
  Console.WriteLine("Sorry, you are not on the dean's list.");
  Console.WriteLine("You missed it by {0} points.", margin);
```

There are no compile-time errors here, but the code does contain an intent error. The final two statements always execute! They do not belong to the if/else statement. If GPA >= 3.5 is false, the code executes as one would expect. However, when this Boolean expression is true, the output is not what is intended. Instead, this rather confusing output shows up:

```
Congratulations, you are on the dean's list.
You made it by 0.152 points.
Sorry, you are not on the dean's list.
You missed it by -0.152 points.
```

Although it is not necessary to do so, always using blocks for the true and false parts of if and if/else statements can help prevent intent errors, such as the one above. It also makes your code more readable and clear. It does have the drawback that when you use blocks this way, there are more lines of code and more sets of curly braces to line up. In addition, the code to execute for the true and false parts is often only one statement. When this is the case, the block is not required, though it is allowed.

5.3   Conditional Logical Operators

C# has three additional conditional operators that let you create more complex Boolean expressions: the binary *and* operator &&, the binary *or* operator ||, and the unary *not* operator !. For example, this Boolean expression shows the Boolean *and* operator && applied to two Boolean operands:

```
(test >= 0) && (test <= 100)
```

The unary *not* operator ! is often used in if/else statements to specify the logical negation of a Boolean expression (the negation of true is false, and the negation of false is true). The following table shows every possible combination of Boolean values and the **Boolean operators** *!* , *||*, and **&&**:

&& Boolean Binary *and* Operator

Expression	Result
true && true	true
true && false	false
false && true	false
false && false	false

|| Boolean Binary *or* Operator

Expression	Result
true || true	true
true || false	true
false || true	true
false || false	false

! Boolean Unary *not* Operator

Expression	Result
!false	true
!true	false

The next example Boolean expression uses the Boolean *and* operator && to ensure that a test is in the range of 0 through 100 inclusive. The Boolean expression evaluates to true when the value of test is greater than or equal to 0 (test >= 0) and is also less than or equal to 100 (test <= 100).

```
if ((test >= 0) && (test <= 100))
   Console.WriteLine("Test is in range");
else
   Console.WriteLine("**Warning--Test is out of range");
```

The Boolean expressions evaluate as follows when test has the value 97 and then 977 (to simulate a user attempting to enter 97, but accidentally pressing the 7 key twice):

When test is **97**:	When test is **977**:
(test >= 0) && (test <= 100)	(test >= 0) && (test <= 100)
(97 >= 0) && (97 <= 100)	(977 >= 0) && (977 <= 100)
true && true	true && false
true	false

Operator Precedence Rules

Programming languages have *operator precedence rules* to determine the order in which operators are evaluated. For example, in the absence of parentheses, the relational operators >= and <= are evaluated before the && operator. This is a very important issue!

The following table lists the C# operators in order of precedence. The dot . and () operators are evaluated first (have the highest precedence), and the assignment operators are evaluated last. This table shows all operators in the C# language (including those not yet introduced).

Precedence Rules for the Operators Presented So Far ('=' evaluates last)

Category	*Operators*		
Primary	x.y	f(x)	new
Unary	+	- !	(Type)x
Multiplicative	*	/ %	
Additive	+	-	
Relational	<	> <=	>=
Equality	==	!=	
Conditional AND	&&		
Conditional OR	||		
Assignment	=		

These elaborate precedence rules are not easy to remember. So if you are unsure, always use parentheses to clarify expressions that use more than one operator, such as (3 * 5) + 7 instead of 3 * 5 + 7. This makes your code more readable and, therefore, more understandable. Readable, understandable code is easier to debug and maintain.

Most operators are grouped (evaluated) in a left-to-right order. For example, a/b/c/d is equivalent to (((a/b)/c)/d). The property that states in which direction an operator is grouped (evaluated) is called its *associativity*. Operators like + and / are grouped from the left and are called left-associative.

One operator that behaves differently is the assignment operator; it is right-associative and therefore evaluates right to left. For example, the multiple assignment a=b=c=d=999 is equivalent to (a=(b=(c=(d=999)))). Indeed, it would not make sense the other way; ((((a=b)=c)=d)=999) does not make sense because an expression such as (a=b) cannot be reassigned the new value as in ((a=b)=c).

This assignment is legal because an assignment can also be used as an expression. This allows several variables to be assigned the same value in one expression, such as this:

```
string first, middle, last;
first = middle = last = "?";

// Three string variables assigned reference to the string object "?"
Console.WriteLine(first == "?");   // True
Console.WriteLine(middle == "?");  // True
Console.WriteLine(last == "?");    // True
```

Self-Check

5-10   Evaluate the following expressions to true or false:

(a) `(false || true)`

(b) `(true && false)`

(c) `(1 * 3 == 4 - 1)`

(d) `(false || (true && false))`

(e) `(3 < 4 && 3 != 4)`

(f) `!false && !true`

(g) `(5 + 2 > 3 * 4) && (11 < 12)`

(h) `!((false && true) || false)`

5-11   Write an expression that is true only when the int named score is in the range of 1 through 10 inclusive.

5-12   Write an expression that is true if test is outside the range of 0 through 100.

5-13   Write the output generated by the following code:

```
double GPA = 1.03;
if (GPA == 4.0)
    Console.WriteLine("President's list");
```

5-14   Write an expression that is true only when the int value stored in anInt is evenly divisible by 5.

5.4 Comparing Objects with **CompareTo**

Relational operators such as < and >= test the relationship between numeric values. However, these operators only compare numeric data types, not most other types of objects. C# objects in general are compared by sending them a special message called **CompareTo**. The CompareTo method is present in many C# types for comparing the relationship between two objects of that type. In addition, you can create a CompareTo method for your own user-defined types.

A CompareTo message is called on an object, and it accepts another object of the same type as an argument. An example would be `"Abc".CompareTo("abc")`. It returns one of these three values:

- ○ 0 if the two objects are considered to be equal
- ○ an integer less than 0 if the object before
     the dot is less than the argument in parentheses
- ○ an integer greater than 0 if the object before
     the dot is greater than the argument in parentheses

For example, the string type has a CompareTo method that compares two strings alphabetically, character by character, from left to right. This is a case-sensitive comparison, and capital letters are considered to be "greater than" lowercase ones. For example, "M" is considered to be greater than "m". If the strings' values are different, either they have at least one different character, they have different lengths, or both.

The CompareTo method returns the following values in the following cases, matching the pattern above:

- ○ 0 if the two strings are equal (have the same characters)
- ○ an integer less than 0 if the string object before the dot comes earlier in alphabetical order than the one in parentheses
- ○ an integer greater than 0 if the string object before the dot comes later in alphabetical order than the one in parentheses

Consider the following messages.

```
"Abc".CompareTo("Abc")            // Returns 0
"Abc".CompareTo("abc")            // Returns greater than 0
"jones".CompareTo("smith")        // Returns less than 0
"Aardvark".CompareTo("Aaron")     // Returns greater than 0
"abcde".CompareTo("abc")          // Returns greater than 0
"meat".CompareTo("meatloaf")      // Returns less than 0
```

A string that precedes another alphabetically is considered to be "less than" the other string. Consider some more examples where the returned value from CompareTo is compared to see if it is less than, equal to, or greater than, 0.

Code Sample: Class Alphabits

```
1  using System;
2
3  class Alphabits
4  {
5     static void Main()
6     {
7        string a = "Able";
8        string b = "Baker";
9
10       if (a.CompareTo("Charlie") < 0)
11          Console.WriteLine("{0} < Charlie", a);
12
13       if (a.CompareTo(b) > 0)
```

```
14          Console.WriteLine("{0} > {1}", a, b);
15
16      if (b.CompareTo(a) > 0)   // False
17          Console.WriteLine("{0} > {1}", b, a);
18
19      if (b.CompareTo(b) == 0)
20          Console.WriteLine("{0} equals {0}", b);
21    }
22 }
```

Output

```
Able < Charlie
Baker > Able
Baker equals Baker
```

The CompareTo method does not evaluate left to right, like the more intuitive a < b does. The CompareTo message forces you to think more like a b < (which is called *postfix notation*). You may find it easier to deal with the CompareTo message if you read the first operand, ①; followed by a relational operator, ②; followed by the second operand, ③.

For example, the following Boolean expression can be read as a < "def":

```
     ①              ③     ②
if (a.CompareTo("def") <   0)
   Console.WriteLine("{0} < def", a);
```

This expression can be read as "def" >= b:

```
     ①              ③    ②
if ("def".CompareTo(b) >= 0)
   Console.WriteLine("def >= {0}", b);
```

This expression can be read as "def" != a:

```
     ①              ③    ②
if ("def".CompareTo(a) != 0)
   Console.WriteLine("def != {0}", a);
```

Many types in the .NET Framework can be compared using CompareTo besides string. For example, the DateTime type, covered in Chapter 3, has a CompareTo method that compares two DateTime objects by date and time. For example, take line 11 below:

```
if (date1.CompareTo(date2) >= 0)
```

If the object before the dot is an earlier date or time than the argument in parentheses, an integer less than 0 is returned. If they are the same date and time, 0 is returned. If the object is a later date or time than the argument, an integer greater than 0 is returned.

Code Sample: Class CompareDates

```
 1  using System;
 2
 3  class CompareDates
 4  {
 5    static void Main()
 6    {
 7      DateTime date1 = new DateTime(2003, 6, 1);
 8      DateTime date2 = new DateTime(2000, 12, 20);
 9      DateTime now   = DateTime.Now;    // current date and time
10
11      if (date1.CompareTo(date2) >= 0)
12        Console.WriteLine("{0} is equal to or after {1}",
13                          date1, date2);
14
15      if (now.CompareTo(date2) < 0)
16        Console.WriteLine("Today's date must be before {0}", date2);
17      else
18        Console.WriteLine("It must be almost holiday break time!");
19    }
20  }
```

Output

```
6/1/2003 12:00:00 AM is equal to or after 12/20/2000 12:00:00 AM
It must be almost holiday break time!
```

Self-Check

5-15   Write the output generated by the following code samples:

```
string option = "A";
```

(a)

```
if (option.CompareTo("A") == 0)
   Console.WriteLine("addRecord");
if (option.CompareTo("D") == 0)
{
   Console.WriteLine("deleteRecord");
}
```

(b)

```
option = "D";
if (option.CompareTo("A") == 0)
   Console.WriteLine("addRecord");
if (option.CompareTo("D") == 0)
   Console.WriteLine("deleteRecord");
```

(c)

```
option = "R";
if (option.CompareTo("M") > 0)
{
   Console.WriteLine("R > M");
}

if (option.CompareTo("D") >= 0))
{
   Console.WriteLine("R >= D");
}
```

5-16   Write the output generated by the following code samples (you may wish to review Chapter 3 to see how DateTime objects are printed):

```
DateTime dt_1 = new DateTime(2000, 1, 1);
DateTime dt_2 = new DateTime(2000, 1, 1);
DateTime dt_3 = dt1.AddDays(4);
```

(a)

```
Console.WriteLine("{0} compared to {1} is: {2}",
   dt_1, dt_2, dt_1.CompareTo(dt_2));
```

(b)

```
if (dt_3.CompareTo(dt_1) <= 0)
   Console.WriteLine("{0} is earlier", dt_3);
else
   Console.WriteLine("{0} is earlier", dt_1);
```

5.5   Multiple Selection (`if/else/if/...`)

"Multiple selection" refers to times when a program needs to select one action from many possible actions. This pattern is summarized as follows:

Algorithmic Pattern: Multiple Selection

Problem: Must execute one set of actions from three or more alternatives.

Outline: if condition 1 is true, then
     execute action 1;
  otherwise if condition 2 is true, then
     execute action 2;
  // ...
  otherwise if condition n-1 is true, then
     execute action n-1
  otherwise
     execute action n

Example:

```
Console.Write("Enter monthly sales: ");
double sales = double.Parse(Console.ReadLine());
string message;
if (sales == 0.0)
   message = "Get to work or be fired";
else if (sales < 10000.00)
   message = "Sales should be 10,000.00 or more";
else if (sales < 20000.00)
   message = "Okay, sales > 10,000 but still under quota";
else
   message = "You've met or exceeded your quota";
```

The following `CollegeStudent` class contains an instance of the *Multiple Selection pattern* in its `ToString` method. It selects from one of three possible actions. Any grade point average (GPA) less than 3.0 (including negative numbers) returns as its result `"Try harder"`. Any GPA less than 4.0 but greater than or equal to 3.0 returns as its result `"Dean's list"`. In addition, any GPA greater than or equal to 4.0 returns as its result `"President's list"`. There is no upper range or lower range defined in this problem.

Code Sample: Class CollegeStudent

```
1  using System;
2
3  class CollegeStudent
4  {
5     private string name;
6     private double gpa;
7
8     public CollegeStudent(string initName, double initGpa)
9     {
10        name = initName;
11        gpa = initGpa;
12     }
13
14     public override string ToString()
15     {
16        string result = name + ": ";
17
18        if (gpa < 3.0)
19           result += "Try harder";
20        else
21        { // The false part of this if/else is another if/else
22           if (gpa < 4.0)
23              result += "Dean's list";
24           else
25              result += "President's list";
26        } // End else
27
28        return result;
29     }
30 }
```

Notice that the false part of the first `if/else` statement is another `if/else` statement. If GPA is less than 3.0, `"Try harder"` is returned, and the program skips over the nested `if/else`. However, if the `Boolean` expression is false (when GPA is greater than or equal to 3.0), the false part executes. This second if/else statement is the false part of the first if/else. It determines if GPA is high enough to qualify for either the dean's list or the president's list.

When implementing multiple selection with if/else statements, it is important to use proper indentation, so that the code executes as its written appearance suggests. Remember, although the C# compiler ignores indentation, the readability that comes from good indentation habits can save you large amounts of time as you write and debug your programs.

To illustrate the flexibility you have in formatting, you could also implement the previous multiple selection in the following preferred manner, to line up the three different paths through this control structure:

```
if (gpa < 3.0)
   result += "Try harder";
else if (gpa < 4.0)
   result += "Dean's list";
else
   result += "President's list";
```

The Most Closely Nested Rule

Sometimes code that uses multiple selection can be written in a way that may seem ambiguous. Consider the following fragment:

```
int x = 5;
string message = "I don't know anything about x yet";

if (x > 0)
   if (x > 10)
     message = "x > 10";
else
   message = "x is negative?";

Console.WriteLine(message);
```

Output

```
x is negative?
```

The code fragment above looks like it will leave the value of message untouched because the outer if statement is true, and the inner one false. Actually, it ends up executing the code in the else statement, so at the end of the above code, message has a value of "x is negative?"!

This happens because the code is interpreted in a way that is misleading, given the indentation above:

The Above Code IS interpreted by C# as:	NOT as:

```if (x > 0)```
```{```
  ```if (x > 10)```
    ```message = "x > 10";```
  ```else```
    ```message = "x is negative?";```
```}```
	```if (x > 0)```
	```{```
	  ```if (x > 10)```
	    ```message = "x > 10";```
	```}```
	```else```
	    ```message = "x is negative?";```

Notice that there are no braces or explicit blocks in the original example. Because of this, the `else` statement bound itself to the most deeply nested `if` statement near it; that is, to `if (x > 10)`. This important fact is sometimes called the *Most Closely Nested Rule*. To avoid intent errors, it is important to remember this when you write code that uses multiple selection.

The indentation in the original example makes it appear that the `else` is actually bound to the outer `if (x > 0)` statement, but C# is not whitespace-sensitive, so the indentation has no effect on the code's meaning. Remember that the compiler cannot catch the mistake if you forget the Most Closely Nested Rule and write incorrect code. This is because the code is still legal syntax; it just behaves differently than you intended.

To solve problems such as the one above, either use braces to create blocks for your `if`/`else` statements to avoid ambiguity, or carefully comment and indent your code to avoid confusion. Some code editors will also help you by indenting your `if` and `else` statements for you; if the editor indents your `else` statement to a different amount than you expect, your code probably has an intent error.

Example—Determining Letter Grades

Consider the problem of adding a `GetLetterGrade` method to the above `CollegeStudent` class. This method will return a `string` with the right letter grade for a given percentage, which is passed in as a `double`. Some schools use a scale like the following to determine the proper letter grade to assign to a student. The letter grade is based on a percentage that represents a weighted average of all of the work for the term.

Based on the following table, all percentage values must be in the range of 0.0 through 100.0.

Value of Percentage	Assigned Grade
$90.0 \leq \text{percentage} \leq 100.0$	A
$80.0 \leq \text{percentage} < 90.0$	B
$70.0 \leq \text{percentage} < 80.0$	C
$60.0 \leq \text{percentage} < 70.0$	D
$0.0 \leq \text{percentage} < 60.0$	F

This problem is an example of choosing one action from more than two different actions—a case of multiple selection. You could implement a method to determine the range that the argument percentage falls into by using separate if statements:

Code Sample: Inelegant GetCourseGrade Solution

```
 1 public string GetLetterGrade(double percentage)
 2 {
 3    string result = string.Format("{0} got {1}% for a grade of ",
 4       name, percentage);
 5
 6    if (percentage >= 90.0 && percentage <= 100.0)
 7       result += "A";
 8    if (percentage >= 80.0 && percentage < 90.0)
 9       result += "B";
10    if (percentage >= 70.0 && percentage < 80.0)
11       result += "C";
12    if (percentage >= 60.0 && percentage < 70.0)
13       result += "D";
14    if (percentage >=  0.0 && percentage < 60.0)
15       result += "F";
16    if (percentage < 0.0 || percentage >  100.0)
17       result += "Out of range";
18
19    return result;
20 }
```

The solution above is correct, but it is inelegant. It requires the evaluation of all six of its complex Boolean expressions each time the code is run, no matter what the grade is. When given the problem of choosing from among five different actions, it is better to use multiple selection, not guarded action. The preferred multiple selection implementation is shown below. Because it uses *nested if/else* statements, the code stops executing as soon as one of the Boolean tests evaluates to true. The true part executes, and all of the remaining nested if/else statements are skipped.

Additionally, the multiple selection pattern shown below is less prone to intent errors. It ensures that an error message will be returned when percentage is outside the range of 0.0 through 100.0 inclusive. There is a possibility, for example, that percentage might be entered as 777 instead of 77. Notice that since 777 >= 90.0 is true, the method in the code above could improperly return an "A" when a "C" would have been the correct result.

The following nested if/else solution first checks if percentage (the argument to the method shown below) is less than 0.0 or greater than 100.0. In this case, an error message is returned instead of a valid letter grade.

Code Sample: Elegant GetCourseGrade solution

```
1  public string GetLetterGrade(double percentage)
2  {
3    string result = string.Format("{0} got {1}% for a grade of ",
4      name, percentage);
5
6    if (percentage < 0.0 || percentage >  100.0)
7      result += "Out of range";
8    else if (percentage >= 90.0)
9      result += "A";
10   else if (percentage >= 80.0)
11     result += "B";
12   else if (percentage >= 70.0)
13     result += "C";
14   else if (percentage >= 60.0)
15     result += "D";
16   else
17     result += "F";
18
19   return result;
20 }
```

When this code runs, if percentage is out of range (less than 0 or greater than 100), the result is an error message. The program then skips the rest of the nested if/else structure, rather than getting an incorrect letter grade.

However, if the first Boolean expression is false, the next if statement executes. This statement checks if percentage represents an A. At this point, percentage is certainly less than or equal to 100.0, so any value of percentage >= 90.0 concatenates and returns an A. The program then skips over all other statements after the first else.

At this point, if the proper range for percentage hasn't been found yet, the program continues down through the elses, until it either finds the correct range or it reaches the last else. If it reaches this final else, this means that percentage < 60.0. The program then executes the action after the final else and "F" is concatenated to result.

Testing Multiple Selection

Consider how many messages must be sent to completely test the GetLetterGrade method with multiple selection—or for that matter, any method or segment of code that uses multiple selection. To test for all possible percentages, the method could be called with all numbers from -1.0 through 101.0. At an extreme, this could require an infinite number of calls for arguments such as 1.000000000001 and 1.999999999999. Testing only integers would be a lot easier, but still tedious. The good news is that such testing is unnecessary.

You can avoid testing all possible values by simply testing every possible *branch* (path through the code) through the nested if/else, so that every statement is executed. This is called *branch coverage testing*.

Always make sure to test the cut-off (boundary) values. This minimal extra effort is worth it. For example, testing the cut-offs might avoid situations where students with 90.0 are accidentally shown to have a letter grade of B, rather than A. This would occur if you accidentally coded the Boolean expression (percentage >= 90.0) as (percentage > 90.0). In the above program, the cut-off values between grades (60.0, 70.0, 80.0, and 90.0) need to be thoroughly tested.

One testing strategy is to select test values that combine branch and boundary testing at the same time. For example, a percentage of 90.0 should return "A". The value of 90.0 not only checks the path for returning an A, it also tests the boundary—90.0—as one cut-off. Counting down by tens to 60 checks all boundaries. However, this still misses one path: the one that sets result to "F". Adding 59.9 to the test values completes the test.

These three things are necessary to perform branch coverage testing correctly:

1. Establish a set of data that executes all branches (all possible paths through the multiple selection) and all boundary (cut-off) values.
2. Execute the portion of the program containing the multiple selection for all selected data values.
3. Make sure that the program segment behaves correctly for all data values.

For example, the following data set executes all branches of GetLetterGrade while also checking the boundaries:

```
-0.1 0.0 59.9 60.0 69.9 70.0 79.9 80.0 89.9 90.0 99.9 100.0 101.1
```

A testing class could start like this (you may wish to review the CollegeStudent class from earlier in this chapter to refresh your memory):

Code Sample: Test class for CollegeStudent GetCourseGrade Method

```
1  using System;
2
3  class TestGrader
4  {
5    static void Main()
6    {
7      CollegeStudent jim = new CollegeStudent("Jim", 1.7);
8
```

```
 9        Console.WriteLine(jim);   // calls ToString
10        Console.WriteLine(jim.GetLetterGrade(-0.1));
11        Console.WriteLine(jim.GetLetterGrade(0.0));
12        Console.WriteLine(jim.GetLetterGrade(59.9));
13        Console.WriteLine(jim.GetLetterGrade(60.0));
14        Console.WriteLine(jim.GetLetterGrade(69.9));
15        Console.WriteLine(jim.GetLetterGrade(70.0));
16        Console.WriteLine(jim.GetLetterGrade(79.9));
17        Console.WriteLine(jim.GetLetterGrade(80.0));
18        Console.WriteLine(jim.GetLetterGrade(89.9));
19        Console.WriteLine(jim.GetLetterGrade(90.0));
20        Console.WriteLine(jim.GetLetterGrade(99.9));
21        Console.WriteLine(jim.GetLetterGrade(100.0));
22        Console.WriteLine(jim.GetLetterGrade(101.1));
23      }
24 }
```

The program output must be examined to verify that every method call returned the proper value. Here is the output from the test code above.

Output

```
Jim: Try harder
Jim got -0.1% for a grade of Out of range
Jim got 0% for a grade of F
Jim got 59.9% for a grade of F
Jim got 60% for a grade of D
Jim got 69.9% for a grade of D
Jim got 70% for a grade of C
Jim got 79.9% for a grade of C
Jim got 80% for a grade of B
Jim got 89.9% for a grade of B
Jim got 90% for a grade of A
Jim got 99.9% for a grade of A
Jim got 100% for a grade of A
Jim got 101.1% for a grade of Out of range
```

Self-Check

5-17   Write the output produced by the following code:

```
int theAnswer = 42;
if (theAnswer % 2 == 0)
  Console.WriteLine("{0} is divisible by 2", theAnswer);
```

```
   else if (theAnswer % 3 == 0)
      Console.WriteLine("{0} is divisible by 3", theAnswer);
   else if (theAnswer % 5 == 0)
      Console.WriteLine("{0} is divisible by 5", theAnswer);
   else if (theAnswer % 6 == 0)
      Console.WriteLine("{0} is divisible by 6", theAnswer);
   else if (theAnswer % 7 == 0)
      Console.WriteLine("{0} is divisible by 7", theAnswer);
   else if (theAnswer % 10 == 0)
      Console.WriteLine("{0} is divisible by 10", theAnswer);
```

5-18   Write a fragment of code that compares three integers stored in variables num1, num2, and num3 and prints the number that is smallest of the three. Use multiple selection. (Could this problem be solved without multiple selection?)

5.6 The `switch` Statement

Nested `if`/`else` statements work well when there are ranges of values to choose from, or when complex Boolean expressions are required. C# also provides a **switch** statement that works well when you need to choose one selection from two or more specific values. The `switch` statement can be useful when there are a large number of choices to select from, or when the action to take is the same for multiple cases. The choices can be whole numbers, characters, or strings.

General Form: The C# switch statement

```
switch (expression)
{
  case constant-expression:
    statement(s);
    jump-statement (s);
  case constant-expression :
    statement(s) ;
    jump-statement (s);

    ...
  default:        // optional
    statement(s);
    jump-statement (s);
}
```

Notes:

○ The *expression* is any expression that evaluates to an integral type[1] or a string.

○ The *constant-expression* is a literal value that must be of the same type as the *expression*.

○ The *jump-statement* typically is break (but it could also be continue, goto, or return) to transfer control out of each case (or default) part.

○ The default part and each case must have a *jump-statement* to avoid this compile-time error:

```
Control cannot fall through from one case label to another
```

○ Each *constant-expression* (after case) must be unique (can't have 1 or 'A' twice).

Example

```
Console.Write("Enter option 1, 2, or 3: ");
int option = int.Parse(Console.ReadLine());

switch (option)
{
  case 1:
    Console.WriteLine("option 1 selected");
    break;
  case 2:
    Console.WriteLine("option 2 selected");
    break;
  case 3:
    Console.WriteLine("option 3 selected");
    break;
  default:
    Console.WriteLine("Option must be 1, 2, or 3");
    break;
} // End switch
```

When a switch statement executes, the *expression* is matched to a *constant-expression* and the statements following the colon (:) execute. Using the example above, inputs of *1* and then *2* result in different statement execution:

---

[1] C# supports nine integral types: sbyte, byte, short, ushort, int, uint, long, ulong, and char. The integral type values are stored in a varying number of bytes and have different ranges of values.

Dialogue 1:

```
Enter option 1, 2, or 3: 1
option 1 selected
```

Dialogue 2:

```
Enter option 1, 2, or 3: 2
option 2 selected
```

If no *constant-expression* matches the *expression*, the default section—if present—executes. If there is no default selection, no code is executed.

Dialogue 3: (No match found for user input of -1)

```
Enter option 1, 2, or 3: -1
Option must be 1, 2, or 3
```

The default section is needed only when you want the program to carry out a specific action when the switch expression does not match any of the case values. Notice that it is possible that no statements will execute inside the switch statement. This occurs when the switch expression does not match any *constant-expression* and there is no default section.

A string can also be used as the constant expression, as shown in the following switch statement. It chooses one of four choices, based on the value of the uppercase equivalent of the string object referenced by option.

Code Sample: Class Options

```
 1 using System;
 2
 3 class Options
 4 {
 5   static void Main()
 6   {
 7     Console.Write("Add Remove Print: ");
 8
 9     // Choose from 1 of 3 valid selections or report invalid option.
10     // Make sure the string has no leading or trailing blanks
11     // that it is also in upper case (easier on the user).
12     string option = Console.ReadLine().Trim().ToUpper();
13
```

```
14      // Choose from 1 of 3 options or report an invalid option.
15      switch (option)
16      {
17        case "ADD":
18          Console.WriteLine("Add selected");
19          break;
20        case "REMOVE":
21          Console.WriteLine("Remove selected");
22          break;
23        case "PRINT":
24          Console.WriteLine("Print selected");
25          break;
26        default:
27          Console.WriteLine("Invalid choice");
28          break;
29      } // End switch
30    }
31 }
```

One Possible Dialogue

```
Add Remove Print: remove
Remove selected
```

Remember that ToUpper() changes all letters to uppercase. If the value read into option is remove or ReMoVe, the program displays Remove Selected and **break** is executed to exit the switch control structure. If the user enters Print (or prinT), Print selected is displayed, and break is executed. Whatever the user enters, each case is evaluated until option matches one of the three values following case. If no match is found (option is any other value), the message Invalid choice is displayed.

Self-Check

5-19   Write the output produced by the following switch statements:

(a)

```
char option = 'A';
switch (option)
{
  case 'A':
    Console.WriteLine("AAA");
    break;
```

```
      case 'B':
        Console.WriteLine("BBB");
        break;
      default:
        Console.WriteLine("Invalid");
        break;
    }
```

(b)

```
int anInt = 2;
switch (anInt)
{
  case 0:
    Console.WriteLine("zero");
    break;
  case 1:
    Console.WriteLine("one");
    break;
  default:
    Console.WriteLine("Neither");
    break;
}
```

5-20   Write the output from (a) above when option is 'B'.

5-21   Write the output from (a) above when option is 'C'.

5-22   Write a switch statement that displays your favorite music if a string called choice is "music", your favorite food if choice is "food", and your favorite teacher if choice is "teacher". Otherwise, display "Invalid choice."

5.7   Adding Selection to BankAccount

In Chapters 3 and 4, the Withdraw method of BankAccount allowed withdrawals for more than the account balance. Withdraw simply subtracts the argument passed to it. No check is made to ensure that the amount requested is less than or equal to the balance.

```
// Debit account by amount even if amount > balance or balance <= 0
// Precondition: amount is positive.
public void Withdraw(double amount)
{
  balance = balance - amount;
}
```

We will now modify the `Withdraw` method to guard against withdrawing more than the current balance or non-positive amounts such as 0.00 or -60.00. `Withdraw` will now become a method with return type of `bool` that returns `true` when the withdrawal is successful. If the amount requested exceeds the balance, `Withdraw` will return `false`. In this case, no change is made to the state of the `BankAccount` object. This design change allows programs that use `BankAccount` to find out if a withdrawal was successful or not. A program using `BankAccount` can then take its own appropriate actions.

Here is the modified version of `Withdraw`:

```
// Debit this account by amount.
// If amount is negative, has no effect on account's balance.
// If amount > account balance, debit by amount and return true.
public bool Withdraw(double amount)
{
  bool result = true;

  if (amount > this.Balance || amount <= 0.00)
    result = false;
  else
    balance = balance + amount;

  return result;
}
```

The alternative action to handle any withdrawal request for any amount is encapsulated in the `Withdraw` method. Although a different type of account could be made to allow overdrafts, this `BankAccount` does not. Notice that the new version starts by assuming that the withdrawal will succeed. The `result` is set to `true` at the start, and only becomes `false` if the withdrawal subsequently fails.

This modified `Withdraw` method will no longer accept negative amounts, which would otherwise credit a negative amount to the account. The following test documents this behavior.

```
// With a negative argument to amount, Withdraw returns false.
if (one.Withdraw(-2.34))
  Console.WriteLine("Withdrawal of -2.34 should have returned false!");

// Withdrawing -2.34 had no effect. Balance is still 1.50.
if (one.Balance != 1.50)
  Console.WriteLine("Balance should be 1.50!");
```

The program using BankAccount has the responsibility to ensure that the argument in the message is valid—that it is a positive amount. The following test shows that the program using BankAccount objects is responsible for ensuring positive withdrawal and deposit amounts.

```
// Depositing a negative amount has no effect
one.Deposit(-2.34);
if (one.Balance != 1.50)
  Console.WriteLine("Balance should be 1.50!");
```

The Deposit method used Math.Max to avoid negative deposits, but the solution was somewhat inelegant because it did not report whether the deposit succeeded or failed. Therefore, we will also modify Deposit to prevent negative deposits (which could otherwise result in less money in the account!).

```
// Credit this account by amount.
// If amount is negative, return false.
public bool Deposit(double amount)
{
  bool result = true;

  if (amount <= 0.00)
    result = false;
  else
    balance = balance + amount;

  return result;
}
```

The following test code shows BankAccount's new behavior for the updated Withdraw and Deposit methods.

Code Sample: Class TestBankAccount

```
1 using System;
2
3 class TestBankAccount
4 {
5   static void Main()
6   {
7     BankAccount one = new BankAccount("One", 1.50);
8     if (one.Balance != 1.50)
9       Console.WriteLine("Balance should be 1.50");
10
11     // Try a successful deposit and withdrawal
```

```
12       if (!one.Deposit(1.00))
13          Console.WriteLine("Deposit should have succeeded!");
14
15       if (one.Balance != 2.50)
16          Console.WriteLine("Balance should be 2.50!");
17
18       if (!one.Withdraw(1.00))
19          Console.WriteLine("Deposit should have succeeded!");
20       if (one.Balance != 1.50)
21          Console.WriteLine("Balance should be 1.50!");
22
23       // BankAccount does not allow withdrawals when amount > Balance
24       if (one.Withdraw(567.89))
25          Console.WriteLine("Withdrawal should have failed!");
26
27       if (one.Balance != 1.50)
28          Console.WriteLine("Balance should be 1.50!");
29
30       // Withdrawals and deposit of negative amounts have no effect
31       one.Withdraw(-2.34);
32       one.Deposit(-2.34);
33       if (one.Balance != 1.50)
34          Console.WriteLine("Balance should be 1.50!");
35    }
36 }
```

Chapter Summary

○ Selection requires Boolean expressions that evaluate to true or false. Boolean expressions often have one or more of the following operators:

$$< \quad > \quad <= \quad >= \quad != \quad == \quad ! \quad || \quad \&\&$$

○ The Guarded Action pattern, implemented with the if statement, allows a program to either execute a collection of statements or skip them, depending on the circumstances.

○ The Alternative Action pattern, implemented with the if/else statement, chooses one action or its alternative. There are exactly two choices.

○ The Multiple Selection pattern, implemented either with nested if/else statements or with the switch statement, chooses one action from multiple alternatives. Multiple selection should be used whenever there are three or more actions to select from.

○ Selection control allows a program to respond to a variety of situations in an appropriate manner.

○ The `bool` type and the Boolean literals `true` and `false` can be used as the `return` type of a method, to conveniently return information about the state of an object. They can be used to answer questions such as "Is the book available?", "Was the `withdraw` message successful or not?", or "Does this equation have real roots?"

○ To test multiple selection, establish a set of data that executes all branches and tests all boundary values.

○ Remember that without thorough testing, a program may appear to work, when in fact there may be one or more values that do not work.

○ The `switch` statement must compare string expressions or values of one of C#'s integral types: `sbyte`, `byte`, `short`, `ushort`, `int`, `uint`, `long`, `ulong`, and `char`. No other type is allowed.

Key Terms

Alternative Action pattern	`break`	nested `if`/`else`
associativity	`CompareTo`	operator precedence rules
`bool` type	Guarded Action pattern	postfix notation
Boolean	`if`	relational operator
`Boolean expression`	`if`/`else`	selection
`Boolean operators ! && ||`	integral types	selective control
branch	Most Closely Nested Rule	`switch`
branch coverage testing	Multiple Selection pattern	

Exercises

1. True or False: When an `if` statement is encountered, the true part always executes.

2. True or False: When an `if` or `if`/`else` statement is encountered, valid boolean expressions are evaluated to either true, false, or maybe.

3. Write the output from the following code fragments:
    (a)

    ```
    double x = 4.0;
    if (x == 10.0)
       Console.WriteLine("is 10");
    else
       Console.WriteLine("not 10");
    ```

(b)

```
string s1 = "Ab";
string s2 = "Bc";
if (s1==s2)
   Console.WriteLine("equal");
if (s1.compareTo(s2) != 0)
   Console.WriteLine("not");
```

(c)

```
int j = 0, k = 1;
if(j != k) Console.WriteLine("abc");
if(j == k) Console.WriteLine("def");
if(j <= k) Console.WriteLine("ghi");
if(j >= k) Console.WriteLine("klm");
```

(d)

```
double x = -123.4,  y = 999.9;
if(x < y) Console.WriteLine("less");
if(x > y) Console.WriteLine("greater");
if(x == y) Console.WriteLine("equal");
if(x != y) Console.WriteLine("not eq.");
```

4. Write the output from the following code fragment:
```
int t1 = 87;
int t2 = 76;
int larger;
if(t1 > t2)
   larger = t1;
else
   larger = t2;
Console.WriteLine("larger: {0}", larger);
```

5. Write the output generated from the following program fragments, assuming the following values:
```
int j = 25;
int k = 50;
```

(a)

```
if (j == k)
    Console.WriteLine(j);
Console.WriteLine(k);
```

(b)

```
if((j <= k) && (j >= 0))
   Console.WriteLine("ONE");
else
   Console.WriteLine("TWO");
```

(c)

```
if ((j > k) || (k < 100))
   Console.WriteLine("THREE");
else
   Console.WriteLine("FOUR");
```

(d)

```
if ((j >= 0) && (j <=100))
   Console.WriteLine("FIVE");
else
   Console.WriteLine("SIX");
```

6. Write a statement that writes "YES" if anInt is positive, "NO" if anInt is negative, or "NEUTRAL" if anInt is zero.

7. Write a statement that adds 1 to the int j when the int counter has a value less than the int n.

8. Write a statement that displays Hello if the int hours has a value less than 8, or that displays Goodbye if hours has any other value.

9. Write code that guarantees that the int variable named amount is even. If amount is odd, increment amount by 1.

10. Write code that adds 1 to the int amount if amount is less than 10. In this case, also display Less than 10. If amount is greater than 10, subtract 1 from amount and display Greater than 10. If amount is 10, just display Equal to 10.

11. Write a LittleStatistician class with a property Largest that returns the largest of any three numbers. The constructor takes three arguments.
```
LittleStatistician ls = new LittleStatistician(1.2, 3.4, 1.2);
if (ls.Largest != 3.4)
```

```
    Console.WriteLine("Largest should be 3.4!");
  LittleStatistician ls2 = new LittleStatistician(-1.2, -3.4, -1.2);
  if (ls2.Largest != -1.2)
    Console.WriteLine("Largest should be -1.2!");
```

12. To test the preceding `Largest` property, walk through your code for each of these sets of arguments in the constructor.

```
(1.0, 2.0, 3.0)   (1.0, 3.0, 2.0)   (2.0, 1.0, 3.0)   (3.0, 3.0, 2.0)
(2.0, 3.0, 1.0)   (3.0, 2.0, 1.0)   (3.0, 1.0, 2.0)   (2.0, 2.0, 3.0)
(3.0, 3.0, 1.0)   (3.0, 1.0, 3.0)   (1.0, 3.0, 3.0)   (3.0, 3.0, 3.0)
```

13. Write the output from the following program fragments, assuming the following values:

```
int j = 25;
int k = 50;
```

(a)

```
if (j == k)
   Console.WriteLine(1);
else if (j < k)
   Console.WriteLine(2);
else
   Console.WriteLine(3);
```

(b)

```
if ((j + 25) < k)
   Console.WriteLine("aaa");
else if (j > k)
   Console.WriteLine("bbb");
else
   Console.WriteLine("ccc");
```

(c)

```
if (j < 10)
   Console.WriteLine("{0} One", j);
else if (j < 20)
   Console.WriteLine("{0} Two", j);
else if (j < 30)
   Console.WriteLine("{0} Three", j);
else
   Console.WriteLine("{0} Four", j);
```

(d)

```
if (k >= 100)
    Console.WriteLine("Five");
else if (k >= 75)
    Console.WriteLine("Six");
else if (k >= 50)
    Console.WriteLine("Seven");
else
    Console.WriteLine("Eight");
```

(e)

```
if (j > 0)
{
    if (j < 50)
        Console.WriteLine("Eight");
    else
        Console.WriteLine("Nine");
}
```

(f)

```
if (k <= 100)   // Be careful
    Console.WriteLine("Ten ");
if (k <= 50)
    Console.WriteLine("Eleven ");
if (k <= 10)
    Console.WriteLine("Twelve ");
else
    Console.WriteLine("Hmmmm");
```

14. Show the output from the previous exercise when j is 30 and k is 10.

15. Show the output from the previous exercise when j is 20 and k is 20.

Programming Tips

1. Use blocks, even when they are not required.

Consider always using curly braces to mark the beginning and end of the true part and the false part of an if/else. You *must* use a block to treat several statements as one. You *may* use a block for readability and to help avoid bugs.

2. Mathematicians write expressions differently than C#.

It is tempting to use standard mathematical notation and write the following code to check to see if a value is in a certain range:

```
int someInt = 2222;
if (0 <= someInt <= 100)...
```

However, this produces an error at compile time. Here is the correct way to write an equivalent expression:

```
if ((0 <= someInt) && (someInt <= 100))
```

3. Testing helps protect against errors.

Use testing classes to completely test methods that use multiple selection. Send arguments that check all boundary values to the various methods. Also, send arguments to ensure that each branch executes at least once.

4. Do not compare strings with < or >.

Although strings can be compared with the equality operators != and ==, the relational operators cannot be used to test the relationship between two strings.

```
string s1 = "0ne";
string s2 = "Another";
if (s1 < s2)    // <- Compile-time error
// ...
```

Instead of relational operators, use CompareTo messages to compare strings:

```
Console.WriteLine("< {0}", (s1.CompareTo(s2) < 0));
Console.WriteLine("> {0}", (s1.CompareTo(s2) > 0));
Console.WriteLine("<= {0}", (s1.CompareTo(s2) <= 0));
Console.WriteLine(">= {0}", (s1.CompareTo(s2) >= 0));
```

5. Avoid unnecessary comparisons.

The following Boolean expression could be simplified by avoiding the unnecessary part of the expression. Notice that ave < 90 must be true, since the only time this would get evaluated is when ave >= 90 is false.

```
if (ave >= 90)
  result = "A"
else if (ave >= 80 && ave < 90)
    result = "I already know ave must be less than 90";
```

6. **Multiple selection can always be done with nested** `if/else` **and can sometimes be done with** `switch`.

The `switch` statement can choose an action from multiple choices only if the `switch` expression is a `string` or is one of C#'s integral types, such as `int` or `char`. You can not compare `DateTime` objects using the `switch` statement, for example.

Programming Exercises

5A   Gross Pay with Overtime

Write a C# program (the `Main` method only) that determines an employee's pay, based on hours worked and hourly rate of pay. Any hours over 40 (overtime) are calculated at 1.5 times the hourly rate. Test your program with several sets of inputs. Assume that the input will always be >= 0.0. Here are three sample dialogues:

```
Hours worked: 38.0
Hourly rate: 10.00
Pay = 380.0

Hours worked: 40.0
Hourly rate: 10.00
Pay = 400.0

Hours worked: 42.0
Hourly rate: 10.00
Pay = 430.0
```

5B   Salary with a Bonus

Write a C# program (the `Main` method only) that determines a salesperson's salary for the month, based on the following table:

Sales	Monthly Salary
Sales ≤ 10,000.0	Base Salary (1,500.00)
10,000.0 < Sales	Base salary plus 5% of sales over 10,000

The base salary is 1500.00. The salary will never be less than 1500.00, even if the user enters a negative sales amount. When sales are over $10,000, commission is added to the base salary. For example, when sales equal 10001.00, the monthly salary is $1500.00 + 5% of 1.00, for a total of

$1500.05. Test your program with several inputs. You may assume that the input is always >= 0.0 (everyone earns at least 1500.00). Here are three sample dialogues:

```
Enter sales: 9999.99
Salary: 1500.0

Enter sales: 10002.00
Salary: 1500.1

Enter sales: 19000.00
Salary: 1950.0
```

5C   Salary Computer with Bonuses

Write a complete C# class named `SalaryComputer` that determines a salesperson's salary for the month, based on the following table:

Sales	Monthly Salary
Sales ≤ 10,000.0	Base salary (1,500.00)
10,000.0 < Sales ≤ 20,000	Base salary plus 5% of sales over 10,000
20,000 < Sales ≤ 30,000	Base salary plus 500.00 plus 8% of sales over 20,000
30,000 < Sales	Base salary plus 1300.00 plus 12% of sales over 30,000

The base salary is $1500.00, which means that getting the `Salary` property returns a value that is never less than 1500.00, even if sales are negative. When sales are over $10,000, a commission is added to the base salary. For example, when sales equal 10001, the monthly salary is $1500.00 + 5% of 1.00, for a total of $1500.05. When sales are $20001, the monthly salary is $1500.00 + 500.00 + 8% of 1.00, for a total of $2000.08.

Use the following testing class to determine the properties that your class must implement. Also, complete the code necessary to completely test the multiple selection.

```
using System;

class TestSalaryComputer
{
  static void Main()
  {
    // You must supply the base salary (1500.00 here) as an argument.
    SalaryComputer s = new SalaryComputer(1500.00);
    Console.WriteLine("{0} salary is ${1}", s.Sales, s.Salary);
```

```
            s.Sales = 10001.00;
            Console.WriteLine("{0} salary is ${1}", s.Sales, s.Salary);

            s.Sales = 20002.00;
            Console.WriteLine("{0} salary is ${1}", s.Sales, s.Salary);

            // Complete this testing class to test all of the code
        }
    }
```

5E   The CollegeStudent Class with GPA and Standing

Create a modified version of the CollegeStudent class from this chapter. Your class should have the following methods and properties:

○ public CollegeStudent(string initName)
  Constructs a new student with this name and with 0 total credits taken so far.

○ public string Name {get; set;}
  The student's name.

○ public double GPA {get;}
  The student's overall GPA, which is computed by the combination of all grades for all courses taken so far. This is a weighted average, because different courses are worth a different number of credits.

A useful notion to use when writing this property is the notion of "quality points," which are used as a measure of the value of one course grade. To find quality points for one course, take the GPA value of that course's grade and multiply it by the number of credits for that course. For example, a B in a 4-credit course is worth 3.0 * 4 = 12.0 quality points. An A in a 2 credit course is worth 4.0 * 2 = 8.0 quality points. The advantage of calculating a running total of quality points is that if you divide quality points by the total credits taken so far, you get the student's overall GPA. For the prior example, the student has 12.0 + 8.0 = 20.0 quality points and has taken 6 units, so the GPA is 20.0 / 6 = 3.333.

○ public int TotalCredits {get;}
  The total number of credits combined for all courses this student has taken so far.

○ `public string Standing {get;}`

The class standing of this `CollegeStudent`. Use the number of total credits the student has taken to determine class standing. Here is the mapping (this school has lower credit requirements than most!):

Credits Completed	String Return Value
Less than 5 credits	"Freshman"
5 to 9 credits	"Sophomore"
10 to 14 credits	"Junior"
15 credits or more	"Senior"

○ `public void RecordCourse(int credits, string letterGrade)`

Records that this student has taken a course worth the given number of credits and has received the given letter grade in the course.

The legal values of `letterGrade`, and their worth in quality points per unit, are:

`letterGrade`	Quality Points Per Course Unit
"A"	4.0
"B"	3.0
"C"	2.0
"D"	1.0
"F" (or any other value)	0.0

○ `public override string ToString()`

Returns a textual representation of this student.

A student with name of `"Mary"`, standing of `"Sophomore"`, and GPA of `2.9` should have the following `ToString` representation (note that the GPA is shown to the nearest 0.01; see Chapter 2's section on format strings to do this):

```
"Mary: Standing = Sophomore, GPA = 2.90"
```

The following test code should work on your `CollegeStudent` class:

```
using System;

class TestCollegeStudent
{
  static void Main()
  {
    CollegeStudent student = new CollegeStudent("Mary");

    student.RecordCourse(3, "A");
    Console.WriteLine(student);

    student.RecordCourse(3, "B");
    Console.WriteLine(student);

    student.RecordCourse(4, "C");
    Console.WriteLine(student);

    student.RecordCourse(3, "A");
    Console.WriteLine(student);

    student.RecordCourse(5, "B");
    Console.WriteLine(student);
  }
}
```

The following should be the output from the above test code:

```
Mary: Standing = Freshman, GPA = 4.00
Mary: Standing = Sophomore, GPA = 3.50
Mary: Standing = Sophomore, GPA = 2.90
Mary: Standing = Junior, GPA = 3.15
Mary: Standing = Senior, GPA = 3.11
```

6

Repetition

Summing Up

You have now seen that classes are collections of related methods and data. You have seen constructors that initialize fields, properties to access object state, and other methods that implement the complex behavior of objects. Additionally, you have seen two important methods of control—sequence and selection. Sequential control occurs when every statement executes one after another. Selection (implemented in C# with the if/ else and switch statements) lets you write code that executes differently under different circumstances.

Coming Up

This chapter introduces the third major control structure—repetition. Repetition is discussed within the context of two general algorithmic patterns—the Determinate Loop and the Indeterminate Loop. Repetition control allows a block of code statements to be repeatedly executed. The repetition can occur either a predetermined number of times, or until some event or condition occurs to terminate it. After studying this chapter, you will be able to

- ○ implement loops in C# with the while, for, do/while, and foreach statements.
- ○ recognize and use the Determinate Loop pattern to execute a set of statements a predetermined number of times.
- ○ recognize and use the Indeterminate Loop pattern to execute a set of statements until some event occurs to stop it.
- ○ use Determinate and Indeterminate loops in your programs, as appropriate.
- ○ design loops of your own to solve programming problems.

6.1   Repetition Concepts

Repetition refers to the repeated execution of a set of statements. It occurs naturally in non-computer algorithms such as these:

- For every student's name on the attendance roster, call the name. Write an "X" if the student is absent, or a checkmark if the student is present.
- Practice playing the piano piece until you can play it well.
- Add the flour ¼ cup at a time, whipping until smooth.
- Run five laps around the school track.

Similarly, you can use repetition in computer algorithms. If something can be done once, it can be done repeatedly. Computer-based uses of repetition include:

- Process many customers at an automated teller machine (ATM).
- Continuously accept reservations.
- While there are more fast-food items, sum the price of each item.
- Compute the course grade for every student in a class.
- Microwave the food until the timer reaches 0, the cancel button is pressed, or the oven door is opened.

This chapter examines repetitive algorithmic patterns and the C# statements that implement them. It begins with a statement that executes a collection of actions a fixed, predetermined number of times. A statement that is used to implement repetition is often called a *loop*. Loops are useful for many tasks: to process report cards *for every* student in a school, to keep prompting for input *until* a valid option is entered, or to keep processing data *while* there is more data to process.

Why Is Repetition Needed?

Many jobs formerly done by hand are now performed much more quickly by computers. Think of a payroll department that produces employee paychecks. With only a few employees, this task could certainly be done by hand. But with thousands of employees, a very large payroll department would be needed to compute and generate that many paychecks, by hand, in a timely fashion. Other situations that require repetition include finding an average, searching a collection of objects for a particular item, alphabetizing a list of names, and processing all the data in a file. Luckily, computers are great for quickly completing such repetitive tasks.

Consider the following code that finds the average of exactly three numbers. No repetitive control is used (this code will be improved shortly):

Code Sample: AverageThree Class

```
1  using System;
2
3  class AverageThree
4  {
5    static void Main()
6    {
7      double sum = 0.0;    // stores the sum of all inputs
8      double input;        // will be read many times below
9
10     // The following statements will be repeated several times.
11     Console.Write("Enter number: ");
12     input = double.Parse(Console.ReadLine());
13     sum += input;
14
15     Console.Write("Enter number: ");
16     input = double.Parse(Console.ReadLine());
17     sum += input;
18
19     Console.Write("Enter number: ");
20     input = double.Parse(Console.ReadLine());
21     sum += input;
22
23     double average = sum / 3.0;
24     Console.WriteLine("Average: {0}", average);
25   }
26 }
```

This program uses a **brute force** algorithm. This means that it uses a straightforward approach, doing each task one after the other, until all tasks are done. There is a drawback to this approach to repetition. This program is not general enough to handle input sets of various sizes. If it ever needs to average a larger set of inputs, it must be modified. As currently written, it repeats the same statements three times (lines 11–13, 15–17, and 19–21). Averaging 100 numbers would require 97 additional copies of these three statements. Also, in line 23, the constant 3.0 in average = sum / 3.0 would have to be changed to 100.0.

A better algorithm would be adaptable to changes, such as needing to average an arbitrary number of terms. To solve this problem, we will use a form of control that can execute one copy of these three statements three times. We could do this writing a method that contained the repeated statements, and calling the method three times. However, if we wanted to call the method 100 times, we would still have to write 100 lines of method calls. This is wasteful, easy to miscount, and hard to modify later.

6.2 The while Loop

Without the selection control structures of the preceding chapter, computers are little more than nonprogrammable calculators. Selection control lets computers adapt to varying situations. But what really makes computers powerful is their ability to repeat the same actions quickly, accurately, and efficiently.

As mentioned previously, a statement that executes code multiple times is called a *loop*. The *while loop statement* is the simplest way to program a loop in C#. A while loop is a sequence of statements that keep executing *while* some Boolean condition is true. Here is its general form:

General Form: while loop statement

while (*Boolean expression*)

{

    statement(s) to execute;

}

Notes:

The braces are optional if only one statement is used.

Examples:

```
int i = 0;
int max = 10;
while (i < max)
{
   Console.WriteLine(i);
   i++;
}

string input = null;
while (input != "OK")
{
   input = Console.ReadLine();
}
```

The *Boolean expression* above is a bool expression that evaluates to either true or false. As with the bodies of if statements (discussed in the preceding chapter), the *statement(s) to execute* may be a block of C# statements, or a single statement.

Most of the examples in this textbook use a block enclosed in { and }, but the following is also legal, as long as only one statement is executed as a result of the while loop:

```
while (input != "OK")        // no {} braces...
  input = Console.ReadLine();  // legal syntax, but discouraged
```

When a while loop is encountered, the *Boolean expression* is evaluated to either true or false. If the expression evaluates to false, the loop is skipped, and the statement(s) inside it is not executed. However, if the expression is true, the statements in the body execute once, after which the *Boolean expression* is evaluated again. This process continues as long as the expression is true. In this way, the statements to execute (the "body" of the loop) can be executed many times, depending on the *Boolean expression* used as the loop's condition.

The following figure shows the flow of execution of a while loop:

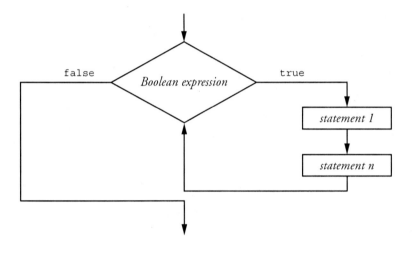

Figure 6.1: while Loop Execution Flow Chart

The statements in the body of a while loop might execute zero times, once, or many times. Each time that the statements in a loop's body execute is called one *iteration* of the loop. A loop that repeats ten times, therefore, has undergone ten iterations.

The AverageThree class from the preceding section can be rewritten using a while loop with three iterations, as follows:

Code Sample: AverageThree Class with while loop

```
 1 using System;
 2
 3 class AverageThree
 4 {
 5   static void Main()
 6   {
 7     double sum = 0.0;    // stores the sum of all inputs
 8     double input;        // will be read many times below
 9
10     int numIterations = 3;
11     int i = 0;
12
13     while (i < numIterations)
14     {
15       // The following statements will be repeated 3 times.
16       Console.Write("Enter number: ");
17       input = double.Parse(Console.ReadLine());
18       sum += input;
19
20       i++;
21     }
22
23     double average = sum / numIterations;
24     Console.WriteLine("Average: {0}", average);
25   }
26 }
```

Looking at the above code, it may not be immediately obvious that it is equivalent to the original program. Walking through the code execution visually is helpful in proving that the code behaves as desired:

```
int numIterations = 3;
int i = 0;

while (i < numIterations)
```

Is i < numIterations true? Currently i has the value 0 and numIterations has the value 3; so yes, this is true. So, the statements in the loop execute once.

```
Console.Write("Enter number: ");
input = double.Parse(Console.ReadLine());
sum += input;

i++;
```

One input is read from the console, and the value of i is increased by 1. Now we start the loop over, by re-evaluating its Boolean expression:

```
while (i < numIterations)
```

Is i < numIterations true? Now i has the value 1 and numIterations has the value 3; so yes, this is still true. The statements in the loop execute a second time.

```
Console.Write("Enter number: ");
input = double.Parse(Console.ReadLine());
sum += input;

i++;
```

A second input is read from the console, and the value of i is again increased by 1. Now we start the loop over, re-evaluating its Boolean expression again:

```
while (i < numIterations)
```

Is i < numIterations true? Now i has the value 2 and numIterations has the value 3; so yes, this is still true. Therefore, the statements in the loop execute a third time.

```
Console.Write("Enter number: ");
input = double.Parse(Console.ReadLine());
sum += input;

i++;
```

A third input is read from the console, and the value of i is again increased by 1. Now we start the loop over, re-evaluating its Boolean expression again:

```
while (i < numIterations)
```

Is i < numIterations true? This time, i has the value 3 and numIterations has the value 3; so *no*, the Boolean expression has now become false. Therefore, the loop stops executing.

Loops are very powerful and can be used to accomplish many programming tasks. Here are some example loops:

```
// 1. read integer from console, and say hello that many times
Console.Write("How many times? ");
int numTimes = int.Parse(Console.ReadLine());
while (numTimes > 0)
{
  Console.WriteLine("Hello!");
  numTimes--;
}
```

One Possible Dialogue

```
How many times? 4
Hello!
Hello!
Hello!
Hello!
```

```
// 2. keep prompting the user until a valid option is given
string option = null;
while (option != "a" && option != "r" && option != "f")
{
  Console.Write("(A)bort, (R)etry, (F)ail? ");
  option = Console.ReadLine();
}
```

One Possible Dialogue

```
(A)bort, (R)etry, (F)ail? q
(A)bort, (R)etry, (F)ail? x
(A)bort, (R)etry, (F)ail? a
```

```
// 3. generate a random number that is divisible by 6
Random rand = new Random();
int randomNumber = rand.Next();
while (randomNumber % 6 != 0)
{
  randomNumber = rand.Next();
  Console.WriteLine(randomNumber);
}
```

One Possible Result

```
342154
145
6042
```

Remember that once a `while` loop starts executing, it executes until the Boolean expression that controls it becomes `false`. The `++`, `+=`, `*=`, and other increment-and-assign operators introduced in Chapter 2 are often used to modify values inside a loop, so that the controlling expression eventually does become `false`. Which operator is appropriate to use depends on the loop's purpose. If the loop is counting something, or if it is repeating an action for every part of a whole, the `++` operator is usually the right choice.

For example, the following code prints each character of a `string` on a separate line:

```
string s = "Howdy";
int index = 0;
while (index < s.Length)
{
   Console.WriteLine("Letter {0} is {1}",
                          index, s[index]);
   index++;
}
```

Output

```
H
o
w
d
y
```

The `+=`, `-=`, and other modify-and-assign operators are useful when you wish to increment (increase) or decrement (decrease) loop control variables by values other than 1. In the next example, the loop control variable `j` increments by 2 at the end of each iteration:

```
int j = 0;
while (j <= 10)
{
   Console.Write("{0}  ", j);
   j += 2;      // Count by twos
}
```

Output
0   2   4   6   8   10

The following example prints powers of 2, up to 1024:

```
int j = 1;
while (j <= 1024)
{
  Console.Write("{0}   ", j);
  j *= 2;
}
```

Output
1   2   4   8   16   32   64   128   256   512   1024

Self-Check

6-1   Write the output generated by the following code:

(a)

```
int j = 1;

while (j <= 5)
{
   Console.Write(j);
   j++;
}
```

(b)
```
int j = 5;

while (j > 0)
{
   j--;
   Console.Write(j);
}
```

6-2   Rewrite the following code fragments to use `while` loops:

(a)

```
Console.WriteLine(2);
Console.WriteLine(1);
Console.WriteLine(0);
```

(b)

```
Console.WriteLine("a");
Console.WriteLine("aa");
Console.WriteLine("aaa");
```

(c)

```
Console.WriteLine(1);
Console.WriteLine(2);
Console.WriteLine(4);
Console.WriteLine(8);
```

(d)

```
Console.WriteLine(2);
Console.WriteLine(4);
Console.WriteLine(16);
Console.WriteLine(256);
```

6-3   Write code that asks the user to enter an integer, and then sums all integers that the user enters, until a negative integer is entered.

6-4   Write code that asks to user to enter integers, until the difference between two consecutive integers is greater than 100. Assume that there are always at least two inputs. The number of inputs may be even or odd and can range from 2 inputs to many. Print the values of the first two consecutive numbers that differ by more than 100.

Infinite Loops and Empty Loops

It is possible that a `while` loop will never execute, if its Boolean expression is `false` initially. It is also possible that a `while` loop will never terminate. A loop that never stops running (unless the program is forcefully shut down) is called an *infinite loop*.

Infinite loops are usually undesirable. The simplest example of an infinite loop is the `while` `(true)` loop, shown below:

```
while (true)
{
   Console.WriteLine("This is an infinite loop!");
}
```

Since the Boolean expression for the above loop is simply `true`, the loop's condition will never be `false`. The loop will continue executing forever.

Unfortunately, it is also possible to write infinite loops unintentionally, as shown in the following example. The loop below is an infinite loop; the condition, `i >= 0`, is initially `true`, and (as currently written) the loop body will never cause it to become `false` (`i = i;` should be `i = i + 1;`).

```
int i = 0;
while (i <= 10)
{
  Console.WriteLine(i);
  i = i;  // Need to update the value of i
}
```

When you write programs that use loops, it is easy to accidentally write an infinite loop. Usually, infinite loops are easy to spot, because the program will print endless output or will hang indefinitely.

To avoid infinite loops, always check the following things:
- ○ Are the variables before the loop initialized correctly?
- ○ Is the loop test correct?
- ○ Does the body of the loop perform some action that will eventually terminate the loop?

Unfortunately, it is also legal to write a loop with an empty body; this loop will do nothing! This type of loop is called an *empty loop*. Most of the time, an empty loop occurs as a result of a typing or intent error. Empty loops often end up also being infinite loops. Because their body is empty, they cannot perform any update step to make the loop terminate.

The following is an empty (and infinite) loop:

```
int i = 0;
while (i < 10)
{
  // no statements in the loop body!
}
```

It might seem easy to identify empty infinite loops, but they can be tricky to spot. For example, the following is also a legal loop, whose body consists of a single empty statement:

```
int i = 0;
while (i < 10)     // the loop's body is the semicolon below
  ;
```

Because C# is not sensitive to whitespace, and because method calls usually have semicolons after them, programmers often write something like the following, by mistake:

```
int i = 0;
while (i < 10);    // The loop's body is the semicolon on this line!
  i++;             // The programmer wanted this to be the body!
```

As you can see, it is easy to accidentally write an infinite or empty loop without intending to do so. As mentioned above, the symptom of such a loop is that the program either prints endless output, or it runs forever, without producing output.

If either of these things happens, close the program manually and inspect each loop carefully to correct mistakes like those above. Also, follow the steps outlined in this section for making sure that each loop will eventually terminate. This is also a strong argument for always using the braces { and } around the body of a loop, even if it only contains one statement. The preceding errors would not be possible with such a brace-surrounded block of statements.

Self-Check

6-5   Write the output from the following C# program fragments:

(a)

```
int n = 3;
int counter = 1;
while (counter <= n)
{
   Console.Write("{0}  ", counter);
   counter++;
}
```

(b)

```
int last = 10;
int j = 2;
while (j <= last)
{
   Console.Write("{0}  ", j);
   j += 2;
}
```

(c)

```
counter = 10;
// Tricky, but an easy-to-make mistake
while (counter >= 0);
{
   Console.WriteLine(counter);
   counter++;
}
```

6-6   Write the number of times that "Hello" is printed. "Zero" and "Infinite" are valid
        answers.

(a)

```
int counter = 1;
int n = 20;
while (counter <= n)
{
   Console.Write("Hello ");
   counter++;
}
```

(b)

```
int counter = 1;
int n = 0;
while (counter <= n)
{
   Console.Write("Hello ");
}
```

(c)

```
int counter = 1;
int n = 5;
while (counter <= n)
{
   Console.Write("Hello ");
   counter++;
}
```

(d)

```
int n = 5;
int j = 1;
while (j <= n)
```

```
Console.Write("Hello ");
j++;
```

(e)

```
int j = 1;
int n = 5 ;
while (j <= 5)
{
   Console.Write("Hello ");
   n++;
}
```

(f)

```
int j = 2;
int n = 1024;
while (j <= n)
{
   Console.Write("Hello ");
   j = j * 2;
}
```

6-7 Describe how to fix each of the following infinite loops:

```
int sum = 0;
int j = 1;
```

(a)

```
while (j <= 100)
{ // Sum the first 100 integers
   sum += j;
}
```

(b)

```
while (j <= 100);
{ // Sum the first 100 integers
   sum += j;
   j++;
}
```

(c)

```
while (j <= 100)
   // Sum the first 100 integers
   sum += j;
   j++;
```

6.3 Determinate and Indeterminate Loops

By looking at the many `while` loop examples in the previous section, you can see that loops can be categorized based on how many times they will execute. Some loops never execute at all; some execute a fixed number of times; some execute an unfixed number of times until a condition is met; and some execute forever!

A key observation here is that many loops execute a specific number of times. For example, to find the average of 142 test grades, you would repeat a set of statements exactly 142 times. To pay 89 employees, you would repeat a set of statements 89 times. To produce grade reports for 32,675 students, you would repeat a set of statements 32,675 times. This generalizes; if there are *n* students, you would repeat the statements *n* times to print the reports.

To create a loop that executes a fixed number of times, you must put that number in the C# program code. This number should be stored either as a literal integer, or as a variable's value. It must be established before the loop begins to execute. Executing statements a predetermined number of times this way is referred to here as the ***Determinate Loop pattern***.

Algorithmic Pattern: Determinate Loop

Problem: Do something exactly *n* times, where *n* is known in advance.

Outline: Determine *n* as the number of times to repeat the actions.
Repeat the following *n* times.
Execute the actions to be repeated.

Example:
```
double sum = 0.0;
double input;
int count = 0;
while (count < 10)
{
    // these statements will be executed 10 times
    Console.Write("Enter a number: ");
    input = double.Parse(Console.ReadLine());
    sum += input;
    count++;
}
```

The Determinate Loop pattern uses an `int` variable—named n here—to represent how often the actions must repeat. However, you can use any appropriate variable name, such as `numberOfEmployees`.

The first thing to do in the Determinate Loop pattern is to determine the number of iterations. This number might be known at compile time. In this case, it would be written into the code as a constant value, such as the constant 10 in the code example above. Alternatively, the number of repetitions might come from user input, such as `int n = int.Parse(Console.ReadLine());`. The value might even be passed as an argument to a method, as in `public void Display(int n)`. Once the number of repetitions is set, another `int` variable (named `count` in the program above) controls the number of loop iterations.

However, not all loops are determinate; sometimes it is not possible to know exactly how many times a loop will execute. However, just because a loop executes an unknown number of times does not mean it is an infinite loop. Consider the following example:

```
// generate a random number that is divisible by 6
Random rand = new Random();
int randomNumber = rand.Next();
while (randomNumber % 6 != 0)
{
    randomNumber = rand.Next();
}
```

How many times will the above loop execute? Is it an infinite loop? One could imagine a scenario where the `rand` number generator produces infinitely many numbers that are not divisible by 6. This would cause the loop to keep executing forever. However, this becomes more and more unlikely as more random numbers are chosen, so over time there is only an infinitely small chance that a number divisible by 6 will not have been chosen. Therefore, the above loop would not be considered the infinite loop.

Although the Determinate Loop pattern occurs in many algorithms, it has a serious limitation. Somehow, you must determine the number of repetitions in advance. Quite often this is impossible, or at least is very inconvenient or difficult. For example, an instructor may have a different number of tests to average as attendance varies between school terms. A company may not have a constant number of employees because of hires, fires, layoffs, transfers, and retirements. Also, consider a program with a loop based on user input: perhaps the program loops until the user enters a certain string or number (such as "quit" or −1). How many times should this loop run? The result is not fixed and cannot be predicted ahead of time.

The *Indeterminate Loop pattern* describes this idea of repetition, where the number of iterations is not constant or is not known in advance. With indeterminate loops, repetitions can continue an arbitrary number of times. Generally, an indeterminate loop continues executing until some special event occurs, or some special unpredictable condition is met.

Algorithmic Pattern: Indeterminate Loop

Pattern:	Indeterminate Loop
Problem:	A process must repeat an unknown number of times, so some event is needed to terminate the loop.
Outline:	while the termination event has not occurred,
	{
	Perform these actions.
	Do something to bring the loop closer to termination.
	}

Example:

```
// Continue until user wants to quit.
int n = 0;
while (n != -1)
{
    Console.Write("Enter a number (-1 to quit): ");
    n = int.Parse(Console.ReadLine());
    Console.WriteLine("You entered {0}", n);
}
```

Extended examples of determinate and indeterminate loops will be shown later in this chapter.

6.4 The `for` Loop

As discussed in the previous section, for many loops the number of iterations is known in advance; these are called determinate loops. Also, it is very common to declare a special "counter variable" that is used only to govern the number of loop iterations. At the end of the loop, the counter variable is updated in some way that brings the loop closer to termination. The loop below should look similar to many in this chapter:

```
int j = 0;                        // initialize counter variable
while (j < 10)                    // boolean test
{
    Console.Write("{0}  ", j);    // loop body
    j++;                          // increment counter variable
}
```

Since this determinate pattern of loop is so common, C# includes an additional looping statement that is tailored to this pattern. C#'s for statement provides a loop that is designed to implement the Determinate Loop pattern. The for statement begins with the keyword for, followed by a three-part parenthesized section: an initialization, a Boolean test for determining when to stop repeating, and an update step to perform after each repetition. The update step is generally used to bring the loop one step closer to terminating.

The for loop was added to programming languages because the Determinate Loop pattern arises so often. Here is the general form of the C# **for loop statement**:

General Form: for loop statement

for (*initialization statement; Boolean expression; update statement(s)*)
{
    statement(s) to execute;
}
Notes:
The braces are optional if only one statement is used.

Examples:

```
for (int j = 0;  j < 10;  j++)
{
    Console.WriteLine(j);
}

double sum = 0.0;
for (double pow = 10.0;  pow >= 1.0;  pow -= 2.0)
{
    sum += Math.Pow(2, pow);
    Console.WriteLine("Sum so far is {0}", sum);
}
```

The for statement's syntax is admittedly confusing at first. But it is a useful statement because it combines several individual steps into a single compact entity. The confusing part about its syntax is understanding what is executed when.

When a for loop is first encountered, the *initialization statement* is executed first, exactly one time. Next, the *Boolean expression* is evaluated to either true or false; this is done before each iteration of the loop. Assuming that the Boolean test is initially true, the *statement(s) to execute* are executed. After these statement(s) have been executed, the program executes the *update statement(s)* After the update, the Boolean test is re-evaluated. If it is still true, the loop executes again. This process continues until the loop test evaluates to false. Here is a description of the flow of execution of a `for` loop:

1. Execute initialization statement.
2. Evaluate Boolean expression.
3. If Boolean test is false, stop.
4. Otherwise (if the test is true),
   ○ Execute statement(s) to execute.
   ○ Execute update statement(s).
   ○ Go back to step 2.

The following figure also summarizes the behavior of a `for` loop:

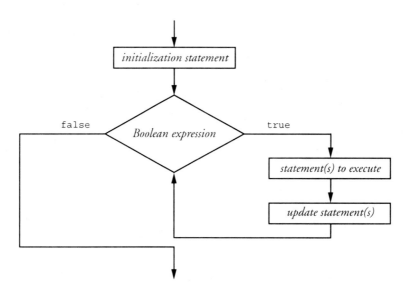

Figure 6.2: For loop flow chart

Here is the `while` loop shown at the start of this section, converted into an equivalent `for` loop:

```
for (int j = 0; j < 10; j++)
{
  Console.Write("{0}  ", j);        // loop body
}
```

Output

```
0  1  2  3  4  5  6  7  8  9
```

In the preceding `for` loop, `j` is first assigned the value of 0. Next, the Boolean test `j < 10` is evaluated; it results in a value of `true`, because 0 < 10; so the block executes. When the statements inside the block are done, the update step is executed, incrementing `j` by 1 (`j++`). These three components ensure that the block executes precisely n times. To recap:

```
int j = 0;      // Initializes the counter
j < 10;         // A test to see if the loop should continue repeating
j++             // Updates the counter
```

Like an `if` statement or `while` loop, a `for` loop can have a single statement as its body, rather than an entire block of code. The loop above could have been written as:

```
for (int j = 0; j < 10; j++)
   Console.Write("{0}  ", j);       // 1-line loop body, no braces
```

However, as stated before, consider always using a block with braces when writing a `for` loop. This helps avoid difficult-to-detect logic errors.

Legal syntax, but discouraged:
```
for (int i = 0; i < 10; i++)
   Console.WriteLine(i);
```

Encouraged:
```
for (int i = 0; i < 10; i++)
{
      Console.WriteLine(i);
}
```

The `for` loop is shown next in the context of a small program that improves the design of the task to average a set of numbers. In this example, the `for` statement implements the repetition needed to solve the problem.

Code Sample: DoAverage Class

```
1  using System;
2
3  // This class accumulates and averages numbers.
4  class Averager
5  {
6    private int n = 0;
7    double sum = 0.0;
```

```
 8
 9     // Adds the given number to the running total.
10     public void AddNumber(double num)
11     {
12       n++;
13       sum += num;
14     }
15
16     // The current average of all numbers entered so far.
17     public double Average
18     {
19       get
20       {
21         if (n == 0)
22           return 0.0;
23         else
24           return sum / n;
25       }
26     }
27 }
28
29 // Demonstrates a determinate loop using the Averager class.
30 class TestAverage
31 {
32    static void Main()
33    {
34      Averager averager = new Averager();
35
36      Console.Write("How many numbers do you need to average? ");
37      int n = int.Parse(Console.ReadLine());
38
39      // Now accumulate n numbers
40      for (int j = 0;  j < n;  j++)
41      {
42        // Repeat these statements n times
43        Console.Write("Enter number: ");
44        double input = double.Parse(Console.ReadLine());
45        averager.AddNumber(input);
46      }
47
48      // Compute the average only when there is at least one input
49      Console.WriteLine("Average of {0} numbers is {1:F1}",
50                         n, averager.Average);
51    }
52 }
```

Dialogue

```
                              Dialogue
How many numbers do you need to average? 4
Enter number: 70.0
Enter number: 80.0
Enter number: 90.0
Enter number: 86.0
Average of 4 numbers is 81.5
```

The following trace of the execution shows how the sum variable in the Averager class accumulates the numbers as the loop repeats the block of statements four times.

Loop Number	j	input	sum
Before loop	NA	?	0.0
1	1	70.0	70.0
2	2	80.0	150.0
3	3	90.0	240.0
4	4	86.0	326.0

Self-Check

6-8   Does a for loop execute the update step at the beginning of each iteration?

6-9   Must an update step increment the loop counter by + 1?

6-10   Do for loops always execute the repeated part at least once?

6-11   Describe a situation when the loop test j <= n of a for loop never becomes false and the loop never terminates on its own.

6-12   Write the output generated by the following for loops.

(a)

```
for (int j = 1; j < 5; j = j + 1)
{
   Console.Write("{0} ", j);
}
```

(b)

```
int n = 5;
for (int j = 1; j <= n; j++)
{
    Console.Write("{0} ", j);
}
```

(c)

```
int n = 3;
for (int j = -3; j <= n; j += 2)
{
    Console.Write("{0} ", j);
}
```

(d)

```
for (int j = 0; j < 5; j++)
{
    Console.Write("{0} ", j);
}
```

(e)

```
for (int j = 5; j >= 1; j--)
    Console.Write("{0} ", j);
```

(f)

```
int n = 0;
Console.Write("before ");
for (int j = 1; j <= n; j++)
{
    Console.Write("{0} ", j);
}
Console.Write(" after");
```

6-13   Write a for loop that displays all of the integers from 1 to 100 inclusive, on separate lines.

6-14   Write a for loop that displays all of the integers from 10 down to 1 inclusive, on separate lines.

Equivalence of `while` and `for` Loops

Though `while` and `for` loops look very different, they have the same computational and expressive power. To convert a `for` loop into an equivalent `while` loop, first move the initialization to before the `while` loop. Then move the update step to the bottom of the repeated statements to execute.

```
initialization
while (Boolean-test)
{
  // Activities to be repeated
  update-step
}
```

The following code represents an alternate implementation of a determinate loop:

```
// Sum the first n integers
int sum = 0;        // Initialization
int j = 1;          // Initialization
int n = 5;          // Initialization
while (j <= n)      // Loop test
{
   sum += j;         // Action
   j++;             // Update step
}

Console.WriteLine("Sum of the first {0} integers is {1}", n, sum);
```

Converting a `while` loop to an equivalent `for` loop is similar. Though not all `while` loops seem to follow the pattern that `for` loops require (a counter variable that is initialized and updated at each step), any `while` loop can be converted to a `for` loop that has the exact same behavior. Consider the following `while` loop:

```
// generate a random number that is divisible by 6
Random rand = new Random();
int num = rand.Next();
while (num % 6 != 0)
{
  num = rand.Next();
}
```

The equivalent `for` loop would look like this:

```
Random rand = new Random();
for (int num = rand.Next();  num % 6 != 0;   num = rand.Next())
{
}
```

Notice that the `for` loop body here is empty! This does not mean that the loop serves no purpose, however. Its purpose is that its update step, `num = rand.Next()`, will keep executing until the Boolean test `num % 6 != 0` becomes `true`.

The syntax of `for` loops is somewhat flexible. Any of the three parts of the `for` loop header (the initialization, the Boolean test, and the update step) may be left empty (the initialization, test and update must still be separated by semicolons, even if empty). If the initialization is omitted, no initialization is performed. If the Boolean test is omitted, the test is assumed to be `true` (which generally leads to infinite loops!). If the update step is omitted, the loop starts each iteration without any update being performed. So the infinite `for` loop (sometimes called the "forever loop") equivalent to the infinite `while (true)` loop looks like this:

```
for (;;)      // no initialization, test, or update steps
{
  // do something here
  Console.WriteLine("This is an infinite loop!");
}
```

Also, the initialization statement and update statements can actually be multiple initializations and updates, separated by commas.

```
for (int pow = 1, result = 2; pow < 10; pow++, result *= 2)
{
  Console.WriteLine("2 to the {0} = {1}", pow, result);
}
```

Output

```
2 to the 1 = 2
2 to the 2 = 4
2 to the 3 = 8
2 to the 4 = 16
2 to the 5 = 32
2 to the 6 = 64
2 to the 7 = 128
2 to the 8 = 256
2 to the 9 = 512
```

Although the `while` loop can implement determinate loops, the `for` loop is more concise and convenient. It is recommended that you use the `for` loop when the number of iterations is known in advance. When this cannot be determined, use the `while` statement instead.

6.5 Loop Examples and Applications

This section shows how loops can be used to solve larger programming problems. One major example is shown for the Determinate Loop pattern, and one for the Indeterminate Loop pattern. A key concept from this section is that it is important to analyze a problem to decide what type of repetition, if any, is needed to solve it, and to choose the appropriate loop to solve the problem.

Application of Determinate Loop Pattern: Temperature Ranges

Problem: Write a program that determines a range of temperature readings. "Range" is defined as the difference between the highest and lowest. The number of temperature readings will be known in advance. One dialogue would look like this:

Dialogue

```
Enter 6 temperature readings:
11
15
19
23
20
16
Range: 13
```

To find the range without the aid of a computer (this is easier with a small number of temperature readings), you could look at the list of numbers and simply keep track of the highest and lowest ones, while scanning the list from top to bottom.

Let's walk through some temperatures. `aTemp` is the name assigned to the user input.

aTemp	highest	lowest
-5	-5	-5
8	8	-5
22	22	-5
-7	22	-7
15	22	-7

For this set of data, range = highest – lowest + 1 = 22 - (-7) + 1 = 30.

Let the number of temperature readings be n. Again, the variable named aTemp stores the individual temperature readings as each is read in. The range of temperature readings is the difference between the highest and lowest temperature readings in the list of inputs, + 1. The following table summarizes the problem:

Problem Description	Variable Name	Sample Values	Input/Output
Compute the range of	n	5	Input
temperature readings	aTemp	-5, 8, 22, -7, 15	Input
	highest	22	
	lowest	-7	
	range	30	Output

For a large list—an approach more suited to a computer—the algorithm mimics the repetition of the hand-operated version just suggested. It uses a determinate loop to compare every temperature reading in the list to the highest and the lowest readings, and to update these readings, if necessary.

Algorithm: Determining the range for each temperature reading

```
for each temperature reading
{
    input aTemp from user
    if aTemp is greater than highest so far,
        store it as highest
    if aTemp is less than lowest so far,
        store it as lowest
}
range = highest - lowest + 1
```

As usual, it is a good idea to walk through the algorithm to verify its soundness.

1. Input the number of temperature readings (n == 5).
2. Input aTemp from the user (aTemp == -3).
3. If aTemp is greater than highest so far (-3 > . . .). Whoops!

There is no value yet for highest! And there is no value yet for lowest. To fix this, let's assume that the program will initialize both highest and lowest to 0:

1. Initialize lowest and highest to 0 (`lowest = 0; highest = 0;`).
2. Input the number of temperature readings (`n == 5`).
3. Input `aTemp` from the user (`aTemp == -3`).
4. If `aTemp` is greater than highest (`-3 > 0`), store `aTemp` as `highest` (highest stays the same).
5. If `aTemp` is less than lowest so far (`-3 < 0`), store `aTemp` as `lowest` (`lowest = -3`).

This seems to work. Consider one more iteration.

1. Input `aTemp` from the user (`aTemp == 8`).
2. If `aTemp` is greater than `highest` so far (`8 > 0`), store it as `highest` (`highest == 8`).
3. If `aTemp` is less than `lowest` so far (`8 < -3`), store it as `lowest` (`lowest` stays `-3`).

This seems okay. Now try the next three inputs to verify that `highest` and `lowest` are correct. Finally, the last step in the algorithm (after the repetition) produces the range: `range = highest - lowest + 1`.

Self-Check

6-15   Using the previous algorithm, determine the range when `n` is 4 and the user inputs the four temperature readings *3*, *4*, *2*, and *6*.

If you did the previous self-check question correctly, you noticed that our algorithm is not totally correct yet: `lowest` stays 0. The initial value of `lowest` is less than all subsequent inputs. The first test set before the self-check only worked because a negative temperature was input (something lower than the initial value for `lowest`, which is 0). But this algorithm does not work on a warmer day, when all temperatures are positive.

To solve this problem, instead of initializing both `highest` and `lowest` to 0, consider setting `highest` to something ridiculously low, like `-999`. This is so low that any input will have to be higher. Similarly, set `lowest` to something ridiculously high, like `999`, so that any input will have to be lower. Remember, though, that these mysterious values have no real meaning. Also, if you wanted a generalized loop that would find the range of any set of numbers, the algorithm would not always work.

A better alternative is to read in the first input, and then set both `highest` and `lowest` to that value. This is no longer phony. The first input is the highest and the lowest read in so far (assuming that the user is seeking the range of more than zero inputs). The second input can then be compared to the first. Now, walk through the modified algorithm with n == 4 and inputs of *3*, *4*, *2*, and *6* to verify that the algorithm works.

Algorithm: Finding the range of n integers

input aTemp from the user
set highest so far to aTemp
set lowest so far to aTemp
for each of the remaining (2 through *n*) temperature readings
{
   input aTemp from the user
   if aTemp is greater than highest so far,
     store it as highest
   if aTemp is less than lowest so far,
     store it as lowest
}
range = highest - lowest + 1

From Algorithm to Implementation

The problem stated that the number of inputs (*n*) would be known in advance. If *n* is 5, the user is prompted for five integers. This is an instance of the Determinate Loop pattern.

Code Sample: Class DemonstrateDeterminateLoop

```
 1  // Read n integers and display the range of inputs
 2  using System;
 3  public class DemonstrateDeterminateLoop
 4  {
 5    static void Main()
 6    {
 7      int aTemp;
 8      int n = 5;  // Only works with 5
 9
10      // Input first integer and record it as highest and lowest
11      Console.WriteLine("Enter {0} numbers ", n);
12      aTemp = int.Parse(Console.ReadLine());
13      int highest = aTemp;
14      int lowest = aTemp;
15
```

```
16        // Process n inputs. Since the first was already
17        // processed, start the loop counter at 2
18        for (int j = 2; j <= n; j++)
19        {
20           // Get the next input
21           aTemp = int.Parse(Console.ReadLine());
22
23           // Update the highest so far, if necessary
24           if (aTemp > highest)
25              highest = aTemp;
26
27           // Update the lowest so far, if necessary
28           if (aTemp < lowest)
29              lowest = aTemp;
30        }
31
32        int range = highest - lowest + 1;
33        Console.WriteLine("Range: {0}", range);
34     }
35 }
```

Dialogue

```
Enter 5 numbers
67
78
89
101
95
Range: 35
```

Testing the Implementation

To test this code, you should compare many hand-checked results with the range displayed by the program. For example, one set of inputs could include values that are all the same—the range should be 1. With two temperatures to check, the range should be computed as one more than the difference between those two values. Another test is the entry of one temperature only. This should result in the range of 1. The testing should also include a set of values where the number of inputs is greater than 2. This leads to many possible test sets, especially when you are attempting to input all possible orderings. Three inputs have six orderings, four inputs have 24 orderings, and in general n inputs have $n!$ (n factorial) orderings, or ($n * (n - 1) * (n - 2) *, \ldots, * 3 * 2 * 1$). Such exhaustive testing is impractical. It is also unnecessary.

305

A tester begins to gain confidence in the code by picking an arbitrary number of tests—for example, when *n* is 5 and the inputs were -5, 8, 22, -7, and 15. In this set of inputs, the difference between the highest and lowest is (22 - (-7) + 1), or 30. Looking at the dialogue and seeing that the range is 30 could lead us to believe that the algorithm and implementation are correct. However, the only thing that is sure is this: when those particular five temperatures are entered, the correct range is returned.

However, always keep in mind that testing only reveals the presence of errors, not the absence of errors. If the range were shown as an obviously incorrect answer (-11, for example), hopefully you would detect the presence of an error.

Debugging Loops with Output Statements

When you detect an intent error, and a loop is involved, consider displaying the important values that might be incorrectly calculated. The program developed in the preceding sections tries to find the lowest and highest value from a group of *n* numbers. However, it would be easy to write it with an intent error, so it would be useful to print relevant variables' values such as `highest` and `lowest`. Writing an output statement inside the loop lets you see the changing values during each iteration of the loop. This simple debugging tool is called a ***debugging output statement***. By showing you what is happening, it can make your task much easier.

A well-placed debugging output statement can be very revealing. For example, you could include one at the bottom of the loop below to show what is going on during the loop. The dialogue would look like this (some sections of the program are omitted with . . .):

```
. . .
for (int j = 1; j <= n; j++)
{
  . . .

  else if (currentInput < lowest)
    lowest = aTemp;

  // DEBUGGING: Add a WriteLine to help aid debugging
  Console.WriteLine("Lowest: {0}  Highest: {1}", highest, lowest);
}
```

Dialog

```
Enter 3 integers
5
Lowest: 5  Highest: 999
12
Lowest: 12  Highest: 999
```

```
16
Lowest: 16   Highest: 999
Range: -983
```

The debugging output statement vividly shows that the highest value is not changing, even though 5, 12, and 16 are all less than 999. This suggests that the program's intent error is in the code that updates the variable `highest`.

Self-Check

Use this code to answer the questions that follow.

```
highest = -999;
lowest = 999;
int n = 5;
for (int j = 1; j <= n; j++)
{
   currentInput = int.Parse(Console.ReadLine());
   if (currentInput > highest)
     highest = aTemp;
   else if (currentInput < lowest)
     lowest = aTemp;
}
range = highest - lowest + 1;
```

6-16   Trace through the code above using these inputs:

-5   8   22   -7   15

Predict the value stored in range. Is it correct?

6-17   Trace through the same code with these inputs:

5   4   3   2   1

Predict the value stored in range. Is it correct?

6-18   Trace through the same code with these inputs:

1   2   3   4   5

Predict the value stored in range. Is it correct?

6-19   When is range incorrectly computed?

   (a) When the input is entered in descending order.

   (b) When the input is entered in ascending order.

   (c) When the input is in neither ascending nor descending order.

6-20   What must be done to correct the error?

The Fencepost Problem

Consider the problem of writing a method `PrintLetters` that prints the characters in a string, with a comma between each character. On the surface, it sounds simple to solve: write a loop that prints each letter followed by a comma. An initial implementation might look something like this:

```
// an incorrect implementation
public static void PrintLetters(string arg)
{
  for (int index = 0;  index < arg.Length;  index++)
  {
    Console.Write("{0}, ", arg[index]);
  }
  Console.WriteLine();  // end the line once
}
```

But as shown here, the output is not quite correct:

```
PrintLetters("Mississippi");
```

Output
M, i, s, s, i, s, s, i, p, p, i,

Notice the comma following the final i in `Mississippi`. It looks like the method is implemented incorrectly. The first thought many programmers have at this point is that the comma in `Console.Write("{0}, ", arg[index]);` should not have been placed after the letter, but before it. This suggests a second attempted implementation:

```
// sadly, also incorrect
public static void PrintLetters(string arg)
{
  for (int index = 0;  index < arg.Length;  index++)
```

```
{
    Console.Write(", {0}", arg[index]);
}
Console.WriteLine();   // end the line once
}
```

But this one has a new problem:

```
PrintLetters("Mississippi");
```

Output
, M, i, s, s, i, s, s, i, p, p, i

Now there is a comma before the first M in "Mississippi"! Neither of the above solutions is quite right.

This simple example demonstrates a common problem that arises in computer science, called the *fencepost problem.* The fencepost problem takes its name from the idea that every picket fence needs exactly one more post than the number of connecting areas between posts. The diagram below shows a fence with five posts and four connecting areas:

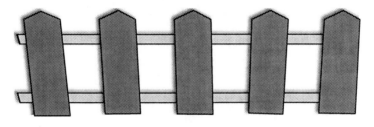

Figure 6.3: Fenceposts

The analogy of the fence can be applied to problems like the PrintLetters method just shown. The method needs to print every letter, with a comma in between, just as a picket fence needs every post to have a connecting area between it and the next. The letters of the string arg are the fence posts, and the commas are the connecting areas. But there should be no comma before the first letter or after the last letter, just as there should be no connecting area before the first fence post or after the last.

The two algorithms shown previously for PrintLetters were incorrect because they were essentially equivalent to the following algorithm for building a fence:

How to build a fence, with N posts. (attempt 1)

  1. *Repeat the following actions N times:*

   ○ *Place a post.*

   ○ *Place a connecting area.*

If this algorithm were followed to build a fence with 4 posts, it would incorrectly look like the following figure.

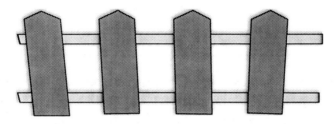

Figure 6.4: Fence with wrong number of posts

What was wrong with the algorithm? It needed to not place a connecting area after the last post. A second algorithm for building a fence might look like this:

How to build a fence, with N posts. (attempt 2)

  1. *Repeat the following actions N times:*

   ○ *Place a post.*

   ○ *If I am not on post #N (the last post), place a connecting area.*

This algorithm works correctly, despite being a bit verbose. The code for `PrintLetters` would look something like this, if it used the preceding algorithm:

```
public static void PrintLetters(string arg)
{
  for (int index = 0;  index < arg.Length;  index++)
  {
    Console.Write("{0}", arg[index]);
    if (index < arg.Length - 1)
      Console.Write(", ");
  }
  Console.WriteLine();  // end the line once
}
```

The second fencepost algorithm is correct, but it can be improved and made simpler. A third way to fix the fencepost problem is with the following algorithm:

How to build a fence, with N posts. (attempt 3)
1. *Repeat the following actions N - 1 times:*
   ○ *Place a post.*
   ○ *Place a connecting area.*
2. *Place one final post to complete the fence.*

This third algorithm is somewhat better, because it does not require the fence builder to check how many posts have been placed every time. However, the algorithm has a minor incorrectness: if the builder were asked to place a fence with 0 posts, she would skip Step 1 entirely and then execute Step 2, incorrectly placing one post. A minor modification is needed to ensure the algorithm's correctness:

How to build a fence, with N posts. (attempt 4)
1. *Repeat the following actions N - 1 times:*
   ○ *Place a post.*
   ○ *Place a connecting area.*
2. *If there is a dangling last connecting area that needs a last fence post, that is, If N is greater than 0, then place one final post to complete the fence.*

This last algorithm is the most common solution to the fencepost problem, and is commonly called the "loop-and-a-half" solution. It is named this way because the code is usually implemented as a loop that does most of the work, and then a last step that does the final "half" iteration, which is slightly different from the others (following the analogy, it is the iteration that places only a fence post, and not a connecting area).

Implementing the loop-and-a-half solution to the fencepost problem gives a `PrintLetters` method like the following:

Code Sample: Class Fencepost

```
1 using System;
2
3 class Fencepost
4 {
5   public static void PrintLetters(string arg)
6   {
7     // write all letters of the string except the last one
```

```
 8        // (place all fence posts and connecting areas but last one)
 9        for (int index = 0;   index < arg.Length - 1;   index++)
10        {
11           Console.Write("{0}, ", arg[index]);
12        }
13
14        // last "half" loop iteration; write last letter
15        if (arg.Length > 0)
16           Console.Write(arg[arg.Length - 1]);
17
18        Console.WriteLine();   // end the line once
19     }
20
21     static void Main()
22     {
23        PrintLetters("Mississippi");
24     }
25  }
```

Output

M, i, s, s, i, s, s, i, p, p, i

Sentinel Loops: Indeterminate Loops and Fencepost Problem

The fencepost problem is often seen when solving problems involving sentinel loops. A *sentinel* is a specific input value used to terminate a loop. The loop that uses the sentinel value is called a *sentinel loop*. For example, perhaps a program repeatedly reads numbers from the user until the user enters -1 to stop, then averages all of the numbers the user entered. Sentinel loops like this one are indeterminate, because it is unknown how many numbers the user will enter before entering the sentinel value.

Dialogue

```
Enter test scores or -1 to quit:
80
90
70
-1
Average of 3 tests = 80.0
```

A sentinel value is of the same type of data as the other input; in this case, an integer -1 just like the other integers the user enters. However, the sentinel itself is not an input number that the program is supposed to process. The user does not actually want -1 to be included when calculating the average of the numbers. Because of this, the sentinel value must not be treated the same as other input. If -1 were included with the scores just shown, the average would be considerably lower than 80.0, and the student would be graded unfairly.

An incorrect algorithm for solving such a problem essentially looks like this (the variable SENTINEL is written in all uppercase because it will be implemented as a class constant):

```
number = something other than the SENTINEL;
while (number != SENTINEL)
{
   // Read the next number...

   // Process input...
}
```

The algorithm just shown has a problem. The last time through the loop, when the user enters the sentinel value, it will be processed just like the rest of the numbers. Since this is incorrect, the algorithm could be modified as follows to produce a correct, yet clunky, solution:

```
number = something other than the SENTINEL;
while (number != SENTINEL)
{
   // Read the next number...

   if (number != SENTINEL)
   {
      // Process input...
   }
}
```

This second algorithm is technically correct because it will not process the sentinel, and the loop will then terminate at the start of the next iteration. However, it is awkward because the loop test of number != SENTINEL must be repeated redundantly during each iteration through the loop. In addition, initializing the variable number to something other than the sentinel is also bad style, because if the sentinel ever changes, number might accidentally be initialized to the sentinel's value, which would break the program's correctness. This is poor coding style.

A better implementation of the algorithm uses the loop-and-a-half solution.

```
number = // Read the first number...

while (number != SENTINEL)
{
  // Process input...

  // Read the next number...
}
```

In this last implementation, the loop has been turned on its head. The "half" loop iteration is done first, by prompting the user and reading the first number. Then the loop begins; if the first number entered by the user is the sentinel, the loop is skipped. Otherwise, the number is processed, another number is read, and the loop starts over. If the newly read number is the sentinel, the loop test fails, and the loop terminates.

This last implementation solves the problems of the one before it; it does not repeat the loop test twice, and it does not initialize the number variable to an otherwise arbitrary value. The following program demonstrates the sentinel loop. This program asks the user either to enter data in the range of 0 through 100 inclusive, or to enter -1 to signal the end of the data. With sentinel loops, you should always display a message that tells the user how to notify the program to terminate the loop when there is no more input. In the dialogue above, -1 is the sentinel. This could easily have some been other value.

For this algorithm, the value for number must be read once before the loop test is made. This is called a "priming read," which goes before the first iteration of the loop. Immediately after the ReadLine message at the bottom of the loop, number is always compared to SENTINEL. When the sentinel value -1 is entered, the loop terminates, rather than attempting to process the number -1 or attempting to add one too many to the counter n. The odd part of the algorithm is that the loop processes the valid data from the *previous* iteration of the loop (or, in the case of the first iteration of the loop, it is processing the data that was read just before the start of the loop).

Code Sample: DemonstrateIndeterminateLoop Class

```
 1  using System;
 2
 3  // Find average by using SENTINEL of -1 to terminate loop
 4  // that counts number of inputs and accumulates them.
 5  class DemonstrateIndeterminateLoop
 6  {
 7    public static readonly int SENTINEL = -1;
 8
 9    static void Main()
10    {
```

```
11      Console.WriteLine("This program computes an average on");
12      Console.WriteLine("numbers entered before {0}", SENTINEL);
13      Console.WriteLine();
14
15      int number;
16      double accumulator = 0.0;
17      int n = 0;
18
19      Console.Write("Enter number or {0} to quit: ", SENTINEL);
20      number = int.Parse(Console.ReadLine());
21      while (number != SENTINEL)
22      {
23        // Process input
24        accumulator += number;
25
26        // Read the next string to be processed as a number or
27        // the sentinel value that terminates the loop
28        Console.Write("Enter number or {0} to quit: ",
29                      SENTINEL);
30        number = int.Parse(Console.ReadLine());
31
32        n++;
33      }
34
35      if (n == 0)
36        Console.WriteLine("Can't average zero numbers");
37      else
38        Console.WriteLine("Average {0:F1}", accumulator / n);
39  }
40 }
```

Dialogue

```
This program computes an average on
numbers entered before -1

Enter number or -1 to quit: 76
Enter number or -1 to quit: 92
Enter number or -1 to quit: 93
Enter number or -1 to quit: 80
Enter number or -1 to quit: -1
Average 85.3
```

The following table traces the changing state of the important variables, to simulate execution of the previous program. The variable named accumulator maintains the running sum of the test scores. The loop also increments n by +1 for each valid number entered by the user. Notice that the number -1 is not processed.

Location in Code	number	accumulator	n	loop test
First loop test	76	0.0	0	true
End of Iteration 1	92	76.0	1	true
End of Iteration 2	93	168.0	2	true
End of Iteration 3	80	261.0	3	true
End of Iteration 4	-1	341.0	4	true
Final Loop test	-1	341.0	4	false

At this point, accumulator and n are the correct values, and the loop terminates when the user wishes. A check is made to ensure that there was at least one valid number entered before computing the average.

Self-Check

6-21 Determine the value assigned to average for each of the following code fragments by simulating execution when the user inputs 70.0, 60.0, 80.0, and -1.0. For both code segments, assume the following:

```
double currentInput;
int n = 0;
double accumulator = 0.0;
double SENTINEL = -1.0;
```

(a)

```
currentInput = double.Parse(Console.ReadLine());
while (currentInput != SENTINEL)
{
   currentInput = double.Parse(Console.ReadLine());
   accumulator += currentInput; // Update accumulator
   n++;                         // Update total # of inputs
}
double average = accumulator / n;
```

(b)

```
currentInput = double.Parse(Console.ReadLine());
while (currentInput != SENTINEL)
{
```

```
    accumulator += currentInput; // Update accumulator
    n++;                         // Update # of inputs
    currentInput = double.Parse(Console.ReadLine());
}
double average = accumulator / n;
```

6-22   Explain why the values are different for parts (a) and (b) of the last question. If you answered 70.0 for both (a) and (b) above, redo both until you get different answers for (a) and (b).

6-23   How many iterations of the loop just shown will occur when the user enters the sentinel (-1.0) as the very first input?

6-24   What activity should be added to the previous while statement, so that each loop iteration brings the loop one step closer to termination?

6.6   More Loops: do/while and foreach

The for loop is useful for processing determinate loops. Other C# looping statements exist for specialized types of loops. These additional loop statements are equivalent in power to the existing loops presented, but they are sometimes cleaner or more concise when implementing certain types of algorithms.

The do/while Loop Statement

The *do/while loop statement* is similar to the while loop. It allows a collection of statements to be repeated while an expression is true. The primary difference is the time at which the loop test is evaluated. Whereas the while loop test is evaluated at the beginning of each iteration, the do/while statement evaluates the loop test at the end of the loop. This means that the do/while loop always executes its repeated part at least once.

Here is the general form of the do/while loop.

General Form: do/while loop statement

do
{
   statement(s) to execute;
}
while (*Boolean expression*);

Notes:

The braces are *not* optional, even if only one statement is used!

Example:

```
string option = "?";
do
{
   Console.Write("Enter <yes> or <no>: ");
   option = Console.ReadLine().Trim();
}
while (option != "yes" && option != "no" );
```

Dialog

```
Enter <yes> or <no>: Huh?
Enter <yes> or <no>: y
Enter <yes> or <no>: YES
Enter <yes> or <no>: yes
```

Note the semicolon after the `while` line of the `do/while` loop! It is easy to forget, but it is required for the syntax to be correct.

When a `do/while` statement is encountered, all statements execute within the block, from `{` to `}`. The *Boolean-test* evaluates at the *end* of the loop—not at the beginning. If the test expression is `true`, the *statement(s)-to-execute* execute again. If the test expression is `false`, the loop terminates.

Here is an example of the `do/while` loop. To help visualize the execution, this loop displays the increasing value of `counter`.

```
int counter = 1;
int n = 4;
Console.WriteLine("Before loop...");

do
{
   Console.WriteLine("Loop #{0}", counter);
   counter++;
}
while (counter <= n);

Console.WriteLine("...After loop");
```

Output

```
Before loop...
Loop #1
Loop #2
Loop #3
Loop #4
...After loop
```

You can write a nearly equivalent while loop, including having a pre-test, as follows:

```
int counter = 1;
int n = 4;
Console.WriteLine("Before loop...");
while(counter <= n)
{
   Console.WriteLine("Loop #{0}", counter);
   counter++;
}
Console.WriteLine("...After loop");
```

However, there are times when a post-test loop is better. Although the while loop shown above produces the same exact output as its do/while counterpart when n is greater than or equal to counter, consider what happens when n = 1 is replaced with n = 0. Now, the while loop does not execute its iterative part; but the do/while loop executes its iterative part once, even when n is 0:

```
Before loop...
Loop #1
...After loop
```

The do/while loop is a good choice for repetition whenever a set of statements must be executed at least once to initialize objects that are used later in the loop test. The do/while loop is the preferred statement when asking the user of the program to enter one of several options. For example, in the following example, the do/while loop in the method GetNextOption repeatedly asks the user to enter one of three choices. The loop does not terminate until the user enters a valid option. The Main method also uses a do/while loop to process as many deposits and withdrawals as the user wants.

Code Sample: DoWhileLoopDemo Class

```
 1 using System;
 2
 3 class DoWhileLoopDemo
 4 {
 5   public static readonly double AMOUNT = 10.00;
 6
 7   static void Main()
 8   {
 9     BankAccount account = new BankAccount("Smith", 100.00);
10     string choice = "";
11
12     do
13     {
14       choice = GetNextOption();  // Call the method in the loop
15
16       switch (choice)
17       {
18         case "W":
19           account.Withdraw(AMOUNT);
10           Console.WriteLine("Withdrew {0}", AMOUNT);
20           break;
21         case "D":
22           account.Deposit(AMOUNT);
23           Console.WriteLine("Deposited {0}", AMOUNT);
24           break;
25         case "P":
26           Console.WriteLine("Account: {0}", account);
27           break;
28         default:
29           Console.WriteLine("Have a nice day :)");
30           break;
31       }
32     }
33     while (choice != "Q");
34   }
35
36   // Prompts until user chooses an uppercase W, D, or Q
37   public static string GetNextOption()
38   {
39     string option = "";
40
41     // loop until one of the valid inputs is read
42     do
43     {
44       Console.Write("W)ithdraw, D)eposit, P)rint or Q)uit: ");
```

```
45
46           // get the first no blank character in upper case
47           option = Console.ReadLine().ToUpper();
48
49           // end loop if option is not any of the three valid choices
50       }
51       while (option != "W" && option != "D"
52             && option != "P" && option != "Q");
53
54       return option;
55   }
56 }
```

Dialogue

```
W)ithdraw, D)eposit, P)rint or Q)uit: invalid
W)ithdraw, D)eposit, P)rint or Q)uit: x
W)ithdraw, D)eposit, P)rint or Q)uit: p
Account: Smith $100.00
W)ithdraw, D)eposit, P)rint or Q)uit: d
Deposited 10
W)ithdraw, D)eposit, P)rint or Q)uit: d
Deposited 10
W)ithdraw, D)eposit, P)rint or Q)uit: p
Account: Smith $120.00
W)ithdraw, D)eposit, P)rint or Q)uit: w
Withdrew 10
W)ithdraw, D)eposit, P)rint or Q)uit: p
Account: Smith $110.00
W)ithdraw, D)eposit, P)rint or Q)uit: q
Have a nice day :)
```

Because at least one character must be obtained from the keyboard before the test expression evaluates, a do/while loop is used in GetNextOption instead of a while loop—the loop must iterate at least once. In addition, a do/while loop is used in Main to get an option, because it needs at least one user input to evaluate what the user wants to do.

Self-Check

6-25   Write the output produced by the following code:

(a)

```
int counter = 1;
do
{
   Console.Write("{0} ", counter);
   counter++;
}
while (counter <= 3);
```

(b)

```
string str = "abcdef";
do
{
   Console.WriteLine(str);
   str = str.Substring(1, str.Length);
}
while (str.Length > 0);
```

6-26   Rewrite the following `while` loop to use an equivalent `do/while` loop:

```
// generate a random number that is divisible by 6
Random rand = new Random();
int randomNumber = rand.Next();
while (randomNumber % 6 != 0)
{
   randomNumber = rand.Next();
   Console.WriteLine(randomNumber);
}
```

6-27   Write a `do/while` loop that prompts for and inputs integers until the integer input is in the range of 1 through 10, inclusive.

The `foreach` Loop Statement

The **foreach** *loop statement* is a specialized instance of the `for` loop, designed as a determinate loop that iterates over each element of a collection. The major collection that will be seen is this book is the array. However, arrays are not introduced until the next chapter. For now, the collection will be a `string` object, which is a collection of many `char` characters that represent the letters in the string.

    Consider the following `for` loop:

```
string str = "Howdy";
for (int index = 0;   index < str.Length;   index++)
{
   Console.WriteLine(str[index]);
}
```

Semantically, the real meaning of the above loop is to print each letter of the string on its own line. The `for` loop's somewhat ugly syntax makes it somewhat hard to decipher what the code is doing. The solution is to use a `foreach` loop, whose syntax in this case is closer to the meaning of the code.

General Form: foreach loop statement

foreach (*variable-type variable-name* **in** *collection-name*)
{
  statement(s) to execute;
}
Notes:
The braces are optional if only one statement is used.

Example:
```
string message = "Hi there!";
foreach (char ch in message)
{
   Console.WriteLine("Letter is: {0}", ch);
}
```

Note that the `foreach` loop does not need any update step or Boolean expression test. The update step is implicitly to move the counter variable forward to the next element of the collection—in this case, to the next character of the string. The Boolean expression test is implicitly to stop when the loop has exhausted all elements in the collection—all characters in the string, in this case.

The previous `for` loop example could be rewritten with a `foreach` loop like this:

```
string str = "Howdy";
foreach (char letter in str)
{
   Console.WriteLine(letter);
}
```

Not all `for` loops can be replaced by `foreach` loops! This is possible only with `for` loops that operate on elements in a collection, which in this case are characters of a `string`. Its usefulness is limited now, but in later chapters, when you see more collections, the `foreach` loop will prove to be a handy statement.

Self-Check

6-28   Write the output produced by the following code:

(a)

```
string message1 = "Hello";
string message2 = "";
foreach (char ch in message1)
{
   message2 = ch + message2;
}
Console.WriteLine(message2);
```

(b)

```
string str = "abcdef";
string str2 = "";
foreach (char letter in str)
{
   str2 += letter;
   str2 += letter;
}
Console.WriteLine(str2);
```

6-29   Rewrite the following `for` loop to use an equivalent `foreach` loop:

```
string myName = "amanda banana ranna";
for (int index = 0;  index < myName.Length;  index++)
{
   // only do this code on letters
   if (myName[index] >= 'a' && myName[index] <= 'z')
   {
      int letterNum = myName[index] - 'a' + 1;
      Console.WriteLine("{0} is letter {1} in the alphabet",
        myName[index], letterNum);
   }
}
```

6-30   Which kind of loop best accomplishes these tasks?

   (a) Sum the first five integers (1 + 2 + 3 + 4 + 5).

   (b) Find the average value for a set of numbers when the size of the set is known.

   (c) Find the average for a set of numbers when the size of the set cannot be determined until the data has been completely entered.

   (d) From the user, obtain a character that must be an uppercase S or Q.

Chapter Summary

- ○ Repetition is an important method of control for all programming languages. Typically, the body of a loop has statements that may change the state of one or more variables during each loop iteration, so that the loop can terminate.
- ○ The for loop is often used to implement the Determinate Loop pattern, which requires that the number of repetitions be known before the loop is encountered.
- ○ Determinate loops rely on a value representing the number of repetitions (n perhaps) and a properly initialized and incremented loop counter (j perhaps) to track the number of repetitions. The loop counter is compared to the known number of iterations at the start of each loop. The counter is automatically updated at the end of each for loop iteration.
- ○ There are a number of ways to determine the number of loop iterations before a loop executes. The number of iterations may be input from the user, passed as an argument to a method, initialized in advance, or may be part of the state of some object. For example, every string object knows how many characters it has at any given moment.
- ○ The Determinate Loop pattern is so common that a specific statement—the for loop—is built into almost all languages.
- ○ Indeterminate loops rely on some external event for their termination. The terminating event may occur at any time.
- ○ Indeterminate loops are used when a program is unable to determine, in advance, the number of times a loop must iterate. The terminating events include sentinels read from the keyboard (such as -1 as a test or "Q" in a menu selection). These types of loops allow any number of users to execute any number of transactions, for example.

❍ Although you often need one repetitive statement to solve any computer problem, the for loop is the most convenient one under certain circumstances. The for loop requires the program to take care of the initialization, loop test, and repeated statement all at once. The compiler protests if one of these important steps is missing. The for loop provides a more compact and less error-prone determinate loop than some other looping structures.

❍ Remember these steps if you are having trouble designing loops:
  ❍ Determine which type of loop to use.
  ❍ Determine the loop test.
  ❍ Write the statements to be repeated.
  ❍ Bring the loop one step closer to termination.
  ❍ Initialize variables if necessary.
  ❍ Use debugging output statements to discover and fix intent errors. (Make sure to remove or comment them out later!)

Key Terms

brute force
debugging output statement
Determinate Loop pattern
do/while loop statement

empty loop
fencepost problem
for loop statement
foreach loop statement
Indeterminate Loop pattern
infinite loop

iteration
loop
repetition
sentinel
sentinel loop
while loop statement

Exercises

1. How many times will the following loops execute Console.Write("Hello");? For this question, "Zero" and "Infinite" are legitimate possible answers.

   (a)

   ```
   int n = 5;
   for (int j = 1; j <= n; j++)
   {
      Console.Write("Hello ");
   }
   ```

(b)

```
int n = 0;
for (int j = 5; j >= n; j--)
{
    Console.Write("Hello ");
}
```

(c)

```
int n = 5;
for (int j = 1; j <= n; j--)
{
    Console.Write("Hello ");
    j++;
}
```

(d)

```
int n = 0;
for (int j = 1; j <= n; j++)
{
    Console.Write("Hello ");
}
```

2. Write the output produced by these for loops:
```
for (int counter = 1; counter <= 5; counter++)
    Console.Write(" {0}", counter);
Console.WriteLine(" Loop One");

for (int counter = 10; counter >= 1; counter--)
    Console.Write(" {0}", counter);
Console.WriteLine(" Blast Off ");
```

3. Write loops to produce the outputs shown.
    (a)   10 9 8 7 6 5 4 3 2 1 0
    (b)   0 5 10 15 20 25 30 35 40 45 50
    (c)   -1000 -900 -800 -700 -600 -500 -400 -300 -200 -100 0

4. Write the output generated by the following code:
```
int j = 0;
while (j < 5)
{
    Console.Write(" {0}", j);
    j++;
}
```

5. Write a `for` loop that sums all the integers between start and stop inclusive that are input from the keyboard. You may assume that start is always less than or equal to stop. If the input were 5 for start and 10 for stop, the sum would be 5 + 6 + 7 + 8 + 9 + 10 (45).

6. How many times will `Hello` be displayed using the following program segments? For this question, "Zero," "Unknown," and "Infinite" are legitimate possible answers.

(a)
```
while (j <= 10)
   Console.Write("Hello");
```

(b)
```
int j = 1;
while (j <= 7)
{
   Console.Write("Hello");
   j++;
}
```

(c)
```
int j = 7;
while (j <= 1)
{
   Console.Write("Hello");
}
```

(d)
```
int j = 1;
while (j <= 5)
   Console.Write("Hello");
   j++;
```

7. Write a while loop that produces this output:
```
-4  -3  -2  -1  0  1  2  3  4  5  6
```

8. Write a loop that displays 100, 95, . . ., 5, and 0 on separate lines.

9. Write a loop that counts how many perfect scores (scores of 100) are entered from the keyboard.

10. Convert the following code to its `for` loop counterpart:
```
Console.Write("Enter number of ints to be summed: ");
int n = int.Parse(Console.ReadLine());
```

```
int counter = 1;
int sum = 0;

Console.WriteLine("Enter {0} integers on separate lines: ", n);
while (counter <= n)
{
    int anInt = int.Parse(Console.ReadLine());
    sum += anInt;
    counter++;
}
Console.WriteLine("Sum: {0}", sum);
```

11. Write a loop that counts the number of lines input by a user until the user enters the string ENDOFDATA (must be uppercase letters, no spaces) on a line by itself. The words will be entered one string per line.

12. Write the complete output generated by the following code when the user enters 1, 2, 3, 4, and -999 on separate lines.
```
double sum = 0.0;
Console.Write("Enter tests or a negative number to quit: ");
double test = double.Parse(Console.ReadLine());
while(test >= 0.0)
{
  sum += test;
  test = double.Parse(Console.ReadLine());
}
Console.Write("Sum: {0}", sum);
```

13. Write the output generated by the following code:
```
string choice = "BDWBQDW";
for (int j = 0; choice[j] != 'Q'; j++)
{
    Console.WriteLine("Opt: {0}", choice[j]);
}
```

14. How many times will the following loops print "Hello "? For this question, "Zero," "Unknown," and "Infinite" are legitimate possible answers.

(a)
```
int j = 1;
int n = 10;
do
{
  Console.Write("Hello ");
```

```
    }
    while (j > n);

    (b)
    int n = 10;
    int j = 1;
    do
    {
      Console.Write("Hello ");
      j = j - 2;
    }
    while (j <= n);

    (c)
    int j = -1;
    do
    {
      Console.Write("Hello ");
      j++;
    }
    while (j != j);

    (d)
    int j = 1;
    do
    {
      Console.Write("Hello ");
      j++;
    }
    while (j <= 100);
```

15. Write a do/while loop that produces this output:

```
10  9  8  7  6  5  4  3  2  1  0
```

16. Write the output generated by the following program:

```
    int j = -2;
    do
    {
      Console.WriteLine("{0} ", j);
      j--;
    }
    while (j > -6);
```

17. Rewrite the following do/while loop as a pretest while loop (the loop test is first, before the body):

```
int counter = 0;
do
{
   Console.WriteLine(counter);
   counter++;
}
whilecounter <= 100);
```

18. Complete a method EvenNumber that prompts for, and returns, an even integer in the range of two integer arguments (assume that it is called from another method in the same class). If the user enters an odd number, or an integer that is out of the range, inform the user of the error until they enter an even number that is in the range.

```
using system;
public class EvenNumberLoop
{
   // Return even number in range of min through max inclusive
   public static int EvenNumber(int min, int max)
   {
      // Complete this code
   }

   static void Main()
   {
      int size = EvenNumber(1, 20);
      Console.WriteLine("You entered {0}", size);
   }
}
```

Dialogue
Enter an even integer in the range of 1 through 20: *-1*
Integer was not even
Integer was out of range
Enter an even integer in the range of 1 through 20: *0*
Integer was out of range
Enter an even integer in the range of 1 through 20: *1*
Integer was not even
Enter an even integer in the range of 1 through 20: *21*
Integer was not even
Integer was out of range
Enter an even integer in the range of 1 through 20: *20*
You entered 20

Programming Tips

1.   Pick the type of loop you want to use.

After recognizing the need for repetition, decide if the number of repetitions can be determined in advance. If so, use a determinate loop, which is best implemented with a `for` loop. If the number of iterations cannot be determined in advance, determine the event that terminates the loop. For example, the loop might terminate when the user enters the word STOP. In this case, the termination condition is `word == "STOP"`. The loop test is the logical negation `word != "STOP"`.

```
while (word != "STOP")
{ // ...
}
```

2.   Beware of infinite loops.

Watch out for infinite loops. They are easy to create, and sometimes they are very difficult to find. Can you spot why these are infinite loops?

```
while (j <= 100)
{ // Sum the first 100 integers
   sum += j;
}
j++;

for (j = 0; j <= 100; j++)
{ // Sum the first 100 integers
   sum += j;
   j--;
}

for (j = 1; j <= 10; j++);
   Console.WriteLine(j);
```

3.   Always write a block for the iterative part of `while` loops.

This provides you a better chance of including any increment statement as part of the loop, rather than accidentally leaving it outside of the loop.

4. Use debugging outputs to find out what is going on in a loop.

Use debugging output statements inside a loop to display one or more variables that should be changing. This can be very revealing. Sometimes you'll spot an infinite loop. Other times you might spot that the loop test is never true.

```
while (. . .)
{ // ...
   mid = (lo + hi) / 2.0;
   Console.WriteLine("In loop, mid equals {0}", mid );
   // ...
}
```

5. Loops may not always execute the iterative part.

It is possible that a loop will execute zero times, or less than you might have thought.

```
int n = 3;
for (int j = 1; j >= n; j++)   // 1 >= n is false
{
   Console.Write("You'll not see me!");
}

for (int j = 1; j <= n; j++);   // Get rid of ;
{
   Console.Write("You see me only once, not thrice");
   Console.Write("for I'm not part of the for!");
}
```

Programming Projects

6A   Wind Speed

Write a program (a class with the `Main` method only) that determines the lowest, highest, and average of a set of wind speed readings. Prompt the user for the number of wind speed readings in the set. After the set has been entered, compute and display the high, low, and average. Assume that the user always enters at least one wind speed reading. Round the average (after `Ave:`) to the nearest integer. (Use the `Math` class to do this.)

```
     Enter number of wind speed readings:  4
     4
     6
     8
     3

      High:  8
       Low:  3
     Count:  4
       Ave:  5
```

6B   Factorial

Write a program (a class with the `Main` method only) that asks for a number and displays N! (N factorial) where N! is the product of all the positive integers from 1 to N. For example, 5! = 1 x 2 x 3 x 4 x 5 = 120; 4! = 1 x 2 x 3 x 4 = 24; and 0! = 1 (by definition). Test your program with these arguments: 0, 1, 2, and 7. Here is one log of execution when the user enters 4:

```
Enter n:  4
4! is 24
```

6C   Squaring Integers

The square of an integer value n can be found by adding the first n positive odd integers. For example, both 4 squared and -4 squared are the sum of the first four positive odd integers (1 + 3 + 5 + 7 = 16). Write a program (a class with the `main` method only) that reads an integer and displays the square of that integer, using this algorithm. Do not use the built-in method `Math.Pow` or the multiplication operator `*`. Test your program with various inputs, including negative integers and zero. Here is one sample log of execution:

```
     Enter integer:  -4
     -4 squared is 16
```

6D   The Elevator Class

Complete the `Elevator` class with a constructor that places an elevator with an ID at a selected floor. The constructor requires exactly three arguments:

1. a `string` as the elevator ID
2. an `int` as the starting floor
3. an `int` as the top floor

The lowest floor that can be selected is 1. The `Select` method allows floors to be selected and issues an error message when the wrong floor is selected—stating that the selected floor is either too high or too low. For every floor, the elevator ID should be displayed before the message "going up" or "going down" and the current floor of the elevator.

The sample output shown below gives you an idea of what one simulated `Elevator` object must look like on your screen. Notice that a message is displayed when both elevators are constructed. The output also shows that there are several places where the constructor and the `select` method must check for and report errors.

```
1  // Test drive the Elevator class by constructing one
2  // Elevator object and sending several select(floor)
3  // messages, some of which are invalid.
4  class TestElevator
5  {
6    static void Main()
7    {
8      Elevator error1 = new Elevator("No way 1", 1, -1);
9      Elevator error2 = new Elevator("No way 2", 3, 2);
10     Elevator error3 = new Elevator("No way 3", 0, 9);
11     Elevator liftOne = new Elevator("West", 2, 12);
12     Elevator liftTwo = new Elevator("East", 1, 6);
13
14     liftOne.Select(5);
15     liftTwo.Select(3);
16     liftOne.Select(5);   // 5 is current floor; open at 5 again
17     liftTwo.Select(7);
18     liftOne.Select(1);
19     liftTwo.Select(1);
20     liftOne.Select(13); // Out of range--elevator does not change
21     liftOne.Select(0);  // Out of range--elevator does not change
22   }
23 }
```

Output

```
**ERROR** max floor for 'No Way 1' must be greater than 1
**ERROR** starting floor for 'No Way 2' must be in range of 1..2
**ERROR** starting floor for 'No Way 3' must be in range of 1..9
West begins at floor 2
East begins at floor 1
West going from 2 up to 5
  going up to: 3
  going up to: 4
  going up to: 5
West open at 5
East going from 1 up to 3
  going up to: 2
  going up to: 3
East open at 3
West door opens at 5 (current floor == selected floor)
**ERROR** 7 not in range of 1..6 for East
East open at 3
West going from 5 down to 1
  going down to: 4
  going down to: 3
  going down to: 2
  going down to: 1
West open at 1
East going from 3 down to 1
  going down to: 2
  going down to: 1
East open at 1
**ERROR** 13 not in range of 1..12 for West
West open at 1
**ERROR** 0 not in range of 1..12 for West
West open at 1
```

6E   Mini-Teller

Write a program (a class with the Main method only) that allows a user to make as many withdrawals, deposits, and balance queries as desired to one BankAccount object that you construct. Your program should notify the user of insufficient funds if the withdrawal fails due to lack of funds. Use the following dialogue to help you understand the problem specification, which assumes that your single BankAccount was constructed like this:

```
BankAccount currentAccount = new BankAccount("Jackson", 100.00);
```

Dialogue

```
Intitial balance for Jackson is 100.0

W)ithdraw, D)eposit, B)alance, or Q)uit: d
Enter deposit amount: 1.00

W)ithdraw, D)eposit, B)alance, or Q)uit: b
Current balance: 101.0

W)ithdraw, D)eposit, B)alance, or Q)uit: w
Enter withdrawal amount: 2.00

W)ithdraw, D)eposit, B)alance, or Q)uit: b
Current balance: 99.0

W)ithdraw, D)eposit, B)alance, or Q)uit: w
Enter withdrawal amount: 100.00
**Amount requested exceeds account balance**

W)ithdraw, D)eposit, B)alance, or Q)uit: b
Current balance: 99.0

W)ithdraw, D)eposit, B)alance, or Q)uit: q
Have a nice day :)
```

Also, notice that upper- and lower-case choices are to be allowed. You might wish to use one of the `string` methods in Chapter 3 to convert the user's input to uppercase, to avoid having to check for both options such as q and Q.

6F   Wind Speed Again

Write a program (a class with the `Main` method only) that determines the lowest, highest, and average of a set of wind speed readings that are all positive or zero. Terminate the loop with any negative input. Be sure that you notify the user how to terminate data entry. Compute and display the high, the low, the number of inputs (initially undetermined), and the average (rounded to the nearest tenth). Here is one sample dialogue:

```
Enter wind speed readings or a number less than 0 to quit:
4
6
8
3
-5

 High:  8
  Low:  3
Count:  4
  Ave:  5.3
```

6G   Guessing Game

Write a C# class that implements a guessing game. Ask the user to guess a random number that you have generated, in the range of 1 through 100, inclusive. If the guess is larger than the number, tell the user that the guess was too high. If the guess is too low, tell that to the user. When the guess matches the random number, tell that to the user, state how many guesses the user took, and terminate the program. Here is one sample dialogue:

```
Play one game
Pick a number from 1..100: 50
50 is too high
Pick a number from 1..100: 25
25 is too high
Pick a number from 1..100: 12
12 is too low
Pick a number from 1..100: 18
18 is too high
Pick a number from 1..100: 15
15 is just right
Congrats, you needed 5 guesses
```

The name of the class is GuessingGame. The method named PlayOneGame must get one guessing game going. The NumberOfGuesses property must return the number of guesses the user has taken at any moment (starts at 0 and increases each time the user makes a guess).

```
GuessingGame aGuessingGame = new GuessingGame();

aGuessingGame.PlayOneGame();

Console.WriteLine("#Tries {0}", aGuessingGame.NumberOfGuesses);
```

This project requires the use of random numbers. Use the `Random` class covered in Chapter 3 for this.

6H   Piggy Bank

As we have seen in this chapter, loops are useful when writing classes that need repetitive behavior. Consider a child's piggy bank in countries that have penny, nickel, dime, and quarter coins. Imagine that a child wants you to add a minimum number of money, in cents. You can add any of the four different types of coins to get to this minimum, and you can even go over the minimum requested.

The following dialogue shows that the input continues until the desired minimum is reached. There are many ways to get to the minimum shown here—this is just one:

```
Piggy bank has 0 cents, desired minimum 61
Add coins to reach a minimum of 61

Add P)enny N)ickel D)ime Q)uarter: Q
25 cents, desired minimum 61

Add P)enny N)ickel D)ime Q)uarter: q
50 cents, desired minimum 61

Add P)enny N)ickel D)ime Q)uarter: d
60 cents, desired minimum 61

Add P)enny N)ickel D)ime Q)uarter: p
61 cents, desired minimum 61
```

The `while` loop shown below keeps asking for money until the `PiggyBank` has at least the minimum coins required (`PiggyBank` members are in boldface).

Code Sample: TestPiggyBank Class

```
 1  using System;
 2
 3  class TestPiggyBank
 4  {
 5    static void Main()
 6    {
 7      // PiggyBank with 0 cents and a desired minimum of 61 cents
 8      PiggyBank bank = new PiggyBank(0, 61);
 9
10      // Prompt the user to get things going
11      Console.WriteLine("Piggy bank has {0}", bank);
12      Console.WriteLine("Add coins to reach a minimum of {0}",
13                        Bank.Minimum);
14
15      // loop goes until the bank does not need more cents
16      while (bank.NeedsMore())
17      {
18        // Add a penny, nickel, dime, or quarter
19        bank.AddMoreMoney();
20
21        // Show updated state of the PiggyBank
22        Console.WriteLine(bank);
23        Console.WriteLine();
24      }
25    }
26  }
```

After a `PiggyBank` object is constructed, with an arbitrary number of cents (0) and a desired minimum amount (61), the `while` loop repeats until the `PiggyBank` has at least the minimum number of cents requested (it could get more). This loop may execute from 0 to many times. The exact number of loop iterations cannot be predetermined. The minimum may vary, and/or the user may enter different combinations of coins.

Write the `PiggyBank` class for this programming project so that it works with the above test code.

Arrays

Summing Up

Almost all of the objects studied so far either represent a single value (e.g., `double` and `int`) or contain two or more possibly different types of values (e.g., `BankAccount` objects store two `strings` and a `double`).

Coming Up

This chapter introduces the C# array for storing collections of objects, such as a collection of twenty thousand `BankAccounts`. After studying this chapter, you will be able to

- O declare and use arrays to store reference or primitive values.
- O implement algorithms to process a collection of objects.
- O use the sequential search algorithm to locate a specific element in an array.
- O build a collection class to manage a collection of objects for an application.
- O employ the faster binary search.
- O arrange elements of any array into ascending or descending order.
- O declare and use multi-dimensional arrays.
- O use a selection sort to sort arrays.

7.1 The C# Array Object

Consider a program that needs to manipulate three integer values. To write such a program, you could declare and use three `int` variables to store the data.

Code Sample: Class ThreeInts

```
 1  using System;
 2
 3  class ThreeInts
 4  {
 5    static void Main()
 6    {
 7      int num1;
 8      int num2;
 9      int num3;
10
11      // now use them
12      // ...
13    }
14  }
```

But what about writing a program that manipulates a hundred integer values? Or a million? It would not be possible or practical to declare so many variables. However, there are times when such a program must be written. For example, imagine a program that needs to read 100 students' test grades as inputs from the user and then find statistics about them, such as the average, median, and standard deviation. You could create 100 variables to store all the test scores, but this would be an awkward solution.

A better design comes form using a C# *array* object, which can be thought of as a group or list of values. Arrays are declared like other variables, by giving them a name and type. Arrays have a length specified to indicate the maximum number of values they can store.
Once an array is created, the values in it are referred to through a zero-based integer *index*, which points to its position in the array. Each value is called an array *element*. Arrays are homogeneous, which means that every element in an array is the same type. Arrays are declared and/or constructed using square brackets [and].

General Form: Declaring and Constructing array objects

```
// Array declared, but not constructed
type[] array-name;


// Declare and construct
type[] array-name = new type[capacity];
```

Notes:

The *type* specifies the type of value to be stored. The *type* may be any value or reference type.
The *array-name* is any valid C# identifier.

The *capacity* is an integer expression representing the maximum number of elements that can
be stored in the array. The capacity is always available through a property named Length that is
referenced as *array-name*.Length.

Array Declaration Examples:

```
int[] arrayOfInts;
BankAccount[] accountHolder;
```

Array Construction Examples:

```
int[] testScores = new int[10];        // Store 100 integers
double[] numbers = new double[10000]; // Store 10000 numbers
string[] names = new string[500];      // Store 500 strings
BankAccount[] accts = new BankAccount[1000];  // 1000 accounts
```

When an array is declared and constructed, all array elements are initialized to the default
value of their type. So the array named testScores above has 10 elements that are set to the
default value of 0. The array named numbers stores 10,000 double elements that are all set to
the default value of 0.0. The arrays names and accts now store null values for every element.

Arrays can be pictured as connected boxes, where each box representing one array element.
The elements are numbered by index; the first is element 0, the second is element 1, and so on.
Because of this, an array that is declared with capacity of *n* has a last element with the index
n - 1. The figure below shows an array of integers being declared and initialized.

```
int[] testScores = new int[10];

testScores
```

index	*value*
0	0
1	0
2	0
3	0
4	0
5	0
6	0
7	0
8	0
9	0

Figure 7.1: Array Declaration and Initialization

Arrays are reference type objects. Like other reference types, arrays must be initialized before they can be used. An attempt to access an array that has been declared, but not initialized, results in a compile-time error.

```
BankAccount[] accountHolder;    // declared but not initialized (null)
Console.WriteLine(accountHolder[0]);

Error: Use of unassigned local variable 'accountHolder'
```

Accessing Individual Elements of an Array

Arrays support random access. Individual array elements can be accessed—set or retrieved—by writing the array variable's name, followed by the desired index as an integer, placed between [and]. This is also called *subscript* notation.

General Form: Accessing one array element

array-name [*index*]

Examples:

```
// assigning values to individual array elements
```

```
testScores[0] = 91;
names[1] = "Josie";

// using array elements in expressions
Console.WriteLine(numbers[4]);
Console.WriteLine("{0} | {1} | {2} | {3}",
                  testScores[0], names[1], numbers[9999], accts[23]);
double bal = accts[23].Balance;
```

The example below assigns values to some of the elements of the testScores array of integers, which was declared in the previous section.

```
int[] testScores = new int[10];

// assigning values to the array elements
testScores[0] = 95;
testScores[1] = 87;
testScores[7] = 100;
```

testScores

index	value
0	95
1	87
2	0
3	0
4	0
5	0
6	0
7	100
8	0
9	0

```
// accessing elements' values from the array
Console.WriteLine(testScores[0]);
int highScore = testScores[7];
Console.WriteLine(highScore);
```

Figure 7.2: Accessing and Modifying Array Element Values

Consider the following array named x, which will be used as an example in the following sections. This array can store up to eight floating-point numbers.

```
double[] x = new double[8];
```

The special symbols [and] represent the mathematical subscript notation. Instead of x_0, x_1, and x_{n-1}, C# uses x[0], x[1], and x[n-1]. So the reference to an array element written in C# as x[0] can be read as "x, element zero" or "x, sub zero".

Because the indexes used with arrays are zero-based, the valid range for an index is an integer value between 0 and the array's capacity minus one. Therefore, the individual elements of the array x are referenced with the indexes 0, 1, 2, ... 7.

This code assigns values to the first two array elements:

```
// Assign new values to the first two elements of the array named x:
x[0] = 2.6;
x[1] = 5.7;
```

If a program tried to access the array x with the indexes -1 or 8, it would raise an ***IndexOutOfRangeException***, meaning that the program tried to access an array with a subscript that is too large or small.

Subscript notation allows individual array elements to be displayed, used in expressions, and modified with assignment and input operations. In fact, you can do anything to an individual array element that can be done to a variable of the same type. The array is simply a way to package together a collection of values.

The familiar assignment rules apply to array elements. For example, a string constant cannot be assigned to an array element that was declared to store double values:

```
// ERROR: Cannot implicitly convert type 'string' to 'double'
x[2] = "Wrong type of literal";

// C# implicitly converts 'int' to 'double'
x[2] = 123;    // Okay
```

Since any two double values can use the arithmetic operators, array elements of type double can also be used in arithmetic expressions, like this:

```
x[2] = x[0] + x[1];    // Store 8.3 into the third array element
```

Keyboard input can also be used to store a value into an array element, like this:

```
Console.Write("Enter x[3]: ");
x[3] = double.Parse(Console.ReadLine());

Console.Write("Enter x[4]: ");
x[4] = double.Parse(Console.ReadLine());
```

Dialogue

```
Enter x[3]: 9.9
Enter x[4]: 5.1
```

After a user inputs 9.9 and 5.1 into the fourth and fifth array elements x[3] and x[4], and given the previous assignments that were made to the first three array elements, the state of the array named x looks like the table below:

State of x (all elements are initialized to 0.0 when the array is constructed)

index	value
0	2.6
1	5.7
2	8.3
3	9.9
4	5.1
5	0.0
6	0.0
7	0.0

Arrays do not always have to be filled to capacity with meaningful values. In the array shown above, if the elements x[5] through x[7] are never used, it doesn't matter what is in them. Often, a programmer declares an array with a maximum capacity that is only a prediction of the maximum number of elements expected. You will often use a separate integer variable—n is used here often—to store the number of meaningful elements. An array will often have meaningful values only in the elements referenced from 0 through n - 1, rather than from 0 through its *capacity* -1.

Out-of-Range Indexes

As mentioned above, array indexes are checked to ensure that they are within the proper range of 0 through *capacity* -1. The following assignment results in an exception:

```
x[8] = 4.5;   // This out-of-range index causes an exception
```

The program terminates prematurely, with a message like the one shown below (the output shows the out-of-range index, which is 8 for array x):

```
Unhandled exception of type 'System.IndexOutOfRangeException' occurred
```

This might seem to be a nuisance. However, without this subscript range checking, out-of-range indexes would otherwise destroy the state of other objects in memory in a seemingly random manner. This causes difficult-to-detect bugs in your applications. More dramatically, it could make the computer hang or crash. In C#, you get the more acceptable occurrence of an IndexOutOfRangeException message, as shown above.

Array Processing with Loops

Programmers must frequently access many consecutive array elements. For example, you often must reference every meaningful element in an array. The C# for loop provides a convenient way to do this. If n is the number of meaningful elements, the number of repetitions is known in advance (n). The loop-counting variable (index below) can range from 0 through n - 1.

```
int n = 5; // n represents the number of meaningful elements

// Display the meaningful elements of x, the first n elements
Console.WriteLine("The first {0} elements of x: ", n);

for (int index = 0;  index < n;  index++)
{
   Console.WriteLine(x[index]);
}
```

Output

```
The first 5 elements of x:
2.6
5.7
8.3
9.9
5.1
```

In the above program, the first n elements of x are accessed by changing the int variable named index. This variable acts both as the loop counter, and as an array index inside the for loop (x[index]). With index serving both roles, the specific array element accessed as x[index] depends on the current value of index. For example, when index is 0, x[index] accesses the first element in the array named x; when index is 4, x[index] accesses the fifth element.

Here is another way to access the elements of an array. This for loop inspects the meaningful (0 through n - 1) array elements to find the largest value:

```
// Assume the first element is the smallest.
// If n==0, the smallest will be 0.
double largest = x[0];

// Set the largest to be the value less than all other doubles
// Compare all other array elements, x[1] through x[n-1]
for (int index = 1;  index < n;  index++)
{
   if (x[index] > largest)
      largest = x[index];
}

// Display the largest
Console.WriteLine("Largest number in the array is {0}", largest);
```

Output

```
Largest number in the array is 9.9
```

Remember that an array often stores fewer meaningful elements than its capacity. Therefore, you will need to maintain an int variable to store the number of elements in the array that have been given meaningful values. In the previous code, n was used for this purpose. Only the first five elements were searched, since those were the only ones with meaningful values. If the search had not been limited to the meaningful elements (indexed as 0 through n - 1), the smallest element would not be 2.6 (x[0]). Instead, it would be 0, which is the value of the three elements at the end of the array. If this program had been looking for the smallest value, it would have ended up with the wrong result.

The C# foreach loop also works effectively on arrays, because arrays can be considered collections. Recall the general form of the foreach loop:

foreach (*variable-type variable-name* **in** *collection-name*)
{
  statement(s) to execute;
}

349

To use a `foreach` loop on an array, write the array's name as the *collection-name* field of the loop header, and use the array elements' type as the *variable-type* field. The following example demonstrates this:

Code Sample: Class UseForeach

```
 1  using System;
 2
 3  class UseForeach
 4  {
 5    static void Main()
 6    {
 7      int[] numbers = new int[4];
 8      numbers[0] = 42;
 9      numbers[1] = 10;
10      numbers[2] = 8;
11      numbers[3] = 1;
12
13      foreach (int num in numbers)
14      {
15        Console.WriteLine("The element's value: {0}", num);
16      }
17    }
18  }
```

Output

```
The element's value: 42
The element's value: 10
The element's value: 8
The element's value: 1
```

The only word of caution when using a `foreach` loop with an array is that it iterates over every element in the array, not just the ones with meaningful values. Consider, for example, the task of finding the smallest element of an array; it could be written with a `foreach` loop, but this loop would also consider the elements past the end of the meaningful elements. This might cause the program to get an answer other than the intended one.

The following program demonstrates this mistake:

Code Sample: Class MisuseForeach

```
1  using System;
2
3  class MisuseForeach
4  {
5    static void Main()
6    {
7      // find the smallest element value; expected result is 2
8      int[] numbers = new int[10];
9      numbers[0] = 15;
10     numbers[1] = 2;
11     numbers[2] = 29;
12     numbers[3] = 101;
13
14     int smallest = numbers[0];
15
16     foreach (int element in numbers)
17     {
18       if (element < smallest)
19         smallest = element;
20     }
21
22     Console.WriteLine("Smallest number in the array is {0}",
23                       smallest);
24   }
25 }
```

Output

```
Smallest number in the array is 0
```

The preceding program did not have the expected result of 2 because elements 4 through 9 of the array numbers still had their initial default value of 0. This value was smaller than 2 when the loop examined those elements. Remember that foreach loops are useful for concise iteration through an entire array, but should be used only when every element in the array has a valid value that you want the program to examine. When the array is not completely populated with meaningful values, a for loop is preferred.

As shown in this section, the Determinate Loop pattern makes it easy to perform *array processing*—the inspection of, or modification of, a selected number of array elements. The foreach loop looks at all elements of an array. You can process only array elements that have valid values by using a `for` loop and limiting the range to a predetermined number of elements (n here).

In the rest of this chapter, various array processing algorithms will be covered. These include:

- Displaying all array elements
- Finding the sum, average, or highest of all array elements
- Searching for a given value in an array (with two different algorithms)
- Arranging elements in a certain order (ordering numbers from largest to smallest, or alphabetizing an array of strings from smallest to largest)

Self-Check

Use this initialization to answer the questions that follow:

```
int[] x = new int[100];
```

7-1   How many integers may be properly stored in x?

7-2   Which integer is used as the index to access the first element in x?

7-3   Which integer is used as the index to access the last element in x?

7-4   What is the value of x[23]?

7-5   Write code that stores 78 into the first element of x.

7-6   Write code that stores 1 into x[99], 2 into x[98], 3 into x[97], ..., 99 into x[1], and 100 into x[0]. Use a `for` loop.

7-7   Write code that displays all elements of x on separate lines. Use a `for` loop.

7-8   What happens when this code executes: x[-1] = 100;

7-9   Write the output generated by the following code:

```
int max = 10;
int[] intArray = new int[max];
for (int j = 0; j < max; j++)
{
    intArray[j] = j;
}
int low = 0;
int high = max - 1;
while (low < high)
{
```

```
    Console.WriteLine("{0} {1}", intArray[low] ,intArray[high]);
    low++;
    high--;
}
```

Arrays of Objects

The examples so far have focused on arrays of simple types such as `int` and `double`, but arrays can also store elements of more complex types, like `string` or `DateTime`. Just as with the simpler types, you can use subscript notation to identify the individual elements of these more complex types. Combining the array subscript notation with the standard *object-name . property-or-method-name* notation gives the desired effect.

General Form: Sending messages to individual array elements

array-name[index].property-name
array-name[index].method-name(arguments)
Examples:
```
string[] names = new string[3];
names[0] = "Jody";
names[0] = names[0].ToUpper();


BankAccount[] accts = new BankAccount[100];
accts[7] = new BankAccount("Hall", 0.00);
accts[7].Deposit(10.00);
Console.WriteLine(accts[7].Balance);
```

The `index` distinguishes the specific object that the message is to be sent to. For example, the uppercase equivalent of `name[0]` (this element has the value `"Jody"`) is returned with this expression:

```
names[0].ToUpper() // The first name in an array of strings
```

The expression `names.ToUpper()` (without the `[0]` subscript) is a syntax error because it attempts to find the uppercase version of the entire array, not one of its `string` elements. The `ToUpper` method is not defined for an array object, only for a `string` that is an element of an array.

We will now see how you could deposit a $5.00 bonus to all `BankAccount` elements in an array. The program will first set up a miniature database of four `BankAccount` objects. *Note:* A constructor call—with new—can generate a reference to any type of object. Therefore, a statement such as the one shown below can be used to construct one of the BankAccount elements. This assignment constructs a BankAccount object with the ID "Hall" and a balance of 0.0. The same technique is used to construct the other three BankAccount objects that will be used, but with different initial balances.

```
// Construct object, assign reference
accts[0] = new BankAccount("Hall", 0.00);
```

The reference to this object is stored in the first array element, accts[0]. After all four BankAccount objects are created, a Deposit message will be sent to each element in the array of references to BankAccount objects.

Code Sample: Class AnArrayOfAccounts

```
 1  // Deposit 5.00 to each array element and then show all elements
 2  using System;
 3
 4  public class AnArrayOfAccounts
 5  {
 6    static void Main()
 7    {
 8      BankAccount[] accts = new BankAccount[100];
 9
10      // Initialize the first n elements
11      accts[0] = new BankAccount("Hall", 0.00);
12      accts[1] = new BankAccount("Small", 100.00);
13      accts[2] = new BankAccount("Ewall", 200.00);
14      accts[3] = new BankAccount("Westphall", 300.00);
15      int n = 4;
16      // Only the first n elements of account are meaningful
17
18      // Deposit 5.00 to all BankAccount objects
19      for (int index = 0;  index < n;  index++)
20      {
21        accts[index].Deposit(5.00);
22        Console.WriteLine(accts[index]);
23      }
24    }
25  }
```

Output

```
Hall $5.00
Small $105.00
Ewall $205.00
Westphall $305.00
```

The same idea applies to properties. To get the balance of any individual array element, just apply the `Balance` property to an individual element, using a subscript. The following loop adds up the assets of all `BankAccount` elements by getting the balance of each array element and adding it to the sum.

```
double assets = 0;
for (int index = 0; index < n; index ++)
{
   assets += accts[index].Balance;
}
Console.WriteLine("Assets {0:C}", assets);
```

Output

```
Assets $620.00
```

What Arrays Actually Store: Values vs. References

C# arrays store both general categories of C# types: value types and reference types. If an array is declared to store value types such as `int []`, `double[]`, or `char[]`, the integer, double and character values are stored directly in the array. However, if an array is declared to store a reference type, such as `string[]` or `BankAccount []`, references to those objects are stored directly into the array.

The following code constructs two arrays and initializes all five elements of both arrays. Because `balance` is a `double` type, its values are stored in the array. Because `name` is a `string` type, references to string objects are stored in this array.

```
// Declare two arrays with the capacity to store up to five elements
double[] balance = new double[5];
string[] name = new string[5];
```

```
// Store the actual double values.
balance[0]  =  0.00;
balance[1]  =  111.11;
balance[2]  =  222.22;
balance[3]  =  333.33;
balance[4]  =  444.44;

// Store references to string objects.
name[0]  =  "Jody";
name[1]  =  "Rachael";
name[2]  =  "Troy";
name[3]  =  "Neha";
name[4]  =  "Jim";
```

The values referenced by the arrays can be pictured as follows, indicating that the arrays
balances and names store five different values. In this case, balances is a collection of double
values, and name stores five references to string objects. The following figure shows the values
of each array element.

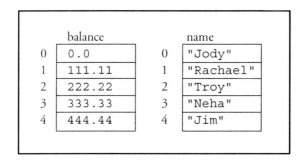

Figure 7.3: Values of Array Elements

Although the picture for the double values of the arrays is accurate, the actual values stored
in names are reference values, not the state shown. A more accurate picture of names is shown
below, where the arrows represent the references to the string objects, located elsewhere in
memory.

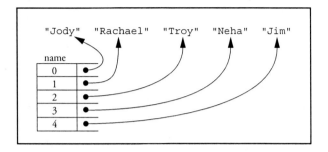

Figure 7.4: References to Array Elements

The same assignment rules apply for array elements as for individual variables. If a value type is assigned to an array element, a copy of the value is stored into the array element. If a reference type is assigned to an array element, the reference to the object is copied. Value type variables have their own copy of the data. An operation on one variable does not affect other variables. However, more than one reference type variable can refer to the same object. Therefore, operations on one reference variable can affect the same object that is referred to by another variable. Consider the following code. It eventually has two references to the same object with the id of "b".

Code Sample: Class ArrayReferenceExample

```
 1 using System;
 2
 3 class ArrayReferenceExample
 4 {
 5   static void Main()
 6   {
 7     BankAccount[] accounts = new BankAccount[3];
 8
 9     // Store references to 5 new BankAccount objects
10     accounts[0] = new BankAccount("a", 1.00);
11     accounts[1] = new BankAccount("b", 2.00);
12     accounts[2] = new BankAccount("c", 3.00);
13
14     Console.WriteLine("b's balance {0:C}", accounts[1].Balance);
15
16     // Have two array elements refer to the same object
17     accounts[0] = accounts[1];
18
```

```
19        // Send a message to an object referenced by accounts[0]
20        accounts[0].Deposit(555.55);
21
22        // see that the object reference by accounts[1] has changed
23        Console.WriteLine("b's balance {0:C}", accounts[1].Balance);
24    }
25 }
```

Output

```
b's balance $2.00
b's balance $557.55
```

After the assignment of the reference value in accounts[1] to accounts[0], both accounts[0] and accounts[1] store a reference to the same BankAccount. The Deposit message to accounts[0] also changed the object referenced by accounts[1].

Self-Check

7-10 Using the two arrays just shown, write the output generated by the following program fragment:

```
BankAccount[] tinyBank = new BankAccount[5];
// Store references to 5 new BankAccount objects
tinyBank[0] = new BankAccount(name[0], balance[0]);
tinyBank[1] = new BankAccount(name[1], balance[1]);
tinyBank[2] = new BankAccount(name[2], balance[2]);
tinyBank[3] = new BankAccount(name[3], balance[3]);
tinyBank[4] = new BankAccount(name[4], balance[4]);

// Send messages to each array element
for (int j = 0; j < 5; j++)
{
  Console.WriteLine("{0} {1}",
  tinyBank[j].ID, tinyBank[j].Balance);
}
```

7-11 Write code that displays the ToString version of all BankAccount objects referenced by tinyBank that have a balance greater than 150.00.

7-12 Write the output generated by the following code:

```
int n = 8;
int[] x = new int[n];
for (int j = 0; j < n; j++)
{
  x[j] = j * 2;
}

for (int j = 0; j < n; j = j + 2)
{
  x[j] = x[j + 1];
}

for (int j = 0; j < n; j++)
{
  Console.Write("{0} ", x[j]);
}
```

7-13   Write the output generated by the following code:

```
string[] s = new string[10];
// Initialize the first n elements of s
int n = 4;
s[0] = "First";
s[1] = "Second";
s[2] = "Third";
s[n - 1] = "FourthAndFinal";

// Do something with all four array elements
for (int j = 0; j < n; j++)
{
  Console.WriteLine(s[j].Substring(s[j].Length-2), 2);
}
```

Array Initializers

C# provides a quick and easy way to construct and initialize arrays without using new or declaring a capacity: declare the array as variable, and assign a collection of values (separated by commas) between curly braces. This is called an *array initializer*. For example, the following code initializes an array of int values:

```
int[] test = {76, 74, 100, 62, 89};
```

The compiler sets the capacity of test to be the number of elements between { and }; in the preceding case, the number of elements would be five. The first value is assigned to test[0], the second value to test[1], and so on. Therefore, the previous *initializer list* is equivalent to the following six lines of code:

```
int[] test = new int[5];
test[0] = 76;
test[1] = 74;
test[2] = 100;
test[3] = 62;
test[4] = 89;
```

General Form: Declaring / Initializing an array with an Array Initializer List

type[] *array-name* = {*value0*, *value1*, ..., *value N*};

Examples:

```
string[] names = {"Bill", "Melinda", "Steve"};
int[] coolNums = {1, 42, 17, 63};
BankAccount[] accts = {
   new BankAccount("Account 0", 0.00),
   new BankAccount("Account 1", 1.00)
};
```

To use an initializer list with complex object types like BankAccount, the syntax is similar, but it has a separate new instance for each object created. The constructor for that type of object is called to initialize each complex object in the array:

```
BankAccount[] accounts = { new BankAccount("Kelly", 1234.56),
                           new BankAccount("Barney", 234.56),
                           new BankAccount("Chris", 34.56) };

// Display the ToString version of each
Console.WriteLine(accounts[0]);
Console.WriteLine(accounts[1]);
Console.WriteLine(accounts[2]);
```

Output

```
Kelly $1,234.56
Barney $234.56
Chris $34.56
```

The Length Property

The *Length property* returns the capacity of an array. It is often used to avoid out-of-range index exceptions. For example, the index range of the previous array named `accounts` is 0 through `accounts.Length` - 1. The capacity is referenced as the array name, a dot, and the read-only property named `Length`.

```
// Output: Capacity of accounts is 3
Console.WriteLine("Capacity of accounts is {0}", accounts.Length);
```

This next example constructs an array of `string` objects and uses the `Length` property in a loop.

Code Sample: ShowTAs Class

```
 1 using System;
 2
 3 public class ShowTAs
 4 {
 5   static void Main()
 6   {
 7     string[] TAs = {
 8       "Kelly Heffner", "Barney Boisvert", "*Canceled*",
 9       "Chris Schulte", "*Canceled*", "Stuart Smith",
10       "Andy Lenards", "Brent Haas", "Stuart Smith"
11     };
12
13     Console.WriteLine("CS227 TAs for {0} sections", TAs.Length);
14     Console.WriteLine("Sec#  TA name");
15     Console.WriteLine("====  ==============");
16     for (int j = 0; j < TAs.Length; j++)
17     {
18       Console.WriteLine(" #{0}   {1}", (j + 1), TAs[j]);
19     }
20   }
21 }
```

Output

```
CS227 TAs for 9 sections
Sec#  TA name
====  ==============
 #1   Kelly Heffner
 #2   Barney Boisvert
 #3   *Canceled*
 #4   Chris Schulte
 #5   *Canceled*
 #6   Stuart Smith
 #7   Andy Lenards
 #8   Brent Haas
 #9   Stuart Smith
```

Note that using a foreach loop might have eliminated the need for using TAs.Length in the for loop above. One of C#'s nice features is that it is powerful enough that there is usually more than one way to solve a given problem.

Arrays as Parameters to Methods

You may sometimes find it useful to write a class with a method that takes an array as an argument. For example, you could write a method Max that takes an array of numbers and returns the element in the array with the highest value. For a method to take an array as an argument, the following syntax must be used:

General Form: Method declaration with Array parameter

return-type method-name(type[] *array-parameter-name*)

Examples:
```
void ApplyInterest(BankAccount[] accounts)
int Max(int[] numbers)
void Sort(int startIndex, int endIndex, double[] nums)
static void Main(string[] args)
```

Notice that a method that has an array parameter can also take other, non-array parameters if necessary.

Calling a method that requires an array argument is the same as calling other methods, except that the name of an array of the right type must be used as one of the arguments. For example, to call the Sort method above, one would need code like the following:

```
double[] myNumbers = {2.4, 1.7, -3.5, 2.817, -15.9};
Sort(0, myNumbers.Length - 1, myNumbers);    // call the Sort method
```

The following method accepts an array of strings as an argument. It then prints each array element on a separate line, with an increasing amount of leading white space.

Code Sample: Class ArrayParameter

```
1  using System;
2
3  class ArrayParameter
4  {
5    static void Main()
6    {
7      string[] strs = {"First", "Second", "Third", "Fourth"};
8      PrintStaggered(strs);
9    }
10
11   static void PrintStaggered(string[] args)
12   {
13     string spacer = "";
14     foreach (string arg in args)
15     {
16       Console.WriteLine("{0} {1}", spacer, arg);
17       spacer += "  ";
18     }
19   }
20 }
```

Output

```
First
   Second
      Third
         Fourth
```

The reference to `strs` is passed as an argument to the `Print` method. Inside the `Print` method, the parameter `args` refers to the same array object that is referenced by `strs` in `Main`. This is important to notice because it means that an array passed as a parameter to a method could have its elements modified by the method.

The following method is similar to the previous one. It prints each array element on a separate line, with an increasing amount of white space. Then, it does the same with a capitalized version of each array element.

Code Sample: Class ArrayParameter2

```
 1  using System;
 2
 3  class ArrayParameter2
 4  {
 5    static void Main()
 6    {
 7      string[] strs = {"First", "Second", "Third", "Fourth"};
 8      PrintStaggered(strs);
 9      Capitalize(strs);
10      PrintStaggered(strs);
11    }
12
13    // Makes all strings in the given array be upper case.
14    static void Capitalize(string[] args)
15    {
16      for (int index = 0; index < args.Length; index++)
17        args[index] = args[index].ToUpper();
18    }
19
20    static void PrintStaggered(string[] args)
21    {
22      string spacer = "";
23      foreach (string arg in args)
24      {
25        Console.WriteLine("{0} {1}", spacer, arg);
26        spacer += "   ";
27      }
28    }
29  }
```

Output

```
First
    Second
        Third
            Fourth
 FIRST
     SECOND
         THIRD
             FOURTH
```

Command-Line Arguments

In the programs in this textbook, you have seen `Main` methods with the following heading:

```
static void Main()
```

However, it is also legal to declare `Main` in other ways. For starters, it is legal to put the public access modifier on `Main`. In fact, many people write `Main` as public for clarity. But more importantly, it is legal to declare `Main` to have a parameter, which is an array of strings.

```
static void Main(string[] args)
```

This array `args` (it can be called anything you like) represents an optional array of command-line arguments that are passed to the program. A *command-line argument* is a value typed on the console when the program is run, which gets passed in to `Main` in its `args` array. If no arguments are passed, `args` is an empty 0-element array; otherwise, each whitespace-delimited argument passed to the program occupies an element in the `args` array. Here is an example:

Code Sample: Class WriteArguments

```
1 using System;
2
3 class WriteArguments
4 {
5     static void Main(string[] args)
6     {
7         foreach (string arg in args)
```

```
 8          {
 9              Console.WriteLine("argument: {0}", arg);
10          }
11      }
12  }
```

The above program writes every argument passed to it on the screen. If it is compiled into an executable program named `WriteArguments.exe` in the folder `C:\My Documents\Ch7` and the program is executed on the console like this,

`C:\My Documents\Ch7> WriteArguments Here are a bunch of arguments!`

then the output will be as follows:

```
argument: Here
argument: are
argument: a
argument: bunch
argument: of
argument: arguments!
```

The parameter `args` will be passed a reference to the array of strings that have been entered from the command line (see dialogue below). The number of arguments entered at the command line is known as `args.Length`. The array named `args` references the array of strings built by C# when the program runs.

The following similar program shows the number of arguments and information about each one:

Code Sample: Class CommandLine

```
 1  // This program is in the file named CommandLine.cs
 2  using System;
 3
 4  class CommandLine
 5  {
 6      static void Main(string[] args)
 7      {
 8          Console.WriteLine("Number of command line parameters = {0}",
 9                          args.Length);
10
11          for(int index = 0; index < args.Length; index++)
12          {
13              Console.WriteLine("args[{0}]: {1}", index, args[index]);
```

```
14
15        }
16     }
17 }
```

C:\My Documents\Ch7> CommandLine one two three four

Dialogue 1

Number of command line parameters = 4

args[0]: one

args[1]: two

args[2]: three

args[3]: four

Dialogue 2

C:\My Documents\Ch7> CommandLine c:\temp C:\C#Project

Number of command line parameters = 2

args[0]: c:\temp

args[1]: C:\C#Project

Dialogue 3

C:\My Documents\Ch7> CommandLine

Number of command line parameters = 0

See Appendix B for a more detailed explanation about how to run C# programs and pass arguments to them.

Self-Check

7-14   Write the output generated by this code:

```
string[] names = { "Abe", "Bev", "Cy", "Deb" };
foreach (string name in names)
   Console.WriteLine(names[j].ToUpper());
```

7-15   Write the output generated by the following code:

```
int[] temp;
int[] x = new int[3];
int newCapacity;

x[0] = 11;
x[1] = 22;
x[2] = 33;
Console.WriteLine("current length of x: {0}", x.Length);
Console.WriteLine(x[0]);
Console.WriteLine(x[1]);
Console.WriteLine(x[2]);

newCapacity = 2 * x.Length;

temp = new int[newCapacity];
for (int j = 0;  j < x.Length;  j++)
   temp[j] = x[j];
x = temp;
temp = null;
Console.WriteLine("current length of x: {0}", x.Length);
Console.WriteLine(x[0]);
Console.WriteLine(x[1]);
Console.WriteLine(x[2]);

newCapacity = x.Length / 2;
temp = new int[newCapacity - 1 ];   // Be careful
for (int j = 0;  j < temp.Length;  j++)
   temp[j] = x[j];
x = temp;
temp = null;
Console.WriteLine("current length of x: {0}", x.Length);
Console.WriteLine(x[0]);
Console.WriteLine(x[1]);
Console.WriteLine(x[2]);   // Be careful!
```

7.2 Array Fields

Arrays are often used as fields. An object containing an array field can store a collection of elements. These objects can also keep track of the number of meaningful elements as new elements are added.

Consider the following QuizScores class that stores a collection of numbers. The quiz field is an array of int values to represent individual quizzes. The size field stores the number of quizzes stored in any `QuizScores` object. Both fields are declared inside the class, but not inside a method. They are both available to all methods of the class.

Code Sample: QuizScores Class

```
1  using System;
2
3  // Build a class to demonstrate a class with an array field
4  public class QuizScores
5  {
6    // Fields
7    private int[] quiz;   // array is declared, but not constructed
8    private int size;
9
10   // Build an empty list of
11   public QuizScores()
12   {
13     quiz = new int[100];
14     size = 0;
15   }
16
17   // Place the new quiz score as the last element in the array
18   public void Add(int aQuiz)
19   {
20     quiz[size] = aQuiz;
21     size++;
22   }
23
24   // Determine the average of all quiz scores so far.
25   // Return -1.0 when there are no quizzes to average.
26   public double Average()
27   {
28     // Find sum
29     double sum = 0.0;
30     for (int index = 0;  index < size;  index++)
31     {
32       sum += quiz[index];
33     }
34
35     // Return average or -1 if no quizzes have been added yet.
36     if (size == 0)
37       return -1.0;
38     else
39       return (sum/size);
40   }
41
42   // for testing
```

369

```
43    static void Main()
44    {
45      QuizScores quiz1 = new QuizScores();
46      QuizScores quiz2 = new QuizScores();
47
48      // Add a few quiz scores to the first quiz
49      quiz1.Add(90);
50      quiz1.Add(84);
51      quiz1.Add(80);
52
53      // Add a couple of quiz scores to the second quiz
54      quiz2.Add(100);
55      quiz2.Add(82);
56
57      Console.WriteLine("Average for quiz 1 {0:F1}", quiz1.Average());
58      Console.WriteLine("Average for quiz 2 {0:F1}", quiz2.Average());
59    }
60
61  } // End class QuizScores
```

Output

```
Average for quiz 1 84.7
Average for quiz 2 91.0
```

Both fields are initialized in the constructor. Each new QuizScore object should have zero elements. Therefore, size is initialized to 0. As shown by the constructor, the programmer has predicted that there will never be more than 100 quiz scores stored in any one QuizScores object.

Meaningful elements (actual quiz scores) are put into the array with the Add method. When size is zero, aQuiz is added at quiz[0] and size is incremented to 1 to indicate that there is one quiz in the array. When a second quiz is added, the int argument passed during the Add message will be stored into quiz[1] before size increments to 2.

Any attempt to add more than 100 quizzes to a newly constructed QuizScores object will result in an IndexOutOfRangeException (a more graceful alternative for adding when the array is filled to capacity is shown later in this chapter).

The Average method shows that array processing can be hidden inside a method. The testing code shows that there may be more than one QuizScore object. Two are constructed, with a few quiz scores added before showing the average for both.

Arrays can store references to any type in C#. For example, an array of `QuizScores` is now possible, since a `QuizScores` type has been built:

```
int n = 2;
QuizScores[] allQuizzes = new QuizScores[n];
allQuizzes[0] = quiz1;
allQuizzes[1] = quiz2;
```

Moreover, you can ask each array element of type `QuizScore` for its `Average`.

```
// Find average of all quizzes
double sum = 0.0;
for (int index = 0; index < n;  index++)
{ // Ask each QuizScore object for the average of quiz scores.
  sum += allQuizzes[index].Average();
}

Console.WriteLine("Average for {0} quizzes = {1:F1}%", n, (sum/n));
```

Output

```
Average for 2 quizzes = 87.8%
```

Self-Check

7-16 Write class `RestaurantBill` that keeps track of all menu items of a bill at a restaurant. The class must have a method named `Add` to add items ordered from the menu to the bill. It must also have a method named `Show` to show all individual items, the sum of all items, the tax (at 6%), and the total (all items plus the tax). The code shown here must generate the output below.

```
RestaurantBill aBill = new RestaurantBill();
aBill.Add(10.00);
Console.WriteLine(aBill);


RestaurantBill bill2 = new RestaurantBill();
bill2.Add(3.25);
bill2.Add(4.75);
bill2.Add(10.00);
Console.WriteLine(bill2);
```

OUTPUT

```
===Restaurant Bill===
1) 10.00
Tax: $0.60
Total: $10.60

===Restaurant Bill===
1)  3.25
2)  4.75
3) 10.00
Tax: $1.08
Total: $19.08
```

7.3   Sequential Search

When references to many objects are stored in an array, the elements are stored in the computer's memory. Because access to memory is fast, the objects can be accessed conveniently, quickly, and frequently. Often a collection will be searched for a particular element. Examples include, but certainly are not limited to, searching for a student name in the registrar's database, looking up the price of an item in an inventory, or obtaining information about a bank account.

One algorithm used to "look up" an array element is called sequential search. The *sequential search* algorithm attempts to locate a given element by comparing the element being sought to every object in the array. The algorithm searches in a sequential (one-after-the-other) fashion, until either the element is found or there are no more array elements left to search.

This sequential search algorithm will be demonstrated by finding a string in an array of string objects. Although the search element here is a person's name, the array being searched could contain other types of objects—numbers, students, or employees, for example. First, consider a class that constructs an array of references to string objects, which begins like this:

Code Sample: Class FriendList

```
1  using System;
2
3  // Build a class to demonstrate sequential search
4  public class FriendList
5  {
6    private string[] my_friends;
7    private int my_size;
8
9    // Build a list of friends with the same data each time. This is
10   // not realistic, but makes it easier to show sequential search.
11   public FriendList()
```

```
12   {
13     // Make the array capable of storing up to 10 references
14     my_friends = new string[10];
15     // All 10 elements have default object value of null.
16
17     // Now set the number of meaningful elements in the array.
18     my_size = 5;
19
20     // Now initialize the first my_size elements of the array.
21     my_friends[0] = "DEBBIE";
22     my_friends[1] = "JOEY";
23     my_friends[2] = "BOBBIE";
24     my_friends[3] = "SUSIE";
25     my_friends[4] = "MIKEY";
26     // my_friends[5] through my_friends[9] are null
27   }
28
29   // To be arranged. It currently returns null just
30   // so this class compiles. Later on it will
31   // return null only if searchName is not found.
32   public string Find(string searchName)
33   {
34     return null; // This will be designed in the next section
35   }
36
37   // for testing
38   static void Main()
39   {
40     FriendList myFriendList = new FriendList();
41
42     Console.Write("Enter name to search for [UPPERCASE]: ");
43     string searchName = Console.ReadLine().Trim().ToUpper();
44
45     // Determine if searchName is in myFriendList
46     string reference = myFriendList.Find(searchName);
47
48     // Report success or failure
49     if (reference != null)
50       Console.WriteLine(reference + " found");
51     else
52       Console.WriteLine(searchName + " not found");
53
54   } // End Main
55 } // End class FriendList
```

Dialogue (the find method is not yet working—it always returns null)

```
Enter name to search for [UPPERCASE]: BOBBIE
BOBBIE not found
```

Self-Check

7-17   What is the value of each of the following expressions?

(a) my_friends[3]

(b) my_friends[4]

(c) my_friends[9]

(d) my_friends[10]

(e) myFriendList.find("JOEY");

(f) myFriendList.find("MIKEY");

Before searching for something, you need to know what that is. The test code above prompts the user for a name from the keyboard. The object named myFriendList and the test code will be used in the next few sections.

Searching When The Element Is in the Array

When searching for an object called searchName in an array, there are at least these two possibilities:

1. searchName is in the array
2. searchName is *not* in the array

First, assume that searchName has the same value as a string in the array named my_friends. With index initialized to 0, the following code begins by comparing searchName to the first array element, also known as my_friends[0]:

```
// This modified version of find from the FriendList
// class works only if searchName is in the array.
public string Find(string searchName)
{
  // Sequential search begins at the first array location
  int index = 0;

  // The loop will terminate as soon as the string is found
  while (searchName != my_friends[index])
```

```
{ // searchName has not yet been found in the array my_friends
  // so prepare to compare searchName to the next array element.
  index++;
}

// Assume the string was found (this will be changed later)
return my_friends[index];
}
```

The loop test, searchName != my_friends[index], evaluates to true as long as the element being searched for has not been found in the searched portion of the array. Each loop iteration increments an array index with index++ to prepare for a comparison of searchName to the next array element. The searchName is first compared to my_friends[0], then my_friends[1], then my_friends[2], and so on. The loop iterates as long as searchName is not found. This code works fine, but only if the string being searched for is in the array. After the search loop terminates, the reference to the existing name is returned.

Dialogue (using the test Main method in FriendList)

```
Enter name to search for [UPPERCASE]: BOBBIE
BOBBIE found
```

The following table traces a successful search for the string "BOBBIE":

		Search for "BOBBIE"		
Iteration	searchName	my_size	index	Array Element Being Compared
Before loop	"BOBBIE"	5	0	N/A
1	"BOBBIE"	5	0	"DEBBIE"
2	"BOBBIE"	5	1	"JOEY"
3	"BOBBIE"	5	2	"BOBBIE"
After loop	"BOBBIE"	5	2	N/A

Self-Check

7-18   What happens in the code above if searchName is not in the array?

Searching When the Element Is Not in the Array

Now consider what happens if the string is not in the array. Each iteration of the loop increments index by +1. However, what will stop the comparisons if searchName is not found in my_friends?

			Example Search: "SOMEONE"	
Loop Iteration	searchName	my_size	index	Array Element Being Compared
Before loop	"SOMEONE"	5	0	N/A
1	"SOMEONE"	5	0	"DEBBIE"
2	"SOMEONE"	5	1	"JOEY"
3	"SOMEONE"	5	2	"BOBBIE"
4	"SOMEONE"	5	3	"SUSIE"
5	"SOMEONE"	5	4	"MIKEY"
6	"SOMEONE"	5	5	null
7	"SOMEONE"	5	6	null
8	"SOMEONE"	5	7	null
9	"SOMEONE"	5	8	null
10	"SOMEONE"	5	9	null

As currently written, the sequential search algorithm does not consider that searchName might not be found. The program terminates with IndexOutOfRangeException. This occurs when the array index == 10 in the loop test. At this point, "SOMEONE" is compared to my_friends[10]. The loop test in the sequential search evaluates like this when index becomes 10:

```
searchName != my_friends[index]

searchName != my_friends[10]   // index 10 is out of range
```

We can improve the sequential search loop by having it terminate when there are no more meaningful elements to look at. This can be accomplished by using my_size to prevent unnecessary comparisons when the element being searched for is not in the array. The loop test can be made to guard against referencing my_friends[index] when index reaches my_size. Both termination conditions are used in the following corrected implementation of the sequential search:

```
// A correct find method to be added to the FriendList class
public string Find(string searchName)
{
  // Sequential search begins at the first array location
  int index = 0;

  // The loop will terminate as soon as the string is found.
  // However, now a check is first made to terminate the loop
  // when index == size. The loop continues as long as there
  // are more elements to look at (indexes 0..size-1) and the
  // searchName does not equal the array element being compared.
  while ((index < my_size) && (searchName != my_friends[index]))
  {
    // searchName has not yet been found in the array my_friends
    // so prepare to compare searchName to the next array element.
    index++;
  }

  // Return a reference to the string or null if not found in array
  if(index < my_size)
    return my_friends[index];
  else
    return null;
}
```

Now Find returns a reference to the string in the array, or it returns null to indicate that the argument searchName was not found. The following dialogues show some possibilities:

Dialogue 1

```
Enter name to search for [UPPERCASE]:  SOMEONE
SOMEONE not found
```

Dialogue 2

```
Enter name to search for [UPPERCASE]:  BOBBIE
BOBBIE found
```

A Special Case: Searching a Full Array

Consider what happens when the array is filled to capacity (add five more names and change my_size from 5 to 10). What happens when the search name is not in the array? The index goes to the capacity in the final while loop evaluation.

```
// Assume the array capacity == my_size and searchName is not in
// my_friends. The index will go to 10 in the final loop test.
while ((index < my_size) && (searchName != my_friends[index]))
         10 <    10    &&             not  evaluated
             false
```

This shows that the order in which tests are done can be important. The subexpression in the loop (index < my_size) was placed first to avoid evaluating my_friends[index] when index == 10. Only when this first subexpression is true will the second subexpression be evaluated. If index < my_size evaluates to false, the comparison of string values is not made.

This is due to *short circuit Boolean evaluation*. Since (false && *anything*) is always false, the second subexpression does not need to be evaluated, and is ignored. This short circuiting built into C# to make programs run faster. Not evaluating unnecessary subexpressions improves runtime performance. And here, it also helps avoid evaluating an expression that when would otherwise cause an exception.

The following evaluation shows what happens when searchName is not found in an array that is filled to capacity. This illustrates the second reason for comparing index to my_size before evaluating the array index.

```
while ((searchName != my_friends[index]) && (index < my_size))
       ("SOMEONE" != my_friends[10])    && (10 <    10 ))
```

Output

Unhandled exception of type 'System.IndexOutOfRangeException' occurred

---

Other Implementations of `Find`

Without this trick of short circuit Boolean evaluation, the code would have to be written another way to ensure that index is never used when it is equal to my_size. Here is an alternative implementation that uses a bool variable named found that avoids this special case.

```
public string Find(string searchName)
{
  int index = 0;
  bool found = false;

  while ((index < my_size) && (!found))
  {
```

```
   if(searchName == my_friends[index])
     found = true;
   else
     index++;
}

if(found)
  return my_friends[index];
else
  return null;
}
```

However, because a program can have multiple `return` statements, the sequential search can also be shortened as follows. Here, the `for` loop increments `index`. As soon as `searchName` is found, the array reference is returned. If there is no match, the `for` loop terminates when `index` reaches `my_size`. At that point, `null` can be returned.

```
// This is perhaps the shortest implementation of sequential search.
public string Find(string searchName)
{
   for(int index = 0; index < my_size; index++)
   {
     if(searchName == my_friends[index])
        return my_friends[index];
   }
   return null;
}
```

Self-Check

7-19 How many comparisons (iterations of the search loop) are necessary when `searchName` matches `my_friends[0]`?

7-20 How many comparisons are necessary when `searchName` matches `my_friends[3]`?

7-21 How many comparisons are necessary when `searchName` is not in `my_friends`?

7-22 How many sequential search comparisons occur when the array has no useful data in it, that is, when `my_size == 0`?

7.4 Developing a Collection Class

As you continue your study of computing fundamentals, you will spend a fair amount of time exploring ways to manage collections of data. The C# array is but one of several major data storage structures. There are also classes such as ArrayList, Hashtable, Queue, and Stack to manage collections of objects with higher-level messages such as Add, Remove, BinarySearch, Enqueue, Push, and Pop. These classes are known as *collection classes* because they group many elements into a single object. Collection classes have the following characteristics:

    ○ The main responsibility of a collection class is to store a collection of objects.
    ○ Objects may be added and removed from a collection.
    ○ A collection class allows clients to access the individual elements.
    ○ A collection class may have search-and-sort operations for locating a particular item.
    ○ Some collections allow duplicate elements, other collections do not.

Collections are realized in a variety of ways. For example, the C# array uses subscript notation to access individual elements. The author-supplied AccountList class developed in this section exemplifies a collection class approach for storing a collection of objects. It presents users with messages, and it hides the array processing details inside the methods.

An instance of the AccountList class allows a large number of BankAccounts to be stored under one name. The AccountList class has the following characteristics:

    ○ An AccountList object can store references only to BankAccount objects.
    ○ AccountList elements have unique IDs. An attempt to add a BankAccount with an existing ID will fail.
    ○ BankAccount elements need not be in any particular order.
    ○ Elements can be removed from the collection (if the given ID exists).
    ○ Elements can be retrieved with the ID.
    ○ All elements can be seen with a ToString.
    ○ An AccountList object has a Size property to answer how many elements are in the collection.
    ○ An AccountList object can store any number of BankAccount objects (up to the memory capacity of the computer).

The methods and behavior of the class about to be developed are shown in the following code (messages are shown in boldface):

```
1 using System;
2
3 class TestAccountList
```

```
 4 {
 5   static void Main()
 6   {
 7     AccountList accounts = new AccountList();
 8     Console.WriteLine("Size = {0}", accounts.Size);
 9     Console.WriteLine("Elements = {0}", accounts);
10     // Output:
11     // Size = 0
12     // Elements = []
13
14     BankAccount a1 = new BankAccount("Kim", 100.00);
15     BankAccount a2 = new BankAccount("Devon", 200.00);
16     BankAccount a3 = new BankAccount("Chris", 300.00);
17     BankAccount a4 = new BankAccount("Chris", 400.00);
18     accounts.Add(a1);
19     accounts.Add(a2);
20     accounts.Add(a3);
21     accounts.Add(a4);   // ID Chris exists so a4 will not be added
22     Console.WriteLine("Size = {0}", accounts.Size);
23     Console.WriteLine("Elements = {0}", accounts);
24
25     // Output:
26     // Size = 3
27     // Elements = [Kim $100.00, Devon $200.00, Chris $300.00]
28
29     BankAccount currentAccount = accounts.GetAccountWithID("Chris");
30     Console.WriteLine("Before deposit: {0}", currentAccount);
31     // Output:
32     // Before deposit: Chris $300.00
33
34     currentAccount.Deposit(999.99);
35     currentAccount = accounts.GetAccountWithID("Chris");
36     Console.WriteLine("After deposit: {0}", currentAccount);
37     // Output:
38     // After deposit: Chris $1,299.99
39
40     accounts.RemoveAccountWithID("Chris");
41     accounts.RemoveAccountWithID("Devon");
42     accounts.RemoveAccountWithID("Not Here");
43     Console.WriteLine("Size = {0}", accounts.Size);
44     Console.WriteLine("Elements = {0}", accounts);
45     // Output:
46     // Size = 1
47     // Elements = [Kim $100.00]
48   }
49 }
```

The `AccountList` Constructor

The private fields of the `AccountList` class include an array named `accountArray` for storing a collection of `string` objects, and an integer named `size` to maintain the number of meaningful elements that have been added to the collection. The `AccountList` methods frequently need both of these fields to accomplish their responsibilities. The constructor establishes an empty `AccountList` object by setting `size` to zero. The capacity is set to the arbitrary initial capacity of 10.

```
// A class for storing a collection of BankAccount objects.
public class AccountList
{
  private BankAccount[] accountArray;  // Stores the elements
  private int size;           // Number of elements in this collection

  // Construct an empty (zero elements) collection
  public AccountList()
  {
    accountArray = new BankAccount[10];  // Initial capacity is 10
    size = 0;                 // No elements have been added
  }

  // ...
```

`public bool Add(BankAccount accountToAdd)`

We need a way to add an element at the end of the array, or more specifically, at the first available array location of `accountArray`. The two-step algorithm shown below summarizes how a new `BankAccount` can be added to the first available array position:

Algorithm: Adding an element

`accountArray[size]` = the BankAccount passed to the add method

increment `size` by +1

Both `size` and `accountArray` will be available to the `add` method, since all methods have access to the private fields of their class.

The argument passed to the `add` method is stored in the proper array location, using `size` as the index. Then `size` is incremented to reflect the new addition. Incrementing `size` maintains the correct number of elements in the collection.

Incrementing `size` also conveniently sets up a situation where the next added element is inserted into the proper array location. The array location at `accountArray[size]` is the next place to store a newly added element. This is demonstrated in the following view of the fields before and after adding a fourth `BankAccount` with the ID `"Fourth"`.

Before:

Field	State of accounts, an instance of AccountList
size	3
accountArray[0]	Kim $100.00
accountArray[1]	Devon $200.00
accountArray[2]	Chris $300.00
accountArray[3]	null // accountArray[size] is the next available spot
accountArray[4]	null
. . .	. . .
accountArray[9]	null

After this message is sent to the `AccountList`, the reference to this new `BankAccount` is added at `accountArray[size]`.

```
accounts.Add(new BankAccount("Fourth", 444.44));
```

After:

Field	State of accounts
size	**4**
accountArray[0]	Kim $100.00
accountArray[1]	Devon $200.00,
accountArray[2]	Chris $300.00
accountArray[3]	**Fourth $444.44**
accountArray[4]	null // accountArray[size] is the next available spot
accountArray[5]	null
. . .	. . .
accountArray[9]	null

Before the new `BankAccount` is added, a check is made to ensure that the ID does not already exist (using a private helper method named `IndexOf`). In this case, the `Add` method will return `false`. If the ID of the new account is found in the array, the code checks to ensure that there is enough capacity to add another element. If there is no room, the capacity of the array is doubled with the private helper method `DoubleArrayCapacity`. The new element is then added, and the method returns `true` to indicate a successful add.

```
// Add a BankAccount at the end if its ID is unique to all others
// accountToAdd: Any BankAccount you want to store in this collection.
public bool Add(BankAccount accountToAdd)
{
  bool result = true;

  // First check if the ID is already in the collection.
  // indexOf returns -1 if the ID is not found in accountArray
  if (IndexOf(accountToAdd.ID) != -1)
    result = false; // ID already exists, don't allow
  else
  { // Add the account with an ID property that is
    // unique to all others. First check to ensure
    // array has the capacity to add a new element.
    if (size == accountArray.Length)
      DoubleArrayCapacity();

    // Always add accountToAdd (unless the computer
    // runs out of memory) at the "end" of the
    // meaningful elements in the array
    accountArray[size] = accountToAdd;

    // Make sure size is always increased by one
    size++;
  }

  // Return false only if the account had an ID that already existed
  return result;
}
```

The private helper method `IndexOf` employs a sequential search algorithm to find if another existing element has the same ID. `IndexOf` returns -1 if the ID is not found (the same method will also be used by another method of this class).

```
// Return the index of the first occurrence of accountID as an ID.
// Otherwise return -1 if accountID is not in this collection.
private int IndexOf(string accountID)
```

```
{
  int result = -1;

  // Perform a sequential search on this unordered collection
  int subscript = 0;
  while(subscript < size && result == -1)
  {
    if (accountID == accountArray[subscript].ID)
      result = subscript;
    else
      subscript++;
  }

  // Return -1 if the ID was not found in any array element
  return result;
}
```

If size is at the array's capacity (that is, if size == accountArray.Length), there is not enough room to add the new element. In this case, the array capacity is doubled. The object sends a DoubleArrayCapacity message to itself. The accountArray field will now reference an array with twice the capacity. The original contents (accountArray[0] through accountArray[count - 1]) are copied, so that the collection remains intact. All elements have the same indexes as before.

```
// Change accountArray to have the same elements
// in indexes 0..size - 1 with twice as many
// array locations to store elements.
private void DoubleArrayCapacity()
{
  // Construct a new array with twice the current capacity.
  BankAccount[] temp = new BankAccount[2 * accountArray.Length];

  // Copy all existing elements into the new larger array
  for (int j = 0; j < size; j++)
    temp[j] = accountArray[j];

  // Store reference to the new larger array into this object's field.
  accountArray = temp;
}
```

Size Property

The Size property returns the precise number of elements that are currently in the collection. The private field size is maintained by incrementing it (adding 1) in successful add messages, and decrementing it (subtracting 1) in successful `remove` messages. The constructor initialized `size` to zero to indicate an empty collection.

```
// A property to return the number of elements in this collection
public int Size
{
  get { return size; }
}
```

ToString Method

The `ToString` method is overridden to show all elements, with a comma separating them.

```
public override string ToString()
{
  string result = "[";

  // Concatenate all but the last element as one big string
  for (int j = 0;  j < Size - 1;  j++)
    result += accountArray[j] + ", ";

  // Do not concatenate ", " to the last element
  if (Size > 0)
    result += accountArray[Size-1];

  result += "]";

  return result;
}
```

The loop concatenates the `ToString` version of each element with a separating `", "` between elements, except at the end. Then, if there is at least one element, the last element is concatenated without `", "`.

public BankAccount GetElementWithID(string ID)

The method `GetElementWithID` will return a reference to the `BankAccount` element whose ID matches the ID that is passed as an argument. With this method, any valid `BankAccount` message can be sent to any element stored by the collection. Given the correct ID, this will allow programs using this collection class to find balances, and to allow withdrawals and deposits, for any object.

```
BankAccount currentAccount = accounts.GetAccountWithID("Kim");
Console.WriteLine("Account: {0}", currentAccount);
currentAccount.Deposit(999.99);
currentAccount.Deposit(555.55);
Console.WriteLine("Balance: {0}", currentAccount.Balance);
Console.WriteLine("ID: {0}", currentAccount.ID);
currentAccount.PIN = "0001";
Console.WriteLine("ID: {0}", currentAccount.PIN);
```

Output

```
Account: Kim $100.00
Balance: 1655.54
ID: Kim
ID: 0001
```

The GetElementWithID method uses the private helper method IndexOf to find the account with the string ID. If the index is -1, the ID was not found, and null is returned.

```
public BankAccount GetAccountWithID(string accountID)
{
  BankAccount result = null;    // Assume accountID is not in the array

  int subscript = IndexOf(accountID);

  if(subscript != -1)
    result = accountArray[subscript];  // ID was found

  return result;
}
```

public bool RemoveElementWithID(string ID)

Now consider the method that removes an element. In order to concentrate on the algorithm, remember that accountArray (an array of BankAccount objects) and size (the number of elements) are always available to any AccountList object. The following method heading also provides the ID of the BankAccount to be searched for, and to be removed if found:

```
// Remove the BankAccount with ID == accountID if found.
// Return true if the object was successfully removed or
// false if accounted was not found in this collection.
public bool RemoveAccountWithID(string accountID)
```

If `accountID` is found to equal the ID of one of the array elements, `RemoveAccountWithID` effectively takes out the reference to the object with the given ID. Assuming that the collection currently has the four accounts that were added above, the fields would look like this:

	Before:
Field	**State of `accounts`, an instance of `AccountList`**
`size`	4
`accountArray[0]`	Kim $100.00
`accountArray[1]`	Devon $200.00
`accountArray[2]`	Chris $300.00
`accountArray[3]`	Fourth $444.44
`accountArray[4]`	null // accountArray[size] is the next available spot
`accountArray[5]`	null
. . .	. . .
`accountArray[9]`	null

Assume that the following message is sent to the `AccountList`:

```
accounts.RemoveAccountWithID("Devon");
```

The reference to the `BankAccount` with this ID will be erased by copying the reference to the last `BankAccount` over it.

	After:
Field	**State of `accounts`**
`size`	3
`accountArray[0]`	Kim $100.00
`accountArray[1]`	~~Devon $200.00~~ **Fourth $444.44**
`accountArray[2]`	Chris $300.00
`accountArray[3]`	~~Fourth $444.44~~ **null** // next available spot to add
`accountArray[4]`	null
`accountArray[5]`	null
. . .	. . .
`accountArray[9]`	null

Once found, the reference stored in `accountArray[index]` must somehow be removed from the array, which is currently `accountArray[1]`. The simplest way to do this is to move the last element into the position where the matching ID was found. It is okay to destroy the reference in `accountArray[1]`, because this is the object to be removed from the `AccountList`. Also, since there is no ordering requirement, it is also okay to move `accountArray[count - 1]`, the last meaningful element in the array.

Notice that the field `size` must be changed to reflect the removal. Here are the three statements that do it:

```
// index is the array location of the item to be removed
accountArray[subscript] = accountArray[size - 1];

// No longer need a reference in the last array location, so make it null
accountArray[size - 1] = null;

// Make sure size is decreased to complete the removal of one element
size--;
```

Although the elements are not in the same order as they were (this was not a requirement), the same elements exist after the requested removal. But because the last element has been relocated, `size` must be decreased by one. There are now only three, not four, elements in this collection.

```
// Remove the first occurrence of accountToRemove if found.
// Return true if the object was successfully removed or
// false if accountToRemove was not found in this collection.
public bool RemoveAccountWithID(string accountID)
{
  bool result;
  int subscript = IndexOf(accountID);

  if(subscript == -1)
    result = false;
  else
  {
    // index is the array location of the item to be removed
    accountArray[subscript] = accountArray[size - 1];

    // No longer need two references to same object, so make it null
    accountArray[size - 1] = null;

    // Decrease the size by 1 to complete the removal of one element
    size--;
```

```
    // Let this method return true to where the message was sent
    result = true;
  }

  // Return true if element removed, false if ID was not found

  return result;
}
```

Self-Check

7-23   Write the output of the following code:

```
AccountList accounts = new AccountList();
accounts.Add(new BankAccount("One", 1.00));
accounts.Add(new BankAccount("Two", 2.00));
accounts.Add(new BankAccount("Three", 3.00));
accounts.Add(new BankAccount("Three", 4.00));
Console.WriteLine("Size = {0}", accounts.Size);

BankAccount currentAccount = accounts.GetAccountWithID("One");
currentAccount.Deposit(20.00);
currentAccount = accounts.GetAccountWithID("Three");
currentAccount.Withdraw(0.01);
Console.WriteLine("Elements = {0}", accounts);
accounts.RemoveAccountWithID("One");
accounts.RemoveAccountWithID("Two");
accounts.RemoveAccountWithID("Not Here");
Console.WriteLine("Size = {0}", accounts.Size);
```

7-24   What happens when an attempt is made to Add a BankAccount with an ID of an account that is already in the collection?

7-25   What happens when an attempt is made to remove an element that is not in the collection?

7-26   Using the implementation of RemoveElementWithID just given, what happens when an attempt is made to remove an element from an empty collection (size == 0)?

7-27   Write a complete program that adds and then removes an account with an ID that is your name.

7-28   Must RemoveElementWithID always maintain the elements in the same order as that in which they were originally added?

7.5 Binary Search

This section presents the *binary search* algorithm. This algorithm finds objects much more quickly than a sequential search. However, one requirement for a successful binary search is that the array must already be sorted. An array is sorted when the array elements are arranged in order from smallest to largest (sorting is presented in the next section).

Whereas a sequential search eliminates one array element at each comparison, a binary search can eliminate half of the remaining array elements from further searches each time that a comparison is made. This makes binary searches much quicker. The algorithm begins by comparing the element in the middle of a sorted array to the search element. If this is the element being sought, the search terminates. Because the array is sorted, the binary search algorithm knows if the element being sought is more (alphabetically) than the middle element, or if it is less than the middle element. The binary search then confines its search to the appropriate half of the sorted array by eliminating the "impossible" half, either above or below the middle element. Here is a first cut at the algorithm:

Algorithm: Binary search (to be used on sorted arrays)

while the element is not found and it still may be in the array
{

    if the element in the middle of the array is the element being searched for
      store the reference and terminate the loop
   else
      eliminate the correct half of the array from further search

}

Each time the search element is not the element in the middle, the search can be narrowed. If the search item is less than the middle element, you search only the half that precedes the middle element. If the search item is greater than the middle element, you search only the half that follows the middle element. Either way, this effectively eliminates half of the remaining array elements from the search. By contrast, the sequential search only eliminates one element from the search field with each comparison.

Assuming that an array of strings is sorted in alphabetical order, sequentially searching for `"Ableson"` does not take long, because it is likely to be located near the front of the array elements. However, sequentially searching for `"Zevon"` takes much more time, especially if the array is very big (with millions of elements). The sequential search algorithm must first compare all of the names beginning with A through Y before arriving at any names beginning with Z.

Because it eliminates half of the remaining elements with each comparison, a binary search gets to "Zevon" much more quickly. When an array is very large, binary search is much faster than sequential search.

The binary search algorithm has the following preconditions:

○   The array must be sorted (in ascending order, for now).

○   The indexes that reference the first and last elements must represent the entire range of meaningful elements.

The index of the element in the middle is computed as the average of the first and last indexes. These three indexes—named first, mid, and last—are shown in the code fragment below:

```
// This array is initialized so the element at index 0 is less than
// all of the others and the largest index stores a reference
// to the element that is larger than all of the other elements.
int n = 7;
string[] name = new string[n];
name[0]  =  "ABE";
name[1]  =  "CLAY";
name[2]  =  "KIM";
name[3]  =  "LAU";
name[4]  =  "LISA";
name[5]  =  "PELE";
name[6]  =  "ROY";

// Binary search needs several assignments to get things going
int first = 0;
int last = n - 1;
int mid = (first + last) / 2;
string searchString = "LISA";

// -1 will mean that the element has not yet been found
int indexInArray = -1;
```

Here is a more refined algorithm that will search as long as there are more elements to look at, and the element has not been found:

Algorithm: Binary search (more refined)

while indexInArray is -1 and there are more array elements to look through
{
    if searchString is equal to name[mid] then
        let indexInArray = mid // *This indicates the array element equaled searchString*
    else if searchString alphabetically precedes name[mid]
        eliminate mid . . . last elements from the search
    else
        eliminate first . . . mid elements from the search
    mid = (first + last) / 2; // *Compute a new mid for next loop iteration (if there is one)*
}
// At this point, indexInArray is either -1, indicating that searchString was not found,
// or in the range of 0 through n - 1, indicating that searchString was found.

As the search begins, one of three things can happen (the code is searching for a `string` that equals `searchString`):

   ○ The element in the middle of the array equals `searchString`. The search is complete. Store `mid` into `indexInArray` to indicate where the `string` was found.

   ○ `searchString` is less than (alphabetically precedes) the middle element. The second half of the array can be eliminated from the search (`last = mid - 1`).

   ○ `searchString` is greater than the middle element. The first half of the array can be eliminated from the search field (`first = mid + 1`).

In the following code, the first part of the loop test checks to see if the string being searched for has been found (if `indexInArray == -1` is `true`, it has not been found). As soon as an array element is found to equal `searchString`, `IndexinArray` is set to the spot where the element was found, and the loop terminates. The second part of the loop test stops the loop when there are no more elements to look at. This happens when `first` becomes greater than `last`, which means that the entire array has been examined.

```
// Binary search if searchString
// is not found and there are more elements to compare.
while (indexInArray == -1 && (first <= last))
{
  // Check the three possibilities
  if (searchString.CompareTo(name[mid]) == 0)
    indexInArray = mid; // 1. searchString is found
```

```
  else if (searchString.CompareTo(name[mid]) < 0)
    last = mid - 1;      // 2. searchString may be in first half
  else
    first= mid + 1;      // 3. searchString may be in second half

  // Compute a new mid
  mid = (first + last) / 2;

} // End while

// indexInArray is now either -1 to indicate the string is
// not in the array or is the index of the first equal string.
```

At the beginning of the first loop iteration, the variables first, mid, and last are initialized as shown below. Notice that the array is in ascending order. A binary search does not work if the array is not sorted.

Data before Comparing searchString ("LISA") to name[mid] ("LAU")

name[0]	"ABE"	← first == 0
name[1]	"CLAY"	
name[2]	"KIM"	
name[3]	"LAU"	← mid == 3
name[4]	"LISA"	
name[5]	"PELE"	
name[6]	"ROY"	← last == 6

After comparing searchString to name[mid], first is increased from 0 to mid + 1, or 4; last remains 6; and a new mid is computed as (4 + 6) / 2 = 5.

name[0]	"ABE"	Because "LISA" is greater than name[mid],
name[1]	"CLAY"	the objects name[0] through name[3] no longer
name[2]	"KIM"	need to be searched and can be eliminated from
name[3]	"LAU"	future searches. That leaves three possibilities.
name[4]	"LISA"	← first == 4
name[5]	"PELE"	← mid == 5
name[6]	"ROY"	← last == 6

With mid == 5, "LISA".compareTo("PELE") < 0 is true. So last is decreased (5 - 1 = 4), first remains 4, and a new mid is computed as mid = (4 + 4) / 2 = 4.

```
name[0]     "ABE"
name[1]     "CLAY"
name[2]     "KIM"
name[3]     "LAU"
name[4]     "LISA"     ← mid == 4    ← first == 4    ← last == 4
name[5]     "PELE"
name[6]     "ROY"      Because "LISA" is less than name[mid], eliminate name[6].
```

Now name[mid] does equal searchString ("LISA".equals("LISA")), so indexInArray = mid. The loop terminates, because indexInArray is no longer -1. The following code after the loop, and the output, confirm that "LISA" was found in the array.

```
if (indexInArray == -1)
    Console.WriteLine("{0} not found", searchString);
else
    Console.WriteLine("{0} found at index {1}",
                    searchString , indexInArray);
```

Output
LISA found at index 4

Terminating When searchName Is Not Found

Now consider the possibility that the data being searched for is not in the array—if searchString is "DEVON", for example.

```
// Get the index of DEVON if found in the array
string searchName = "DEVON";
```

This time the values of first, mid, and last progress as follows (the first column counts iterations of the loop) :

first	mid	last	Comment
#1	0	3	6	Compare "DEVON" to "LAU"
#2	0	1	2	Compare "DEVON" to "CLAY"
#3	2	2	2	Compare "DEVON" to "ABE"
#4	2	-1	1	first <= last is false—loop ends

When the searchString ("DEVON") is not in the array, last becomes less than first (first > last). The two indexes have crossed each other, and the search terminates. Here is another way to trace the binary search shown above:

		#1	#2	#3	#4
name[0]	"ABE"	← first	← first		
name[1]	"CLAY"		← mid		**last**
name[2]	"KIM"		← last	← first, mid, last	**first**
name[3]	"LAU"	← mid			
name[4]	"LISA"				
name[5]	"PELE"				
name[6]	"ROY"	← last			

After searchString ("DEVON") is compared to name[2] ("KIM"), no further comparisons are necessary. Since DEVON is less than KIM, last becomes mid-1, or 1. The new mid is computed, but it is never used as an index. The second part of the loop test terminates the loop (2 <= 1 is false).

```
while(indexInArray == -1 && (first <= last))
```

Since first is no longer less than or equal to last, the searchString cannot be in the array. The indexInArray remains -1 to indicate that the element was not found.

Comparing Running Times

The binary search algorithm can be much more efficient than the sequential search algorithm. Whereas a sequential search only eliminates one element from the search per comparison, a binary search eliminates half of the remaining elements for each comparison. For example, when the number of elements (n) == 1,024, a binary search eliminates 512 elements from further search in the first comparison, 256 during the second comparison, then 128, 64, 32, 16, 4, 2, and 1.

When n is small, a binary search is not much faster than a sequential search. However, when n gets large, the difference in the time required to search for something can make the difference between selling the software and having it flop. Consider how many comparisons are necessary when n grows by powers of two. Each doubling of n would require potentially twice as many comparisons for a sequential search. However, the same doubling of n would require potentially only one more comparison for a binary search.

The Maximum Number of Comparisons during Two Different Search Algorithms

Power of 2	n	Sequential Search	Binary Search
2^2	4	4	2
2^4	16	16	4
2^8	256	256	8
2^{12}	4,096	4,096	12
2^{24}	16,777,216	16,777,216	24

As n gets very large, a sequential search has to do a lot more work. The numbers above represent the maximum number of iterations to find an element, or to realize that it is not there. The difference between 24 comparisons and almost 17 million comparisons is quite dramatic, even on a fast computer.

In general, as the number of elements to search (n) doubles, a binary search requires only one more iteration. The growth of this function is said to be logarithmic.

Self-Check

7-29   Give one advantage of a binary search over a sequential search. Are there any disadvantages to a binary search over sequential search?

7-30   What is the maximum number of comparisons (approximately) performed on a list of 1,024 elements during a binary search? (*Hint:* After one comparison, only 512 array elements need be searched; after two searches, only 256 elements need be searched, and so on.)

7-31   During a binary search, what condition signals that the search element does not exist in the array being searched?

7-32   What changes would need to be made to the binary search algorithm when the elements are sorted in descending order?

7.6 One Sorting Algorithm: Selection Sort

The binary search algorithm works correctly only when all array elements are arranged in a specific order. The array must be arranged into either ascending or descending order, through a process known as *sorting*. Sorting is a very important process that is used across many areas of computer science.

There are many sorting algorithms. Even though others are more efficient (run faster), the relatively simple selection sort is presented here. The goal is to arrange an array of `double` values into ascending order, the natural ordering of numbers.

Object Name	Unsorted Array	Sorted Array
data[0]	76.0	62.0
data[1]	91.0	76.0
data[2]	100.0	89.0
data[3]	62.0	91.0
data[4]	89.0	100.0

With the *selection sort* algorithm, the largest integer must end up in `data[n - 1]` (where n is the number of meaningful array elements). The smallest number should end up in `data[0]`. In general, an array x of size n is sorted in ascending order if `x[j] <= x[j + 1]` for `j = 0` to `n - 2`.

The selection sort begins by locating the smallest element in the array, by searching from the first element (`data[0]`) through the last element (here, it is `data[4]`). The smallest element, `data[3]` in this array, is then swapped with the top element, `data[0]`. Once this is done, the array is sorted at least through the first element.

Placing the Smallest Value in the "Top" Position (index 0)

top == 0	Before	After	Sorted
data[0]	76.0	62.0	?
data[1]	91.0	91.0	
data[2]	100.0	100.0	
data[3]	62.0	76.0	
data[4]	89.0	89.0	

The task of finding the smallest element is accomplished by examining all array elements and keeping track of the index with the smallest integer. After this, the smallest array element is swapped with `data[0]`. Here is an algorithm that accomplishes these two tasks:

Algorithm: Finding smallest in array and swapping it with topmost element

// At first, assume that the first element is the smallest
(a) top = 0

// Check the rest of the array (data[top + 1] through data[n - 1])

(b) indexOfSmallest = top
(c) for index ranging from top + 1 through n - 1
    (c1) if data[index] < data[indexOfSmallest]
               indexOfSmallest = index

// Place the smallest element into the first position and place the first array
// element into the location where the smallest array element was located.
(d) swap data[indexOfSmallest] with data[top]

The following algorithm walkthrough shows how the array is sorted through the first element. The smallest integer in the array will be stored at the "top" of the array—data[0]. Notice that indexOfSmallest changes only when an array element is found to be less than the one stored in data[indexOfSmallest]. In the following walkthrough, this happens the first and third times that step c1 of the algorithm executes.

Step	top	indexOf Smallest	index	[0]	[1]	[2]	[3]	[4]	my_size
?	?	?	?	76.0	91.0	100.0	62.0	89.0	5
(a)	0	"	"	"	"	"	"	"	"
(b)	"	0	"	"	"	"	"	"	"
(c)	"	"	1	"	"	"	"	"	"
(c1)	"	1	"	"	"	"	"	"	"
(c)	"	"	2	"	"	"	"	"	"
(c1)	"	"	"	"	"	"	"	"	"
(c)	"	"	3	"	"	"	"	"	"
(c1)	"	2	"	"	"	"	"	"	"
(c)	"	"	4	"	"	"	"	"	"
(c1)	"	"	"	"	"	"	"	"	"
(c)	"	"	5	"	"	"	"	"	"
(d)	"	"	"	62.0	"	"	76.0	"	"

This algorithm walkthrough shows indexOfSmallest changing twice to represent the index of the smallest integer in the array. After the entire array is traversed, the smallest element is swapped with the top array element. Specifically, the preceding algorithm swaps the values of the first and fourth array elements, so 62.0 is stored in data[0] and 76.0 is stored in data[3]. The array is now sorted through the first element. Not much, but it is a good start.

The same algorithm can be used to place the second smallest element into data[1]. The second traversal must begin at the new "top" of the array—index 1 rather than 0. This is accomplished by incrementing top from 0 to 1. Now a second traversal of the array begins at the second element, rather than the first. The smallest element in the unsorted portion of the array is swapped with the second element. A second traversal of the array ensures that the first two elements are in order. In this example array, data[3] is swapped with data[1] and the array is sorted through the first two elements.

top == 1	Before	After	Sorted
data[0]	62.0	62.0	←
data[1]	91.0	76.0	←
data[2]	100.0	100.0	
data[3]	76.0	91.0	
data[4]	89.0	89.0	

This process repeats a total of n - 1 times.

top == 2	Before	After	Sorted
data[0]	62.0	62.0	←
data[1]	76.0	76.0	←
data[2]	100.0	89.0	←
data[3]	91.0	91.0	
data[4]	89.0	100.0	

And an element may even be swapped with itself.

top == 3	Before	After	Sorted
data[0]	62.0	62.0	←
data[1]	76.0	76.0	←
data[2]	100.0	89.0	←
data[3]	91.0	91.0	←
data[4]	89.0	100.0	

When top goes to data[4], the outer loop stops. The last element need not be compared to anything. It is unnecessary to find the smallest element in an array of size 1. This element in data[n - 1] must be the largest (or equal to the largest), since all of the elements preceding the last element are already sorted in ascending order.

top == 3	Before	After	Sorted
data[0]	62.0	62.0	←
data[1]	76.0	76.0	←
data[2]	100.0	89.0	←
data[3]	91.0	91.0	←
data[4]	89.0	100.0	←

Therefore, the outer loop changes the index top from 0 through n - 2. The loop to find the smallest index in a portion of the array is nested inside a loop that changes top from 0 through n - 2 inclusive.

Algorithm: Selection Sort

```
for top ranging from 0 through n - 2
{
    indexOfSmallest = top
    for index ranging from top + 1 through n - 1
    {
        if data[indexOfSmallest] < data[index] then
            indexOfSmallest = index
    }
    swap  data[indexOfSmallest] with data[top]
}
```

Here is the C# code that uses a selection sort to sort the array of numbers shown. The array is displayed. Then the array is sorted into ascending order and is displayed again.

Code Sample: Class UseSelectionSort

```
1 using System;
2
3 class UseSelectionSort
4 {
5    static void Main()
6    {
7        // Build a small array to work with
8        double[] data = { 76.0, 91.0, 100.0, 62.0, 89.0 };
9        int n = data.Length;
10
11       Console.Write("Before sorting: ");
```

```
12       for(int j = 0; j < data.Length; j++)
13          Console.Write(data[j] + " ");
14       Console.WriteLine();
15
16       int indexOfSmallest = 0;
17
18       for(int top = 0; top < n - 1; top++)
19       {
20          // First assume that the smallest is
21          // the first element in the subarray
22          indexOfSmallest = top;
23
24          // compare all of the other elements, looking for smallest
25          for(int index = top + 1; index < data.Length; index++)
26          { // Compare elements in the subarray
27             if(data[index] < data[indexOfSmallest])
28                indexOfSmallest = index;
29          }
30
31          // make sure the smallest from data[top] through data.size
32          // is in data[top]. This message swaps two array elements.
33          double temp = data[top];   // Hold on to value temporarily
34          data[top] = data[indexOfSmallest];
35          data[indexOfSmallest] = temp;
36       }
37
38       Console.Write(" After sorting: ");
39       for (int j = 0; j < data.Length; j++)
40          Console.Write(data[j] + " ");
41       Console.WriteLine();
42    }
43 }
```

Output

```
Before sorting: 76 91 100 62 89
 After sorting: 62 76 89 91 100
```

Sorting an array usually involves elements that are more complex. The sorting code is most often located in a method. This more typical context for sorting will be presented later.

This selection sort code arranges the array into ascending numeric order. Most sort routines arrange the elements from smallest to largest. However, with just a few simple changes, any primitive type of data (such as int, char, and double) may be arranged into descending order, by using the > operator instead of the < operator.

```
if (data[index] < data[indexOfSmallest])
  indexOfSmallest = index;
```

becomes

```
if (data[index] > data[indexOfLargest])
  indexOfLargest = index;
```

Many C# types can be sorted with the relational operators < and >. To sort arrays of other types, you might need to use the object's CompareTo method to check the relationship of two objects. Consider a small array of BankAccount objects, for example:

```
int n = 3;
BankAccount[] data = new BankAccount[n];
data[0] = new BankAccount("zero", 1.00);
data[1] = new BankAccount("middle", 2.00);
data[2] = new BankAccount("first", 3.00);
```

The following code shows the two differences needed to sort an array of objects when the < and > operators are not defined for the type of array elements being sorted.

```
for (int index = top + 1;  index < data.Length;  index++)
{ // Compare two BankAccounts (based on the IDs)
   if(data[index].CompareTo(data[indexOfSmallest]) < 0)
     indexOfSmallest = index;
}

BankAccount temp = data[top]; // Hold on to this value temporarily
```

Many C# classes define a CompareTo method. If it does not already have one, you could add a CompareTo method to your class. Or you could define the < and > operators for your class, which is beyond the scope of this textbook.

Self-Check

7-33   Alphabetizing an array of strings requires a sort in which order, ascending or descending?

7-34   If the smallest element in an array already exists as first, what happens when the code to swap two array elements executes for the first time (when top = 0)?

7-35   Write code that searches for and stores the largest element of array x into largest. Assume that all elements from x[0] through x[n - 1] have been given meaningful values.

7.7 Two-Dimensional Arrays

Consider this table of data that represents a score sheet of six quizzes for 11 students.

This data will be used in several examples of 2-D array processing.

Quiz#	0	1	2	3	4	5
0	67.8	56.4	88.4	79.1	90.0	66.0
1	76.4	81.1	72.2	76.0	85.6	85.0
2	87.8	76.4	88.7	83.0	76.3	87.0
3	86.4	54.0	40.0	3.0	2.0	1.0
4	72.8	89.0	55.0	62.0	68.0	77.7
5	94.4	63.0	92.9	45.0	75.6	99.5
6	85.8	95.0	88.1	100.0	60.0	85.8
7	76.4	84.4	100.0	94.3	75.6	74.0
8	57.9	49.5	58.8	67.4	80.0	56.0
9	86.1	76.0	72.0	88.1	55.6	71.3
10	87.2	95.5	98.1	97.0	98.0	99.0

This data could be processed in a variety of ways:
- ○ Use one column to determine one quiz average.
- ○ Use one row to determine the quiz average for one particular student.
- ○ Use the entire table to determine the overall average.

Declaring Two-Dimensional Arrays

Data that conveniently presents itself in this kind of tabular format can be represented using an array with two subscripts, henceforth called a *two-dimensional array*. Two-dimensional arrays are constructed as follows:

General Form: A two-dimensional array declaration

variable-type[,] *identifier* = **new** *variable-type*[*rows*, *columns*];
Notes:
variable-type must be one of the primitive types or the name of any class.
identifier is the name of the two-dimensional array.
rows specifies the total number of rows.
columns specifies the total number of columns.

Examples:
```
double[,] matrix = new double[4, 8];
string[,] name = new string[5, 10];


// Construct with int constants or expressions
int rows = 10;
int columns = 20;
BankAccount[,] acctMap = new BankAccount[rows, columns];
```

These declarations allocate memory to store 32 floating-point numbers, 50 strings, and 200 `BankAccount` objects, respectively.

Two-dimensional arrays can also be declared and initialized with initializers by using similar syntax to that of one-dimensional arrays, but with nested braces.

```
int[,] numbers = {{10, 20}, {30, 40}, {50, 60}};
```

The previous declaration creates an array with three rows, each with two columns.

Arrays can be declared with more than two dimensions. The general term for an array with more than one dimension is a ***multi-dimensional array***. This textbook will limit its discussion to two-dimensional arrays only.

Referencing Individual Items with Two Subscripts

A reference to an individual element of a two-dimensional array requires two subscripts. By convention, programmers use the first subscript for the rows. The second subscript represents the columns. Each subscript must be bracketed individually.

General Form: Accessing individual two-dimensional array elements

two-dimensional-array-name[*rows*, *columns*]
○ *rows* is an integer value in the range of 0 through the number of *rows* - 1
○ *columns* is an integer value in the range of 0 through the *number of columns* - 1

Examples:
```
string[,] name = new string[5, 10];
name[0, 0] = "Upper Left";
name[4, 9] = "Lower Right";
Console.WriteLine("At row 0, column 0: {0}", name[0, 0]);
```

```
Console.WriteLine("At row 4, column 9: {0}", name[4, 9]);
Console.WriteLine("{0}  {1}", name[0, 0].ToUpper(),
                  name[4, 9].ToUpper());
```

Output:

```
At row 0, column 0: Upper Left
At row 4, column 9: Lower Right
UPPER LEFT  LOWER RIGHT
```

Nested Looping with Two-Dimensional Arrays

Nested looping, in which one loop executes inside another, is commonly used to process the data of two-dimensional arrays. The following initialization allocates enough memory to store 40 floating-point numbers—a two-dimensional array with five rows and eight columns. C# sets all values to 0.0.

```
double[,] table = new double[5, 8];  // all set to 0.0
```

Arrays have a method named the *GetLength method*, which returns the length of the array in a given dimension. GetLength should be used instead of the Length property when looping over a 2D array, because the Length property returns the total number of elements in the entire array. In the initialization shown above for the array table, the Length value would be 40. But to do nested loops over an array, it is best to use the number of rows, and the number of columns in each row, obtained with GetLength.

The nested for loops shown below initialize all 40 elements to -1.0, with help from the GetLength method. (C# initialized all elements to 0.0 when the table was constructed with new.) GetLength(0) returns the length in the first dimension—the number of rows; GetLength(1) returns the length in the second dimension—the number of columns.

```
// Initialize all elements to -1.0
for (int row = 0;  row < table.GetLength(0);  row++)
{
  for (int col = 0;  col < table.GetLength(1);  col++)
  {
    table[row, col] = -1.0;
  }
}
```

Note that it would *not* have been correct to try to initialize the elements of the array using a `foreach` loop like this:

```
// this code does not work!
foreach (double element in table)
{
   element = -1.0;
}
```

The `foreach` will not have any effect on the array, because declaring the `double element` variable merely stores a copy of the table element's value; assigning a new value to `element` does not affect the original array element's value. This is why a set of nested `for` loops is used.

The following code assigns some values to elements in the two-dimensional array. It then uses nested loops to display each row on its own separate line:

```
table[1, 1]  = 1.1;
table[2, 2]  = 2.22;
table[3, 3]  = 33.3333;
table[4, 4]  = 444.444444;
table[4, 5]  = 4.5;
table[4, 6]  = 4.6;
table[4, 7]  = 4.7;
table[0, 7]  = -7;
table[1, 7]  = 171.7;

for(int row = 0;  row < ROWS;  row++)
{ // Display one row
   for(int col = 0;  col < COLUMNS;  col++)
   {
      // Numbers are seven columns wide with two decimal places
      Console.Write("{0,7:F2}", table[row, col]);
   }
   Console.WriteLine();
}
```

Output
-1.00 -1.00 -1.00 -1.00 -1.00 -1.00 -1.00 -7.00
-1.00   1.10 -1.00 -1.00 -1.00 -1.00 -1.00 171.70
-1.00 -1.00   2.22 -1.00 -1.00 -1.00 -1.00 -1.00
-1.00 -1.00 -1.00 33.33 -1.00 -1.00 -1.00 -1.00
-1.00 -1.00 -1.00 -1.00 444.44   4.50   4.60   4.70

Self-Check

Use this construction to answer the following questions:

```
int[,] a = new int[3, 4];
```

7-36   Are the subscript ranges checked when referencing elements in a?

7-37   How many ints are properly stored by a?

7-38   What is the row (first) subscript range for a?

7-39   What is the column (second) subscript range for a?

7-40   Write code to initialize all of the elements of a to 999.

7-41   Write code to display all of the rows of a on separate lines, with eight spaces for each element.

7-42   Declare a two-dimensional array named sales such that 120 floating-point numbers are stored in 10 rows.

7-43   Declare a two-dimensional array named sales2 such that 120 floating-point numbers are stored in 10 columns.

7.8   2D Arrays and Class Design

A two-dimensional array manages tabular data that is typically processed by row, by column, or in totality. These forms of processing will be examined by designing the following example class named GradeTable, which manages a grade book for a group of students on a set of assignments. The data consists of six assignments for each of the 11 students. The 66 assignments shown below in the table entitled "input (shown here as a table)" are used throughout this section to demonstrate several ways to process data that is stored in two-dimensional arrays.

The assignment average for each student is computed by processing a 2-D array one row at a time—using *row-by-row processing*. The average, highest, and lowest score of each assignment is found by processing the data one column at a time—using *column-by-column processing*.

The overall assignment average for all students on all assignments is computed only after referencing all meaningful elements. However, before any processing occurs, the two-dimensional array must be declared and given a defined state. These forms of array processing are represented in the context of a class. Here is an outline of the methods needed in the `GradeTable` class to accomplish this task.

GradeTable constructor and methods

```
public GradeTable(int nrows, int ncols)
```
Constructs a grade table holding the given number of rows (students) and the given number of columns (assignments).

```
public override string ToString()
```
Returns a string representation of the grade table, including all rows and columns aligned properly.

```
public double GetScore(int row, int col)
```
Returns the score for the given row (student) on the given column (assignment).

```
public void SetScore(int row, int col, double value)
```
Sets the score for the given row (student) on the given column (assignment) to be the given value.

```
public void PrintStudentStatistics()
```
Prints all students' assignment averages.

```
public void PrintAssignmentStatistics()
```
Prints stats about each assignment, including the high, low, and average score.

```
public double GetAssignmentAverage()
```
Returns the overall average on all assignments for all students.

Sometimes when implementing a class like this, it is useful to see how the class could be used. The `GradeTable` class should work with the following test class. The expected input is shown, and the desired output follows.

Code Sample: Class TestGradeTable

```
1 class TestGradeTable
2 {
3   static void Main()
4   {
5     int numRows = int.Parse(Console.ReadLine());
6     int numCols = int.Parse(Console.ReadLine());
7
```

```
 8        GradeTable table = new GradeTable(numRows, numCols);
 9
10     // initialize the data in the table
11      for (int row = 0;  row < numRows;  row++)
12      {
13         for (int col = 0;  col < numCols;  col++)
14         {
15            double score = double.Parse(Console.ReadLine());
16            table.SetScore(row, col, score);
17         }
18      }
19
20      Console.WriteLine(table);            // uses ToString method
21      table.PrintStudentStatistics();
22      table.PrintAssignmentStatistics();
23      Console.WriteLine("Assignment Average: {0:F1}",
24         table.GetAssignmentAverage());
25   }
26 }
```

---

input (shown here as a table)

```
11 6
67.8    56.4    88.4     79.1    90.0    66.0
76.4    81.1    72.2     76.0    85.6    85.0
87.8    76.4    88.7     83.0    76.3    87.0
86.4    54.0    40.0      3.0     2.0     1.0
72.8    89.0    55.0     62.0    68.0    77.7
94.4    63.0    92.9     45.0    75.6    99.5
85.8    95.0    88.1    100.0    60.0    85.8
76.4    84.4   100.0     94.3    75.6    74.0
57.9    49.5    58.8     67.4    80.0    56.0
86.1    76.0    72.0     88.1    55.6    71.3
87.2    95.5    98.1     97.0    98.0    99.0
```

Output

	0	1	2	3	4	5
0	67.8	56.4	88.4	79.1	90.0	66.0
1	76.4	81.1	72.2	76.0	85.6	85.0
2	87.8	76.4	88.7	83.0	76.3	87.0
3	86.4	54.0	40.0	3.0	2.0	1.0
4	72.8	89.0	55.0	62.0	68.0	77.7

```
  5    94.4    63.0    92.9    45.0    75.6    99.5
  6    85.8    95.0    88.1   100.0    60.0    85.8
  7    76.4    84.4   100.0    94.3    75.6    74.0
  8    57.9    49.5    58.8    67.4    80.0    56.0
  9    86.1    76.0    72.0    88.1    55.6    71.3
 10    87.2    95.5    98.1    97.0    98.0    99.0


Student      Average
====================
      0        74.6
      1        79.4
      2        83.2
      3        31.1
      4        70.8
      5        78.4
      6        85.8
      7        84.1
      8        61.6
      9        74.9
     10        95.8


Assignment   High    Low    Average
===================================
      0      94.4    57.9      79.9
      1      95.5    49.5      74.6
      2     100.0    40.0      77.7
      3     100.0     3.0      72.3
      4      98.0     2.0      69.7
      5      99.5     1.0      72.9


Assignment Average:  74.5
```

Initializing Two-Dimensional Arrays with Input Data

In programs that require little data, reading the input from the user is reasonable. However, initialization of large arrays often involves large amounts of data. The input would have to be typed in from the keyboard many times during implementation and testing. That much interactive input would prove to be tedious and error-prone. For large amounts of data, it is best to read the data from an external file instead.

File input is not introduced until the next chapter. The next best thing would be to redirect the program's standard input so that it comes from a file, rather than from the keyboard (see Appendix B for a detailed discussion of input and output redirection). This way, the program will

read the input from the file, rather than having to manually prompt the user 66 times to popu-
late the entire 11-by-6 grid. For this program, the input desired is stored in the file
`inputdata.txt`, which is on the downloadable source code at **www.fbeedle.com/csharp/
code.exe**.

The input starts with two numbers, one for the number of rows (students) and one for the
number of columns (assignments). These are read first by the test class, so that the program
knows what arguments to pass to the constructor of the `GradeTable` object.

```
int numRows = int.Parse(Console.ReadLine());
int numCols = int.Parse(Console.ReadLine());

GradeTable table = new GradeTable(numRows, numCols);
```

Seeing this usage of the `GradeTable` constructor gives some insight about how the class
should be designed. It looks like the class should have a 2D array of type `double` to store the
score data, and perhaps should store the number of rows and columns.

Let's implement the fields and constructor:

```
using System;

class GradeTable
{
  private double[,] scores;
  private int numRows, numCols;

  // Constructs a grade table holding the given number of rows
  // (students) and the given number of columns (assignments).
  public GradeTable(int nrows, int ncols)
  {
    numRows = nrows;
    numCols = ncols;
    scores = new double[numRows, numCols];
  }
```

This is a good start toward implementing the `GradeTable` class. Going back to the test class,
the table data is read into the program from standard input. Nested loops are used to do this,
reading one value per line for each of the 11 rows of 6 columns.

```
// initialize the data in the table
for (int row = 0;  row < numRows;  row++)
{
  for (int col = 0;  col < numCols;  col++)
  {
```

```
        double score = double.Parse(Console.ReadLine());
        table.SetScore(row, col, score);
    }
}
```

The code above uses the `SetScore` method of the `GradeTable` object. The `SetScore` method needs to store the score given into the desired row and column of the array.

Let's implement it:

```
// Sets the score for the given row (student) on the given
// column (assignment) to be the given value.
public void SetScore(int row, int col, double value)
{
    scores[row, col] = value;
}
```

The `GetScore` method should do the opposite—fetching and returning the value from the row and column specified. This is also straightforward to implement:

```
// Returns the score for the given row (student) on the given
// column (assignment).
public double GetScore(int row, int col)
{
    return scores[row, col];
}
```

Next, the test class calls the `ToString` method of the `GradeTable` by passing it to `Console.WriteLine`. This lets us examine the data, to ensure that the `GradeTable` is correctly it.

```
Console.WriteLine(table);              // uses ToString method
```

The `ToString` method is larger than the parts of the class that have been written so far. It must iterate over every row and column and build a string that contains the scores, aligned properly. To build such a formatted string, we can use nested `for` loops to access each score, and the `string.Format` method to build the aligned strings for each score. The method is challenging to write and likely requires several attempts to get just right. Here is a working implementation:

```
public override string ToString()
{
    string result = "     ";
```

```
// a header with the assignment numbers
for (int col = 0;  col < numCols;  col++)
{
   result += string.Format("{0,7}", col);
}
result += "\n";  // end of line

// each student's scores
for (int row = 0;  row < numRows;  row++)
{
   // a header showing the student number
   result += string.Format("{0,4}", row);

   for (int col = 0;  col < numCols;  col++)
   {
      double score = GetScore(row, col);
      result += string.Format("{0,7:F1}", score);
   }

   result += "\n";  // end of line
}

result += "\n";  // one final blank line
return result;
}
```

This two-dimensional array is now correctly initialized and stores 66 assignment scores. Each row represents the record of one student. Each column in that row represents the score of one assignment for that student.

When working with two-dimensional arrays, take a little extra time to output all of the elements and the number of assigned elements. Do this immediately after the code that initializes the objects. Do not continue until you are satisfied that the two-dimensional array has been properly initialized. Otherwise, you may end up wasting a lot of effort debugging your code, when the problem is really with the data. It may appear that there is a bug later on in the program, when in fact, the array was never initialized correctly to begin with.

Student Statistics (Row-by-Row Processing)

The average for one student can be found by adding all of the elements of one row and dividing by the number of assignments (the number of columns; 6 in this case). Since the data for each student are stored in one row of the two-dimensional array, they can be processed in a row-by-row manner.

Row-by-row processing is characterized by nested loops, where the row subscript changes in the outer loop, and the column subscript changes (more quickly) in an inner loop. Each complete row of data is processed before proceeding to the next row.

The following code shows the implementation of PrintStudentStatistics, which shows row-by-row processing (as well as an example of a very long method name!).

```
// Prints all students' assignment averages.
public void PrintStudentStatistics()
{
  Console.WriteLine("Student    Average");
  Console.WriteLine("==================");

  for (int row = 0;  row < numRows;  row++)
  {
    // outer loop; iterates over all students (row processing)
    double sum = 0.0;

    for (int col = 0;  col < numCols;  col++)
    {
      // inner loop; calculates sum for this student
      sum += GetScore(row, col);
    }

    double average = sum / numCols;
    Console.WriteLine("{0,7}{1,11:F1}", row, average);
  }
  Console.WriteLine();
}
```

Assignment Statistics (Column-by-Column Processing)

Column-by-column processing occurs when the data of a two-dimensional array are processed such that all the rows of one column are examined before proceeding to the next column. The row subscript changes faster than the column subscript. Since each assignment is represented as one column, processing the data column by column can be used to generate assignment statistics such as the lowest, highest, and average scores for each assignment. The expected output follows.

		Output	
Assignment	High	Low	Average
=================================			
0	94.4	57.9	79.9
1	95.5	49.5	74.6
2	100.0	40.0	77.7
3	100.0	3.0	72.3
4	98.0	2.0	69.7
5	99.5	1.0	72.9

The implementation of PrintAssignmentStatistics is left as a programming project.

Overall Assignment Average (Processing All Elements)

Finding the overall average of all assignment scores is done by summing every element in the two-dimensional array and then dividing by the total number of assignments. The following message shows the output that follows:

```
Console.WriteLine("Assignment Average: {0:F1}",
   table.GetAssignmentAverage());
```

Output
Assignment Average: 74.5

The implementation of GetAssignmentAverage is also left as a programming project.

Self-Check

7-44   In row-by-row processing, which subscript increments more slowly, row or column?

7-45   In column-by-column processing, which subscript increments more slowly, row or column?

7-46   Given the following declaration:

```
. . .
int[,] t = new int[rows, cols];
. . . // (t is populated with data)
```

write code that determines the sum of all of the elements in t.

7-47   Write code that displays the largest element in each row of t.

Chapter Summary

- ❍ Arrays store collections of elements in a list-like manner, where elements are accessed through indexes.
- ❍ Individual array elements are referenced with subscript notation. In a C# array, the integer expression in a subscript should be in the range of 0 through the array capacity - 1. For example, the valid index range of the `double[] x = new double[100]` is 0 through 99 inclusive.
- ❍ Out-of-range indexes are detected at runtime. The program terminates with an `IndexOutOfRangeException`.
- ❍ An integer to count the number of meaningful elements, which is often named n (or `size`) is an important piece of data that must be maintained in addition to the array elements themselves. The number of meaningful elements is important in any array-processing algorithm.
- ❍ The capacity of an array almost always differs from the number of meaningful elements. An array of capacity 1,000 may only be using the first 739 elements to store meaningful data.
- ❍ The array `Length` property returns an `int` representing the current capacity (not the number of meaningful elements) of the array.
- ❍ Some of the new ideas presented with data stored in a two-dimensional array format include:
  - ❍ A two-dimensional array manages data that is logically organized in a tabular format—that is, in rows and columns.
  - ❍ The first subscript of a two-dimensional array specifies the row of data in a table; the second represents the column.
  - ❍ The elements stored in a two-dimensional array can be processed row by row, column by column, or by both rows and columns.
  - ❍ One or more `for` loops are commonly used to process arrays. In the case of a two-dimensional array being processed row by row, the outer loop usually increments the row index and the inner loop usually increments the column index.
- ❍ C# Arrays can have many dimensions. One-dimensional arrays are the most common, but occasionally it becomes convenient to store data in a two-dimensional array, and perhaps even in a three-dimensional array.

Key Terms

array

array initializer

array processing

binary search

collection class

column-by-column processing

command line argument

element

GetLength method

index

IndexOutOfRangeException

initializer list

Length property

multi-dimensional array

row-by-row processing

selection sort

sequential search

short circuit Boolean evaluation

sorting

subscript

two-dimensional array

Exercises

1. Write the output generated by the following code:
```
int MAX = 10;
int[]  x = new int[MAX];

for (int j = 0; j < 3; j++)
  x[j] = j * 2;

for (int j = 3; j < MAX; j++)
  x[j] = x[j - 1] + x[j - 2];

for (int j = 0; j < MAX; j++)
Console.WriteLine("{0}. {1}", j, x[j]);
```

2. How many elements will have meaningful values (other than null) in an array with a capacity to store references to 100 objects?

3. Declare a C# array called arrayOfInts that stores 10 integers with indexes 0 through 9.

4. Write the code that determines the largest number in the following array, assuming that the first 52 values are meaningful:
```
double[]  y = new double[75];
// Assume y[0] through y[51] are meaningful
int n = 52;
```

5. Write the code that determines the average of the following array, assuming that only the first 43 elements are meaningful:

```
double[] z = new double[100];
// Assume z[0] through z[42] are meaningful
int n = 43;
```

6. Write the code that declares and initializes an array of strings using lines of input from the keyboard. First, ask the user how many lines of input there will be. Then, display the lines in reverse order. Your dialogue should look like this:

```
How many lines? 4

Enter 4 lines of input:
First Line
Second Line
Any string input data you want
Fourth

Lines reversed:
Fourth
Any string input data you want
Second Line
First Line
```

7. Write the code that sets a bool variable found to true if a string named searchName is found in the array. If a string is not in the array, let found remain false. Assume that only the first n array elements have meaningful values.

```
string[] s = new string[200];
int n = 97;
// Assume n elements (s[0] through s[96]) are initialized
string searchName = Console.ReadLine().Trim();
bool found = false;
// Assign true to found if searchName is in s
```

8. How many comparisons does a sequential search make when the search element is stored in the first array element and there are 1,000 meaningful elements in the array?

9. How many comparisons does a sequential search make when the search element does not match any array element and there are 1,000 meaningful elements in the array?

10. Assuming that a large number of sequential searches are made on an array, and that it is just as likely that an element is found in the first position as in the last position, approximate the average number of comparisons after 1,000 searches, when there are 1,000 meaningful elements in the array.

11. Write the output generated by the following code:

```
public class TestMystery
{
  private string[] accountArray = {"c", "b", "e", "d", "a"};
  private int size;

  public TestMystery()
  {
    size = accountArray.Length;
  }

  public void Rearrange()
  {
    int last = size - 1;
    for (int j = 0; j < size / 2 + 1; j++)
    {
      string temp = accountArray[j];
      accountArray[j] = accountArray[last];
      accountArray[last] = temp;
      last--;
    }
  }

  public override string ToString()
  { // Show all meaningful elements of data
    string result = "";

    for (int j = 0; j < size; j++)
      result += accountArray[j] + " ";

    return result;
  }

  static void Main()
  {
    TestMystery tm = new TestMystery();
    Console.WriteLine(tm);
    tm.Rearrange();
    Console.WriteLine(tm);
  }
}
```

12. Write the output of this program that uses the `DebuggingBinarySearcher` class. The output statements are in boldface.

```csharp
using System;

class DebuggingBinarySearcher
{
  static void Main()
  {
    DebuggingBinarySearcher list =
                      new DebuggingBinarySearcher();
    list.Add(new BankAccount("ABE" , 0.00));
    list.Add(new BankAccount("CLAY", 1.00));
    list.Add(new BankAccount("KIM" , 2.00));
    list.Add(new BankAccount("LAU" , 3.00));
    list.Add(new BankAccount("LISA", 4.00));
    list.Add(new BankAccount("PELE", 5.00));
    list.Add(new BankAccount("ROY" , 6.00));

    // Get a reference to LISA or null if
    // searchName is not in the array
    string searchID = "LISA";
    BankAccount reference = list.ReferenceTo(searchID);

    // Display the results
    if(reference != null)
      Console.WriteLine( "{0} has a balance of {1:F2}",
                      reference.ID, reference.Balance);
    else
      Console.WriteLine(searchID + " not found");
  }

  // Store a collection of BankAccounts
  private BankAccount[] accountArray;
  private int my_size;

  public DebuggingBinarySearcher()
  { // Construct an empty collection
    accountArray = new BankAccount[1000];
    my_size = 0;
  }

  public void Add(BankAccount newAcct)
  { // Add a bankAccount to this collection
    accountArray[my_size] = newAcct;
    my_size++;
  }
```

```
public BankAccount ReferenceTo(string searchID)
{ // Return a reference to the BankAccount
  // that has the ID searchID. If not found
  // return null. PLEASE NOTE THE DEBUGGING OUTPUT.
  BankAccount result = null;
  int first = 0;
  int last = my_size - 1;

  Console.WriteLine("First Mid Last");
  // Perform a binary search

  while (result == null && (first <= last))
  {
    // If n == 7, mid = (0 + 6) / 2 = 3
    int mid = (first + last) / 2;
    Console.WriteLine("{0}       {1}    {2}", first, mid, last);

    // Check the three possibilities
    if (searchID.CompareTo(accountArray[mid].ID) == 0)
      result = accountArray[mid];
    else if (searchID.CompareTo(accountArray[mid].ID) < 0)
      last = mid - 1;
    else
      first= mid + 1;
  } // End while

  return result;
}
}
```

13. Write the output generated by the preceding program when searchID is initialized
    with each of the following string constants:

       (a)   `searchID = "ROY";`

       (b)   `searchID = "CLAY";`

       (c)   `searchID = "LAURIE";`

       (d)   `searchID = "KIM";`

(e)   `searchID = "PELE";`

(f)   `searchID = "ABE";`

14. List at least one condition that must be true before a successful binary search can be implemented.

15. Using a binary search, what is the maximum number of comparisons (approximately) that will be performed on a list of 256 sorted elements? (*Hint:* After one comparison, only 128 array elements need be searched; after two comparisons, only 64 elements need be searched; and so on.)

16. Write the output generated by the following code:

```
string[] str = new string[10];
int n = 5;
str[0] = "Aimee";
str[1] = "Bob";
str[2] = "Lauren";
str[3] = "Alex";
str[4] = "Morgan";

for (int top = 0; top < n - 1; top++)
{
    int index = top;
    for (int j = top + 1; j <= n-1; j++)
    {
        if (str[j].CompareTo(str[index]) < 0)
            index = j;
    }
    string temp = str[index];
    str[index] = str[top];
    str[top] = temp;
}

for (int j = 0; j <= n - 1; j++)
{
    Console.WriteLine(str[j]);
}
```

17. Write the output generated by the following program:

```
using System;
public class Mystery
{
    static void Main()
    {
        Mystery m = new Mystery();
        m.traceMe();
    }

    private int[] x;
    private int n;

    public Mystery()
    {
        x = new int[100];
        x[0] = 2;
        x[1] = 4;
        x[2] = 6;
        x[3] = 8;
        x[4] = 10;
        x[5] = 12;
        x[6] = 14;
        x[7] = 16;
        n = 8;
    }

    public void traceMe()
    {
        int first = 0;
        int last = n - 1;
        while (first <= last)
        {
            Console.WriteLine("{0} {1}", x[first], x[last]);
            first++;
            last--;
        }
    }
}
```

18. Write the output generated by the following program using the Huh class.

```
class Huh
{
    static void Main()
    {
```

```
    Huh h = new Huh(4, 4);
    h.Show();
}

private int lastRow;
private int lastCol;
private int[,] m;

public Huh(int initLastRow, int initLastColumn)
{
    lastRow = initLastRow;
    lastCol = initLastColumn;
    // array of arrays must be initialized in constructor
    m = new int[lastRow, lastCol];
    for (int row = 0;  row < lastRow;  row++)
    {
        for (int col = 0;  col < lastCol;  col++)
        {
            m[row, col] = (row + 1) + (col + 1);
        }
    }
}

public void Show()
{
    for (int row = 0;  row < lastRow;  row++)
    {
        for (int col = 0;  col < lastCol;  col++)
        {
            Console.Write("{0,5}", m[row, col]);
        }

        Console.WriteLine();
    }
}
}
```

19. Add a method to Huh that is named IncrementBy and that adds the value of the parameter named increment to every element in the two-dimensional array. The message h.IncrementBy(5) must add 5 to every element in the array.

20. Add a method to Huh that is named RowSum and that returns the sum of all the elements in a given row. A valid call to RowSum is shown in this output statement:
```
int sumOfRow2 = h.RowSum(2);
```

21. Declare a two-dimensional array with three rows and four columns of floating-point numbers.

22. Write the C# code to accomplish the following tasks:

    (a) Declare a two-dimensional array named aTable that stores 10 rows and 14 columns of floating-point numbers.

    (b) Set every element in aTable to -1.0.

    (c) Write a for loop that sets all of the elements in the fourth row (index 3) to 9.9.

23. Show the output from the following program:

```
class TableOfInts
{
  static void Main()
  {
    TableOfInts aTable;
    Console.WriteLine("a.");
    aTable= new TableOfInts(2, 3);
    Console.WriteLine(aTable);

    Console.WriteLine("b.");
    aTable = new TableOfInts(3, 2);
    Console.WriteLine(aTable);

    Console.WriteLine("c.");
    aTable = new TableOfInts(3, 2);
    Console.WriteLine(aTable);

    Console.WriteLine("d.");
    aTable = new TableOfInts(4, 4);
    Console.WriteLine(aTable);

    Console.WriteLine("e.");
    aTable = new TableOfInts(1, 1);
    Console.WriteLine(aTable);
  }

  private int[,] my_data;
  private int my_lastRow;
  private int my_lastCol;
```

```
    public TableOfInts(int maxRow, int maxCol)
    {
      my_lastRow = maxRow;
      my_lastCol = maxCol;
      my_data = new int[my_lastRow, my_lastCol];

      // Initialize the two-dimensional array elements
      for (int row = 0;  row < my_lastRow;  row++)
      {
        for (int col = 0;  col < my_lastCol;  col++)
        {
          my_data[row, col] = row * col;
        }
      }
    }

    public override string ToString()
    { // Display the table elements
      string result = "";
      for(int row = 0; row < my_lastRow; row++)
      {
        for(int col = 0; col < my_lastCol; col++)
        {
          result += string.Format("{0,5}", my_data[row, col]);
        }
        result += "\n";
      }
      return result;
    }
}
```

24. Using this two-dimensional array named t:

```
int nRows = 12;
int nCols = 15;
int[,] t = new int[nRows, nCols];
// Assume that all 12*15 elements of t are initialized
```

and assuming that all of the elements of t have been properly initialized, write code that displays the range of elements (highest to lowest) for each row, on its own separate line.

Programming Tips

1. Remember that C# begins to index at 0.

The first array element is referenced with index 0, not 1 as is done in some other programming languages.

2. An array often has a capacity greater than its number of meaningful elements.

Sometimes arrays are initialized to store more elements than are actually needed. In this case, only the first *n* elements are meaningful. Process the elements numbered 0 through *n* - 1, not the elements numbered 0 through capacity - 1.

3. The last array element in an array x with n elements is x[n - 1], not x[n].

Do not reference x[n]. This can be done by accidentally writing the for loop so the index is out of bounds (writing < rather than <=).

```
// Antibugging tip: Verify that the array and n are
// properly initialized
Console.WriteLine("You entered {0} numbers.", n);
for (int j = 0; j <= n; j++)
{ // Whoops: Throw an exception at x[n]
   Console.WriteLine(x[j]);
}
```

4.   Take the time and effort to display an array after initialization.

This helps ensure that your array is properly initialized before continuing with array processing algorithms. This tip is particularly helpful even in the relatively simple programming exercises in this chapter. This test could be done in the code in Programming Tip 3 by writing this for loop:

```
// Verify that the array and n are properly initialized
for (int j = 0; j < n; j++)
{
   Console.WriteLine(x[j]);
}
```

5. There are searching algorithms other than sequential and binary search.

The sequential search algorithm is only one of several known searching algorithms. For small amounts of data, sequential search works very nicely. For larger amounts of data stored in sorted arrays, the binary search algorithm can be used. In addition, there are other ways to store large amounts of data that can be searched rapidly—hash tables and binary search trees, for example. These topics are typically presented in a second programming course.

6. **The searching algorithm presented here only works with data stored in arrays.**
There is quite often a need to sort and search data stored on a disk (the data could even be on a server in a different country). The algorithms presented here only work on data stored in the computer's main memory. The values disappear when the program finishes. The array processing algorithms are intended only to present the notions of storing a collection until the program terminates.

7. **Many of the programming tips for arrays with one dimension can be applied to two- and three-dimensional arrays:**
   a. Subscripts must be integers.
   b. The range of subscripts is 0 to capacity - 1 (initialized size - 1).
   c. Subscript range-checking is always in force.

Programming Exercises

7A   Reverse

Write a C# program (a class with a Main method only) that inputs an undetermined number of integers (a maximum of 100) and then displays them in reverse order. The user may not supply the number of elements, so a sentinel loop must be used. Here is one sample dialogue:

```
Enter up to 100 ints using -1 to quit:
70
75
90
60
80
-1
Reversed:   80   60   90   75   70
```

7B   Showing the Items That Are Above Average

Write a C# program (a class with a Main method only) that inputs an undetermined collection of numbers, determines the average, and displays every value that is greater than or equal to the average. The user may not supply the number of elements, so the Indeterminate Loop pattern must be used. You may assume that the user will never enter more than 100 numbers. Here is one sample dialogue:

```
Enter numbers or -1 to quit
70.0
75.0
90.0
60.0
80.0
-1
Average: 75.0
Inputs >= average:   75.0   90.0   80.0
```

7C   Fibonacci

The Fibonacci numbers start as 1, 1, 2, 3, 5, 8, 13, 21, and so on. The first two numbers are 1, and any successive Fibonacci number is the sum of the preceding two. Write a C# program (a class with a Main method only) that properly initializes an array named fibonacci to represent the first 20 Fibonacci numbers (fibonacci[1] is the second Fibonacci number). Do not use 20 assignment statements to do this. Three should suffice.

7D   Modify AccountList's RemoveElementWithID 1

Modify the RemoveElementWithID method of the AccountList class so that it maintains the order of elements after the element is removed. If the fields look like this (BankAccounts are represented by their ID; the word "Kim" below implies an account with ID of "Kim"):

```
accountArray        size: 3
[0]    [1]    [2]    [3]    [4]    [5]    [6]    [7]    [8]    [9]
Kim    John   Sally  null   null   null   null   null   null   null
```

then the following message should change the fields to look as shown below:

```
accounts.RemoveAccountWithID("Kim");
```

```
accountArray        size: 3
[0]    [1]    [2]    [3]    [4]    [5]    [6]    [7]    [8]    [9]
John   Sally  null   null   null   null   null   null   null   null
```

In other words, you may not simply move the last account (Sally's account, in this case) to fill the hole left by the removed element. Instead, use a loop to slide all elements after the one that is being removed one position to the left.

7E   Modify `AccountList`'s `RemoveElementWithID` 2

Modify the `RemoveElementWithID` method of the `AccountList` class so that it decreases the array capacity by half when the `size` is 10 elements less than half of the capacity. The following table shows the size and the array capacity before and after certain successful removals of one element.

Size Before	Capacity Before	Size After	Capacity After
10	10	9	10
10	40	9	20
490	1000	489	500
489	500	488	500

7F   Odd-Sized Magic Squares

A magic square is an n-by-n array where each integer from 1 to n^2 appears exactly once, and the sum of the integers in every row, every column, and on both diagonals, is the same. For example, the following is a 7-by-7 magic square. Notice that each row, each column, and both diagonals total 175 (in general, the sum is $n * (n^2 + 1) / 2$):

```
30   39   48    1   10   19   28

38   47    7    9   18   27   29

46    6    8   17   26   35   37

 5   14   16   25   34   36   45

13   15   24   33   42   44    4

21   23   32   41   43    3   12

22   31   40   49    2   11   20
```

Implement `MagicSquare` with a constructor and a `Display` method. With the algorithm given below, the argument must be odd. Ignore the possibility of invalid sizes.

```
class MagicSquare
{
  public static readonly int MAX_SIZE = 19;
  // ...
```

```
public MagicSquare(int initSize)
{
  // ...
```

The following code should generate output like that shown above:

```
MagicSquare magic = new MagicSquare(7);
magic.Display();
```

Also test other magic square sizes:

```
MagicSquare magic3 = new MagicSquare(3);
magic3.Display();

MagicSquare magic5 = new MagicSquare(5);
magic5.Display();
```

You should be able to construct an n-by-n magic square for any size from 3 through 19. Use j as a counter for the numbers that you place in the magic square. You'll also need variables to keep track of row and column.

When j is 1, place the value of j in the middle of the first row. Then, for j ranging from 2 to n^2, move up one row and to the right by one column and store value of j there, unless one of the following events occurs (*Note:* There are other algorithms for handling even numbers):

1. When the row variable becomes 0, set the row variable to n - 1. Store the value of j there.
2. When the column variable becomes n, set the column variable to 0. Store the value of j there.
3. If the array element that is up one row and one row to the right is already filled, or if you have just placed a value in the upper-right corner element, place the next value (j) in the position that is one row below the position where the last counter value was placed.

7G GradeTable's GetAssignmentAverage

Write the GetAssignmentAverage method left missing from the GradeTable class implemented in the "2D Arrays and Class Design" section of this chapter. The method should return the overall assignment average of all assignments completed by all students.

```
Console.WriteLine("Assignment Average: {0:F1}",
  table.GetAssignmentAverage());
```

Output

```
Assignment Average: 74.5
```

7H GradeTable's PrintAssignmentStatistics

Implement `GradeTable.PrintAssignmentStatistics`. This method must generate a report for all of the assignments, with output like that shown below. For each assignment, show the highest and lowest scores, followed by the average.

```
table.PrintAssignmentStatistics();
```

Output

```
Assignment   High    Low  Average
=================================
         0   94.4   57.9     79.9
         1   95.5   49.5     74.6
         2  100.0   40.0     77.7
         3  100.0    3.0     72.3
         4   98.0    2.0     69.7
         5   99.5    1.0     72.9
```

File Input/Output (I/O) and Exceptions

Summing Up

You have learned how to control your programs' structure using conditional statements like `if`/`else` and `switch`, as well as loop structures like `while` and `for`. You have also learned how to store large sets of data into arrays. However, the interaction in your programs so far has been limited to keyboard input.

Coming Up

This chapter presents a method for reading input from files and writing output to files. You will also see how very large objects can be written to a file before a program terminates, so they can be read back in to the most recent state when the program starts up later. After studying this chapter, you will be able to:

- ○ use some of C#'s input/output classes to read and write files.
- ○ save data to a file for later use.
- ○ understand C#'s exception-handling mechanism.
- ○ learn to try, throw, catch, and avoid exceptions.
- ○ save and restore objects using serialization and deserialization (optional).

8.1 Files, Streams, Readers, and Writers

When a program is running, it stores and updates data—such as variables, objects, and so on—in memory. Memory is sometimes referred to as *primary storage* in a computer because it is often the first place data is stored. However, primary storage in memory is not permanent. When a program terminates, the memory associated with that program is cleared. The data is lost.

You will often need to save data after a program ends, or to read data from a source outside the program. Usually this data comes from a disk storage device such as a hard disk, shared network drive, CD-ROM, or floppy disk. These kinds of storage devices are called *secondary storage*. They are more permanent than primary storage in memory, because if a program saves data to a disk, the data remains after the program terminates.

Data on secondary storage devices is organized into files. A *file* is a named collection of bytes. The file ends with a special byte marker called an *end-of-file marker* (often called *EOF* for short), so that programs can tell how big the file is, and when to stop reading data from it. A *directory* (also sometimes called a *folder*) is a collection of files. A directory can also contain other directories. The following figure shows a file that contains *n* bytes of data:

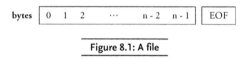

Figure 8.1: A file

You have worked with files before. Each C# program you have written was a file with a name ending in .cs. In this chapter, you write programs that save their data to be used after the program ends. Two common methods are to write the data into a file on the computer's hard disk, or on a network drive. The next time it runs, the program can read the data back from the same file.

C# has libraries of classes for reading and writing data to files. However, in C# the focus is not on the source of the data (the file), but instead on the transmission of data from one place to another. Input and output have been generalized in C#. This means that the methods and classes used to read data from the screen or from a file on a hard disk are the same as the methods and classes used to read data from other sources, such as the Internet or a CD-ROM.

In C#, data channels from one point to another are represented by objects called streams. A *stream* is a transmission channel through which a sequential group of bytes can be read or written from one place to another. Usually, streams are used in conjunction with *readers* and *writers*. These are unidirectional data transfer objects that can send data to, or read data from, a stream.

To read a file in a C# program, you must:

1. create a stream object that represents a connection to that file
2. get a reader for that stream
3. read the bytes in order from the reader

435

Fortunately, you can open a stream to almost any data source, such a connection over a local network, a Web page, or even directly from memory. This lets you read data from almost anywhere.

The C# libraries for reading and writing data using streams are found in the `System.IO` namespace. To use streams, readers, and writers in your code, you must put `using System.IO;` at the top of your program.

Reading Files with `StreamReader`

Formally, the correct way to read a file is to construct a stream that represents a connection to that input source, such as a file. Then you connect the stream to a reader that reads data from the stream. However, C# also makes it easier to read a file without these multiple steps. The easier way is to construct a `StreamReader` object by passing a `string` for the file you want to read. Here is the general form for doing this:

General Form: Constructing a StreamReader to read from a file

StreamReader *variable-name* **= new StreamReader**(*file-name*)**;**

Examples:

```
StreamReader reader = new StreamReader("input.txt");
StreamReader reader2 = new StreamReader("C:\\data\\taxes.dat");
```

Notes:

If *file-name* is not found, trying to construct the stream reader will throw a `FileNotFoundException`, which will terminate the program.

`StreamReader` objects have many useful methods. Here is a partial list:

StreamReader constructor

```
public StreamReader(string filename)
```

Constructs a new stream reader to read data from the specified file.

StreamReader object (instance) methods

```
public void Close()
```

Shuts down the reader and stops reading data from the stream.

```
public int Peek()
```

Looks ahead to the current character of data in the stream and returns it as an int, without advancing the reader; returns −1 if end of stream has been reached.

`public int Read()`
Reads one byte of data from the stream and returns it as an int; returns −1 if end of stream has been reached.

`public string ReadLine()`
Reads many bytes of data as characters until an end-of-line (\n) character is reached, and returns the characters as a string; returns null if end of stream has been reached.

`public string ReadToEnd()`
Reads characters from the reader's current position to the end of the file or data source, and returns the characters as a string; returns null if end of stream has been reached.

To visualize how a reader reads data from a file, picture it as having a reading head that points to a particular place in the file. As you read bytes or lines from the file, the reader advances its reading head through the file. Peeking ahead one byte does not move the reading head. The head cannot go past the end-of-file marker at the end of the stream's data.

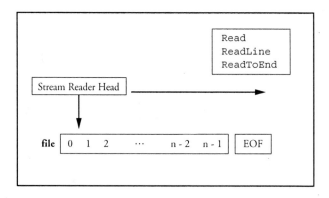

Figure 8.2: Stream reader diagram

Since files can contain arbitrarily large amounts of data, programs usually read files by using an indeterminate `while` loop that grabs the next character or line. After data is read, the loop's condition tests if the file has more data; if so, it then reads the next piece of data. As we will see, it is important to see if the file has more data or not. This can be done in several ways. One way is to use the `Peek` method to see if the next byte in the file is −1; if so, the reader has reached the end of the file, and reading should stop. Another way is to call `ReadLine` or `ReadToEnd` and see if they return a `null` string. If so, the end of the file has been reached.

The following program reads a file input.txt and writes its contents to the screen. For the program to work, there must be a file named input.txt in the same folder as the folder from which the program is run.

Code Sample: Class ReadEntireFile

```
 1  using System;
 2  using System.IO;
 3
 4  class ReadEntireFile
 5  {
 6    static void Main()
 7    {
 8      // open a stream reader to read the file
 9      StreamReader reader = new StreamReader("input.txt");
10
11      // keep track of line numbers
12      int lineNum = 1;
13
14      // read each line from the file and print it with its number
15      while (reader.Peek() != -1)
16      {
17        string line = reader.ReadLine();
18        Console.WriteLine("Line {0}: {1}", lineNum, line);
19        lineNum++;
20      }
21
22      // done reading; close the file
23      reader.Close();
24    }
25  }
```

Input file "input.txt"

```
here are two lines
of text
here is            another

that last one was a blank line

so was that one
this is the last line
```

Output

```
Line 1: here are two lines
Line 2: of text
Line 3: here is              another
Line 4:
Line 5: that last one was a blank line
Line 6:
Line 7: so was that one
Line 8: this is the last line
```

Self-Check

8-1   Name two sources of data for which a C# stream can be constructed to read the data.

8-2   What does it mean when a call to Peek on a stream reader returns -1?

8-3   What could you assume if a stream reader returned -1 from its Peek method the very first time Peek was called, before any information was even read from the file?

Specifying Path Names

The previous example used input.txt as the file name to read. No folder or directory information was given about where input.txt existed on the disk. When no folder name is given, the input file input.txt must be in the same folder as the executable program.

When the input file is in a different folder than the executable program, you must put a folder name before the file name, such as myfiles\inputdata\input.txt. If this string were passed to the StreamReader, it would look for a file named input.txt in the myfiles\inputdata subfolder of the folder from which the program was run. These kinds of file name specifications, which may specify no folder at all, or which may specify a folder that is a subfolder of the current directory, are called *relative paths*.

Beware of the common mistake of the leading backslash when specifying relative paths. A relative path of myfiles\inputdata\input.txt is very different from a relative path of \myfiles\inputdata\input.txt. (note the leading backslash). The former refers to the file input.txt in the myfiles\inputdata subfolder of the current folder; if the program was run from the folder C:\school\programs, the entire path would be C:\school\programs\myfiles\inputdata\input.txt. The latter refers to the file input.txt in the \myfiles\inputdata folder on the current drive (regardless of the current working folder); if the program was run from the same folder `C:\school\programs`, the entire path would be `C:\myfiles\inputdata\input.txt`. In almost all cases, the intention is *not* to use the leading backslash; be cautious when specifying paths to avoid this very common and confusing mistake.

It is also legal to specify a fully qualified path to the file name. A fully qualified path, or *absolute path*, includes the entire path to the file, including the drive letter (if applicable) and all folders and subfolders that the file is in. An example of an absolute path would be `C:\programs\myfiles\inputdata\input.txt`.

The advantage of specifying an absolute path is that the input file does not have to be in the same folder as the executable program, or in a subfolder of that folder. The disadvantage is that the file location is fixed. If the file is moved to a different folder, the absolute path string is out of sync and must be changed. For simplicity and versatility, all examples in this chapter use relative paths for their input and output files.

Since folder names are separated by \ characters on Windows systems, and \ specifies special escape sequences in C#, it can be inconvenient to express file paths as strings. For example, to specify the above absolute path, the following string would be needed:

```
"C:\\programs\\myfiles\\inputdata\\input.txt"
```

The C# compiler interprets each double backslash (\\) as being a single backslash. Without the double backslashes, the string would not compile correctly.

However, there is an easier way to specify paths. To do so, place the @ character before the path name. Instead of the above string with double-backslashes, you can write a string like:

```
@"C:\programs\myfiles\inputdata\input.txt"
```

Using this type of string tells the C# compiler not to interpret the backslashes as control characters. Such a string is called an *uninterpreted string*, because special character combinations such as \n and \\ are not interpreted as special characters. Using uninterpreted strings lets you write more convenient and readable code for constructing stream readers to read long path strings, such as:

```
StreamReader reader = new StreamReader(@"H:\home\programs\data.dat");
```

You must be careful when you place a quotation mark character in an uninterpreted string. Using \" will not work, because the \ will no longer be interpreted as a special character. Because of this, the first quotation mark encountered will be interpreted as making the end of the string. Instead, in an uninterpreted string, always use two quotation mark characters back-to-back ("") to indicate a quotation mark character:

```
string str = @"Bob said, ""Hello there!"" to me.";
Console.WriteLine(str);
```

Output

```
Bob said, "Hello there!" to me.
```

Reading and Processing a File of Data

Often a file represents a list of entries of data. The data entries can be read one-by-one in your program and processed individually. All the ways that you learned in previous chapters for reading and parsing input from the console will also work here. The only difference is that with files, the contents are usually fixed before your program runs, not generated on-the-fly by users at the keyboard. With keyboard input, you can use the Prompt and Input pattern to prompt the user for input in a particular format. But with file input, you cannot do this. This is not a large problem; if you know the format of the data in the file ahead of time, you can write code to correctly read that data and process it.

Consider the following `Accumulator` class, which maintains a running sum and average of a group of numbers. When a new number is added to the `Accumulator`, it increments its count of how many numbers have been added, and it adds the number to its running sum. This allows the program to compute the sum and average.

Code Sample: Class Accumulator

```
 1  using System;
 2
 3  // Adds numbers and reports the count, sum, and average.
 4  class Accumulator
 5  {
 6    private double sum;     // fields
 7    private int count;
 8
 9    public Accumulator()
10    {
11      sum = 0.0;             // initialize fields
12      count = 0;
13    }
14
15    // The sum of all the numbers accumulated so far.
16    public double Sum
17    {
18      get { return sum; }
```

```
19   }
20
21   // The count of how many numbers have been accumulated.
22   public int Count
23   {
24      get { return count; }
25   }
26
27   // Determine average; 0.0 when there are no numbers
28   public double Average
29   {
30      get
31      {
32         if (count > 0)
33            return sum / count;
34         else                        // avoid division by zero
35            return 0.0;
36      }
37   }
38
39   // Add one number to this accumulator.
40   public void Add(double number)
41   {
42      sum += number;
43      count++;
44   }
45 }
```

Now that there is an Accumulator to work with, imagine a file full of numbers to read, named numbers.txt. A C# program can be written that reads each number from this file and then turns it over to the Accumulator to add to its running sum. After each number is added, stats can be written on the screen about the numbers that have been read, and about the accumulator data.

Code Sample: Class UseAccumulator

```
1 using System;
2 using System.IO;
3
4 class UseAccumulator
5 {
6    static void Main()
7    {
8       Accumulator accum = new Accumulator();
9       StreamReader reader = new StreamReader("numbers.txt");
```

```
10
11      // write an output header
12      Console.WriteLine("{0,10}{1,10}{2,10}{3,10}",
13                        "COUNT", "NUMBER", "SUM", "AVERAGE");
14      Console.WriteLine(new string('=', 40));
15
16      // read each line of input and write a summary line of output
17      while (reader.Peek() != -1)
18      {
19        double number = double.Parse(reader.ReadLine());
20        accum.Add(number);
21        Console.WriteLine("{0,10}{1,10:F1}{2,10:F1}{3,10:F1}",
22                          accum.Count, number, accum.Sum,
23                          accum.Average);
24      }
25
26      reader.Close();
27    }
28 }
```

---

input file "numbers.txt"

```
12.0
23.2
16.7
55.3
34.0
27.1
63.4
6.0
75.9
41.4
83.3
19.0
```

Output

COUNT	NUMBER	SUM	AVERAGE
===	=======	====	=====
1	12.0	12.0	12.0
2	23.2	35.2	17.6
3	16.7	51.9	17.3
4	55.3	107.2	26.8

5	34.0	141.2	28.2
6	27.1	168.3	28.1
7	63.4	231.7	33.1
8	6.0	237.7	29.7
9	75.9	313.6	34.8
10	41.4	355.0	35.5
11	83.3	438.3	39.8
12	19.0	457.3	38.1

Self-Check

8-4   If a C# program is running from the `C:\Programs\Test` folder, give an absolute and relative (if possible) path string to represent each of the following:

(a) `C:\Programs\Test\MyCode.cs`

(b) `C:\Programs\Test\input\debug\data.txt`

(d) `D:\WINNT\SYSTEM32\MSHTML.DLL`

8-5   Write a complete C# program that reads the file input.dat and grabs the first letter of each line in the file. The program must concatenate the letters together to form a combined string. For example, if `input.dat` contains this text:

```
students
have
always
respected
programmers
```

The output from the program is:

```
Message: sharp
```

Complex Input and String Splitting

The preceding example read an input file that contained numbers, one per line. The format of the file made it relatively easy to read it into the program. However, sometimes you must deal with more complex input, such as a file that contains multiple pieces of data on each line. When this is the case, the `Split` method of a `string` object can be very useful. `Split` is a method that tokenizes a string; to *tokenize* means to break it into separate pieces or tokens. `Split` breaks a string into smaller pieces, based on the criteria you give it. It returns the pieces as an array of `strings`. When calling `Split`, you must pass a group of `char` characters that represent the markers that tell `Split` where to chop the string up. These markers are called the *delimiters*.

One common use of Split is to split a line into words, based on whitespace. The figure below shows how the following string is split into an array of smaller strings:

```
"Hello, how are you doing?"
```

Sending a Split message to this string, and passing in as delimiters ' ' (blank space character), ',' (comma), and '?' (question mark) causes these three characters to be seen as places to chop the string. The delimiters are not included in the broken smaller strings returned by Split. Consecutive occurrences of the same delimiter are treated as one delimiter, but consecutive occurrences of different delimiters are treated separately. So, the ", " between Hello and how is considered two delimiters, with an empty string of "" between them.

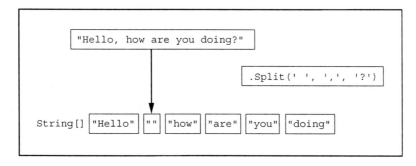

Figure 8.3: Splitting a string

```
string str = "Hello, how are you doing?"
string[] tokens = str.Split(' ', ',', '?');
foreach (string token in tokens)
   Console.WriteLine(token);
```

Output
Hello
how
are
you
doing

String splitting is very useful when you process complex input files. For example, consider an input file named students.txt in the following format. The data in the file represents a list of students, listing each student's name, ID, and GPA.

```
Jones, Cindy          5193     3.75
Spattery, Thomas      3267     2.47
Richards, Marcy       2359     2.98
Millor, Jesse         0976     3.16
```

It would be very tedious to parse such a file using previous `string` methods, like `IndexOf` and `Substring`, to extract the pieces of information from each line. However, using `Split` with the right delimiters makes the parsing much easier.

To remove all unwanted characters from the string, it is important to specify the proper set of delimiters. In the sample data shown above, the regions containing the student IDs and GPAs line up because there is a tab character after the students' names. So, using the tab character as a delimiter (`'\t'`) is a good start. You also need to specify as delimiters the standard space character (`' '`), which precedes the last names and the GPAs, and the comma (`','`), which separates the last names from the first names.

The following program reads `students.txt` and splits the lines to extract the useful tokens. Each student's information is put into a `Student` object, which is then written to the screen.

Code Sample: Class Student

```
 1 using System;
 2 using System.IO;
 3
 4 // Represents a student and his/her grades and student ID.
 5 class Student
 6 {
 7    private string name;
 8    private int id;
 9    private double gpa;
10
11    public Student(string init_name, int init_id, double init_gpa)
12    {
13      name = init_name;   // initialize fields
14      id = init_id;
15      gpa = init_gpa;
16    }
17
18    public override string ToString()
19    { // returns string with student's name, ID, GPA
20      return string.Format("[Name={0,-16}  ID={1:D4}   GPA={2:F2}]",
21                           name, id, gpa);
22    }
23 }
24
25 // Reads student information from a file and creates
26 // Student objects to store it.
27 class ReadStudentsFromFile
```

```
28 {
29   static void Main()
30   {
31     StreamReader reader = new StreamReader("students.txt");
32
33     while (reader.Peek() != -1)
34     {
35       string line = reader.ReadLine();
36       string[] tokens = line.Split(' ', '\t', ',');
37
38       // now tokens array looks like this:
39       // ["Jones" "" "Cindy" "5193" "3.75"]
40
41       // build name from last name and first name
42       string name = tokens[2] + " " + tokens[0];
43
44       int id = int.Parse(tokens[3]);
45       double gpa = double.Parse(tokens[4]);
46
47       Student stu = new Student(name, id, gpa);
48       Console.WriteLine("Student: {0}", stu);
49     }
50
51     reader.Close();
52   }
53 }
```

	Output
Student: [Name=Cindy Jones   ID=5193 GPA=3.75]
Student: [Name=Thomas Spattery ID=3267 GPA=2.47]
Student: [Name=Marcy Richards ID=2359 GPA=2.98]
Student: [Name=Jesse Millor   ID=0976 GPA=3.16]

File I/O with Command-Line Arguments

As discussed in the previous chapter, it is legal to declare Main to have a parameter, which is an array of strings for command-line arguments.

```
static void Main(string[] args)
```

Command-line arguments (parameters entered after the program name on the command line) are particularly useful when you write a program that reads files. For example, rather than hard-coding the file names being read, as in the previous programs in this chapter, the Main method can

447

read the file names as command-line arguments to the program. To ensure that an argument is passed, you can check the Length property of the args array to ensure that it is non-zero.

Code Sample: Class FileDisplayer

```
1  // Displays a file with line numbers on each line.
2  using System;
3  using System.IO;
4
5  class FileDisplayer
6  {
7    static void Main(string[] args)
8    {
9      if (args.Length == 0)
10        Console.WriteLine("Usage: FileDisplayer [file-name]");
11      else
12      {
13        // open the file
14        string filename = args[0];
15        StreamReader reader = new StreamReader(filename);
16
17        int lineNum = 1;
18        while (reader.Peek() != -1)
19        {
20          // read a line
21          string line = reader.ReadLine();
22
23          // write the line with a line number at the start
24          Console.WriteLine("{0,3} {1}", lineNum, line);
25          lineNum++;
26        }
27      }
28    }
29 }
```

The following output is generated when this command is entered at the command line:
FileDisplayer FileDisplayer.cs

Output (the line numbers are part of the output)

```
1 using System;
2 using System.IO;
3
4 class FileDisplayer
5 {
6   static void Main(string[] args)
7   {
```

```
 8        if (args.Length == 0)
 9          Console.WriteLine("Usage: FileDisplayer [file-name]");
10        else
11        {
12          string filename = args[0];
13          StreamReader reader = new StreamReader(filename);
14          int lineNum = 1;
15          while (reader.Peek() != -1)
16          {
17            string line = reader.ReadLine();
18            Console.WriteLine("{0,3} {1}", lineNum, line);
19            lineNum++;
20          }
21        }
22      }
23  }
```

Self-Check

8-6 How many elements are in each of the following arrays, given the following variable declaration?

```
string msg = "Marty $12.50 | Kate $50.00 | Julie $20.56";
```

     (a) `msg.Split(' ')`

     (b) `msg.Split('|')`

     (c) `msg.Split(' ', '|')`

     (d) `msg.Split('$', '.', '|')`

8-7 Write a complete C# program that accepts any number of file names as arguments and writes each file's entire contents to the screen. You may assume that two arguments are passed to the program.

8-8 Write a complete C# program that takes an absolute file path as its argument and constructs a tree output format of the path hierarchy. If the program is run with an argument of "C:\Documents\Csharp\Program1.cs", the output would be

```
C:
|
+--Documents
   |
   +--Csharp
      |
      +--Program1.cs
```

Assume that the argument is in the proper format.

Writing to Files with `StreamWriter`

Just as there is a `StreamReader` that can be used to read files, there is a `StreamWriter` to write data to a stream, such as a file.

General Form: Constructing a StreamWriter to write to a file

`StreamWriter` *variable-name* = **new** `StreamWriter`(*file-name*);

Example:

`StreamWriter writer = new StreamWriter("output.txt");`

Note:

If the file with *file-name* does not exist, a new one is created. If a file with *file-name* does exist, it is erased (or new text can be added to it, if true is given as a second argument in the constructor).

Here is a summary of the useful methods and properties found in a `StreamWriter`:

StreamWriter constructors

`public StreamWriter(string fileName)`
Constructs a new StreamWriter to write data to the stream represented by the given file name. By default, overwrites any data previously in the file.

`public StreamWriter(string fileName, bool append)`
Constructs a new `StreamWriter` to write data to the stream represented by the given file name. If append is true, existing contents of the file are kept and new data is written after them. Otherwise, new data replaces the existing contents of the file.

StreamWriter object (instance) properties

`public bool AutoFlush {get; set;}`
Represents whether this writer should commit its writes immediately to the underlying stream by calling `Flush` after each call to `Write`.

StreamWriter object (instance) methods

`public void Close()`
Shuts down the reader and stops reading data from the stream.

`public void Flush()`
Clears any possible buffers in the writer and forces its data through the underlying output stream.

```
public void Write(string str)
```
Writes all characters in str to this writer's output stream.

To write data to a file, construct a `StreamWriter` to write to that file's stream, then call `Write` on a `StreamWriter` and pass it a `string` to write into the file. If the file does not exist, it will be created. If the file already exists and has contents, the contents will be erased and replaced by what you write into the file (unless `append` is set to `true`, which is not done in the following examples).

You might be tempted to use a `StreamWriter` much like you use `Console.WriteLine`, but there are a few differences in the syntax. First, there is no `WriteLine` in a `StreamWriter`, only `Write`. So if you want to move to the next line, you must do so manually by using a `\n` character. Second, the `Write` method in `StreamWriter` takes only a `string`, not a format string with parameters following it. If you want complex formatted output like you have used with `Console.WriteLine`, use `string.Format` to build a format string, then `Write` that string. The following short program shows an example of writing to a file named `output.txt`.

Code Sample: Class WriteToFile

```
1  // Writes some data to a file using a StreamWriter.
2  using System;
3  using System.IO;
4
5  class WriteToFile
6  {
7     static void Main()
8     {
9        StreamWriter writer = new StreamWriter("output.txt");
10       writer.Write("Here is a line of text.\n");
11       writer.Write("\n");      // need \n to move to next line
12       writer.Write("That last one was a blank line!\n");
13       writer.Write(string.Format("A format string: {0:C} {1:F2}\n",
14                                  2.0, 1.234));
15       writer.Write("This is the end of the file.");
16       writer.Close();
17    }
18 }
```

Output to file "output.txt"

```
Here is a line of text.

That last one was a blank line!
A format string: $2.00 1.23
This is the end of the file.
```

It is important to remember to close the output stream by calling `Close` on the stream writer. If this is not done, there is a chance that the lines you write to the file may be lost. On some C# implementations, output is buffered. This means that it is held in a special area of memory and is not actually written out until the stream is flushed or closed. To *flush* a stream means to force all bytes through it immediately, which causes its output to be written. Closing a stream writer flushes its stream, as does calling the `Flush` method on the writer. You can also set the `AutoFlush` Boolean property to `true` to force each `Write` to be committed to the file immediately.

Self-Check

8-9   A `StreamWriter` has only `Write`, not `WriteLine`, and its `Write` method only takes one argument: the string to write. How can you get around these differences from `Console.WriteLine` and still go to the next line, or use formatted text strings?

8-10   What should you always do after finishing writing to a stream writer, to ensure that the data actually gets written?

8-11   Write a complete C# program that accepts two file names as arguments. The program reads the first file and writes each of its lines, reversed, into the other file. If your program is run with `in.txt` and `out.txt` as its arguments, and `in.txt` has the following contents:

```
hello
how are you
```

After the program is run, `out.txt` will contain the following contents:

```
olleh
uoy era woh
```

8.2 Exceptions

When programs run, errors occur. Perhaps the user enters a string that is supposed to be a number. When it gets parsed, the `int.Parse` or `double.Parse` method discovers that the string does not represent a valid number. Or perhaps an arithmetic expression results in division by zero. Or an array subscript is out of bounds. Perhaps there is attempt to read a file from a floppy disk, but there is no disk in the floppy drive. Perhaps a file with a specific name does not exist. In C#, an error that occurs while the program is running is called an *exception*.

You have probably already seen the word "exception" several times, since it is part of the error output that is written to the screen when a program crashes. The act of an exception occurring is called the ***throwing*** of an exception. When an exception is thrown and nothing is done to stop or correct it, the program crashes (which you have no doubt experienced first-hand by now!).

Exceptions in C# are represented by objects with type names that are representative of the type of error. Consider what happens when a user enters a `string` input that does not represent a valid number. During the `Parse` method call, the code recognizes this exceptional event and throws a `FormatException`:

Code Sample: Class CauseException

```
1  // Demonstrates causing an exception when input is not a number.
2  using System;
3
4  class CauseException
5  {
6    static void Main()
7    {
8      Console.Write("Enter an integer: ");
9
10     string numString = Console.ReadLine();
11     int anInt = int.Parse(numString);
12
13     Console.WriteLine("{0} stored in number as {1}",
14                       numString, anInt);
15     Console.ReadLine();
16   }
17 }
```

Dialogue (when the integer is valid)

```
Enter an integer: 123
123 stored in number as 123
```

Dialogue (when the integer is not valid)

```
Enter an integer: oops!
An unhandled exception of type 'System.FormatException' occurred in
mscorlib.dll
Additional information: Input string was not in a correct format.
```

It is impossible to predict when a user will enter an invalid number. But the chances are very good that it will happen at one point or another. This type of problem can be dealt with in several ways. The first is the way you have dealt with exceptions so far: to ignore it. This solution is easy on the programmer, but it leaves the program not robust to errors, and more likely to crash during execution.

The next technique is to try your best to avoid errors beforehand by carefully checking conditions whenever possible. For example, you could look at each character in the string read in with the ReadLine method call, checking if it is a digit; this might help to ensure that the string was a valid number and could be parsed. This technique is called *exception avoidance*. Exception avoidance is important and should be used when possible, but it can be more trouble than it is worth. Can you imagine how tedious it would be to check every letter of every line read in from the keyboard, just to avoid a FormatException and a program crash?

Not only is exception avoidance inconvenient at times, but it is sometimes impossible. For example, when you try to open a file to read it using a StreamReader, the construction of the stream reader can throw a FileNotFoundException if the file you specify does not exist. But using the classes we have discussed so far, you cannot accurately avoid this exception ahead of time. There is no easy way to confirm that the file exists before trying to read it, using the data types discussed so far.

Exception Handling

If exception avoidance is difficult or impossible, you can use another technique: *exception handling*. Just as the occurrence of an exception is called throwing, the handling of an exception is called *catching* the exception. To catch an exception in C#, you must enclose a group of statements in a special block called a **try block**. A try block is written by writing the keyword try, then a pair of braces with statements between them. A try block must be followed by a *catch block*, which specifies what types of exception(s) you intend to handle, and what you intend to do about them. If any statement in the `try` block throws an exception for which you have a `catch` block, the code in the `catch` block is executed, and the program does not crash.

Here is the general form for exception handling in C# using `try` and `catch` blocks:

General Form: Exception handling

```
try
{
  code that may possibly throw an exception
}
catch (exception-type variable-name)
{
  code to handle the exception
}
```

Example:

```
try
{
   Console.WriteLine("Enter two numbers");
   int number1 = int.Parse(Console.ReadLine());
   double number2 = double.Parse(Console.ReadLine());
}
catch (FormatException exception)
{
   Console.WriteLine("A problem occurred with the input!");
   Console.WriteLine("Details: {0}", exception.Message);
}
```

The *variable-name* that declares a name for the exception variable is optional; you should only give the exception variable a name if you intend to use it in the `catch` block. A common way to use the exception variable in the `catch` block is to write it to the screen, or to print its contained error message.

The *exception-type* specifies a C# type representing some kind of exception. There are many types of exception objects in C#. Here is a partial list:

Type	Description
Exception	general errors that happen during program execution
ArgumentException	an argument passed to a method was invalid
ArithmeticException	inability to perform arithmetic, cast, or conversion
DivideByZeroException	attempt to divide an integer value by zero
FileNotFoundException	attempt to access a file that does not exist on disk
FormatException	incorrectly formatted string, number, etc.
IndexOutOfRangeException	attempt to access outside the bounds of an array
IOException	failure to perform I/O, such as to the hard disk
NullReferenceException	attempt to send a message to a null reference variable
OutOfMemoryException	not enough memory to continue running the program
OverflowException	arithmetic operation goes outside range of int type

Of the exceptions shown above, IOException and FileNotFoundException belong to the namespace System.IO. The rest shown belong to the System namespace.

Exception objects in C# contain state that represents the type of error that occurred, as well as more information about the error. Here is a partial list of useful methods and properties that you can use on an exception object. The exception object only exists inside its corresponding catch block.

Object (instance) properties found in exception objects

```
public string Message {get;}
```
Returns a string representation of the error that occurred.

```
public string Source {get; set;}
```
Returns a string representation of the application or object that caused the error.

Object (instance) methods found in exception objects

```
public override string ToString()
```
Returns a string representation of this exception, plus the list of methods that led to the error.

The following Main method provides an example of handling a FormatException. The exception handling code (in the catch block) executes only when the code in the try block throws an exception. This avoids premature program termination when the input string contains an invalid number.

Code Sample: Class HandleException

```
1  // Demonstrates handling one exception (FormatException).
2  using System;
3
4  class HandleException
5  {
6    public static readonly double DEFAULT_VALUE = -1.0;
7
8    static void Main()
9    { // read a number
10     Console.Write("Enter an integer: ");
11     string numString = Console.ReadLine();
12     double number;
13
14     try
15     { // convert the number from string to double
16       number = double.Parse(numString);
17       Console.WriteLine("Number parsed successfully.");
18     }
19     catch (FormatException fe)
20     {
21       // Execute this code whenever Parse throws an exception
22       Console.WriteLine("Error with value {0}: {1}",
23                           numString, fe.Message);
24       Console.WriteLine("Setting number to {0}", DEFAULT_VALUE);
25       number = DEFAULT_VALUE;  // reset to -1
26     }
27
28     Console.WriteLine("{0} stored as {1}", numString, number);
29   }
30 }
```

Dialogue (when the exception does not occur)

```
Enter a number: 101
Number parsed successfully.
101 stored as 101
```

Dialogue (when the exception is handled)

```
Enter an integer: walrus
Error with value walrus: Input string was not in a correct format.
Setting number to -1
walrus stored as -1
```

Instead of ignoring the possibility of exceptional events at runtime, this program now handles potential exceptions by setting the number to an arbitrary error value of -1.0. Notice that the code in the catch block only executes if the exception is actually thrown; otherwise it is skipped. Also, notice that when the exception does occur, the program stops executing code from the try block and immediately jumps to the catch block. This is why the output, "Number parsed successfully." is not shown when the exception occurs.

It is never mandatory to catch a possible exception in C#, even if you are fairly sure it will occur. This kind of exception—one that you do not need to catch if you do not so desire—is called a *runtime exception* or an *unchecked exception.* Some programming languages also have *checked exceptions*, which must be caught in order for the code to compile. Checked exceptions force the programmer to deal with error cases explicitly, but they can be constricting and annoying in cases where the programmer does not want to handle them. In C#, all exceptions are unchecked and need not be caught if you do not wish to do so.

To catch exceptions intelligently, you need to know which statements can throw which types of exceptions. Most normal statements run a small chance of generating an exception. Some of the more common possible exceptions that can be generated by normal code include dividing by zero (DivideByZeroException), dereferencing a null variable (NullReferenceException), and indexing an array improperly (IndexOutOfRangeException). But many method calls on various objects and classes run higher risks of generating exceptions.

Luckily, in the .NET Framework Reference Documentation, every method lists all the exceptions that it may throw. Here is an excerpt from the documentation on the int.Parse method:

Exceptions that can be thrown by int.Parse

Exception Type	Condition
ArgumentException	The argument is a null reference.
FormatException	The argument does not consist solely of an optional negative sign followed by a sequence of digits ranging from 0 to 9.
OverflowException	The argument represents a number less than int.MinValue or greater than int.MaxValue.

Self-Check

8-12 What exceptions, if any, could be thrown by each of the following statements?

(a) `double x = 7.0 / y;`

(b)
```
int i = int.Parse(Console.ReadLine());
int j = 7 / i;
```

(c)
```
string[] names = new string[5];
names[0] = "Austin";
Console.WriteLine(names[1].ToUpper());
```

(d) `StreamReader reader = new StreamReader("exception.txt");`

8-13 Accessing an array throws an `IndexOutOfRangeException` exception when there is no element at the index specified. Consider the following program:

```
using System;

class HandleArrayIndices
{
  static void Main()
  {
    string[] names = new string[] {"Jane", null, "Mary"};
    Console.Write("Index? ");

    int index = int.Parse(Console.ReadLine());
    Console.WriteLine(names[index].ToUpper());
  }
}
```

Dialogue

Index? **5**

```
Unhandled Exception: System.IndexOutOfRangeException:
  Index was outside the bounds of the array.
    at HandleArrayIndices.Main()
```

Currently, the program crashes when the user types an index that is outside the bounds of the array. Rewrite the code in `Main` so that when the index is out of bounds, the `IndexOutOfRangeException` exception is caught, and "Index out of range" is output.

459

Handling Multiple Exceptions

Sometimes one statement or group of statements could throw many different exceptions. When this is the case, you can write a `try` block that handles multiple types of exceptions by having multiple `catch` blocks. When an exception occurs, it jumps to the code for its corresponding catch block, if any. Here is the general form for catching multiple exceptions:

General Form: Multiple exception handling

```
try
{
    code that may possibly throw an exception
}
catch (exception-type1  variable-name1)
{
    code to handle an exception-type1
}
catch   (exception-type2  variable-name2)
{
    code to handle an exception-type2
}
```

Example:
(see class `MultipleExceptions` that follows)

Just as with an individual exception, you can handle multiple exceptions with or without giving names to the exception variables. If you give names to the variables, you must use them in some way in the `catch` block; if you do not, a compiler warning will result.

The following program catches multiple potential exceptions in the same `try` block. This is useful because the code in the `try` block could have many different types of errors, such as the user inputting an invalid number, inputting a number for an array index past the bounds of the array, or choosing indexes such that a division by zero occurs. For any exception that has a `catch` block, an error message is printed. The exception's message is also written to the screen to provide additional information.

Code Sample: Class MultipleExceptions

```
1  // Shows handling multiple exceptions in one try block.
2  using System;
3
4  class MultipleExceptions
5  {
6    static void Main()
7    {
8      int[] numberArray = {1, 2, 3, 0, 4, 5};
9      string line = null;
10
11     try
12     {
13       // read two indices
14       Console.Write("Enter a first index: ");
15       line = Console.ReadLine();
16       int index1 = int.Parse(line);
17
18       Console.Write("Enter a second index: ");
19       line = Console.ReadLine();
20       int index2 = int.Parse(line);
21
22       // do some math on the array, and write the answer
23       int result = numberArray[index1] / numberArray[index2];
24       Console.WriteLine("Result of division is: {0}", result);
25     }
26     catch (FormatException fe)
27     { // execute this code if the string is not a number
28       Console.WriteLine("Error: Invalid number entered: {0}",
29                          line);
30       Console.WriteLine(fe.Message);
31     }
32     catch (IndexOutOfRangeException ioore)
33     { // execute this code if the numberArray[index] is bad
34       Console.WriteLine("Error: Invalid index.");
35       Console.WriteLine(ioore.Message);
36     }
37     catch (DivideByZeroException dbze)
38     { // execute this code if numberArray[3] is the denominator
39       Console.WriteLine("Error: division by zero!");
40       Console.WriteLine(dbze.Message);
41     }
42   }
43 }
```

Output (when no exception occurs)

```
Enter a first index: 5
Enter a second index: 1
Result of division is: 2
```

Output (when FormatException occurs)

```
Enter a first index: umbrella
Error: Invalid number entered: umbrella
Input string was not in a correct format.
```

Output (when IndexOutOfRangeException occurs)

```
Enter a first index: 15
Enter a second index: -1
Error: Invalid index.
Index was outside the bounds of the array.
```

Output (when DivideByZeroException occurs)

```
Enter a first index: 5
Enter a second index: 3
Error: division by zero!
Attempted to divide by zero.
```

Alternatively, you can catch an exception of ANY type by specifying a general class of exception to catch, rather than any specific exceptions. A `catch` block that catches type `Exception` will catch any possible exception that occurs in the `try` block.

It may seem like a great idea to always catch `Exception`, since this will make your code handle any exception that could occur. However, it is often not a good idea to use exception handling that is this general. First, different errors should be usually be handled in different ways; trying to handle them all the same way is likely to produce mediocre results. Second, catching `Exception` is also dangerous because there are usually errors that cannot be handled gracefully, and that should be allowed to crash the program.

Here is an example of catching `Exception` to handle multiple errors:

Code Sample: Class CatchGeneralException

```
1  // Catches any exception that occurs. (bad design)
2  using System;
3
4  class CatchGeneralException
5  {
6    static void Main()
7    {
8      string[] names = new string[] {"Jane", null, "Mary"};
9      Console.Write("Index? ");
10
11     try
12     {
13       // read a number and try to print that array element
14       int index = int.Parse(Console.ReadLine());
15       Console.WriteLine(names[index].ToUpper());
16     }
17     catch (Exception ex)    // catch ANY error that happens
18     {
19       Console.WriteLine("An error occurred: {0}", ex.Message);
20     }
21   }
22 }
```

Output (when invalid number is typed (FormatException))

```
Index? Billy Bob
An error occurred: Input string was not in a correct format.
```

Output (when names[index] is null (NullReferenceException))

```
Index? 1
An error occurred: Object reference not set to an instance of an object.
```

Self-Check

8-14   Write code that repeatedly prompts for a number, until a valid number is entered from the keyboard. The program should re-prompt (and not crash with an exception) if an invalid number is entered. One dialog could look like this:

```
Enter a number: 1o1.0
Invalid number, try again
Enter a number: huh?
Invalid number, try again
Enter a number: 4.5
Valid number: 4.5
```

Throwing Exceptions

You have now seen how to catch exceptions caused in methods that you call. It is also important to know how to create, or throw, exceptions of your own. You might ask, "Why would I want to throw an exception? That will crash the program!" The reason you would want to throw exceptions is to alert others who are using your code of errors that occur. For example, in the BankAccount class, when a withdrawal was made that exceeded the account balance, or when a negative withdrawal was made, the BankAccount simply ignored the transaction or withdrew as much as it could. A better way to handle this situation would have been to alert the caller that the amount to withdraw was invalid. The correct way to cause such an alert is by throwing an exception.

To throw an exception in C#, you must write a throw statement. A **throw statement** is a line of code that creates an exception object and causes the exception to occur, using the throw keyword. Here is the general form for throwing an exception:

General Form: Throwing an exception

throw new *exception-type*("*description of error*");

Example:

```
throw new Exception("Invalid data!");
throw new ArgumentException("The value must be positive");
```

The Withdraw method in BankAccount could be modified to throw an exception when the amount is invalid. Since amount is an argument, a suitable type of exception to throw would be an ArgumentException. Here is a possible modified Withdraw method:

```
public void Withdraw(double amount)
{
  if (amount < 0.0)
    throw new ArgumentException("amount is negative");
  else if (amount > balance)
```

```
      throw new ArgumentException("amount exceeds balance");
   else
      balance -= amount;    // successful
}
```

Now any code that tries to make such a withdrawal will crash the program. Here is an example:

```
BankAccount acct = new BankAccount("Starving Student", 1.00);
acct.Withdraw(10.00);
```

Output

Unhandled Exception: System.ArgumentException: amount exceeds balance
    at BankAccount.Withdraw(Double amount)
    at TestBankAccount.Main()

Why is this useful? For starters, it makes people who call your methods (including you!) more careful. If you know that an invalid withdrawal will crash the program, you will probably check more carefully not to do it in the first place. In other words, you are enforcing sensible coding by encouraging exception avoidance. Also, by having exceptions in your methods, you can allow the programmer to catch them and deal with them intelligently. You are allowing for intelligent exception handling. Before, there was no sophisticated way to discover if a withdrawal was valid, or successful, without doing a lot of mandatory manual checking of amounts and balances. Now, a caller can simply try a withdrawal and deal with its potential failure intelligently with a well-written catch block.

Self-Check

8-15   Write a static method named TryIt that throws an ArgumentException whenever its BankAccount argument is null. When the argument is not null, print the ToString version of the argument. The following code should generate output similar to that shown:

```
TryIt(new BankAccount("Srini", 100.00));
TryIt(null);
```

Output

```
Srini $100.00
Unhandled Exception: System.ArgumentException
```

8-16   Modify the `BankAccount` class so that the `Deposit` and `Withdraw` methods throw an `ArgumentException` if the amount to deposit or withdraw is invalid. Invalid amounts are negative, or withdrawals that are greater than the balance of the account).

8.3   Advanced Topic: Persistent Objects with Serialization

The following section discusses an advanced C# topic called serialization, which allows objects to be saved and restored from the hard disk. Serialization is very powerful, but it is also somewhat complex to use in C#, because it requires a brief introduction to several topics that have not yet been covered in this textbook. Among the topics mentioned below are enumerations, attributes, typecasting, and a new .NET Framework namespace and type. Because of the number of new and advanced topics in this section, it may be considered an advanced optional topic.

You have now seen how to write text data to a file. Using the streams described above, the state of various objects can be saved to a disk by taking them apart, field by field, and writing the pieces to the disk. Although this has not been covered yet, objects could then be restored by reading in the pieces from the disk and constructing them again. But this is a lot of unnecessary work; when the objects have arrays and other complex structures, it can be very difficult. Fortunately, C# has a much more elegant solution for saving and restoring objects: serialization and deserialization. *Serialization* is the process of packaging an object and pushing it through a stream. To serialize an object, the bytes of the object are first converted into a binary format, which is then sent, in order, through the stream. Serialization allows an entire object to be saved to a file and then restored later. The object can be as simple as a string, or as complex as a collection with millions of elements.

Restoring the object later is called *deserializing* the object. This allows objects to have their state live on through multiple executions of a program. Such an object is called a ***persistent object***. Persistent objects are very powerful, because they allow easy transfer of objects to files on a disk, through a network, or even to and from the Web.

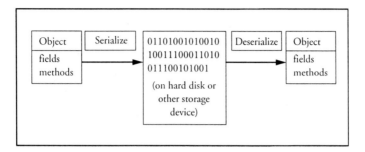

Figure 8.4: Serialization and deserialization of an object

In C#, object serialization is accomplished through the use of a `BinaryFormatter` object. A `BinaryFormatter` object has methods to save or restore an object with a stream. `BinaryFormatter` is part of the lengthily named `System.Runtime.Serialization.Formatters.Binary` namespace.

To use the `BinaryFormatter` class, your program should contain the following `using` directive at the top:

```
using System.Runtime.Serialization.Formatters.Binary;
```

The `BinaryFormatter` has two useful methods, `Serialize` and `Deserialize`, that will respectively allow you to save and load an object from the hard disk or other storage area. Both `Serialize` and `Deserialize` require a `FileStream` object as their first argument, so that the `BinaryFormatter` knows what file to read or write. In the case of `Serialize`, there is a second argument, which specifies the object you want to save. In the case of `Deserialize`, there is no second argument; instead, the object is loaded from the file and is returned as the result of the method.

The `FileStream` constructor takes two arguments: a file name string, and a mode that explains what you wish to do with the file. For example, to construct a `FileStream` object that represents a file named `input.data`, first create a `FileStream` object like this:

```
FileStream aStream =
    new FileStream("input.data", FileMode.Create);
```

The second argument, of type `FileMode`, is a special type called an *enumeration*. Enumerations are types that only contain a fixed set of unique named instances. Enumerations are useful to represent unique states or mutually exclusive modes. A detailed discussion of enumerations is outside the scope of this textbook; you only need to know which `FileMode` value to pass to the `BinaryFormatter` for it to do its work.

Here is the general form for saving and restoring objects to a file, using serialization and deserialization:

General Form: Serializing an object to a file

FileStream *stream-name* =
   new FileStream(*file-name*, **FileMode.Create**);
BinaryFormatter *formatter-name* = **new BinaryFormatter**();
formatter-name.**Serialize**(*stream-name*, *variable-name*);

Example:

```
FileStream stream = new FileStream("account.dat",
                                    FileMode.Create);
BinaryFormatter formatter = new BinaryFormatter();
formatter.Serialize(stream, new BankAccount("Joe", 1.00));
```

General Form: Deserializing an object from a file

FileStream *stream-name* =
   new FileStream(*file-name*, **FileMode.Open**);
BinaryFormatter *formatter-name* = **new BinaryFormatter**();
type variable-name =
   (*type*) *formatter-name*.**Deserialize**(*stream-name*);

Example:

```
FileStream stream = new FileStream("account.dat",
                                    FileMode.Open);
BinaryFormatter formatter = new BinaryFormatter();
BankAccount joe = (BankAccount)formatter.Deserialize(stream);
```

One bizarre thing about the syntax for `Deserialize` is that the object's type must be written in parentheses before the method call, such as the `(BankAccount)` in the example above. This is because the `BinaryFormatter` can load any type of object and therefore needs information from you about what type of object it is deserializing. This syntax in general is called a type-cast, which is not covered in detail in this textbook.

Allowing Your Own Classes to be Serialized

There is one catch to object serialization: for it to be legal to serialize a given type of objects, the class must be tagged with a special Serializable attribute. An *attribute* is an identifier placed between square brackets [and] at the top of a class or method, which provides special information about the class. In this case, the **Serializable** attribute simply tells the .NET virtual machine that it is okay for objects of your class to be saved and loaded using serialization. Serialization involves saving an object and all of its state. This means that when you serialize an object, not only is the object itself saved, but also the values of all fields of the object. Because of this, you must make sure that all fields of any object you intend to serialize are themselves objects of serializable types. Fortunately, many of C#'s existing types are already serializable, such as string, DateTime, Random, and all of the basic value types like int and double. The .NET Framework Class Library Reference documentation for a particular type will state whether the type is serializable or not.

Here is the general form for adding the Serializable attribute to a class:

General Form: Serializable Attribute (allows objects to be saved)

```
[Serializable]
class class-name
{
   // the code for the class ...
```

Example:

```
[Serializable]
class BankAccount
{
   string id;
```

The following program creates and saves two Student objects to a file using serialization, then loads them back from the file, using deserialization. This would not work if the Student type did not have the [Serializable] attribute attached.

Code Sample: Classes Student and SerializeStudents

```
1  using System;
2  using System.IO;
3  using System.Runtime.Serialization.Formatters.Binary;
```

```
 4
 5  // Represents a student and his/her grades and student ID.
 6  [Serializable]
 7  class Student
 8  {
 9    private string name;
10    private int id;
11    private double gpa;
12
13    public Student(string init_name, int init_id, double init_gpa)
14    {
15      name = init_name;  // initialize fields
16      id = init_id;
17      gpa = init_gpa;
18    }
19
20    public override string ToString()
21    { // returns string with student's name, ID, GPA
22      return string.Format("[Name={0,-16}   ID={1:D4}   GPA={2:F2}]",
23                              name, id, gpa);
24    }
25  }
26
27  // Writes two students to disk using serialization.
28  class SerializeStudents
29  {
30    static void Main()
31    {
32      Student student1 = new Student("Billy Bob", 1234, 2.0);
33      Student student2 = new Student("Jimmy Ray", 5678, 3.1);
34
35      FileStream stream = new FileStream("students.dat",
36                                          FileMode.Create);
37      BinaryFormatter formatter = new BinaryFormatter();
38
39      // serialize them
40      Console.WriteLine("Writing Student: {0}", student1);
41      formatter.Serialize(stream, student1);
42
43      Console.WriteLine("Writing Student: {0}", student2);
44      formatter.Serialize(stream, student2);
45
46      stream.Close();
47
48      // wipe out the variables to show the deserialization works
49      student1 = null;
50      student2 = null;
```

```
51
52      // read the two students back from the disk (deserialize)
53      Console.WriteLine();
54      stream = new FileStream("students.dat", FileMode.Open);
55
56      student1 = (Student)formatter.Deserialize(stream);
57      Console.WriteLine("Read a Student: {0}", student1);
58
59      student2 = (Student)formatter.Deserialize(stream);
60      Console.WriteLine("Read a Student: {0}", student2);
61
62      stream.Close();
63    }
64 }
```

Output

```
Writing Student: [Name=Billy Bob        ID=1234   GPA=2.00]
Writing Student: [Name=Jimmy Ray        ID=5678   GPA=3.10]

Read a Student:  [Name=Billy Bob        ID=1234   GPA=2.00]
Read a Student:  [Name=Jimmy Ray        ID=5678   GPA=3.10]
```

The program may not seem terribly impressive, since its output merely writes out the data for the same pair of students twice. However, it's useful because the two Student objects are saved in the students.dat file even after the program ends. This program, or another, can then be run at a later date to retrieve them.

Here is a modified version of the program:

Code Sample: Class DeserializeStudents

```
1 using System;
2 using System.IO;
3 using System.Runtime.Serialization.Formatters.Binary;
4
5 class DeserializeStudents
6 {
7    static void Main()
8    {
9       // read the two students saved earlier back from the disk
10      FileStream stream = new FileStream("students.dat",
11                                         FileMode.Open);
```

```
12        BinaryFormatter formatter = new BinaryFormatter();
13
14        Student student1 = (Student)formatter.Deserialize(stream);
15        Console.WriteLine("Read a Student: {0}", student1);
16
17        Student student2 = (Student)formatter.Deserialize(stream);
18        Console.WriteLine("Read a Student: {0}", student2);
19
20        stream.Close();
21    }
22  }
```

Output

```
Read a Student: [Name=Billy Bob       ID=1234   GPA=2.00]
Read a Student: [Name=Jimmy Ray       ID=5678   GPA=3.10]
```

When you are deserializing objects back from a file, they must be deserialized in the same order they were serialized. For example, if you serialize a BankAccount and then a Student, you must deserialize the BankAccount first and then the Student. Trying to deserialize them in the wrong order produces an exception when trying to cast the reference to the proper type.

Code Sample: Class SerializeObjects

```
1  using System;
2  using System.IO;
3  using System.Runtime.Serialization.Formatters.Binary;
4
5  class SerializeObjects
6  {
7    static void Main()
8    {
9      // serialize two objects
10     FileStream stream = new FileStream("objects.dat",
11                                        FileMode.Create);
12     BinaryFormatter formatter = new BinaryFormatter();
13     formatter.Serialize(stream,
14       new Student("Billy Bob", 1234, 2.0));
15     formatter.Serialize(stream, new BankAccount("Jethro", 50.0));
16     stream.Close();
17
18     // try to deserialize the objects (in the wrong order)
19     stream = new FileStream("objects.dat", FileMode.Open);
```

```
20      BankAccount jethro = (BankAccount)formatter.Deserialize(stream);
21      Student billy = (Student)formatter.Deserialize(stream);
22  }
23 }
```

Output

```
Unhandled Exception: System.InvalidCastException: Specified cast is not
valid.
    at SerializationExceptionExample.Main()
```

Self-Check

8-17   How could serialization be used to maintain a persistent high score list for a guessing game?

8-18   Write code to create and serialize two `DateTime` objects to a file named `dates.dat`.

8-19   Now write the code to retrieve the two `DateTime` objects from the file, using deserialization.

Chapter Summary

- ○ A file is a named collection of bytes. C# represents connections to files with objects called streams, which are manipulated using objects named readers and writers. These objects are found in the `System.IO` namespace.
- ○ Files can be read by calling `ReadLine` on a `StreamReader` object.
- ○ Through parsing and string splitting, you can process an input file that is in a complex format, or which has many fields of different types on each line.
- ○ Files can be written to by calling `Write` on a `StreamWriter` object.
- ○ Objects can be read and written through streams by using the process called serialization. This makes them persistent objects that live on after the program stops running.
- ○ To make a type that you have created serializable, you must put the `[Serializable]` attribute atop its class header.
- ○ Use the `Serialize` and `Deserialize` methods of a `BinaryFormatter` object (from the `System.Runtime.Serialization.Formatters.Binary` namespace) in con-

junction with a `FileStream` to save and load objects using serialization and deserialization.

○ When programs run, errors often occur; in C#, such errors are called exceptions.

○ Causing an error is called throwing an exception; handling the error is called catching it.

○ Exceptions may often be avoided, but in other cases it is better to handle them using `try` and `catch` blocks. One `try` block may catch multiple exceptions, and may catch general categories of exceptions in order to handle many errors the same way.

Key Terms

absolute path	exception	secondary storage
attribute	exception avoidance	`Serializable`
catch	exception handling	serialization
`catch` block	file	stream
checked exception	flush	tokenize
delimiter	folder	`throw`
deserialize	persistent object	`try` block
directory	primary storage	unchecked exception
end-of-file marker	reader	uninterpreted string
eof	relative path	writer
enumeration	runtime exception	

Exercises

1. Explain the concept of a stream and why it is useful.

2. Given the following input file input.txt:

   ```
   val1:val2:val3:::val4
       second line !!!
   ```

   what would be the output from the following code?

   ```
   StreamReader reader = new StreamReader("input.txt");
   string line = reader.ReadLine();
   string[] tokens = line.Split(':');
   Console.WriteLine(tokens[1]);                    // (a)
   Console.WriteLine(tokens[4]);                    // (b)
   line = reader.ReadLine();
   ```

```
Console.WriteLine(line.Trim().ToUpper());        // (c)
tokens = line.Split(' ');
Console.WriteLine(tokens[1]);                    // (d)
Console.WriteLine(reader.Peek());                // (e)
```

3. What happens when a C# program constructs a `StreamReader` object that tries to read a file that does not exist? Be specific.

4. What does the `Peek` method of a `StreamReader` return if it has reached the end of the file? What does `ReadLine` return in the same situation?

5. What new C# namespace must be included when using the input/output classes such as `StreamReader` and `StreamWriter`?

6. Are the following paths relative or absolute?
(a) `"foo.txt"`
(b) `"C:\\documents\\files\\chapter8\\foo.txt"`
(c) `"chapter8\\foo.txt"`
(d) `"files\\chapter8\\foo.txt"`
(e) `"H:\\foo.txt"`

7. Write the equivalent strings from the previous question, but write them as uninterpreted strings with the @ modifier.

8. Write a method `CountLines` that takes a string argument representing a file name, counts the number of lines in that file, and returns the number of lines as an `int`. Blank lines should also be counted. Your method should work with the following test code:

```
using System;
class Lines
{
    static void Main()
    {
        int lines1 = CountLines("file1.txt");
        int lines2 = CountLines("file2.txt");
        Console.WriteLine("# of lines in file 1 = {0}", lines1);
        Console.WriteLine("# of lines in file 2 = {0}", lines2);
    }
}
```

9. Write a method CountWords, similar to the CountLines method from the previous question, but which counts the number of words in the file whose name is passed to it. A word is defined as any nonempty sequence of characters separated by whitespace (the space character, the tab character, or the new line character).

10. Write class FileSwapper with method public void Swap(string file1, string file2) that will swap the contents of two text files. That is, after the swap, file1 will contain what used to be the contents of file2, and file2 will contain what used to be the contents of file1.

11. Assume that the string method Split did not exist. Write your own Split method that takes a string to be split, and char characters for the delimiters, and that returns an array of strings representing the same results that String.Split would have returned. The delimiters should not be part of the result array. For example, calling your method with Split("hello, are you there,, Suzy?", ',') should return the following array of strings:
    {"hello", " are you there", "", " Suzy?"}

    Perhaps this goes without saying, but do not use String.Split to write your solution.

12. Write a program that takes two file names as command-line arguments. The program should read the first file, and then write each line reversed into the second file. For example, if your program is named ReverseIt and is run with the following command line:
    ReverseIt file1.txt file2.txt

    and if the contents of file1.txt are the following:
    this is a line
    here is more text
    1 2 3

    last text here

    after the program runs, file2.txt should have the following contents:
    enil a si siht
    txet erom si ereh
    3 2 1

```
ereh txet tsal
```

If the first argument file is not found, or if not enough arguments are passed, print an error message.

13. Write a program named Compare that takes two file names as command-line arguments and writes "Same" to the console if the two files have the same contents, or "Files differ on line N:" plus each file's line N if the files have a line that does not match. Only print the first non-matching line. For example:

```
Compare readme.txt readme.txt
Same

Compare readme.txt readme2.txt
Files differ on line 4:
readme.txt: Four score and seven years ago
readme2.txt: Fore scour and yeven sears ago
```

If either file is not found, or if not enough arguments are passed, print an error message.

14. Name all the possible exceptions that could happen in the following code:

```
int num = int.Parse(Console.ReadLine());
string[] array = new string[3];
array[1] = array[0].Substring(0, 2) + num;
array[2] = "" + (num / 10);
```

Programming Tips

1. Do not try to read past the end of a file; avoid this by using Peek to make sure that data is still remaining.

The Peek method returns -1 when there is no more data to read, so use it as the test for your loop that reads the file. This way, you can avoid exceptions that would be thrown when trying to read past the end of a file.

2. Use relative path names if possible; they are less prone to errors.

If your program is in the folder C:\My Documents\homework5, and you want to read the file C:\My Documents\homework5\temp\file.txt, ask for a reader that reads "temp\\file.txt" rather than "C:\\My Documents\\homework5\\temp\\file.txt". This way, if your program and its temp folder ever move to a different folder, it will still behave correctly.

3. String splitting works best when the tokens in the string are not separated by multiple delimiters.

The following example input has fields separated by two tabs each. Notice that you cannot distinguish the tab characters from space characters on the screen or on this printed page. If you split a string on the tab character '\t', and your file has input such as this:

```
Smith           Jane            $100.00                 5678
```

the array returned from Split would contain these elements:

```
{"Smith", "", "Jane", "", "$100.00", "", "5678"}
```

If possible, only split strings that are delimited by nonconsecutive occurrences of your delimiters, or else be very certain you know the input format, so that it will be split correctly.

4. Try to avoid exceptions first. Then, if that is not possible, handle them intelligently.

For example, your program will throw an exception when you divide an integer by zero. You could handle this by catching the exception. However, a better solution is to do your best to avoid the exception in the first place by checking the value of numbers before dividing by them. If possible, avoiding exceptions is preferable to trying to catch them.

5. Print verbose and informative error messages from exceptions that occur.

When a program crashes, it is frustrating for the user. It can be even more frustrating for the programmer to debug the code without good information about what went wrong, and how to fix it. Printing exceptions' error messages (with the Message property in the exception object), along with your own message, is a good start toward this goal.

6. Deserialize objects in the same order that they were serialized.

If two objects are serialized, they must be deserialized in the same order. This is especially true of objects of different types, because the code will throw an exception if you try to typecast an object into the wrong type.

7. Add the [Serializable] attribute to any class that you want to serialize.

Most of the C# types covered in this textbook are serializable: string, int, double, char, DateTime, BankAccount, and other types can safely be saved to files. However, if you write your own types and intend to save them to disk, make sure to include the [Serializable] attribute just above the class's header. If the attribute is omitted, an exception will occur when the your program tries to serialize the object.

Programming Projects

8A   Above and Below

Write a C# program (the Main method only) that creates an undetermined number of BankAccount objects and stores them into an array. The input should come from an input file (see the StreamReader class) which contains the initial balance and the ID for each object, as shown below (use Console.ReadLine and the string IndexOf method).

Use the following input file:

```
53.45 Solley
999.99 Kirsten
8790.56 Pantone
0.00 Brendle
1555.76 Kentish
```

After initializing the array and the number of BankAccount objects, display every BankAccount that has a balance greater than 1,000.00. Then display every BankAccount that has a balance less than 500.00.

Your output should look like this if you use the ToString method of BankAccount when the program runs in a country that uses American dollars:

```
Accounts with balances > 1000.00
Pantone $8,790.56
Kentish $1,555.76

Accounts with balances < 500.00
Solley $53.45
Brendle $0.00
```

8B   Frequency

Write a C# program that reads integers from a file and reports the frequency of each integer. As shown in the dialogue below, your program should ask the user for the input file name, and should then print a table of the values in the file, plus how many times each value occurred. Note that the highest numbers should appear first. The input file only has numbers that are in the range of 0 through 100 inclusive. Use this fact to your advantage. You may assume that there are never more than 100 numbers in the file. Use the StreamReader class to read from the disk file.

The File test.dat

```
75
60
75
100
60
75
90
85
90
```

Dialogue

```
Enter file name: test.dat
100: 1
90: 2
85: 1
75: 2
60: 2
```

8C   ReadAmount

Write a static method named ReadAmount that reads input from the keyboard until the user enters a valid currency amount, and then returns that amount. Also give the user a chance to cancel the operation, if so desired, by entering *quit*, in which case the method must return 0. There are three things that your method must check for and report as invalid input:

1. A string that does not successfully parse to a valid number, such as "1x.45".
2. A string that parses to a number with more than 2 decimal places (you will need to write a formula).
3. A string that parses to a negative number, or is 0.0.

The following code should compile and show the valid currency amount (or 0 if the user quits)

```
// This code assumes ReadAmount is a static method in the same class
double number = ReadAmount("Enter a number: ");
Console.WriteLine("Valid number = {0}", number);
```

Output when the user enters four incorrect currency amounts

```
Enter a number: badNumber
'badNumber' is an invalid currency amount.  Enter 'QUIT' or try again.
Enter a number: 1.233
'1.233' must have 2 or fewer decimals.  Enter 'QUIT' or try again.
Enter a number: -1
'-1' must be positive.  Enter 'QUIT' or try again.
Enter a number: 0
'0' must be positive.  Enter 'QUIT' or try again.
Enter a number: 123.45
Valid number = 123.45
```

8D   Grep

Write a program named Grep that takes a file name as its first command-line argument, and a string to search for as its second command-line argument. The program should then print the lines of the file that contain that string, preceded by the line numbers and a colon. If no lines match the string, no output is printed.

For example, if your program was run with Grep gettysburg.txt on (searching for the string on in the file below), your output would be as shown. The string on can occur anywhere in the line; it does not have to be a separate word.

Input file gettysburg.txt

```
Fourscore and seven years ago
our fathers brought forth on this
continent a new nation, conceived
in liberty and dedicated to the
proposition that all men are created equal.
Now we are engaged in a great civil war,
testing whether that nation or any nation so
conceived and so dedicated can long endure.
```

Output

```
2: our fathers brought forth on this
3: continent a new nation, conceived
5: proposition that all men are created equal.
7: testing whether that nation or any nation so
8: conceived and so dedicated can long endure.
```

8E   Doubler

Write a program named `Doubler` that takes a file name as a command-line argument, and in the output doubles every non-whitespace character in the file, and also doubles each line in the file. For example, if your program is run with the command line `Doubler test.txt`, and the file `test.txt` contains the following contents:

```
testing
1 2 3

more data
```

the new contents of test.txt after running Doubler would be:

```
tteessttiinngg
tteessttiinngg
11   22   33
11   22   33


mmoorree   ddaattaa
mmoorree   ddaattaa
```

If not enough arguments are passed, or the file is not found, print an error message. (Note that you will have to catch an exception to do this.) Note that your program must write the doubled text back into the same file; it destroys the file's original contents to read and write the same file at the same time. The two operations must be performed separately, without overlapping.

Recursion

Summing Up

You have now learned how to create programs that can solve complex problems. The key component of this so far has been the ability to control the flow of your programs' execution using structures like selection (`if` statements) and repetition (loops).

Coming Up

This chapter introduces simple recursive methods—methods that invoke another instance of the same method. This brief introduction hints at problems that cannot be easily solved without recursion. After studying this chapter, you will be able to

- compare iterative and recursive solutions to the same problem.
- identify the recursive case and the base case of recursive algorithms and methods.
- implement simple recursive methods.
- solve a problem where the recursive solution is better than the iterative solution.

9.1   Recursion Concepts

One day, a computer science teacher posed the following problem to her students: "Count the number of students in your row of the classroom, without looking at anyone, and without talking to anyone but the people next to you. In a few minutes, I will walk by the rightmost person in each row and ask that person how many students are in her row."

The students complained. "Wouldn't it be easier to just have one person from each row stand up, look down the row, and count the number of students?" said Andy, a disgruntled student in the third row. Grudgingly, the students in each row discussed possible ways to solve the problem.

After some time, Suzanne, another student, pointed out that Andy's algorithm forced one student to do all the work of counting. Perhaps if each student did a small portion of the job, and then everyone combined their work, the problem could be solved more easily.

Then Reggie, the rightmost student in the first row, said, "There's no one to my right, so if I can just find out how many students are to the left of me, and add one for myself, I'll know how many students are in my row." Based on this, Reggie asked Amy, the student to his left, "How many students are there in our row, starting from the left, up to and including you?" Amy did not know the answer, since she was not allowed to look around the room and count. Her only choice was to ask the student to her left the same question that Reggie had asked her, get the answer, add 1 for herself, and then give this information back to Reggie. Reggie waited for Amy's answer, and Amy waited for the answer from the student to her left.

The question rippled down leftward through the row. Eventually, the question, "How many students are there in the row, starting from the left, up to and including you?" reached Leonard, who was sitting in the leftmost seat of the first row. Leonard pointed out that even though he wasn't allowed to look around the room, he knew that he was in the far left seat and that there were no students to his left. "So, in my row, the number of students to my left is zero, plus 1 for me makes a total of 1." He reported this information back to Stuart, the student to his right, who had originally asked him. Knowing Leonard's answer of 1 allowed Stuart to deduce that his own answer to the same question should be 2; 1 for David and 1 for himself. He reported this information back to his right.

The students passed their answers rightward, adding 1 each time. Finally, the student to the left of Amy (second-from-rightmost in the row) reported a value of 22. Amy added 1 for herself and told Reggie, the rightmost student, that there were 23 students, up to and including her. Reggie added a final 1 for himself, then happily reported the answer of 24 to the teacher.

After practicing this exercise a few times, the students got fast enough at it that they could report the overall answer very quickly. "Excellent work," the teacher said. "Now you are thinking recursively. You developed a recursive solution to this problem, rather than your first instinct, which was to solve the problem by iteration."

Let's see how the two algorithms work, and why the recursive solution is better:

First solution (iterative):
NumberOfStudentsInRow(asked to rightmost student) =
    Have one person perform the following actions:
        Start with *count* = 0
    Look at leftmost student
    While I still see a student,
        Increase count by 1,
        and look to the next spot to the right.
    Report *count* as the answer.

Second solution (recursive):
    NumberOfStudentsInRow(asked to rightmost student) =
        If there is no one to my left, then
            Report 1 as the answer.
        Otherwise,
            Find out NumberOfStudentsInRow(asked to the person to my left),
            Add 1,
            And report this total as the answer.

Notice that the recursive solution to NumberOfStudentsInRow actually refers to itself. If there are students to the left, that person must ask the neighbor to the left for her value of NumberOfStudentsInRow in order to find the answer. This idea, that an algorithm can be expressed in terms of itself, is called *recursion*. An algorithm written to use recursion is called a *recursive algorithm*.

The NumberOfStudentsInRow example illustrates many of the important benefits of recursion. For one, the recursive solution is easier to express as an algorithm. Also, the recursive solution makes each student do a bit of the work. This makes the task simpler than requiring one student to do all of the work. Also, because each student has such a simple task that she is unlikely to do it wrong, it is less likely that a mistake will be made in the recursive algorithm.

Perhaps the most important idea behind recursion is that it takes a complex problem and splits it up into smaller subproblems that are easier to solve. The solutions to the subproblems are easier to find than the solution to the overall problem. Once the solutions to the subproblems are found, they can be combined to solve the original overall problem. This is the case with NumberOfStudentsInRow; no one needs to worry about solving the complex task of counting everyone in her row. Instead, each student only needs to worry about finding out how many students are to her left, which can be done by asking a neighbor.

The recursive NumberOfStudentsInRow algorithm has two possible cases: one where there is no one to the left, which is a simpler case; and one where there are people to the left, which requires more work to solve. The second and more complex case of the NumberOfStudentsInRow algorithm is called the *recursive case*, because it is defined in terms of NumberOfStudentsInRow itself. The first and simpler case for the leftmost student is called a *base case*. The base case is more basic than the recursive case, and it does not recursively refer to the algorithm (in this case, NumberOfStudentsInRow) to find its answer.

A recursive algorithm must have a base case to work. Without a base case, the algorithm would never end, because it would continue executing the recursive case (in this example, asking the person to the left) infinitely. A recursive algorithm without a properly defined base case is roughly analogous to an infinite loop, because it will never finish and will never produce a resulting value.

To summarize, there are two important characteristics of recursive algorithms:
1. It must be possible to partition the problem into subproblems that have the same structure as the original problem.
2. A base case must eventually be reached, so that no more recursive calls are made.

There are many recursive algorithms for problems both in and out of computer science. Here is an example:

Recursive Algorithm: Look up a word in a dictionary.
  ◯ Find the word in the dictionary
  ◯ If there is a word in the definition that you do not understand,
    look up that word in the dictionary

  ◯ Example: Look up the word **object**
      ◯ *Look up* **object**, which is defined as "an instance of a **class**."
      ◯ What is a class? *Look up* **class** to find "a collection of **method**s and data."
      ◯ What is a method? *Look up* **method** to find "a **method heading** followed by a collection of programming statements."
      ◯ What is a method heading? *Look up* **method heading** to find "the name of a method and its **return type**, followed by a **parameter list** in parentheses."
      ◯ What is a parameter list? *Look up* **parameter list** to find "a list of **parameters**."
      ◯ *Look up* **list**, *look up* **parameters**, and *look up* **return type**, and you finally get a definition of all of the terms, using the same method you used to *look up* the original term. Now, when all new terms have been defined, you have a definition for **object**.

Recursive Definitions

A *recursive definition* is a definition that includes a simpler version of itself. One example of a recursive definition is shown below: the power method that raises an integer (x) to an integer power (n).

$$x^n \begin{cases} 1 \text{ if } n = 0 \\ x \bullet x^{n-1} \text{ if } x \geq 1 \end{cases}$$

Recursive Definition, Example 1: The mathematical power function

---

This definition is recursive because x^{n-1} is part of the definition itself. For example,

$$4^3 = 4 \times 4^{(n-1)} = 4 \times 4^{(3-1)} = 4 \times 4^2$$

What is 4^2? Using the recursive definition above, 4^2 is defined as:
$$4^2 = 4 \times 4^{(n-1)} = 4 \times 4^{(2-1)} = 4 \times 4^1$$

and 4^1 is defined as
$$4^1 = 4 \times 4^{(n-1)} = 4 \times 4^{(1-1)} = 4 \times 4^0$$

and 4^0 is a base case defined as
$$4^0 = 1$$

The recursive definition of 4^3 includes three recursive definitions. The base case is n == 0:
$$x^n = 1 \text{ if } n = 0$$

To get the actual value of 4^3, work backward and let 1 replace 4^0, 4 * 1 replace 4^1, 4 * 4^1 replace 4^2, and 4 * 4^2 replace 4^3. Therefore, 4^3 is defined as 64.

4^0 is defined as
   1
4^1 is defined as
     4 * 1
4^2 is defined as
     4 * 4
4^3 is defined as
     4 * 16   = 64

To be recursive, an algorithm or method requires at least one recursive case, and at least one base case. The recursive algorithm for power illustrates the characteristics of a recursive solution to a problem.

1. The problem can be decomposed into a simpler version of itself in order to bring the problem closer to a base case.
2. There is at least one base case that does not make a recursive call.
3. The partial solutions are managed in such a way that all occurrences of the recursive and base cases can communicate their partial solutions to the proper locations (values are returned).

Here are some other recursive definitions:

Recursive Definition, Example 2: A definition of a waiting line.
   ○ Empty, or
   ○ someone at the front, followed by a *waiting line.*

Recursive Definition, Example 3: An arithmetic expression is defined as one of these:
   ○ A numeric constant such as 123 or –0.001,
   ○ or a numeric variable that stores a numeric constant,
   ○ or an *arithmetic expression* enclosed in parentheses,
   ○ or an *arithmetic expression* followed by a binary operator (+, -, /, %, or *) followed by an *arithmetic expression.*

Implementing Recursive Algorithms

As stated previously, recursion is implemented in C# as methods that call themselves. If a method M calls M in its body, then M is a *recursive method.* For comparison purposes, this section implements a recursive algorithm, then implements the same algorithm in the usual iterative style.

For many problems involving repetition, a recursive solution exists. Consider the problem of implementing the mathematical power function defined previously (ignoring the fact that C# already includes the Math.Pow method). A recursive solution is shown below, along with an iterative solution. The solutions use the methods PowRecurse and PowLoop, respectively.

Code Sample: Class PowerFunctions

```
1 using System;
2
3 // A class with two methods that do the same thing differently
4 class PowerFunctions
5 {
```

```
 6    // Recursive solution to the Power function.
 7    public static int PowRecurse(int number, int power)
 8    {
 9      // Precondition: number and power are positive && number != 0
10      if (power == 0)
11        return 1;
12      else            // Make this recursive call \\
13        return number * PowRecurse(number, power - 1);
14    }
15
16    // Iterative solution to the Power function.
17    public static int PowLoop(int number, int power)
18    {
19      // Precondition: number and power are positive && number != 0
20      int result;
21      if (power == 0)
22        result = 1;
23      else
24      {
25        result = number;
26        for (int j = 2; j <= power; j++)
27          result = result * number;
28      }
29      return result;
30    }
31
32    static void Main()
33    {
34      Console.WriteLine("PowLoop(number, power)");
35      Console.WriteLine("4^0 is {0}", PowLoop(4, 0));
36      Console.WriteLine("4^1 is {0}", PowLoop(4, 1));
37      Console.WriteLine("4^2 is {0}", PowLoop(4, 2));
38      Console.WriteLine("4^4 is {0}", PowLoop(4, 4));
39
40      Console.WriteLine();  // blank line
41      Console.WriteLine("PowRecurse(number, power)");
42      Console.WriteLine("4^0 is {0}", PowRecurse(4, 0));
43      Console.WriteLine("4^1 is {0}", PowRecurse(4, 1));
44      Console.WriteLine("4^2 is {0}", PowRecurse(4, 2));
45      Console.WriteLine("4^4 is {0}", PowRecurse(4, 4));
46    }
47  }
```

Output

```
PowLoop(number, power)
4^0 is 1
4^1 is 4
4^2 is 16
4^4 is 256

PowRecurse(number, power)
4^0 is 1
4^1 is 4
4^2 is 16
4^4 is 256
```

Notice that `PowLoop` and `PowRecurse` produce the same answers. For both methods to correctly implement the power function, this must be the case. But `PowRecurse` is shorter and cleaner code, and it is much closer to the original mathematical definition than `PowLoop`.

In `PowRecurse`, if n is 0—the base case—the method call evaluates to 1. When n > 0—the recursive case—the method is invoked again with the argument reduced in value by one. For example, `PowRecurse(4, 1)` calls `PowRecurse(4, 1 - 1)`, which immediately returns 1. For another example, the original call `PowRecurse(2, 4)` calls `PowRecurse(2, 3)`, which then calls `PowRecurse(2, 2)`, which then calls `PowRecurse(2, 1)`, which then calls `PowRecurse(2, 0)`, which returns 1. Then 2 * `PowRecurse(2, 0)` evaluates to 2 * 1 or 2, so 2 * `PowRecurse(2, 1)` evaluates to 4, so 2 * `PowRecurse(2, 2)` evaluates to 8, so 2 * `PowRecurse(2, 3)` evaluates to 16, so 2 * `PowRecurse(2, 4)` evaluates to 32.

Tracing Recursive Calls

It can be difficult to understand how recursive methods work, how they produce their answers, and why they are correct or incorrect. A helpful way to understand a recursive method is to follow its chain of nested recursive method calls as it finds the answer to its problem. This is called *tracing* the recursive method. Tracing recursive methods requires diligence, but it can help you understand what is going on.

Consider tracing a call to the recursive power method to get 2^4.

```
Console.WriteLine("2^4 is {0}", PowRecurse(2, 4));
```

Output

```
2^4 is 16
```

After the initial call PowRecurse(2, 4), PowRecurse calls another instance of itself. It keeps doing this until the base case of power == 0 is reached. The following picture illustrates what happens when PowRecurse calls itself. The arrows that go up indicate each time that this happens. When an instance of the method can return something, it returns that value to the instance of the method that called it. The arrows that go down, with the return values written to the right, indicate this.

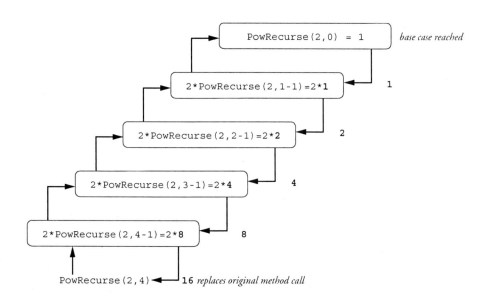

The final value of 16 is returned to the Main method, where the arguments of 2 and 4 were passed to the first instance of PowRecurse.

Self-Check

9-1   What is the value of PowerFunctions.PowRecurse(3, 0)?

9-2   What is the value of PowerFunctions.PowRecurse(3, 1)?

9-3   Fill in the blanks on the following diagram with a trace of the call
      PowerFunctions.PowRecurse(3, 4).

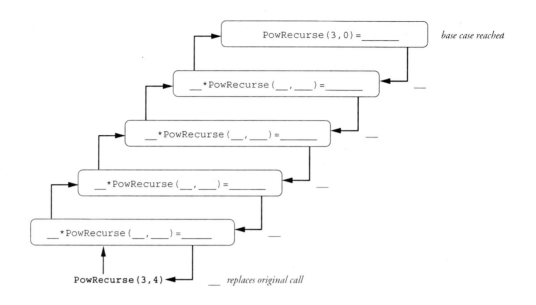

9.2   How Recursion Works

How does a method that calls itself know when to quit calling itself? How does a program know where to continue when a method has finished? Consider the analogy of a pile of boxes that can be stacked one on top of another (without falling down). Each box contains certain vital information that allows a method to execute correctly. At the beginning of a program, there are no boxes on the stack. When a method is called, the vital information needed by that method is stored into a box. This box is then placed onto the stack of boxes.

Next, the computer begins to execute the statements in the method. As the method executes its statements, the information is available from the box on top of the stack. For example, if a change is made to a local variable or the value of a parameter is needed, that information can be found in the box.

When a method has finished executing its own statements, the proper return point must be available in order to continue from the point of the method call. A *return point* is the place that the program returns to when a method has finished executing. More specifically, the return point is the address of the next machine instruction to be executed after the methods has executed.

So where is the value of the return point stored? It is in the box on top of the stack. It was stored there, along with the other vital information, when the method was originally called.

A recursive method is handled in the same manner. When a method calls itself, the vital information is stored into a new box. This box is placed on top of the stack of boxes. The only thing that may appear to be different from what was just described is that the return point happens to be in another instance of the same method that has just been called. The computer then begins executing the statements of the method associated with the vital information in the top box. Every instance of the method is associated with a box on the stack. The stack of boxes "remembers" the vital information for all method calls that have not yet finished executing.

When one instance of a method is finished, the top box is removed from the stack, and the program continues from the correct return point. The vital information for the current method is in the box that is now at the top of the stack. This allows a method to remember its own set of vital information, even though there may previously have been many other boxes piled on top of it.

This stacking of boxes provides a useful tool for tracing recursive methods. Let's illustrate this stack-of-boxes analogy with a simple recursive method that displays the integers 1 through n, where n is a parameter. The recursive method Forward contains a comment to show the return point that is stored into the box at the top of the stack before the recursive call is made.

Code Sample: Class ShowDirection

```
 1  using System;
 2
 3  class ShowDirection
 4  {
 5    public static void Forward(int n)
 6    {
 7      if (n > 1)
 8        Forward(n - 1);
 9
10      // Return Point: RP Forward
11      Console.WriteLine(n);
12    }
13
14    static void Main()
15    {
16      int number = 3;
17      Forward(number);
18
19      // Return Point: RP Main
20      Console.WriteLine("back in Main");
21    }
22  }
```

Before the program begins executing, there are no boxes. When Main is called, the Main method's information is placed on top of the stack of boxes. When Main completes later, the program will be done. This Main method is represented by this box.

```
Program done
number = 3
```

When Forward is invoked from Main, the return point, RP Main, and the value of n (3) are stored into a new box, which is placed on top. The stack of boxes is now represented as two boxes, where the top box contains the return point (RP Main) and the value of the single parameter n.

```
RP Main
   n   3
Program done
number = 3
```

Since n > 1 is true, a recursive call is made that causes the return point and the value of n to be stored into another new box on the top. During the second call to Forward, the recursive call within the if statement executes once again, causing the stack to look like this:

```
RP Forward
   n 2
RP Main
   n 3
Program done
number = 3
```

During the third call to Forward, the recursive call within the if statement executes once again, causing the stack to look like this:

```
RP Forward
   n 1
RP Forward
   n 2
RP Main
   n 3
Program done
number = 3
```

The code in Forward begins to execute again, but now the recursive call within the if statement is skipped, because n > 1 is false. The last statement in the third instance of Forward is executed: `Console.WriteLine(n);`. Even though there are three different values of n, the method knows which one to print. It prints its own value of n (in the box on the top). Therefore, the integer 1 is displayed, and the third execution of `Forward` is completed.

When the program is ready to continue from the return point that is stored in the box on top of the stack, that top box can be removed. Now the stack contains only three boxes, and the program continues executing from `RP Forward` in the previous instance of `Forward`. `RP Forward` is located at the end of the `if` statement. So the next statement executed is the first statement after `RP Forward`: the `WriteLine` in the previous instance. This causes the value of n to be printed. Since the value of this variable was stored in the box at the top, the system knows that n has the value of 2. The output is 2.

Now that the second instance of `Forward` has finished executing, the program returns to `RP Forward` in the first instance of `Forward`. The stack of boxes now looks like this:

```
RP Main
  n 3
Program done
number = 3
```

The value of n (3) is then output, and control returns to `Main` at `RP Main`. The `WriteLine` message in `Main` executes.

Here is the complete output from the program above.

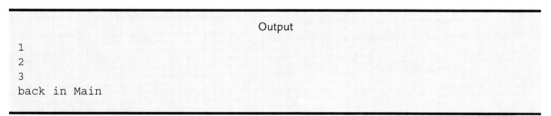

Output
1
2
3
back in Main

The stack of boxes analogy is similar to the stack that is actually used by computer systems to control the execution of methods. The difference is that the computer uses memory to store the vital information. Each time a method is called, more memory is used up, because each method must have its own set of vital information stored (values of parameters, local variables, and the return point). This stack of memory about the methods that are currently being called is named the *call stack*. The space reserved for the call stack has a limit. After some number of recursive calls have been made, the memory allocated to the call stack will be almost used up. If an attempt is then made to store another set of vital information when there is not enough memory available, an `OutOfMemoryException` occurs.

Here is another view that traces this recursive Forward method. It goes left to right.

		RP Forward	*Base Case*	
First call				
to Forward		n == 1	print(1)	
	RP Forward	RP Forward	RP Forward	print(2)
	n == 2	n == 2	n == 2	
RP Forward	RP Forward	RP Forward	RP Forward	RP Forward	print(3)
n == 3	n == 3	n == 3	n == 3	n == 3

The Main method calls Forward, which calls Forward, which calls Forward until the base case is reached. The integer 1 is printed, and the most recently stacked box is removed from the top. Control returns to RP Forward in the new top box, where 2 is printed. Control then returns to the original call to Forward, where 3 is printed. Then control returns to Main, "back in Main" is printed, and the program is done.

Here is another way to look at it:

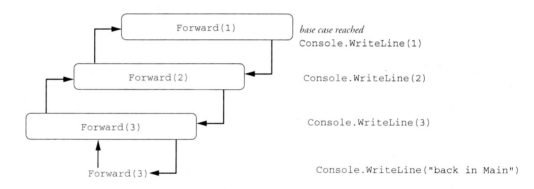

Being able to determine the base case and the recursive case is a requirement of recursive programming. In Forward, the base case occurred when n == 1. When this base case was reached, n was printed; no recursive call was made. Even if nothing happens when the base case is reached, it is critical that a base case is available. Without an appropriate base case, a method may call itself endlessly.

Returning to the first recursive definition, which defined the method of raising an integer to an integer power (x^n), the base case occurred when n == 0. At this point, x^0 was defined as 1. The recursive case occurred whenever n > 0. At that point, x^n was defined as $x * x^{(n-1)}$. Whereas Forward had a do-nothing base case, PowRecurse had a base case of returning 1 back to the method that called PowRecurse(0).

Self-Check

9-4 Write the output from calling `Direction(10)`.

```
public static void Direction(int n)
{
  if (n >= 2)
  {
    Console.Write("{0} | ", n);
    Direction(n - 2);
  }
}
```

9-5 Write the output from calling `ForwardAgain(10)`.

```
public static void ForwardAgain(int n)
{
  if (n >= 2)
  {
    ForwardAgain(n - 2);
    Console.Write("{0} | ", n);
  }
}
```

9-6 Write a method named `Backward` that takes two `int` parameters named `high` and `low` and recursively displays the integers from `high` down to `low`. Use recursion; do not use a loop.

Recursive Method Example: Mystery1

Consider another method, `Mystery1`, that contains two parameters (`Mystery1` serves no useful purpose other than illustrating a recursive method). The recursive definition of mystery is:

$$\text{Mystery1}(j,k) \begin{cases} 1 \text{ if } j <= k) \\ j + k + \text{Mystery1}(j - 1, k + 2) \end{cases}$$

From this definition, the recursive and base cases can be easily determined:

Base Case
```
if (j <= k)
    return 1;
```

Recursive Case

```
else
    return j + k + Mystery1(j - 1, k + 2);
```

When the base case is encountered, `Mystery1` simply returns 1. Otherwise, the method is called recursively with the first argument decreased by one, and the second argument increased by two. Note that the return point after the recursive method call is in an expression. Only after `Mystery1(j - 1, k + 2)` is evaluated can the entire expression be evaluated and then returned.

```
 1  using System;
 2
 3  // Show a silly recursive method
 4  class Mystery
 5  {
 6    public static int Mystery1(int j, int k)
 7    {
 8      if (j <= k)
 9        return 1;
10      else
11        return j + k + /* RP Mystery */ Mystery1(j - 1, k + 2);
12    }
13
14    static void Main()
15    {
16      Console.WriteLine("Mystery1(2, 4) = {0}", Mystery1(2, 4));
17      Console.WriteLine("Mystery1(4, 2) = {0}", Mystery1(4, 2));
18      Console.WriteLine("Mystery1(9, 0) = {0}", Mystery1(9, 0));
19    }
20  }
```

Output

```
Mystery1(2, 4) = 1
Mystery1(4, 2) = 7
Mystery1(9, 0) = 31
```

The first call to `Mystery1` finds the base case immediately and returns 1. The second call returns the sum of its arguments plus `Mystery1(3, 5)`, or 4 + 2 + 1.

Let's trace the third call of `Mystery1(9, 0)`, which finds the recursive case three times before reaching the base case.

Tracing mystery(9, 0)

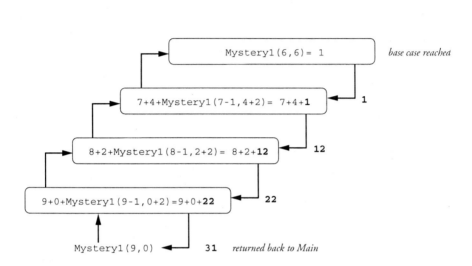

The base case has Mystery1 return 1. Then the previous expression can be returned as 7 + 4 + 1, the value of Mystery1(7, 4). We then move backwards until the first call to Mystery1 returns 9 + 0 + 22 as 31.

Here is another trace, using the stack of boxes analogy, to show how the stack grows and shrinks. When each call to Mystery1 finishes, the expression within the previous method call can finally be evaluated (return values are shown in boldface).

Another Way to Trace the Recursive Method Mystery1

			RP Myst	**1**		
			j == 6	Base case		
			k == 6			
Start		RP Myst	RP Myst	RP Myst	j+k+Mystery1(6,6)	
Point		j == 7	j == 7	j == 7	7+4+ 1 = **12**	
		k == 4	k == 4	k == 4		
	RP Myst	RP Myst	RP Myst	RP Myst	RP Myst	j+k+Mystery1(7,4)
	j == 8	j == 8	j == 8	j == 8	j == 8	8+2+ 12 = **22**
	k == 2	k == 2	k == 2	k == 2	k == 2	
RP Main	RP Main	RP Main	RP Main	RP Main	RP Main	RP Main	j+k+Mystery1(8,2)
j == 9	j == 9	j == 9	j == 9	j == 9	j == 9	j == 9	9+0+ 22 = **31**
k == 0	k == 0	k == 0	k == 0	k == 0	k == 0	k == 0	

Finding Factorials Using Iteration

Consider the mathematical factorial function (designated by !, an exclamation mark). The *factorial* of a number n, labeled n!, has the following nonrecursive definition:

Iterative Definition for Factorial

$$n! \begin{cases} 1 \text{ if n = 0 or n = 1)} \\ n * (n\text{-}1) * (n\text{-}2) * (n\text{-}3) \ldots *3*2*1 \text{ if n > 1} \end{cases}$$

Examples:

0! = 1

1! = 1

2! = 2 * 1 = 2

3! = 3 * 2 * 1 = 6

7! = 7 * 6 * 5 * 4 * 3 * 2 * 1 = 5040

The following Factorial method is written to return n! iteratively, as shown above. It is assumed that the values for n are fairly small (the result of 13! would be too large to be represented in C#, even as an int). The Factorial method is undefined for n < 0.

Code Sample: Class FactorialLoop

```
1  using System;
2
3  // Demonstrate the iterative solution to the factorial function
4  class FactorialLoop
5  {
6    public static int Factorial(int n)
7    { // Precondition: n >= 0 and n is not too large (n < 13)
8        int result = 1;
9        for (int j = 2; j <= n; j++)
10       {
11          result = result * j;
12       }
13       return result;
14   }
15
16   static void Main()
17   {
18       Console.WriteLine(Factorial(0));   // 1
19       Console.WriteLine(Factorial(1));   // 1
20       Console.WriteLine(Factorial(2));   // 2
21       Console.WriteLine(Factorial(3));   // 6
22       Console.WriteLine(Factorial(4));   // 24
23       Console.WriteLine(Factorial(12));  // 479001600
24   }
25 }
```

The Factorial method also has a recursive definition:

$$n! \begin{cases} 1 \text{ if } n = 0 \\ n * (n\text{-}1)! \text{ if } n \geq 1 \end{cases}$$

This definition of the Factorial method uses the method itself as part of the definition, when n > 0. Here are some examples:

```
0! = 1
5! = 5*(5-1)! = 120
```

Now 5! can be calculated by repeatedly bringing the solution one step closer to the base case (n == 0):

```
5! = 5*(4)! = 5*4*(3)! = 5*4*3*(2)! = 5*4*3*2*(1)! = 5*4*3*2*1*(0)!
```

At this time 0! is assigned the value of 1. We can now start moving backwards, by replacing previous calls with the partial solutions:

```
          0!                1!            2!          3!       4!      5!
          |                 |             |           |        |       |
5*4*3*2*1*1   = 5*4*3*2*1 = 5*4*3*2 =   5*4*6 = 5*24 = 120
```

When Main calls Factorial(12), the first occurrence of Factorial sees n == 12. The method will call itself 12 more times for n = 11, 10, 9, . . ., 0, where each recursive call uses the argument n - 1. The base case is finally reached when the method is called with n == 0 and 1 is assigned to the method.

The following code implements the recursive method of finding a factorial. It is followed by a trace of the execution when finding the factorial of 3 (3!).

Code Sample: Class FactorialRecursively

```
 1  using System;
 2
 3  // Demonstrate the iteratice solution to the factorial function
 4  class FactorialRecursively
 5  {
 6    public static int Factorial(int n)
 7    {
 8      // Precondition: n >= 0 and n is not too large
 9      if (n == 0) // Base case
10        return 1;
11      else          // Recursive case
12        return n * Factorial(n - 1)   /* RP Fact */;
13    }
14
15    static void Main()
16    {
17      Console.WriteLine(Factorial(3) /* RP Main */);   // 6
18    }
19  }
```

Tracing factorial(3)

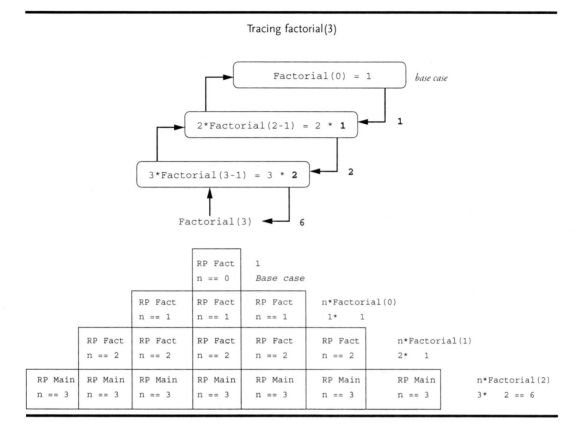

Infinite Recursion

As shown in Chapter 6, "Repetition," care must be taken to avoid infinite loops. Care must also be taken to avoid infinite recursion. *Infinite recursion* occurs when a method keeps calling other instances of itself, without ending up at a base case. For example, the following slight change of – to + in the Factorial method just shown will result in the method going away from, rather than toward, reaching the base case (unless it is called with n <= 0). The arguments to Factorial now get larger, not smaller.

```
public static int Factorial(int n)
{
   // Precondition: n >= 0 and n is not too large
   if (n == 0) // Base case
      return 1;
   else
      return n * Factorial(n + 1);    // Change - to +
}
```

503

Instead of getting the correct answers, the program terminates with an exception. Eventually, there is no memory left to store any more instances of the method.

Self-Check

9-7   Given the following method F, what value is returned from `F(-3)`?

```
public static int F(int n)
{
  if (n < 0)
    return n;
  else
    return n + f(n - 2);
}
```

9-8   What value is returned from `F(1)`?

9-9   What value is returned from `F(3)`?

9-10   What value is returned from `F(7)`?

9-11   What could happen if the recursive call `F(n - 2)` is changed to `F(n + 2)`?

9.3   Finding Palindromes Recursively

Suppose that you had a word and you wanted the computer to check whether or not it was a palindrome. A palindrome is a word that is the same whether read forward or backward: *radar, madam,* and *racecar,* for example. To determine if a word is a palindrome, you could put one finger under the first letter, and one finger under the last letter. If those letters matched, move your fingers one letter closer to each other, and check those letters. Repeat this until two letters don't match, or until your fingers touch because there are no more letters to consider.

The recursive solution is similar to this. To solve the problem using a simpler version of the problem, you can check the two letters on the end. If they match, ask whether the string with the end letters removed is a palindrome.

The base case occurs when the method finds a string of length two with the same two letters. A simpler case would be a string with only one letter, or a string with no letters. Checking for a string with 0 or 1 letters is easier than comparing the ends of a string with the same two letters. This is a general principle; when thinking about a base case, ask yourself, "Is this the simplest case? Or can I get anything simpler?"

The two simplest base cases (the number of characters is 0, or it is 1) can be handled like this (assume that str is the string object being checked):

```
if (str.Length <= 1)
  return true;
```

Another base case is the discovery that the two end letters are different, when `str` has two or more letters:

```
else if (str[0] != str[str.Length - 1])
  return false; // The end characters do not match
```

Now, the method can handle the base cases with `strings` such as `""`, `"A"`, and `"no"`. The first two are palindromes; `"no"` is not.

If a `string` is more than one character in length and its end characters match, no decision can be made, other than to keep trying. But in this circumstance, the same method can now be asked to solve a simpler version of the problem. Take off the end characters and check to see if the smaller string is a palindrome. The `Substring` method of `string` can be used to take the substring of a `string` like `"abba"` to get `"bb"`:

```
// This is a substring of the original string
// with both end characters removed.
return IsPalindrome(str.Substring(1, str.Length - 2));
```

If the original `string` was `"abba"` this message will not resolve on the next call. But when `str` is `"bb"`, the next call is `IsPalindrome("")`, which returns `true`. Our method has reached a base case—length is 0.

Here is a recursive palindrome method inside a class with its own testing method. The expected result is shown after `=?`.

Code Sample: Class PalindromeChecker

```
1  using System;
2
3  // Demonstrate a recursive method that determines if
4  // any string reads the same backward as forward.
5  class PalindromeChecker
6  {
7    // Return true if str is a palindrome or false if it is not
8    public static bool IsPalindrome(string str)
9    {
10     if (str.Length <= 1)
11       // Base case when this method knows to return true
12       return true;
13     else if (str[0] != str[str.Length - 1])
14       // Base case when this method knows to return
```

```
15            // false because the end characters do not match
16            return false;
17         else
18            // The first and last characters are equal so ask
19            // IsPalindrome if the shorter string (a simpler
20            // version of this problem) is a palindrome.
21            return IsPalindrome(str.Substring(1, str.Length - 2));
22     }
23
24     static void Main()
25     {
26        Console.WriteLine("{0} =? true", IsPalindrome(""));
27        Console.WriteLine("{0} =? true", IsPalindrome("A"));
28        Console.WriteLine("{0} =? false", IsPalindrome("no"));
29        Console.WriteLine("{0} =? true", IsPalindrome("abba"));
30        Console.WriteLine("{0} =? true", IsPalindrome("racecar"));
31        Console.WriteLine("{0} =? false", IsPalindrome("oh-no"));
32     }
33 }
```

Output

```
True =? true
True =? true
False =? false
True =? true
True =? true
False =? false
```

If the length of the string is greater than 1 and the end characters match, IsPalindrome calls another instance of IsPalindrome. It continues to do this, with smaller and smaller string arguments, until one of the base cases is reached. Either a string is found that has a length less than or equal to 1, or the characters on the ends are not the same.

The following trace of IsPalindrome("racecar") visualizes the calls that are made in this way.

IsPalindrome Recursive Calls (True result)

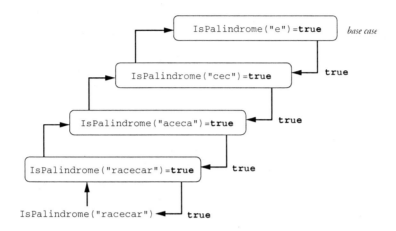

Since the fourth (topmost) call to IsPalindrome is called with the string "e", a base case is found—a string with length 1. This true value gets returned to its caller (the argument was "e"), which in turn returns true back to its caller (the argument was "cec") until true gets passed back to the first caller of IsPalindrome, the method call with the original argument of "racecar"; this now returns the value true.

Now, let's trace the recursive calls for the string "pooltop".

IsPalindrome Recursive Calls (False result)

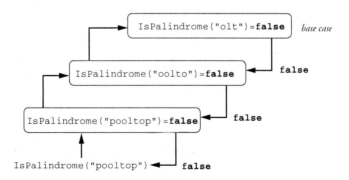

The base case is reached when the method compares the letters at the ends—"o" and "t" do not match. That particular method call returns `false` back to its caller (whose argument was "oolto"), which returns `false` to its caller. The original call to `IsPalindrome("pooltop")` is replaced with a response of `false` to the method that asked if "pooltop" was a palindrome.

Self-Check

9-12 What value is returned from `PalindromeChecker.IsPalindrome("yoy")`?

9-13 What value is returned from `PalindromeChecker.IsPalindrome("yoyo")`?

9-14 Write the output generated by this program.

```
using System;

class SelfCheck
{
  public static string Huh(string str)
  {
    if (str[0] == '-')
      return Huh(str.Substring(1, str.Length-1));
    else if (str[str.Length - 1] == '-')
      return Huh(str.Substring(0, str.Length - 1));
    else
      return str;
  }

  static void Main()
  {
    Console.WriteLine(Huh("+abc+"));
    Console.WriteLine(Huh("-abc-"));
    Console.WriteLine(Huh("-a-b-c-"));
    Console.WriteLine(Huh("------abc-----"));

    Console.ReadLine();
  }
}
```

9.4 Recursion with Arrays

Earlier in this textbook we looked at a sequential search algorithm. This algorithm uses an integer subscript that increases if an element is not found and the index is still in the range (meaning that there are more elements to compare).

The same algorithm can be implemented in a recursive fashion. The two base cases are:

1. If the element is found, return true.
2. If the index is out of range, terminate the search by returning false.

The recursive case is to look in the sub-portion of the array that has not been searched. With a sequential search, it does not matter if the array is searched from the smallest index to the largest, or from the largest index to the smallest. The first call to the `Exists` method below compares the search element to the array element that has the largest valid index. If that is not it, the next call narrows the search field from the back: the recursive call simplifies the problem by decreasing the value of the index by one. If the search element is not in the array, eventually the index goes to -1. At this point, `false` is returned to the preceding call, which returns `false` to the preceding call, until the original method call to `Exists` returns `false` to `Main`.

Code Sample: ShowRecursiveSequentialSearch

```
1  using System;
2
3  // Demonstrate a recursive searching method
4  class ShowRecursiveSequentialSearch
5  {
6    public static bool Exists(string[] array,
7                              int lastIndex,
8                              string searchElement)
9    {
10     if (lastIndex < 0)
11       return false;    // Base case 1: Nothing left to search
12     else if (array[lastIndex] == searchElement)
13       return true;     // Base case 2: Found it
14     else
15       // Recursive case
16       return Exists(array, lastIndex - 1, searchElement);
17   }
18
19   static void Main()
20   {
21     string[] array = {"Kelly", "Mike", "Jen",
22                       "Marty", "Stuart", "Grant"};
23     int n = array.Length - 1;
24
25     Console.WriteLine("{0} =? True", Exists(array, n, "Kelly"));
26     Console.WriteLine("{0} =? True", Exists(array, n, "Jen"));
27     Console.WriteLine("{0} =? False", Exists(array, n, "Not"));
28   }
29 }
```

Output

```
True =? True
True =? True
False =? False
```

Recursive Binary Search

As we saw in an earlier chapter, assuming that an array is sorted, the binary search algorithm can eliminate half of the array from the search with each pass. This is much faster than eliminating just one element per pass with a sequential search. The same binary search algorithm can be implemented in a recursive fashion. The two base cases are:

1. If there is nothing left to compare, terminate the search by returning `false`.
2. If the element is found, return `true`.

With a binary search, there are two recursive cases:
1. If the element is less than the middle element, search only through the lower indexes of the array.
2. If the element is greater than the middle element, search only through the higher indexes of the array.

Each call needs the array being searched, the object being searched for, and two indexes to mark the subarray that needs to be searched. In the beginning, `first` is 0 and `last` should be the array's `Length` minus one.

Code Sample: Class ShowRecursiveBinarySearch

```
1  using System;
2
3  // Demonstrate another recursive searching method
4  class ShowRecursiveBinarySearch
5  {
6    // Return true if searchElement is found in array.
7    public static bool Exists(string[] array,
8                             int first, int last,
9                             string searchElement)
10   {
11     if (first > last)
12       return false;        // Base case 1: Nothing left to search
13     else
14     {
```

```
15          // There is at least one more element to compare
16          int mid = (first + last) / 2;
17
18          if (searchElement == array[mid])
19            return true;      // Base case 2: Found it
20          else if (searchElement.CompareTo(array[mid]) < 0)
21            // Recursive case 1
22            return Exists(array, first, mid - 1, searchElement);
23          else
24            // Recursive case 2
25            return Exists(array, mid + 1, last, searchElement);
26        }
27    }
28
29    static void Main()
30    {
31      // Initialize an array so it is sorted.
32      string[] array = { "Grant", "Jen", "Kelly",
33                         "Marty", "Mike", "Stuart" };
34      int hi = array.Length - 1;
35
36      Console.WriteLine("{0} =? True", Exists(array, 0, hi, "Mike"));
37      Console.WriteLine("{0} =? True", Exists(array, 0, hi, "Grant"));
38      Console.WriteLine("{0} =? False", Exists(array, 0, hi, "Not"));
39    }
40 }
```

Output

```
true =? true
true =? true
false =? false
```

Self-Check

9-15   Write a method called PrintReverse that prints, in reverse order, all objects referenced by the array named x , which has n elements. Use recursion. No loops are allowed. Use this method heading:

```
public static void PrintReverse(Object[] array, int last)
```

9-16   Write a method called PrintForward that prints all objects referenced by the array named x, which has n elements, from the first element to the last. No loops are allowed.

9.5   Backtracking: Escape Obstacle Course

All of the problems presented so far have iterative solutions that do not need recursion. This section presents a problem that has an elegant recursive solution, and that would be rather difficult to do with iteration.

One common use of recursion is finding all of the ways of doing something. In game-playing strategies, recursion is often used to try all of the possibilities, to find the best move. To try all of the possibilities, you must have some form of backtracking available to you. *Backtracking* is the process of taking steps toward the final solution, while recording the details that will allow you to retrace the steps that have been taken. If the desired solution has not been reached, some steps may have to be retraced. This trial-and-error process often requires trying a very large number of possible solutions.

Imagine that you are in a maze, and you want to find the exit. You could try a path and follow it until you either run into a dead end or get out of the maze. If you reached a dead end, you could back up to the most recent place where there was a choice, mark the path you just tried as being no good, and try another direction. You could continue to do this until you either tried all of the paths or got out of the maze. Another way to do this is to keep walking while your left hand touches the wall to your left. If the maze is a proper maze, you will get out eventually, even if you have to try all paths.

Now consider the following problem, which we will use to demonstrate backtracking. Instead of escaping from a maze, this problem finds the path out of an obstacle course. An obstacle course may have multiple paths and exits. But unlike a proper maze, not everything that makes up the obstacle course is connected. Keeping your hand on the wall to the left will not work when the starting position has no nearby wall.

In the diagram below, the path starts at the point marked as S. The picture on the right shows one path out (which in this case is not the shortest one). There is a tendency in this solution to search down first and then to the right.

Initial Obstacle Course	One Path Out (not always the shortest)
`+++++++`	`+++++++`
`+S   + +`	`+SOO+ +`
`+   +`	`+.+OOO`
`+ + + +`	`+.+.+O+`
`+++++ +`	`+++++O+`

The symbols are defined as follows:

'S'	The starting point, where the mover begins.
'+'	A place where the mover cannot go.
' '	A place the mover can still try.
'.'	A place the mover has tried and that may later become part of the path to the exit.
'O'	Part of the path for a successful escape.

It is also possible that there is no path out. Here is an example that shows that all possibilities have been tried. In terms of a recursive algorithm, at this point, one of the base cases has been reached. There are no more paths to attempt.

Initial Obstacle Course	Trying All Possible Paths
`+++++++`	`+++++++`
`+S   + +`	`+S..+.+`
`+ +   +`	`+.+...+`
`+ + + +`	`+.+.+.+`
`+++++++`	`+++++++`

As mentioned above, one possible algorithm to escape a proper maze is to find a wall and keep your left hand on it as you walk. However, this won't always work. In the obstacle course below (which is not a proper maze), you would go around in circles forever if you kept your left hand on the wall in the middle. You would never find any of the four exits.

```
++++ +++
+       +
+       +
    ++
+   S   +
+       +
+++ ++++
```

As you can imagine, finding an iterative solution for this would be difficult. We will use a recursive solution that tries all possibilities.

The heart of this solution will be an escape method named `TryThisWay`. Assume that there is a two-dimensional array of characters in which every element has been initialized to one of the char values shown above: '+', ' ', or 'S'. When another method asks the obstacle course to mark the path to the exit, this escape method will be called.

The initial row and column will be the row and column where the 'S' is located. For each position, the `bool` return result `escaped` will initially be set to `false`. If it is found that a given location is a possible part of the solution, it will be given the symbol ' . ' and its value will be set to TRIED. Then a check will be made to see if the current location may actually represent an exit—if the current row or the current column is on one of the four borders. If the current location is not on a border, the algorithm will then try other possibilities.

In the algorithm below, the first try is to go south. In anticipation of tracing this algorithm, the success of finding an exit by going to the row below is marked with a down arrow ↓. Because the algorithm uses four different return points, they are marked as directional arrows ↓, →, ↑, and ← to indicate the direction the algorithm is trying.

Algorithm: Escaping from the starting point to the first found exit

```
bool TryThisWay(int row, int column)
{
    bool escaped = false;

    if current row and column is a possibility (not blocked and not tried)
    {
        mark current location as being TRIED;

        if current location is on the border, the mover is out so
            set escaped = true
        else
        {
            escaped = result of trying to escape using the square below ↓

            if still not escaped
                escaped = result of trying to escape using the square to the right →

            if still not escaped
                escaped = result of trying to escape using the square above ↑

            if still not escaped
                escaped = result of trying to escape using the square to the left ←
        }

        if escaped is now true, then
            current location = PART_OF_PATH;
    }

    return escaped
} // end TryThisWay
```

If the exit is immediately found below (south), no further recursive calls are made. If not, the algorithm will keep trying to move to the south until one of the base cases occurs:

1. An exit is found.
2. The location is not a possible way out (it may be blocked or already tried).

If the try to the south fails to find an exit, `false` is assigned to the `bool` variable `escaped` marked with ↓. The algorithm then backtracks and tries to the right (east). If the east direction reaches a dead end, `false` is assigned to the `bool` variable `escaped` marked with →. The algorithm then backtracks to try to the north. If an exit is found, `true` is assigned to the `bool` variable `escaped` marked with ↑. At this point, `escaped` is `true`, so there is no attempt to move to the left. Then the most recent intersection (the exit) is assigned the symbol for PART_OF_PATH, which is ‘O’.

```
// This would be skipped
if still not escaped,
  let escaped = result of trying to escape using the square to the left ←
```

Whenever escaped is true, the current location is changed to ‘O’.

```
if escaped is now true, then
 current location = PART_OF_PATH;
```

Then the successful value of `escaped` is returned back to the caller; that row and column intersection is assigned the PART_OF_PATH symbol ‘O’. This assignment process continues back to the original location. The entire path is now marked.

As was suggested earlier, tracing recursive methods requires diligence. Let's take a look at a more concrete example. The arrows shown below have been added to the algorithm above to help trace this very complex recursive algorithm.

Consider the following detailed trace to escape from this obstacle course. In this case, we will start at the second row in the second column. Since this can be represented by a 2-D array, consider this data to be stored in this array:

```
char[,] course = new char[4, 5];
```

The array data will be initialized from a text input file, as shown below.

The Initialized 2-D Array of char Values Used in the Trace That Follows

```
        01234 columns
rows 0  +++++
     1  +S   +
     2  + + +
     3  +++ +
```

Here is a trace of the escape attempt from this small obstacle course. The algorithm begins with TryThisWay(1, 1). This makes a recursive call to try to the south as it calls TryThisWay(row + 1, column). Another recursive call then occurs, to try to the south. It calls TryThisWay(row + 1, column) again, only to discover that there is a block at course[3, 1]. That instance of the method (row == 3, column == 1) is not a possibility. One base case has been reached, and the value of escaped (false) is returned to ↓.

At this point, the trace could look as shown below. Here, the values that are crossed out, such as 'S', have been assigned new values during' the method call (the top call is removed as it returns false, so it can be assigned to escaped near ↓).

↓	'+'	3	1	false
↓	'—' '.'	2	1	~~false~~ false
TryThisWay's caller	~~S~~ '.'	1	1	false
return point	course[row,col]	row	col	escaped?

The algorithm now backtracks to try to the east (col+1) from course[2, 1]. Since this path is blocked, it returns false. The method calls below show the attempt to go east, and its return value.

→	'+'	2	2	False
↓	'.'	2	1	~~false~~ false
TryThisWay's caller	'.'	1	1	False
return point	course[row,col]	row	col	escaped?

The north has already been tried, so going up (row-1) returns false.

↑	'.'	1	1	False
↓	'.'	2	1	~~false~~ false
TryThisWay's caller	'.'	1	1	False
return point	course[row,col]	row	col	escaped?

Finally, the fourth possible move from course[2, 1], to the west (col-1) is blocked; so going west returns false.

←	'+'	2	0	False
↓	'.'	2	1	~~false~~ false
TryThisWay's caller	'.'	1	1	False
return point	course[row,col]	row	col	escaped?

At this point, all recursive calls have been tried. At the end of the method, guarded action prevents the current location from becoming PART_OF_PATH. The algorithm then returns false and backtracks to the original call, so that the east path from course[1, 1] can be tried. At this point the method calls look like this:

TryThisWay's caller	'.'	1	1	~~false~~ false
return point	course[row,col]	row	col	escaped?

and the 2-D array named course now looks like this:

```
        01234 columns
rows 0  +++++
     1  +.  +
     2  +.+ +
     3  +++ +
```

After backtracking to ↓, the direction at course[1, 1], the algorithm checks the column to the right with TryThisWay(row, col + 1).

if still not escaped,
   let escaped = result of trying to escape using the square to the right →

An attempt is now made to go east. Since course[1, 2] is free, it is marked as tried.

```
        01234 columns
rows 0  +++++
     1  +.. +
     2  +.+ +
     3  +++ +
```

Then an attempt is made to go south from course[1, 2], where the return point is the down arrow, ↓. However, this is not a possibility (it is blocked) and false is returned. The method calls now look like this, with the top "box" about to be removed:

↓	'+'		2	2	false	
←	'.'		1	2	false false	
TryThisWay's caller	'.'		1	1	false	
return point	course[row,col]		row	col	escaped?	

At this point, an attempt is made to go east from course[1, 2]. The new top has column == 3, and the space ' ' is changed to the tried character '.'. Then the attempt is made to go south, which is possible. At this point, the trace of method calls looks like this:

↓	'—'	'.'	2	3	false
↓	'—'	'.'	1	3	false
←	'—'	'.'	1	2	false
TryThisWay's caller		'.'	1	1	false
return point	course[row,col]		row	col	escaped?

and the 2-D array course looks like this:

```
      01234 columns
rows 0 +++++
     1 +...+
     2 +.+.+
     3 +++ +
```

From course[2, 3], an attempt is made to go south again. Since this soon-to-be-discovered exit has not been tried, it is marked as tried before the program checks for an exit. At the beginning of this call to TryThisWay, the value of escaped is initially set to false. But then, since the current location is on a border, escaped is set to true, which is a base case. Because of this, the recursive calls in the big else part are skipped. At this point, the following guarded action allows the algorithm to change the current symbol of course[2, 3] to 'O' (PART_OF_PATH):

if escaped is now true, then
  current location = PART_OF_PATH;

Then `true` is returned back to the caller with this action, which always returns `true` or `false`:

return escaped
} // End TryThisWay

The current method calls on the call stack are only those that are part of the path to the first found exit.

return point	*course[row,col]*			*row*	*col*	*escaped?*	
↓	'—'	'÷'	'O'	3	3	false	true
↓	'—'	'.'		2	3	true	
↓	'—'	'.'		1	3	false	
←	'—'	'.'		1	2	false	
TryThisWay's caller	'.'			1	1	false	

The 2-D array named `course` now looks like this:

```
        01234 columns
rows 0  +++++
     1  +...+
     2  +.+.+
     3  +++O+
```

Once an exit has been found, there is no need to try other paths. That is why the same exit at `course[3, 3]` would be found, even if there had been an exit at `course[2, 4]`. Instead, the method returns `true` to assign the direction to `escaped` marked with ↓. Then the remaining recursive calls—to the east, the north, and the west—are skipped, since they are all guarded actions. The value of `true` is returned and assigned to the caller's local `escaped` variable, which causes the other recursive calls to be skipped.

At the end of this method, PART_OF_PATH is stored into `course[2, 3]` and `true` is returned to its caller. The method calls look like this:

return point	*course[row,col]*		*row*	*col*	*escaped?*	
↓	' '	'.'	1	3	false	true
←	' '	'.'	1	2	false	
TryThisWay's caller	'.'		1	1	false	

and the 2-D array named course looks like this:

```
      01234 columns
rows 0 +++++
     1 +...+
     2 +.+O+
     3 +++O+
```

The process continues to return true. This means that the caller can store the success of escaping, skip the other paths, assign PART_OF_PATH into course[row, col], and return true to its caller. This continues until the first call to TryThisWay returns true to the original caller. This indicates the success of the escape attempt.

At the end, the 2-D array named course looks like this.

```
      01234 columns
rows 0 +++++
     1 +OOO+
     2 +.+O+
     3 +++O+
```

Implementing the Escape Obstacle Course Algorithm

The C# solution to this problem is left as a programming project. The file named ObstacleCourse.cs is provided to let you initialize the 2-D array named course by reading from a disk file, and to allow the course to be printed, as follows:

```
+++++
+SOO+
+ +O+
+++O+
```

The code to do this should use the ToString method to print the tried values as spaces again. Also, another method must make the recursive call to TryThisWay and must remember to replace the initial starting position with 'S'.

Chapter Summary

- ○ A recursive definition has some part that includes a simpler definition of itself. Some examples are the power and Factorial methods.
- ○ For many problems, both recursive and iterative solutions exist.

○ The base case of a recursive algorithm refers to the time when a recursive call is not needed.

○ The recursive case occurs when a method invokes another instance of the same method. To avoid infinite recursion, the recursive method call must be able to eventually reach a base case.

○ The characteristics of recursion are:

   ○ The problem can be made into a simpler version of itself, in order to bring the problem closer to a base case.

   ○ There are one or more base cases.

○ Infinite recursion occurs when a method makes recursive calls that do not make progress toward a base case. Eventually the program terminates, when it has no memory left to store any more instances of the method.

○ One common use of recursion is to find all the ways of doing something.

○ Backtracking is a process of taking steps toward the final solution, while recording the details, so that steps can be retraced. This trial-and-error process often requires trying a very large number of possible solutions.

Key Terms

backtracking	recursion	recursive method
base case	recursive algorithm	return point
call stack	recursive case	tracing
infinite recursion	recursive definition	

Exercises

1. Write the output generated when this class runs:

```
using System;
class One
{
    public static int MysteryOne(int n)
    {
        if (n <= 2)
            return 0;
        else if (n == 5)
            return 1;
        else
            return n + MysteryOne(n - 1);
    }

    static void Main()
    {
```

```
        Console.WriteLine(MysteryOne(2));
        Console.WriteLine(MysteryOne(5));
        Console.WriteLine(MysteryOne(7));
    }
}
```

2. Write the output generated when this class runs:
```
using System;
class Two
{
    public static void MysteryTwo(int n)
    {
        if (n >= 1)
        {
            Console.Write("<");
            MysteryTwo(n - 3);
            Console.Write(n);
            Console.Write(">");
        }
    }

    static void Main()
    {
        MysteryTwo(2);
        Console.WriteLine();
        MysteryTwo(5);
        Console.WriteLine();
        MysteryTwo(7);
        Console.WriteLine();
    }
}
```

3. Write the output generated when this class runs:
```
using System;
class Three
{
    public static bool MysteryThree(int a, int b)
    {
        if (a >= 10 || b <= 3)
            return false;
        if (a == b)
            return true;
        else
            return MysteryThree(a + 2, b - 2) || MysteryThree(a + 3,
                                    b - 4);
    }
```

```
   static void Main()
   {
      Console.WriteLine(MysteryThree(14, 7));
      Console.WriteLine(MysteryThree(3, 6));
      Console.WriteLine(MysteryThree(4, 8));
   }
}
```

4. Write the output generated when this class runs:

```
using System;
class Four
{
   public static int MysteryFour(int n)
   {
      if (n < 1)
         return 0;
      else if (n == 1)
         return 1;
      else
         return 2 * MysteryFour(n - 1);
   }

   static void Main()
   {
      Console.WriteLine(MysteryFour(-5));
      Console.WriteLine(MysteryFour( 1));
      Console.WriteLine(MysteryFour( 2));
      Console.WriteLine(MysteryFour( 3));
      Console.WriteLine(MysteryFour( 4));
   }
}
```

5. Write the output generated by the following code:
```
using System;
class Five
{
   public static void MysteryFive(int[] x, int first, int last)
   {
      if (first < last)
      {
         int temp = x[first];
         x[first] = x[last];
         x[last] = temp;
         MysteryFive(x, first + 1, last - 1);
      }
   }
```

```
static void Main()
{
   int x[] = { 1, 2, 3, 4, 5, 6, 7, 8 };
   for (int j = 0; j < x.Length; j++)
     Console.Write("{0} ", x[j]);

   MysteryFive(x, 0, x.Length - 1);

   Console.WriteLine();
   for (int j = 0; j < x.Length; j++)
     Console.Write("{0} ", x[j]);
}
}
```

6. Write a method `Backward` that displays the integers 10, 9, 8, . . ., 1 on separate lines by using the method call `Backward(10)`. Use recursion to implement the iteration.

7. Write a recursive method for the strange numbers, which are defined as

```
            5 if n = 0
strange(n)  3 if n = 1
            2 * strange(n-2) if n > 1
```

   The following code should generate the output shown:
```
Console.WriteLine(strange(0));   // 5
Console.WriteLine(strange(1));   // 3
Console.WriteLine(strange(2));   // 10
Console.WriteLine(strange(3));   // 6
Console.WriteLine(strange(4));   // 20
Console.WriteLine(strange(5));   // 12
```

8. What is the value of `strange(4 )`?

9. List one argument to `strange` that would cause infinite recursion.

10. List the base and recursive cases for the following definition. For each case, list the action taken.

```
                 1 if k = 0
binomial(n, k)   1 if n = k
                 binomial(n-1, k-1) + binomial(n-1, k) if 0 < k < n
```

11. Write a recursive method `Binomial` in C# that implements the recursive definition above.

12. Evaluate Binomial(n, k) for the following values of n and k, or write "Undefined" if
    Binomial is not assigned a value:

n	k	Binomial(n, k)
1	0	
0	1	
8	8	
2	1	

13. The Fibonacci sequence begins as

    1 1 2 3 5 8 13 21 34

    where each Fibonacci number is the sum of the preceding two (except for the first two
    numbers). Write a recursive definition for the Fibonacci function.

14. Write the output generated by the following program:

    ```
    class TestWeird
    {
      public static int AnotherMystery(int x, int y)
      { // Pre: both arguments are >= 1
        if (y == 1)
          return x;
        else
          return x * AnotherMystery(x, y - 1);
      }

      static void Main()
      {
        Console.WriteLine(AnotherMystery(4, 1));
        Console.WriteLine(AnotherMystery(4, 2));
        Console.WriteLine(AnotherMystery(4, 3));
      }
    }
    ```

15. Using recursion, complete the method GoingUp so it displays all the numbers from
    the first argument to the last in ascending order (separated by a space). You cannot use
    a loop. Consider the base case. Consider what the recursive case is, and if the argu-
    ments increase, decrease, or stay the same.

    ```
    using System;
    class TestGoingUp
    {

      // Write the method goingUp

      static void Main()
      {
    ```

```
        GoingUp(1, 5);
        Console.WriteLine();
        GoingUp(2, 7);
        Console.WriteLine();
        GoingUp(3, 3);
        Console.WriteLine();
    }
}
```

Output

```
1 2 3  4  5
2 3 4  5 6 7
3
```

Programming Tips

1. When developing recursive algorithms, identify base and recursive cases.
There may be one or more recursive cases, and one or more base cases. After you identify these, it is easier to develop the algorithm. Don't forget that when a base case is encountered, it is possible that nothing occurs; in other words, no recursive call is made.

2. Make sure each recursive call brings you closer to the base case.
When you write recursive methods, you must have a step that brings the problem closer to the base case. This could involve incrementing or decrementing a parameter for the argument to the next call, or making a string smaller.

```
// Increment an index or decrement an index
Reverse(array, first + 1, last - 1);

// Make the string referenced by str smaller
ShowSmaller(str.Substring(0, str.Length - 1));
```

3. Recursion can be elegant, but it can also be costly.
In future studies, you will find very nice recursive solutions to difficult problems. Examples you would see in a subsequent course might include the recursive quick sort algorithm and the binary tree traversal. While such elegant uses of recursion provide runtime efficiency, some recursive methods are tremendously slow. In some cases, an iterative solution can be much better. You can verify this by completing the programming problem with the Fibonacci numbers and counting how many seconds it takes to compute `Fibonacci(40)` recursively.

Programming Projects

9A   Fibonacci

The Fibonacci sequence begins as

```
1   1   2   3   5   8   13   21   34
```

where each Fibonacci number is the sum of the preceding two (except for the first two). Write a recursive method named `Fibonacci` that returns the correct Fibonacci number for a given argument. For example, `Fibonacci(1)` should return 1, `Fibonacci(2)` should return 1, `Fibonacci(3)` should return 2, and `Fibonacci(8)` should return 21.

9B   Adding Reciprocals

Write a method `AddReciprocals` that takes an integer as a parameter and returns the sum of the first n reciprocals. `AddReciprocals(n)` returns $(1.0 + 1.0/2.0 + 1.0/3.0 + 1.0/4.0 + \ldots + 1.0/n)$.

9C   SumArray

Write a method `SumArray` that uses recursion to return the sum of the integers in the array of integers passed as an argument. You cannot use a loop in this method; you must use recursion. Add another method named `Show` to display the array elements, as shown in the output below.

```
static void Main()
{
  int[] x = {1, 2, 3, 4, 5, 6};
  // Display the array
  Show(x, x.Length);

  // Note: The second argument to sum is the LARGEST legal index in
  // the array. This makes it easier for you to get SumArray correct.
  int sum = SumArray(x, x.Length - 1);

  Console.WriteLine("Sum = {0}", sum);
}
```

Output
`[1 2 3 4 5 6]` `Sum = 21`

9D   ReversePrintString

Write a recursive method `ReversePrintString` that prints out the characters of a string in reverse order. Do not use a loop. The method call `ReversePrintString("abcdef")` should generate the output `fedcba`.

9E   Implementing the Escape Obstacle Course Algorithm

Complete the `ObstacleCourse` class so that it finds a path to an exit. The exit need not be the closest. You are given everything but the recursive method `TryThisWay`. You will probably find it useful to add a few private helper methods for the complex `TryThisWay` method. You will need the files `ObstacleCourse.cs` and `maze.dat` to complete this project.

```
 1 using System;
 2 using System.IO;     // For StreamReader
 3
 4 // This file is on the accompanying disk
 5 class ObstacleCourse
 6 {
 7   private static readonly char TRIED = '.';
 8   private static readonly char PART_OF_PATH = 'O';
 9
10   private char[,] course;
11   private int startRow;
12   private int startColumn;
13   private int rows;
14   private int columns;
15
16   public ObstacleCourse(string fileName)
17   {
18     StreamReader obstacleCourseFile = new StreamReader(fileName);
19
20     rows = int.Parse(obstacleCourseFile.ReadLine());
21     columns = int.Parse(obstacleCourseFile.ReadLine());
22
23     course = new char[rows, columns];
24     for(int r = 0; r < rows; r++)
25     {
26       string line = obstacleCourseFile.ReadLine();
27       for(int c = 0; c < columns; c++)
28       {
29         course[r, c] = line[c];
30         if(course[r, c] == 'S')
31         {
32           startRow = r;
33           startColumn = c;
```

```
34              // Need to make this space available as part of a path.
35              // The ToString method will substitute the S back in.
36              course[r, c] = ' ';
37            }
38          }
39        obstacleCourseFile.ReadLine();
40      }
41    }
42
43    public override string ToString()
44    {
45      string result = "";
46      for(int r = 0; r < rows; r++)
47      {
48        for(int c = 0; c < columns; c++)
49        {
50          if(course[r, c] == TRIED)
51            result += ' ';
52          else
53            result += course[r, c];
54        }
55        result += '\n';
56      }
57      return result;
58    }
59 }
60
61 class TestObstacleCourse
62 {
63    // Write bool TryThisWay and any private helper methods
64    // inside this class
65
66    static void Main()
67    {
68      ObstacleCourse aCourse =
69              new ObstacleCourse("maze.dat");
70
71      Console.WriteLine(aCourse);
72
73      // Call method that calls your private method MarkPathToExit
74      bool foundExit = aCourse.MarkPathToExit();
75
76      if (!foundExit)
77        Console.WriteLine("Could not solve");
78
79      Console.WriteLine(aCourse);
80    }
81 }
```

Output (this is not the shortest path)

```
++  +++  +++++++++++++++
+    +     ++ ++
          +            +++++ ++
+  +       ++  ++++ +  + ++
+  +     + + ++      +++    +
           ++   ++   +  +
+++++ + +         ++   + +
+++++ +++    + +  ++     +
+            + +     +  +
+++++ +    + + +      + +
+++++++++  ++++++++++++
```

```
++  +++  +++++++++++++++
+    +     ++ +++OOOOOOOOO
          +    OOOO+++++ ++
+  +      ++OO++++ +  + ++
+  +     + +O++ OO  +++   +
           O ++OO++    + +
+++++ +    +OOOOOO++   + +
+++++ +++OO+ +OO++     +
+            OO+ + OS +  +
+++++ +    + + + OO   + +
+++++++++  ++++++++++++
```

9F   Ways to Climb a Ladder

Given a ladder with n rungs, that can be climbed in steps of one rung or two rungs, determine
how many ways are there to climb that ladder. A person can climb either one or two rungs at a
time. For example, when rungs == 5, there are eight ways to climb the ladder:

```
1 1 1 1 1
1 1 1 2
1 1 2 1
1 2 1 1
2 1 1 1
1 2 2
2 1 2
2 2 1
```

Other examples include:

```
1    rung      1
2    rungs     1 1 or 2
3    rungs     1 1 1 or 1 2 or 2 1
4    rungs     1 1 1 1 or 1 1 2 or 1 2 1 or 2 1 1 or  2 2
```

Your output should only show the number of ways to climb the ladder, not the actual ways (which is a much more difficult problem). Your output should look just like the output below. Look for the pattern; it's like the Fibonacci sequence described in an earlier Programming Project in this chapter, except that the second number is 2, not 1.

```
Rungs     WaysToClimb
1         1
2         2
3         3
4         5
5         8
6         13
```

9G Showing the Different Ways to Climb a Ladder (Difficult)

For a real challenge, show the different ways to climb a ladder with n rungs. Each step can go up one rung or two rungs. For example, the function call showMeTheWays(5) should generate these eight lines of output (but not necessarily in this order). *Warning:* This is a difficult problem and may take many hours, with no correct result.

```
1 1 1 1 1
1 1 1 2
1 1 2 1
1 2 1 1
2 1 1 1
1 2 2
2 1 2
2 2 1
```

Graphical User Interfaces

Summing Up

So far, you have learned to read and write information using files. You understand arrays for storing collections of data. You have programmed both iterative and recursive solutions to complex problems. And you have learned how to have your programs process arguments that are entered at the command line.

Coming Up

In this chapter you will learn the basics for creating graphical user interfaces (GUIs). This chapter is considered optional for a first course of study. It is included to show the modern way of building applications, with a graphical interface, rather than with a command-line or console-based user interface. You will also see how the same classes that model the bank customers and transactions can be used in the context of a GUI. After studying this chapter, you will be able to

- ○ create programs with a graphical user interface.
- ○ show message boxes, forms, and graphical controls.
- ○ use event-driven programming and C# events.
- ○ cause interactions between different graphical controls in a program.
- ○ make your graphical programs respond
  to mouse clicks and actions from the user.

10.1 GUI Basics

A *graphical user interface*, or *GUI* ("gooey") for short, is a common way for a program to interact with its user. So far, the programs in this textbook have all used a text interface based on the `Console` class. The GUI equivalent to writing to the console is showing a small popup window called a *message box*. In code, the GUI rough equivalent of `Console.WriteLine` is the `MessageBox.Show` method, which takes a string and displays it in a graphical message window. Showing a message box is the simplest way to cause a graphical window to appear, but it is limited in power and usefulness.

General Form: Showing a Message Box

`MessageBox.Show("message");`

Examples:
MessageBox.Show("Testing, 1, 2, 3...");
MessageBox.Show(name + " is the best student at " + school);

The `MessageBox` class is in the `System.Windows.Forms` namespace, so the line `using System.Windows.Forms;` should appear at the start of a program that wishes to call `MessageBox.Show`.

The following short example creates and shows a message box on the screen. Unlike the programs in previous chapters, the programs in this chapter will not write any output to the console. Instead, they will display graphical windows. But to be consistent, the graphical windows will be shown under the heading of "Output."

Code Sample: Class MessageBoxExample1

```
 1 using System;
 2 using System.Windows.Forms;
 3
 4 class MessageBoxExample1
 5 {
 6    static void Main()
 7    {
 8        MessageBox.Show("Hello, world!");
 9    }
10 }
```

Output

The `MessageBox.Show` call causes the window to display. The program waits until the user clicks the OK button, then continues executing the code in `Main`. Since there is no other code in `Main`, the program exits.

`MessageBox.Show` does not have quite the same syntax as `Console.WriteLine`, because `Console.WriteLine` can contain special format specifiers and additional arguments. `MessageBox.Show` only accepts one `string` for its message. To use a formatted string with `MessageBox.Show`, use the `string.Format` method to build the formatted string, and then pass the formatted string:

```
double pi = 3.14159;
int degrees = 180;
MessageBox.Show(
    string.Format("Pi ({0:F2}) radians is {1} degrees",
                  pi, degrees));
```

Output

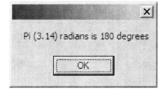

Message boxes are convenient and useful, but they have limitations. They cannot hold content other than messages and buttons. Users cannot interact with them in an interesting way; here, the only possible response is to click the OK button.

The sections below show how you can produce an interface that users can interact with in a meaningful way. Topics include how to create a customizable window of your own, and how to create buttons, messages, and other graphical entities that allow the user to interact with your program.

Forms and Controls

In C#, a graphical window is called a *form*. The widgets inside a form, such as buttons and text boxes, are called *controls*. A form can contain many different controls. In C#, each kind of control is represented by a type in System.Windows.Forms, including forms themselves. Learning about the C# types for forms and controls will make it possible to build programs with sophisticated and powerful graphical user interfaces.

Consider the following form, which has its various controls numbered:

Figure 10.1: Parts of a graphical program

The controls are as follows:

1. **Label**   A *label* is a string of text that generally serves to give a message to the user, or to explain what another control is used for. In the picture above, the labels explain the purpose of the text boxes to their right.

2. **TextBox**   A *text box* is an area in which the user can type information. Text boxes may be constrained to one line, or may span multiple lines.

3. **ComboBox**   A *combo box* is a combination of a text box and a drop-down list of items. Combo boxes are used to provide lists of choices to the user, without taking up a lot of screen space. Combo boxes are not covered in detail in this chapter.

4. **TextBox**   This text box spans many lines and is used to type a large message.

5. **Button**   A *button* is perhaps the most well known control. Clicking a button usually causes some action to occur. A button's text generally indicates its function or behavior.

6. **ScrollBar**   A *scroll bar* is used when the contents of a control are too big to show in the screen space it has been given. Scroll bars are not covered in detail in this chapter.

7. **MainMenu**   A *menu* is a text-based list of program options. A *main menu* consists of one or more high-level text-based options at the top of the form (such as File and Help here). When clicked, each of these choices produces a drop-down list of lower level choices, that, when clicked, execute various commands. Main menus are not covered in detail in this chapter.

8. **Form**   The actual window itself. A form has a title bar, some control buttons, a border that can be used to resize it, and a central area that can hold controls.

The C# namespace `System.Windows.Forms` contains classes to represent forms, all the various controls pictured above, and many more. This group of classes provides the basic framework for you to create rich graphical applications in C#.

To create a graphical program, simply create a `Form` object and set its properties to the appropriate values, then make the form display itself on the screen. To run a program that has one main form, you call the `Application.Run` method and pass the name of the form to show, as a parameter. `Application` is a class in the `System.Windows.Forms` namespace that is related to running graphical applications.

Here is a simple graphical program that creates and shows a form:

Code Sample: Class SimpleGUI

```
1  // A not-so-interesting simple graphical program.
2  using System;
3  using System.Windows.Forms;
4
5  class SimpleGUI
6  {
7    static void Main()
8    {
9      Form window = new Form();        // Construct a Form object
10
11     window.Text = "Window Title";   // Set form properties
12     window.Width = 200;
13     window.Height = 100;
```

```
14
15        Application.Run(window);        // Show Form on screen
16    }
17 }
```

Output

You can decide for yourself which properties of a Form you would like to set. Any properties that you do not set are given default values. For example, the default size of a form is 300 x 300 pixels, the default title is "" (the empty string), and the default background color is your system's predefined window background color (which on many Windows systems is a light gray).

Most of the methods and properties used to construct a form are relatively self-explanatory. Setting a form's Text property changes the text in the window's title, while setting the Size property (or the Width and Height properties) changes the shape of the window on the screen.

But a form by itself is not very interesting. What makes a graphical application have a rich user interface is the set of controls inside the form. Use these steps to put one control inside a form:

1. Create the control object.
2. Set the properties of the control object accordingly.
3. Put the control in the form by calling the Add method of the form's Controls property. The Controls property is a collection of all the controls inside a form.

There is a large set of properties common to all controls. Since a Form is also a control, forms also have the same properties. The common properties are made possible by inheritance, which is not discussed in detail here. It is useful to have a common property set like this, because once you learn the properties in the set, you can use them on any control.

Here is a partial list of properties that are common to all controls:

Properties of All Controls (Partial List)

```
public AnchorStyles Anchor {get; set;}
public Color BackColor {get; set;}
```

```
public Rectangle ClientRectangle {get;}
public Size ClientSize {get; set;}
public ControlCollection Controls {get;}
public Cursor Cursor {get; set;}
public DockStyle Dock {get; set;}
public Font Font {get; set;}
public Color ForeColor {get; set;}
public int Height {get; set;}
public Point Location {get; set;}
public Size Size {get; set;}
public string Text {get; set;}
public int Width {get; set;}
```

In addition to the common properties, particular controls may have unique properties, methods, and constructors of their own. Here is a list of the unique aspects of a Form object:

Form Constructor

```
public Form()
```

Form Properties

```
public bool Enabled {get; set;}
public FormBorderStyle FormBorderStyle {get; set;}
public Icon Icon {get; set;}
public int MaximumSize {get; set;}
public MainMenu Menu {get; set;}
public int MinimumSize {get; set;}
```

Form Methods

```
public void Close()
public void Hide()
public void Show()
```

The following program creates a form and puts some controls (a Label, a Button, and a TextBox) inside it. To save a bit of space, the Width and Height properties are set on the same line, as are the Left and Top. This will be done in the rest of the programs in this chapter.

Code Sample: Class GuiWithControls

```
1  // Create a GUI program as a form with three controls.
2  using System;
3  using System.Windows.Forms;
4
5  class GuiWithControls
6  {
7    static void Main()
8    {
9      // Construct a Label control
```

```
10        Label inputLabel = new Label();
11        inputLabel.Text = "Type your name here:";
12        inputLabel.Width = 160;   inputLabel.Height = 20;
13        inputLabel.Left = 10;     inputLabel.Top = 10;
14
15        // Create a Textbox control
16        TextBox inputArea = new TextBox();
17        inputArea.Text = "Jane Doe";
18        inputArea.Width = 160;    inputArea.Height = 20;
19        inputArea.Left = 10;      inputArea.Top = 30;
20
21        // Construct a Button control
22        Button okButton = new Button();
23        okButton.Text = "OK";
24        okButton.Width = 80;      okButton.Height = 30;
25        okButton.Left = 60;       okButton.Top = 60;
26
27        // Construct a Form to hold these three controls
28        Form window = new Form();
29        window.Text = "My GUI";
30        window.Width = 200;       window.Height = 120;
31
32        // Add three controls inside the one Form
33        window.Controls.Add(inputLabel);
34        window.Controls.Add(inputArea);
35        window.Controls.Add(okButton);
36
37        // Show the Form with its three controls
38        Application.Run(window);
39      }
40 }
```

Output

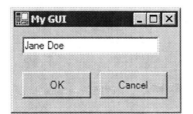

Self-Check

10-1   Write the C# code to show a message box that displays the current time of day. (Hint: Use the `DateTime` class, covered in Chapter 3).

10-2   What classes and namespaces are needed to create a minimal graphical program (not just a message box)?

10-3   Write the C# code to create a form, set its title to `"My first GUI!"`, add any one control to the form, and show it on the screen.

Layout: Position and Size Behavior of Controls

In the preceding examples, each control was given a fixed size and location. However, this can be undesirable, for any of several reasons. For example, what if the form is resized? By default, the controls in the form will retain their original sizes and locations, which may not be desired.

Sometimes it is more desirable to have a control's location and/or size adjust as the window resizes. For example, a window to write a text message may have a large text box that is intended to fill the entire form. Even if the size of the text box is initially set to correctly fill the form, if the user or the program resizes the form, the box may become the wrong size. Enlarging the form will make the text box not fill the entire area. Worse yet, shrinking the form may make the text box disappear off the end of the form!

The following code fragment demonstrates problems with resizing a form:

```
Form window = new Form();
window.Text = "Resizing";
window.Width = 200;
window.Height = 120;

TextBox inputArea = new TextBox();
inputArea.Text = "I am a text box";
inputArea.Multiline = true;

// make text box fill form's available space
inputArea.Size = window.ClientSize;

window.Controls.Add(inputArea);
Application.Run(window);
```

Figure 10.2: Problems with resizing forms

One way to improve the situation described above is to put restrictions on what size the form can be. A `Form` object has `MinimumSize` and `MaximumSize` properties that can be used to keep the form from becoming too small or too large. It is often a good idea to set the Form's `MinimumSize` property to a size just large enough to hold the controls that are in it. This ensures that the user does not shrink the form and obscure its controls.

Another solution to this problem is simply to disallow resizing of the form. If the form's size cannot be tampered with, resizing problems cannot occur. To control resizing of a form, you can adjust its `FormBorderStyle` property. The property holds a value from the `FormBorderStyle` enumeration. This value can be any of `Fixed3D`, `FixedDialog`, `FixedSingle`, `FixedToolWindow`, `None`, `Sizable`, or `SizableToolWindow`. Note that when referring to each form border style, as with any enumeration, you must use its full name, such as `FormBorderStyle.Fixed3D`. For example:

```
Form myForm = new Form();
MyForm.FormBorderStyle = FormBorderStyle.FixedSingle;
```

The following figure demonstrates all possible form border styles, some of which are discussed further below. Some of the styles, such as `FixedSingle` and `Sizable`, or `FixedToolWindow` and `SizableToolWindow`, look almost exactly the same. The difference is that the Fixed styles cannot be resized.

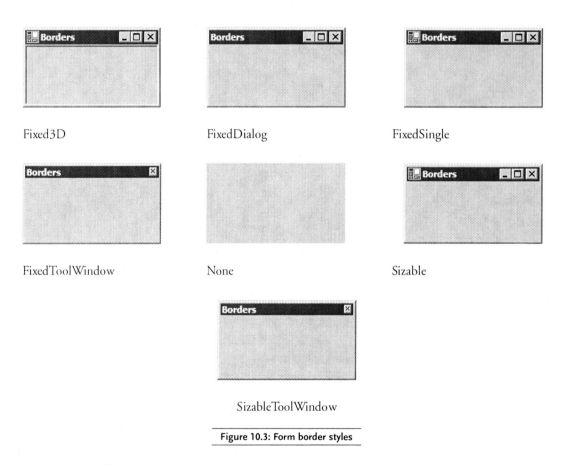

Fixed3D   FixedDialog   FixedSingle

FixedToolWindow   None   Sizable

SizableToolWindow

Figure 10.3: Form border styles

To make a form non-resizable, simply set its border to one of the Fixed borders, such as `FormBorderStyle.FixedSingle`. The ToolWindow borders shown above are for tooltips and toolbars, and are not usually used for forms that represent applications. The `None` border is fun because it removes the window's border entirely, along with its title bar. This lets you create floating windows, without the usual adornments around their edges.

Although making a form non-resizable can solve the resizing problem described above, it is not a very useful solution. Many programs depend on allowing windows to be resized, to provide a satisfactory experience to the user. Imagine if your Web browser were locked to a size of 400 x 300 pixels because the programmer did not want to worry about resizing issues! This would clearly be unacceptable.

An alternate solution is to provide layout information that tells the controls what to do when the form resizes. *Layout* represents the relative positions of controls in a form. In C#, controls may be laid out in several ways. One way to specify layout for a control is to specify an anchor for it. To *anchor* a control to one side of a form means to keep that control's distance from that side of the form constant. For example, anchoring a button to the bottom of a form means that if the bottom of the form moves, the button will move the same distance.

By default, all controls are anchored to the top and left of the form. Here is an example of a text box anchored to the right side of a form, and the subsequent effect when the form is resized:

```
TextBox inputArea = new TextBox();
inputArea.Anchor = AnchorStyles.Right;
```

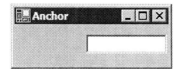 

Figure 10.4: Text box anchored to right side of form

To set an anchor, you modify the `Anchor` property of a control. The `Anchor` property is of type `AnchorStyles`, which is an enumeration of the regions where the control may be attached: `Bottom`, `Left`, `None`, `Right`, and `Top`. The anchor styles may be combined with the bitwise binary OR operator | to produce combined styles. (The bitwise OR operator is not discussed in detail here except to say that it can be used on AnchorStyles to combine them.) For example, to anchor to the bottom right of the window, set the `Anchor` property's value to the following:

```
AnchorStyles.Bottom | AnchorStyles.Right
```

The following program constructs three buttons and anchors them in various areas of the form:

Code Sample: Class AnchorExample2

```
1  // Anchors several buttons.
2  using System;
3  using System.Windows.Forms;
4
5  class AnchorExample2
6  {
7    static void Main()
8    { // construct the buttons, set their properties and anchor
9      Button button1 = new Button();
10     button1.Text = "Right";
11     button1.Width = 80;    button1.Height = 30;
12     button1.Left = 110;    button1.Top = 50;
13     button1.Anchor = AnchorStyles.Right;
14
15     Button button2 = new Button();
16     button2.Text = "Bottom";
17     button2.Width = 80;    button2.Height = 30;
18     button2.Left = 60;     button2.Top = 90;
19     button2.Anchor = AnchorStyles.Bottom;
20
21     Button button3 = new Button();
22     button3.Text = "Left, Right, Top";
23     button3.Width = 150;   button3.Height = 30;
24     button3.Left = 10;     button3.Top = 10;
25     button3.Anchor =
26       AnchorStyles.Top | AnchorStyles.Left | AnchorStyles.Right;
27
28     // Construct form to hold the anchored buttons
29     Form window = new Form();
30     window.Text = "Anchor 2";
31     window.Width = 200;    window.Height = 160;
32     window.Controls.Add(button1);
33     window.Controls.Add(button2);
34     window.Controls.Add(button3);
35     Application.Run(window);
36   }
37 }
```

Output

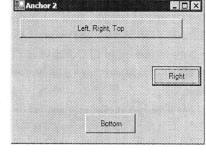

Initial window appearance   After resizing horizontally and vertically

Notice that when the form resizes vertically, the "Right" and "Bottom" buttons move vertically, but the "Left, Right, Top" button stays put, because of its anchor to the top of the form. Since the "Bottom" button is anchored to the bottom, it moves an equal distance to the amount the bottom moves, and since the "Right" button is neither anchored to the top nor to the bottom, it moves at a slower rate, to maintain the correct ratio of space above and below it.

When the form resizes horizontally, the "Left, Right, Top" button expands by the same amount. This is because its anchoring to the left and right sides of the form forces it to keep the same distance from the form's left and right edges when the form resizes. The "Right" button stays glued to the right side of the form. The "Bottom" button is not anchored to the left or right, so it remains roughly in the window's center, to preserve the ratios of space on its left and right sides.

Docking

Another means of layout for controls is through docking. *Docking* forces a control to entirely fill one of the edges of a form, or to fill the form's entire center area. Docking is different from anchoring, because docking is a restriction on both *the position and the size* of a component. A component docked on the top or bottom of a form will stretch horizontally to match the form's width. Similarly, a component docked on the left or right side of a form will stretch vertically to match the form's height. Docking is useful when it is desirable to have one control monopolize all of one edge of the form, such as a text label on the bottom of the window, or a button bar on the left edge of the form (or the entire form in the case of the Center dock style, such as a large image that fills an entire window).

In C#, docking is accomplished by setting the Dock property of the control that you wish to dock. The value of the Dock property can be any of the elements of the DockStyle enumeration, which includes the elements Bottom, Fill, Left, None, Right, and Top. Unlike the AnchorStyles enumeration, a DockStyle is mutually exclusive of other DockStyles, so the elements should not be combined with the binary OR operator, |. To make a control fill the form entirely, set its Dock property to DockStyle.Fill.

The following program demonstrates a text box and a button, docked to the top and bottom of a form, respectively:

Code Sample: Class DockExample1

```
1  // Demonstrates control docking.
2  using System;
3  using System.Windows.Forms;
4
5  class DockExample1
6  {
7    static void Main()
8    {
9      TextBox box = new TextBox();
10     box.Text = "Top";
11     box.Dock = DockStyle.Top;
12
13     Button button = new Button();
14     button.Text = "Bottom";
15     button.Dock = DockStyle.Bottom;
16
17     // Construct a Form object
18     Form window = new Form();
19     window.Text = "Dock";
20     window.Width = 150;
21     window.Height = 80;
22
23     window.Controls.Add(box);
24     window.Controls.Add(button);
25
26     Application.Run(window);
27   }
28 }
```

Output

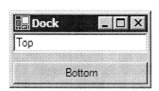

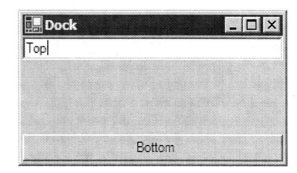

Initial window appearance   After resizing horizontally and vertically

In summary, there are many ways to intelligently control the appearance of a graphical program and its controls. One is by correctly setting the appropriate properties, such as `Left` or `Height`, for the controls, to position them properly. Another is to restrict the resizability of the form using its `MinimumSize`, `MaximumSize`, and `FormBorderStyle` properties. A third way is to make controls respond intelligently to form resizing by setting their `Anchor` and `Dock` properties properly.

Self-Check

10-4   What `DockStyle` should be used to make a button fill an entire form?

10-5   Write the C# code to add a button with text of `"Hello!"`, location of (x = 25, y = 40), and size of 80 pixels wide x 32 pixels high, to a form referred to by variable `myForm`.

10.2 Events and Event-Handling

Even the most attractive GUI is useless unless it actually does something. By default, all the buttons, menus, and other controls on the screen will not do anything when clicked or otherwise interacted with. The programmer must describe the behavior, if any, that each control will have when the user interacts with it.

An *event* is an action that occurs in a graphical program. When the user clicks a button, a button-click event occurs. Similarly, when the user types a character into a `TextBox`, a textual event occurs. Modern graphical programs use the concept of *event-driven programming*, which means that after the GUI appears on the screen, the program's path of execution is driven primarily by the sequence of events caused by the actions of the user.

In C#, the graphical controls have special public properties that are called event objects. An event object can be thought of as a place to attach your method for handling that event. Attaching an *event handler* to an event is done using the `+=` operator. On the left side of the `+=` is the event object to attach to (written, like other properties, as *control-name.event-name*). On the right side of the `+=` goes the method to attach to handle that event.

Actually, that is not entirely correct. What really goes on the right side of the `+=` is an `EventHandler` object. An `EventHandler` object is a wrapper around your method that allows it to be used to handle C# events. An `EventHandler` has a constructor that takes one argument: the name of the method for handling the event.

The overall syntax for handling an event is as follows:

General Form: Attaching an event handler a control's event

control-name.event-name **+= new EventHandler(***method-name***);**

Notes:
The *method-name* must refer to a method with the following signature:
`public void ` *method-name* `(object obj, EventArgs args)`
The method can be static or nonstatic.

Example:
```
public static void ShowBox(object obj, EventArgs args)
{
    MessageBox.Show("Hello there!");
}

. . .

Button myButton = new Button();
myButton.Click += new EventHandler(ShowBox);
```

EventHandler is an example of a C# language feature called a ***delegate***. A delegate can be thought of as an object that holds a method inside it, and that can be used to execute the enclosed method later. Delegates are useful for treating methods as objects, so that they can be passed around in code and executed as needed. Delegates are not discussed in detail in this textbook. The only use of EventHandler that will be needed for this chapter is to be able to construct one and attach it to an event.

To get an EventHandler to respond to a button click:
1. Write a method with the appropriate signature.
2. Construct an EventHandler to represent the method.
3. Attach the EventHandler to the button's Click event, using +=.

Here is an example that shows a message box object whenever the button is clicked. This is done by attaching an event handler to the Click event of the button.

Code Sample: Class ClickEvent

```
1  // Allow a method DisplayMessage to respond to a button click.
2  // When the button is clicked, the code in the method executes.
3  using System;
4  using System.Windows.Forms;
5
6  class ClickEvent
7  {
8    // This method will be used for the event handler
9    static void DisplayMessage(object obj, EventArgs args)
10   {
11     MessageBox.Show("You clicked the button!");
12   }
13
14   static void Main()
15   {
16     // Construct button control
17     Button button = new Button();
18     button.Text = "Click me!";
19     button.Width = 120;
20     button.Height = 30;
21     button.Left = 10;
22     button.Top = 10;
23
24     // attach event handler
25     button.Click += new EventHandler(DisplayMessage);
26
27     // construct form
28     Form window = new Form();
```

```
29        window.Text = "Events";
30        window.Width = 160;
31        window.Height = 80;
32
33        // put controls inside form
34        window.Controls.Add(button);
35
36        Application.Run(window);
37    }
38 }
```

Output

Initial window appearance   User clicks "Click me!" button

The above example responds to the Click event of a button. Just as controls share many common properties and methods, there is also a common set of events that each control object is guaranteed to have. Most of these events use the common EventHandler object, which will be the focus of the event handling in this chapter.

In general, an event is formally described by its event declaration header. This is like a method or property header: it lists the event's name, the type of delegates that may be attached to it, and possibly other information, such as access modifiers.

Here is the general form of an event declaration header:

General Form: Event declaration header

public event *delegate-type event-name*;

In the above form, *delegate-type* represents the type of delegate that may be attached to the event *event-name*. The event keyword always appears on event declarations. Here is a partial list of events common to all graphical controls:

Events for Graphical Controls

```
public event EventHandler Click;
public event EventHandler DoubleClick;
public event EventHandler Enter;
public event EventHandler GotFocus;
public event KeyEventHandler KeyDown;
public event KeyPressEventHandler KeyPress;
public event KeyEventHandler KeyUp;
public event EventHandler Leave;
public event EventHandler LostFocus;
public event MouseEventHandler MouseDown;
public event EventHandler MouseEnter;
public event EventHandler MouseHover;
public event EventHandler MouseLeave;
public event MouseEventHandler MouseMove;
public event MouseEventHandler MouseUp;
public event MouseEventHandler MouseWheel;
public event PaintEventHandler Paint;
public event EventHandler Resize;
public event EventHandler TextChanged;
```

The following program has a GUI that contains a text box, an OK button, and a Cancel button. When the user types an address in the text box and clicks the OK button, a message box pops up, showing the address that the user typed.

Code Sample: Class MultipleEventGui

```
 1  // Responds to click events on multiple buttons.
 2  using System;
 3  using System.Windows.Forms;
 4
 5  class MultipleEventGui
 6  {
 7    static void Main()    // runs the program
 8    {
 9      MultipleEventGui gui = new MultipleEventGui();
10      Application.Run(gui.window);
11    }
12
13    private Form window;
14    private TextBox box;
```

```
15    private Button ok, cancel;
16
17    public MultipleEventGui()
18    {
19      // construct controls
20      box = new TextBox();
21      box.Text = "Type address here";
22      box.Width = 180;
23      box.Height = 30;
24      box.Left = 10;
25      box.Top = 10;
26
27      ok = new Button();
28      ok.Text = "OK";
29      ok.Width = 80;
30      ok.Height = 30;
31      ok.Left = 10;
32      ok.Top = 50;
33
34      cancel = new Button();
35      cancel.Text = "Cancel";
36      cancel.Width = 80;
37      cancel.Height = 30;
38      cancel.Left = 110;
39      cancel.Top = 50;
40
41      // set up event handlers
42      ok.Click += new EventHandler(ok_Click);
43      cancel.Click += new EventHandler(cancel_Click);
44
45      // construct form
46      window = new Form();
47      window.Text = "Send Email";
48      window.Width = 210;
49      window.Height = 120;
50
51      // put controls inside form
52      window.Controls.Add(box);
53      window.Controls.Add(ok);
54      window.Controls.Add(cancel);
55    }
56
57    private void ok_Click(Object sender, EventArgs e)
58    {
59      // A MessageBox will size itself based on the message.
60      // New lines will show up in the Gui.
61      MessageBox.Show("Here is the address you typed!\n\n"
62                       + box.Text);
```

```
63    }
64
65    private void cancel_Click(Object sender, EventArgs e)
66    {
67       Application.Exit();
68    }
69 }
```

Output

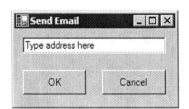

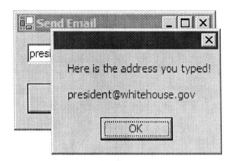

Initial window appearance   After typing an address and clicking OK

The preceding program had some interaction between components. Clicking the OK button caused the text from the text box to appear in a message box. In order for the OK button to be able to do this, the OK button's Click event handling method needed to be able to refer to the text box. For this reason, the program was written as a class, rather than just as a Main method; having the buttons and text box as fields made them accessible from inside the OkClick method.

Self-Check

10-6   Write a C# method with the right signature to be used with an EventHandler object; the method should display a random number between 1 and 10 in a message box.

10-7   Given the following declaration:

```
Button okButton = new Button();
```

using your method from the previous question, write the C# code so that when this button is clicked, your method will execute.

10.3 More Controls: `CheckBox` and `RadioButton`

In the previous sections, the `Button`, `Label`, and `TextBox` controls were introduced. C# contains a large number of other controls that are useful in designing more complex graphical programs.

Check boxes and radio buttons are common controls often seen in graphical programs that let users select and deselect options. *Radio buttons* usually provide a set of mutually exclusive choices, where at most one choice may be selected at any time. Clicking one radio button in a group of buttons selects it, and deselects any other radio buttons in the group. By contrast, check boxes are usually independent; clicking one check box does not affect other check boxes around it. Both radio buttons and check boxes can be thought of as having two distinct states: checked and unchecked.

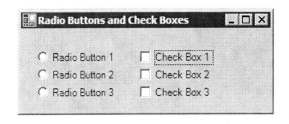

Figure 10.5: Radio Buttons and Check Boxes

Check boxes in C# are implemented using the `CheckBox` control. A `CheckBox` object is like most other controls; you can set its properties, such as `Width`, `Top`, `Text` and so on. However, a `CheckBox` object has some additional helpful features. It has a `Checked` property of type `bool` that indicates whether or not the box is checked. There is also a public event named `CheckedChanged` in each `CheckBox`, so that you can attach an `EventHandler` to execute when the box becomes checked or unchecked.

The following example demonstrates check boxes by using them to change the color of text on the screen. Notice that this program also uses the namespace `System.Drawing`, which contains the *`Color`* type. Colors are named by `Color.`*ColorName*, where *ColorName* can be one of several hundred constant values, such as `Red`, `Green`, `Blue`, `Orange`, `Yellow`, `Purple`, `Black`, `White`, `Brown`, and so on. Color objects can be used to set the `ForeColor` and `BackColor` properties of controls to change their foreground and background color, respectively.

Code Sample: Class CheckBoxExample1

```
1  // Uses check boxes to change a label's color.
2  using System;
3  using System.Drawing;          // for Color type
4  using System.Windows.Forms;
5
6  class CheckBoxExample1
7  {
8    static void Main()    // runs the program
9    {
10     new CheckBoxExample1();
11   }
12
13   private Form window;      // fields
14   private CheckBox cbRed, cbYellow, cbBlue;
15   private Label label;
16
17   public CheckBoxExample1()
18   { // colors can be mixed; e.g red + blue = purple
19     cbRed = new CheckBox();
20     cbRed.CheckedChanged += new EventHandler(UpdateColor);
21     cbRed.Text = "Red";
22     cbRed.Width = 50;    cbRed.Height = 20;
23     cbRed.Left = 10;     cbRed.Top = 10;
24
25     cbYellow = new CheckBox();
26     cbYellow.CheckedChanged += new EventHandler(UpdateColor);
27     cbYellow.Text = "Yellow";
28     cbYellow.Width = 50;    cbYellow.Height = 20;
29     cbYellow.Left = 70;     cbYellow.Top = 10;
30
31     cbBlue = new CheckBox();
32     cbBlue.CheckedChanged += new EventHandler(UpdateColor);
33     cbBlue.Text = "Blue";
34     cbBlue.Width = 80;    cbBlue.Height = 20;
35     cbBlue.Left = 120;    cbBlue.Top = 10;
36
37     label = new Label();
38     label.Text = "This is the label text";
39     label.Dock = DockStyle.Bottom;
40     label.ForeColor = Color.White;
41
42     window = new Form();
43     window.Text = "Check Boxes";
44     window.Width = 200;    window.Height = 100;
```

```
45        window.Controls.Add(cbRed);
46        window.Controls.Add(cbYellow);
47        window.Controls.Add(cbBlue);
48        window.Controls.Add(label);
49
50        Application.Run(window);
51    }
52
53    // Sets a new color for the label by combining the colors
54    // of all currently checked CheckBoxes.
55    public void UpdateColor(object obj, EventArgs args)
56    {
57        if (cbRed.Checked && cbYellow.Checked && cbBlue.Checked)
58          label.ForeColor = Color.Brown;
59        else if (cbRed.Checked && cbYellow.Checked)
60          label.ForeColor = Color.Orange;
61        else if (cbRed.Checked && cbBlue.Checked)
62          label.ForeColor = Color.Purple;
63        else if (cbYellow.Checked && cbBlue.Checked)
64          label.ForeColor = Color.Green;
65        else if (cbRed.Checked)
66          label.ForeColor = Color.Red;
67        else if (cbBlue.Checked)
68          label.ForeColor = Color.Blue;
69        else if (cbYellow.Checked)
70          label.ForeColor = Color.Yellow;
71        else
72          label.ForeColor = Color.White;
73    }
74 }
```

Output

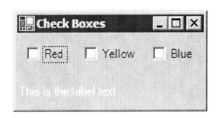
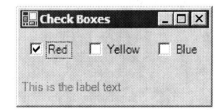

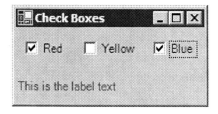

Initial window appearance

Radio buttons in C# are implemented by use of the `RadioButton` control. A `RadioButton` is similar to a `CheckBox`: it has a `Checked` property, a `CheckedChanged` event, and so on. There are two main differences between these objects: first, a radio button looks different than a checkbox (radio buttons are usually circles with dots inside, while check boxes are squares with check marks in them), and second, radio buttons are mutually exclusive from each other, as described previously.

The following program uses three radio buttons to alter the background color of a form. Using radio buttons for this makes sense, because the background can only be one color at a time. Notice that this example uses the `System.Drawing` namespace to have access to the `Color` type.

```
Code Sample: Class RadioButtonExample1
1  // Uses radio buttons to change a form's background color.
2  using System;
3  using System.Drawing;          // for Color type
4  using System.Windows.Forms;
5
6  class RadioButtonExample1
7  {
8    // Runs the program.
9    static void Main()
10   {
11      new RadioButtonExample1();
12   }
13
14   // fields
15   private Form window;
16   private RadioButton rbRed, rbBlue, rbGreen;
17
18   // Sets up the form, controls, and event handlers.
19   public RadioButtonExample1()
```

```
20  {
21    rbRed = new RadioButton();
22    rbRed.Checked = true;
23    rbRed.CheckedChanged += new EventHandler(SetColor);
24    rbRed.Text = "Red";
25    rbRed.Left = 10;   rbRed.Top = 10;
26
27    rbBlue = new RadioButton();
28    rbBlue.CheckedChanged += new EventHandler(SetColor);
29    rbBlue.Text = "Blue";
30    rbBlue.Left = 10;   rbBlue.Top = 30;
31
32    rbGreen = new RadioButton();
33    rbGreen.CheckedChanged += new EventHandler(SetColor);
34    rbGreen.Text = "Green";
35    rbGreen.Left = 10;   rbGreen.Top = 50;
36
37    window = new Form();
38    window.Text = "Radio Buttons";
39    window.Width = 175;   window.Height = 120;
40    window.BackColor = Color.Red;
41    window.Controls.Add(rbRed);
42    window.Controls.Add(rbBlue);
43    window.Controls.Add(rbGreen);
44    Application.Run(window);
45  }
46
47  // Sets the background color by looking at which
48  // radio button is checked.
49  public void SetColor(Object obj, EventArgs args)
50  {
51    if (rbRed.Checked)
52      window.BackColor = Color.Red;
53    else if (rbBlue.Checked)
54      window.BackColor = Color.Blue;
55    else if (rbGreen.Checked)
56      window.BackColor = Color.Green;
57  }
58 }
```

Result

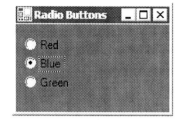

Initial window appearance   After clicking "Blue" button   After clicking "Green" button

By default, RadioButton objects are grouped together and made mutually exclusive to each other; that is, only one can be selected at a time. If finer control is desired (for example, to have several groups of radio buttons, which are mutually exclusive within each group, but do not affect each other), containers such as *GroupBoxes* or Panels must be used. These controls are outside the scope of this chapter, but if you are interested, you can browse the .NET Framework Class Library documentation to learn about them.

CheckBox / RadioButton properties

```
public ContentAlignment CheckAlign {get; set;}
public bool Checked {get; set;}
```

CheckBox / RadioButton events

```
public event EventHandler CheckedChanged;
```

Self-Check

10-8   Which control, CheckBox or RadioButton, would be more suitable for the following cases?

(a) Displaying a list of files to download; the user can download arbitrarily many files, or none at all.

(b) Showing the political parties for an electronic voting program; a voter must be a member of exactly one political party.

(c) A gender selection of male or female.

(d) A list of special offers that the user may be interested in.

10-9   Given these declarations:

```
CheckBox myCheckBox;
Form myForm;
```

write an event handler that, if myCheckBox is checked, sets the background color of the form referred to by myForm to be red. Also, write the code to attach this event handler to myCheckBox's CheckedChanged event.

10.4 A Larger Example: BankTeller

All GUI examples shown so far have focused on the mechanics of laying out a GUI and responding to button clicks. There has been no data being managed. A real application will have data, which is sometimes also called the program's *model*. The next example shows a larger program built with a graphical interface. The model of this program will be an array of BankAccount objects. The program's purpose is to display those BankAccount objects, and to allow the user to open an account, make deposits and withdrawals, and view the account status.

The following is a picture of the way the program should look:

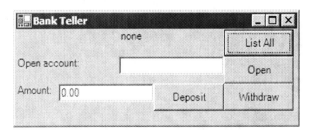

Figure 10.6: Initial appearance of Bank Teller application

Many of the lines of the code for this program are for constructing the controls and setting their properties correctly. Those lines are not shown here; instead, selected parts of the BankTeller code are shown and discussed. The full code can be found on the downloadable source code at **www.fbeedle.com/csharp/code.exe**.

The program depends on a list of accounts that matches the previously shown picture, as well as on having a field to remember which account is currently being accessed. The following array and field contain the accounts needed:

```
private BankAccount[] accounts =
{
```

```
  new BankAccount("David Shawshank", 1.23),
  new BankAccount("Jessica Coors", 4.56),
  new BankAccount("Collen Lint", 7.89),
  new BankAccount("Michael Thomas", 10.11),
  new BankAccount("James Rogers", 14.15),
  new BankAccount("Kelly Huffmar", 12.13),
  new BankAccount("Jeffrey Nagamoto", 14.15)
};

private BankAccount currentAccount = null;
```

When the List All button is clicked, the program should show a message box that lists all the bank accounts in the system. The List All button needs to have an EventHandler attached to its Click event to achieve this. The following method can be used in the event handler. It builds a string out of all the ToString text representations of the accounts in the list, then shows that string in a message box.

```
private void ListAll(object obj, EventArgs args)
{
  string message = "All Accounts:\n\n";
  foreach (BankAccount ba in accounts)
    message += ba.ToString() + "\n";
  MessageBox.Show(message);
}
```

After looking at the list, the user can type an account's name and click the Open button to load it. If the account name typed matches one of the names in the account list, the account is opened. If not, an error message box is displayed:

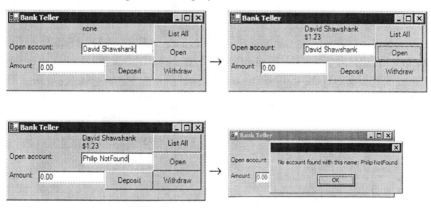

Figure 10.7: Bank Teller application account behavior

When the user types in a correct account name and clicks the Open button, the program should perform several actions. It must find that account from the list (if it exists), set it to be the currently active account for transactions, and display it on the screen. This is achieved here by using a sequential search with a `foreach` loop, which looks at each account and finds the one with the matching name (if any). If no account matches, the variable `found` is set to `false` and an error message box is shown. The following `OpenAccount` method can be attached to the Open button's `Click` event in an `EventHandler` object:

```
private void OpenAccount(object sender, EventArgs args)
{
  bool found = false;

  // sequential search
  foreach (BankAccount ba in accounts)
  {
    // look for account with matching ID
    if (ba.ID == acctNameTextBox.Text)
    {
      // a match; open this account
      currentAccount = ba;
      currAcctLabel.Text = currentAccount.ToString();
      found = true;
      break;
    }
  }

  if (!found)
    MessageBox.Show("No account found with this name: "
      + acctNameTextBox.Text);
}
```

Once an account is opened successfully, the user can deposit or withdraw money from that account by typing an amount into the Amount text box and clicking the appropriate button, either Deposit or Withdraw. If the deposit or withdrawal fails (the user enters a string that is not a number, or an amount that is too large or too small), an error message box is shown.

Here, the user enters 3.20 in the Amount field and clicks the Deposit button:

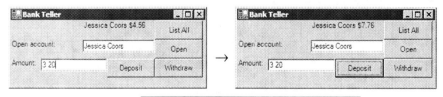

Figure 10.8: Bank Teller application transactions

Here, the user enters `1234.00` in the Amount field and clicks the Withdraw button:

Here, the user enters `not a number` in the Amount field. The result shown happens whether the user clicks the Deposit button or the Withdraw button:

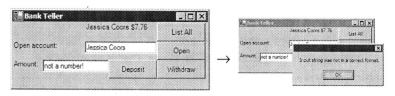

Figure 10.9: Bank Teller application with invalid input

The following code implements the deposit method that can be put into an `EventHandler` and attached to the Deposit button's `Click` event. A similar method can be written for withdrawals. Notice that the method checks for two kinds of failure: a `false` result back from the `Deposit` method on the `BankAccount`, which implies that the deposit amount is invalid; and a `FormatException`, which implies that the user did not type a valid number.

```
private void DepositMoney(object sender, EventArgs args)
{
  try
  {
    double amount = double.Parse(amountTextBox.Text);
    if (currentAccount != null)
    {
      if (!currentAccount.Deposit(amount))
        MessageBox.Show("Deposit failed!");

      // update the label displaying the account's status
      currAcctLabel.Text = currentAccount.ToString();
    }
  }
  catch (FormatException ex)
  {
    MessageBox.Show(ex.Message);
  }
}
```

Self-Check

10-10   How many different controls are there in the BankTeller application? How many kinds of controls are there?

10-11   What sort of change would need to be made to the BankTeller program to cause the account list to display in the window form itself, rather than in a message box?

Chapter Summary

○   A graphical window in C# is called a form.

○   Forms contain items called controls, such as buttons, text labels, and fields. The C# types for controls and forms are in the System.Windows.Forms namespace.

○   To create a graphical program, create a form and set its properties, create the controls desired and set their properties, add the controls to the form, then show the form.

○   Controls have many useful properties, such as Text, Width, Height, Left, Top, Anchor and Dock.

○   Controls can be positioned absolutely or can be laid out relative to other parts of the GUI by setting their anchor and docking styles. These styles are useful to ensure that the form looks correct after it is resized, or on different systems.

○   GUI controls can respond to user events by having specific delegates, called event handlers, attached to them. Event handlers exist for events such as button clicks, mouse movement, key presses, checking and unchecking boxes, and more.

○   A program that relies on user interaction to drive the execution of the code is called an event-driven program.

○   Delegates are C# objects that refer to methods. Delegates are useful for passing a method as an argument in a message, or for attaching methods to handle events.

○   Check boxes provide on/off toggle choices to the user. Radio buttons are similar, except that they are generally mutually exclusive to each other; exactly one member of a group of radio buttons may be checked at a time. Both of these button types have a CheckedChanged event to record when they are checked or unchecked.

○   Some graphical programs manipulate data, which is called a model.

Key Terms

anchor	event-driven programming	main menu
button	event handler	menu
Color	form	message box
combo box	graphical user interface	model
control	GUI	radio button
delegate	group box	scroll bar
dock	label	text box
event	layout	

Exercises

1. What are two limitations of a MessageBox, as compared to a Form?

2. Write a complete C# program named ShowArgs that accepts arguments and then displays each argument in a separate message box. For example, the command ShowArgs how are you should display the following in sequence:

3. What Anchor, Dock, Left, and Top values should be used to place a button in the center of a form, so that its left edge always stays in the same place, and the right edge stretches as the form is resized? The following screen shots illustrate this:

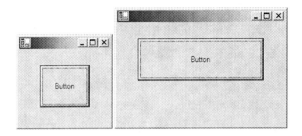

4. Write a C# program that displays a form with a button that occupies the entire top region of the form, no matter how the form is resized. It must also have a Label that appears in the bottom-right corner of the form, no matter how that form is resized. The following screen shots show the appearance of the form at two sizes:

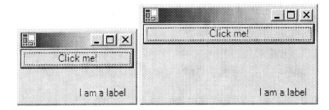

5. Write a method that can be used in an EventHandler that withdraws $10.00 from a BankAccount object and then displays the balance of that BankAccount object in a message box. Assume that the BankAccount object is declared elsewhere.

6. What namespace must be used when dealing with colors?

7. Write C# code to show a form whose background color is blue.

8. Write a program that has a text box and an OK button. The user can type text into the text box. When the user clicks the OK button, the program must examine the text in the text box and do the following: if the text box's text is "Red", the OK button's background color will become red; if the text box's text is "Blue", the OK button's background color will become blue; if the text is anything else, show an error message box. (The program can be case-sensitive; consider the input "RED" to be an error.)

9. Write a method Frustrating that could be used in an EventHandler that could be attached to the CheckedChanged event of a CheckBox variable named cb. When the CheckBox becomes checked, this method immediately unchecks it again!

10. In the previous question, why doesn't the Frustrating method cause an infinite cascade of events? It unchecks the checkbox, which should cause another call to Frustrating, which should cause another call, and so on. Why doesn't it?

Programming Projects

10A Two Handlers

Write a simple GUI that changes the text in a TextBox either to all uppercase letters or to all lowercase letters. When the Upper Case button is clicked, the text in the middle should be shown with all uppercase letters. When the Lower Case button is clicked, the text should be shown with all lowercase letters. At startup, the window should look as shown below, with very wide buttons at the top and bottom (your form need not match exactly). Use this screenshot as a guideline:

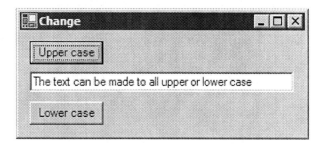

10B Temperature Converter

Write an event-driven program that shows the Fahrenheit equivalent of any Celsius input, and vice versa. When the user enters a new Celsius input and clicks the "C to F" button, the Fahrenheit text field should be updated to show the equivalent Fahrenheit temperature. When the user enters a new Fahrenheit input and clicks the "F to C" button, the Celsius text field should be updated to show the equivalent Celsius temperature. Round all new values to one decimal place. The formula for changing Fahrenheit to Celsius is C = 5/9(F-32). Your form need not match exactly. Use this screenshot as a guideline:

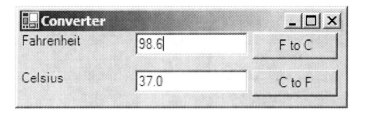

10C   Minimum Coins

Write an event-driven program that shows the minimum number of coins required to make change for a user input (83 cents is shown here). When the user enters a new amount and clicks the Calculate button, update the five `Label` objects to show the new numbers of coins (in the United States).

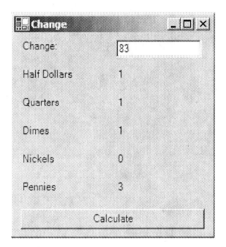

10D   Add Display/Edit of PIN to BankTeller

Starting from the BankTeller example discussed earlier in this chapter, modify the program so that it also displays the account's PIN. It must also display a text box where the user can type a new PIN and then click a Change button to cause the PIN for that account to be updated. In the example below, the PIN is changed from `123` to `456`.

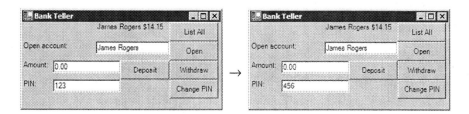

10E Add Persistence to BankTeller

Starting from the BankTeller example discussed earlier in this chapter, modify the program so that it maintains a persistent set of accounts. That is, if the user makes deposits and withdrawals to the `BankAccount` objects, when the program closes, it must save the accounts to disk, using serialization (see Chapter 8). Save the accounts to a file named `accounts.dat`. When the program loads, it should attempt to load the accounts from this same file. If it is unsuccessful (if an exception occurs), it should display an error message of "`Failure loading accounts!`" plus the exception's error message.

To detect when the program closes (so that you can save the accounts), attach a `CancelEventHandler` delegate to the form's `Closing` event. A `CancelEventHandler` delegate has a slightly different header than an `EventHandler`; it requires a `CancelEventArgs` argument, which the body of the method may ignore.

An example would look something like this:

```
// at end of BankTeller constructor
form.Closing += new CancelEventHandler(SaveAccounts);

...

// in BankTeller class
public void SaveAccounts(object sender, CancelEventArgs arg)
{
  // put your code to save the accounts here.

}
```

Form event: Closing

```
public event CancelEventHandler Closing;
```

CancelEventHandler Delegate

```
public delegate void CancelEventHandler(object sender, CancelEventArgs e);
```

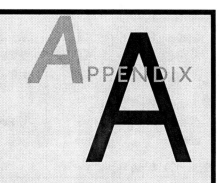

Useful Tables

C# Keywords, the complete list

abstract	delegate	internal	readonly	try
as	do	is	ref	typeof
base	double	lock	return	uint
bool	else	long	sbyte	ulong
break	enum	namespace	sealed	unchecked
byte	event	new	short	unsafe
case	explicit	null	sizeof	ushort
catch	extern	object	stackalloc	using
char	false	operator	static	virtual
checked	finally	out	string	void
class	float	override	struct	volatile
const	for	params	switch	while
continue	if	private	this	
decimal	implicit	protected	throw	
default	int	public	true	

C# Value Types (also known as the Simple Types)

Type	Size (bits)	Value Range
Integers		
sbyte	8	-128 to 127
byte	8	0 to 255
short	16	-32768 to 32767
ushort	16	0 to 65535
int	32	-2,147,483,648 to -2,147,483,647
uint	32	0 to 4,294,967,295
long	64	−9,223,372,036,854,775,808 to 9,223,372,036,854,775,807
ulong	64	0 to 18,446,744,073,709,551,615

Real Numbers

`float`	32	1.5×10^{-45} to 3.4×10^{38} accurate to 7 digits
`double`	64	5.0×10^{-324} to 1.7×10^{308} accurate to 15 digits
`decimal`	128	1.0×10^{-28} to 7.9×10^{28} with 28-29 significant digits

Other

`char`	16	Unicode character set
`bool`	n/a	`true` or `false`

Other C# Value Types

`struct`

`enum`

C# Reference Types

class

array

delegate

interface

Legal C# Implicit Conversions

From:	To:
sbyte	short, int, long, float, double, or decimal
byte	short, ushort, int, uint, long, ulong, float, double, or decimal
short	int, long, float, double, or decimal
ushort	int, uint, long, ulong, float, double, or decimal
int	long, float, double, or decimal
uint	long, ulong, float, double, or decimal
long	float, double, or decimal
char	ushort, int, uint, long, ulong, float, double, or decimal
float	double
ulong	float, double, or decimal

C# Operator Precedence

Category	Operators
Primary	x.y f(x) a[x] x++ x— new typeof checked unchecked
Unary	+ - ! ~ ++x --x (T)x
Multiplicative	* / %
Additive	+ -
Shift	<< >>
Relational and type testing	< > <= >= is as

Equality	==	!=
Logical AND	&	
Logical XOR	^	
Logical OR	|	
Conditional AND	&&	
Conditional OR	||	
Conditional	?:	
Assignment	= *= /= %= += -= <<= >>= &= ^= |=	

Numeric Format Codes

Code	Format	Numeric Argument	Example	Output
c, C	currency		`"{0:C}", 123`	`$123.00`
d, D	decimal	# of digits	`"{0:D8}", 123`	`00000123`
e, E	exponential	# of decimal places	`"{0:E2}", 45.67`	`4.57E+001`
f, F	**fixed precision**	# of decimal places	`"{0:F3}", 45.67`	`45.670`
g, G	general	# of significant digits	`"{0:G2}", 45.67`	`46`
n, N	numeric	# of decimal places	`"{0:N4}", 45.67`	`45.6700`
p, P	percentage	# of decimal places	`"{0:P1}", 0.03`	`3.0 %`
x, X	hexadecimal	minimum # of digits	`"{0:X}", 100`	`64`

Format Codes for DateTime objects

Specifier	Format	Example	Output
d	short date	`{0:d}`	`4/10/2001`
D	long date	`{0:D}`	`Tuesday, April 10, 2001`
f	short full date/time	`{0:f}`	`Tuesday, April 10, 2001 3:51 PM`
F	long full date/time	`{0:F}`	`Tuesday, April 10, 2001 3:51:24 PM`
g	short general date/time	`{0:g}`	`4/10/2001 3:51 PM`
G	long general date/time	`{0:G}`	`4/10/2001 3:51:24 PM`
m, M	month and day	`{0:M}`	`April 10`
t	short time	`{0:t}`	`12:00 AM`
T	long time	`{0:T}`	`12:00:00 AM`
y, Y	year and month	`{0:Y}`	`April, 2001`

Compiling and Running C# Programs

A C# program must be compiled before it can be executed. This section details how to compile and execute a C# program using the free C# compiler from Microsoft. As of this writing, the C# compiler and .NET runtime environment can be downloaded from Microsoft; you will need the following products:

- ○ Microsoft .NET Framework Version 1.1 Redistributable, which contains the .NET runtime environment and .NET class library; this product enables your computer to run C# and .NET programs.
- ○ Microsoft .NET Framework 1.1 Software Development Kit (SDK), which contains the C# compiler and other tools; this product enables you to compile your own C# programs.

Both of the above products can be found on the downloadable source code at **www.fbeedle. com/csharp/code.exe**, or from the following Web site:

http://msdn.microsoft.com/netframework/downloads/updates/default.aspx

If you are using a special editor such as Microsoft Visual Studio .NET, you may not need to download the above programs. Please speak to your instructor to clarify the installation and setup procedure for your environment.

Assuming the use of the products above, the following steps will allow you to compile and execute C# programs:

Writing the C# Source Code

Open your favorite source code editor and type in the source code to a working C# program. If you do not have a source editor, you can use an editor built into your operating system, such as Notepad on Microsoft Windows.

The screenshot below shows a C# program that has been written in the source editor.

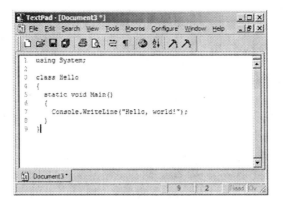

After typing in the file, the file must be saved using the same file name as the name of the class. In the above example, the class is named `Hello`, therefore the file should be named `Hello.cs`.

If a file contains more than one class, the file should be named the same as the class with the `Main` method. When saving the file, also take note of the directory the file is in, because this information will be needed when compiling the file.

Compiling a C# Program

After installing the Microsoft .NET Framework SDK, you will have a C# compiler on your computer named `csc.exe`. This program can be run from your Windows Command Prompt. To do this, open the Command Prompt from the Start Menu (which is usually located under Start, Programs, Accessories).

The Command Prompt shows the name of the current directory it is operating on. You must change this directory so that it points to the drive and directory of your C# program. Change drives by typing a drive letter followed by a colon (:) and pressing Enter. For example, to change to the H drive, type `H:` and press Enter. You do not need to change drives if the Command Prompt already refers to the correct drive (drive C, usually).

Use the `cd` command to change the current directory of the Command Prompt. Type the phrase `cd` followed by a space, and then the directory name in quotation marks (`"`). For example, to change to the **C:\Program Files** directory, use the command `cd "C:\Program Files"`. You should know the directory of your program by looking at where you saved the file; but there are some folders for which it is harder to see the full directory name. For example, on Windows 2000 and higher, the **My Documents** folder on Windows is actually located at **C:\Documents and Settings**_your user name_**\My Documents**; at least, this is the default on most systems; it could be different on your environment. The desktop is usually located at **C:\Documents and Settings**_your user name_**\Desktop**. For example, for a Windows user account named Ursula McDowell, the My Documents folder would be located at **C:\Documents and Settings\Ursula McDowell\My Documents**.

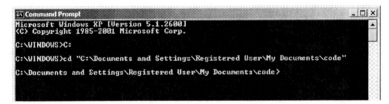

Once you have changed the directory, you should run the compiler program, `csc.exe`. Do this by typing `csc` followed by a space, then any necessary arguments. Generally the only argument you need to provide is the file name to compile. In the case of this example, the file name is `Hello.cs` and the command to type would be:

```
csc Hello.cs
```

If you try to run `csc` and get a failure message such as: _"csc' is not recognized as an internal or external command, operable program or batch file,"_ this means that the `csc.exe` file cannot be found, and likely something is wrong with your installation of Microsoft .NET Framework SDK.

There are other options that may be needed when compiling certain programs. When compiling a program that uses more than one file, their names should all be specified, separated by spaces. For example, when compiling a program that uses files `File1.cs` and `File2.cs`, the command line should be:

```
csc File1.cs File2.cs
```

The other important option that is needed is `/target:winexe`, which is used when compiling programs with a graphical user interface, such as those shown in Chapter 10. For example, to compile a Windows graphical program stored in `WinProg.cs`, the command line should be:

```
csc /target:winexe WinProg.cs
```

A full list of the options to the C# compiler can be found by giving the command `csc /?` at the Command Prompt.

Compiler Output and Syntax Errors

If the compiling process is successful, the C# compiler will simply print its logo information and return to the Command Prompt. (If you do not wish to see the compiler's logo, use the `/nologo` option when running the compiler.) The successfully compiled program will be stored into an executable file. The name of this file will be the same as your class with the `Main` method, but followed by the suffix `.exe`. The name of the compiled `Hello.cs` program would be `Hello.exe`.

If the program has any syntax errors, they will be printed on the Command Prompt console. For example, if the programmer forgot a semicolon in the `Hello.cs` program, a message similar to the one below would be printed.

Running a Compiled C# Program

Once your C# program has been compiled successfully, you can execute it from the Command Prompt. To execute a compiled C# program from the directory where the file is located, type its name at the Command Prompt and press Enter. The name of the program is the same as the name of the class with the `Main` method. To run the `Hello.cs` program from this example, which has been compiled into a file named `Hello.exe`, type either `Hello.exe` or just `Hello` at the Command Prompt.

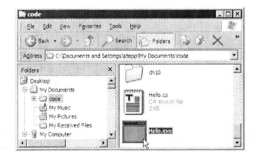

The program's output, if any, will appear on the console and then will return to the Command Prompt.

Compiled C# programs can also be run by locating them in Windows Explorer and double-clicking the program's `.exe` file to run it. However, for programs that print output to the console using `Console.WriteLine`, this may not be a good way to run the program, because the Command Prompt window will pop up and disappear as soon as the program is finished running, making it difficult to see the program's output in time. This procedure does work well for executing graphical Windows programs, though.

Redirecting Input and Output with Files

A program normally accepts its standard input from the keyboard and prints its standard output to the screen. But this does not have to be the case; input and output can be redirected to come to and from files or other devices. When standard output is redirected to a file, any

`Console.WriteLine` statements in the program will write text to that file instead of to the screen. This is useful to capture and save a program's output. When standard input is redirected from a file, any `Console.ReadLine` statements in the program will read their text from this file instead of waiting for the user to type them. This is useful for testing and running quickly a program that needs to read a particular set of input values from the user.

To cause a C# program to redirect its output to a file, at the end of the command to execute the program, write a > sign followed by a space, then the file name redirect the output to. For example, to run the `Hello` program shown previously and to redirect its output to the file `output.txt`, execute the following command:

`Hello > ` **`output.txt`**

After executing the program this way, nothing is printed to the screen; the Command Prompt simply returns. However, looking at the directory, a new file has appeared named `output.txt`, whose contents is the text, "Hello, world!"

The `output.txt` file contains the output that would have been printed to the screen.

The following program reads input from the console, which we'll redirect to come from a file named `input.txt`:

```
using System;

class NumericInput
{
    static void Main()
    {
        int credits;
        double qualityPoints;
```

```
    Console.Write("Enter credits: ");
    credits = int.Parse(Console.ReadLine());

    Console.Write("Enter quality points: ");
    qualityPoints = double.Parse(Console.ReadLine());

    double GPA = qualityPoints / credits;
    Console.WriteLine("Credits completed: {0} total", credits);
    Console.WriteLine("You have {0} quality points",
                        qualityPoints);
    Console.WriteLine("GPA is {0}", GPA);
  }
}
```

The file `input.txt` has been written and saved with the following contents:

```
20
63
```

The program is executed and has its input redirected to come from `input.txt` by executing the following command:

```
NumericInput < input.txt
```

The output is as if the user had typed the numbers, except that the actual typing of the numbers (and the new line breaks that would have followed them) is absent:

```
Enter credits: Enter quality points: Credits completed: 20 total
You have 63 quality points
GPA is 3.15
```

A program can have both input and output redirected, if desired. To run the NumericInput program with input taken from `input.txt` and output written to `output.txt`, execute the following command:

```
NumericInput < input.txt > output.txt
```

Command-Line Arguments to a Program

If your program requires any command-line arguments (as described in Chapter 7), the arguments are written after the program name, separated by spaces. Consider the following program stored in `Hello2.cs`, which prints every argument passed in to it:

```
using System;

class Hello2
{
  static void Main(string[] args)
  {
    foreach (string arg in args)
      Console.WriteLine(arg);
  }
}
```

To run this `Hello2` program and pass arguments to it, first follow the normal compiling process described previously. After the file is successfully compiled into `Hello2.exe`, run it and pass its arguments by writing strings separated by spaces on the command line A string argument containing spaces can be enclosed in quotes. For example, to pass the three arguments `"hi"`, `"how"`, and `"are you"`, execute the following command:

> Hello2 **hi how "are you"**

The output from the program prints to the console, showing the three arguments hi, how, and are you.

If input or output is redirected in a program that accepts arguments, the redirection must be written after the arguments, like so:

```
Hello2 hi how "are you" > outputfile.txt
```

Answers to Self-Check Questions

1-1   A college degree perhaps (other deliverables are possible such as learning, establishing friends, …)

1-2   Input: pounds and perhaps `todaysConversionRate`

      Output: `USDollars`

1-3   `CDCollection, currentSelection`

1-4

Problem	Data Name	Input or Output	Sample
Compute distance	`metersPerSecond`	Input	28.0
traveled	`secondsInFlight`	Input	3.1
`distance`	Output		86.8

1-5

Problem	Data Name	Input or Output	Sample
Compute the	`presentValue`	Input	1000.00
future value of	`periods`	Input	360
an investment	`monthlyRate`	Input	0.0075
`futureValue`		Output	14730.58

1-6   Turn the oven off (or you might recognize some other activity or detail that was omitted).

1-7   No (at least the authors think it's okay)

1-8   No (at least the authors think it's okay)

1-9   No. The `courseGrade` would be computed using undefined values for `test1`, `test2`, and `finalExam`.

1-10   No. The details of the process step are not present. The formula is missing.

1-11   Input: Retrieve values from the user for the three inputs:

```
test1 0
test2 50
finalExam 100
```

      Process: Retrieve the values of the tests and compute courseGrade as follows:

```
courseGrade = (0.25 x test1) + (0.25 x test2) + (0.50 x
finalExam)
              (0.25 x 0.0)    + (0.25 x 50.0)  +    (0.50 x
100.0)
              (0.0            +      12.5       +       50.0)
courseGrade = 62.5
```

      Output: Show courseGrade = 62.5% to the user.

1-12   The program is wrong.

1-13   The prediction is wrong. The problem asked for a weighted average, not a simple average.

1-14   The program is wrong.

2-1   68 plus or minus a few. It is easy to miscount tokens. For example, comments are not tokens and this is only one token: `"A very long string with new, int, double, { }, +, -, /, && * "`

2-2   (a) VALID   (l) Periods (.) are not allowed.
        (b) 1 can't start an identifier.   (m)   VALID
        (c) VALID   (n) Can't start identifiers with a digit.
        (d) . is a special symbol.   (o) A space is not allowed.
        (e) A space is not allowed. (p) VALID
        (f) / is not allowed.   (q) VALID
        (g) ! is not allowed.   (r) VALID (but not meaningful).
        (h) VALID   (s) VALID (but not meaningful).
        (i) () are not allowed.   (t) / is not allowed.
        (j) VALID (double is not)   (u) A space is not allowed.
        (k) VALID   (v) VALID

2-3   +   -   Also   , : ; ! ( ) = {   }

2-4   `/*  */`

2-5   `int    double    Main    Console    Also    ReadLine    WriteLine`

2-6   `thisIsOne and anotherOne`

2-7   (a) string literals: `"H"`   `"1.0"`   `"integer"`
        (b) integer literals: `234`   `-123`
        (c) real number literals: `1.0`   `1.0e+03`
        (d) character literals: `'H'`

2-8   a , d, and e are valid comments

2-9   `double aNumber = -1.0;`
        `double anotherNumber = -1.0;`

2-10   a, d, and e are valid.
        b attempts to store a floating-point literal into an `int` variable.
        c attempts to store a string literal into an `int` variable.
        f attempts to store a string literal into a `double` variable.

2-11   (a) 10.5   (d) -0.75
        (b) 1.75   (e) 0.5
        (c) 3.5   (f) 1.0
        (g) 4.0   (h) 1.25

2-12   0

2-13   (a) 0   (d) 1
        (b) 1   (e) 0
        (c) 0   (f) 0

2-14   (a) 0   (f) 2

            (b) 0.55556   (g) 2.1

            (c) 0.55556   (h) 1.5

            (d) 10   (i) 0.0

            (e) 12   -j 10.0

2-15   (a) number

           (b) 24

           (c) a blank line

           (d) 10.8

           (e) gravity + number

           (f) 33.8

2-16   number24

           10.8gravity + number33.8

2-17

```csharp
using System;
class YourName
{
  static void Main()
  {
    Console.WriteLine("Kim Davies");
  }
}
```

2-18   x is 10 and y is 20

           9 10 11

           30 days have September

           20 / 10 = 2

2-19

```csharp
Console.WriteLine("x{0}y{1}", x, y);
Console.WriteLine("{1} {0} {1} {0}", x, y);
Console.WriteLine();  // blank line
Console.WriteLine("In the year {0}{0}, {0}% were poor.", y);
```

2-20   The argument will become 10 spaces wide, right-justified, in currency format.

2-21

```csharp
Console.WriteLine("{0,12:N}", bigNumber);
Console.WriteLine("{0,12:E2}", biggerNumber);
```

2-22   (a) 3.2   (16.0 / 5.0)

           (b) 3.33   (15.0 / 4.5)

           (c) 0.57   (2.0 / 3.5)

2-23   64.0

2-24   3.0

2-25   2 (an int value)

2-26   2.0 (a double value)

2-27   The average is wrong.

2-28   Change the prompts. "Enter sum: " becomes "Enter number: " and "Enter number: " becomes "Enter sum: ".

3-1 The two characteristics of every object are state and behavior.

3-2 State: an ID of "Sally" and a balance of 75.00

Behavior: account22 understands the methods Deposit, Withdraw, and ToString

3-3 B. Linn: 202.22

N. Li: 545.55

3-4 (a) Missing the second argument in the object construction. Add the starting balance—a number.

(b) Missing = new BankAccount.

(c) Change Account to BankAccount.

(d) Missing a numeric argument between (and).

(e) Missing (, the argument, and).

(f) Wrong type of argument. Pass a number, not a string.

(g) B1 is undefined.

(h) deposit is not a method of BankAccount. Change d to D.

(i) Need an object and a dot before Withdraw.

(j) b4 is undefined.

(k) BankAccount has no method named ID(). The ID property is accessed without using parentheses.

(l) Should be Balance, not GetBalance.

3-5
```
class ShowBankAccountOutput
{
  static void Main()
  {
    BankAccount b1 = new BankAccount("Kerry", 100.00);
    b1.Deposit(1.11);
    b1.Withdraw(2.22);
        Console.WriteLine("{0}: {1}", b1.ID, b1.Balance);
    Console.WriteLine(b1);
        b1.PIN = "1234";
    Console.WriteLine(b1.PIN);
  }
}
```

3-6 (a) String (d) int

(b) Insert (e) String

(c) 2 (f) there are only two arguments

3-7 (a) Valid

(b) String argument can not be assigned to int parameter.

(c) needs 2 arguments

(d) Valid

(e) 1st argument must be int

(f) Valid (error at runtime)

3-8 "tiPme"

3-9 "timeless"

3-10
```
Random rand = new Random();
int randomValue = rand.Next(9998) + 1;
```

3-11
```
Random rand = new Random();
double randomValue = rand.NextDouble() * 1.5 + 0.25;
```

3-12
```
using System;

class CoinFlip
{
  static void Main()
  {
    Random rand = new Random();
    int flip = rand.Next(2);
    Console.WriteLine("Coin Flip (0=heads, 1=tails): {0}",
                      flip);
  }
}
```

3-13   6

3-14   "ef"

3-15   8

3-16   Wheatley, Kay

3-17   (a) error   (d) 3

       (b) error   (e) y S

       (c) error   (f) error (wrong type of argument)

3-18   asdf

3-19   asdf

3-20
```
12 inches is 30.480 cm
.022E+023 is a lot of atoms!
```

3-21
```
using System;
class Message
{
  static void Main()
  {
    BankAccount chris = new BankAccount("Chris", 54.3);
    String message =
     String.Format(
      "Hello Chris, what a pity you only have {0:C} in your
account!",
                                          chris.Balance);
    Console.WriteLine(message);
  }
}
```

3-22   abc123

3-23   ABC123

3-24
```
String aLine = Console.ReadLine();
```

```
3-25    Console.Write("Enter your name: ");
        String fullName = Console.ReadLine();
        int indexOfSpace = fullName.IndexOf(" ");
        String firstName = fullName.Substring(0, indexOfSpace);
        String lastName = fullName.Substring(indexOfSpace + 1);
        Console.WriteLine("Alphabetized name: {0}, {1}",
                          lastName, firstName);
3-26    DateTime specialDay = new DateTime(2001, 10, 8);
        Console.WriteLine(specialDay);
3-27    Console.WriteLine(DateTime.Now);
3-28    Console.Write("Enter a year: ");
        int year = int.Parse(Console.ReadLine());
        int febDays = DateTime.DaysInMonth(year, 2);
        Console.WriteLine("In {0}, February had {1} days.",
                          year, febDays);
3-29    DateTime date = new DateTime(1992, 2, 1);
        date = date.AddDays(120);
        Console.WriteLine(date);
3-30    Console.Write("Enter a month: ");
        int month = int.Parse(Console.ReadLine());
        Console.Write("Enter a day: ");
        int day = int.Parse(Console.ReadLine());
        Console.Write("Enter a year: ");
        int year = int.Parse(Console.ReadLine());
        DateTime date = new DateTime(year, month, day);
        date = date.AddYears(-50);
        Console.WriteLine("50 years before that was {0}", date);
3-31    Console.Write("Enter a date: ");
        DateTime date = DateTime.Parse(Console.ReadLine());
        date = date.AddYears(-50);
        Console.WriteLine("50 years before that was {0}", date);
```

3-32   (a) 5

(b) 2

(c) The b1, b3, and b4 variables refer to the same BankAccount object with ID of "Jim" and balance of 50.00. b2 and b5 refer to an object with ID "Sally" and balance of 20.00.

```
3-33    BankAccount b1 = new BankAccount("Bill", 1.00);
        BankAccount b2 = b1;
        b2.Deposit(9.00);
        Console.WriteLine("b1/b2's account balance: {0}", b1.Balance);
```

3-34   Less code to write.

Abstraction allows us to think of what the method does, not the details of the implementation.

3-35   Using the phone without worrying about how the sound travels to the other end.

-or- Walking around without sweating the details about how you are walking and breathing.

4-1   `private int numTransactions;`

4-2   Private. Public fields are legal but are not used; they violate the principle of encapsulation.

4-3   No. Only an object can see its fields (technically, other objects of the same type can peek at the fields, but doing so is discouraged since it violates encapsulation).

4-4   `'Early Bird' by Joist`
       `'Night Hawk' by Floris`

4-5
```
public BankAccount(String init_id, double init_balance, String
init_pin)
{
  id = init_id;
  balance = init_balance;
  pin = init_pin;
}
```

4-6   `Getting borrower's value of —-`
       `Main: Borrower is —-`
       `Setting borrower to Kim`
       `Getting borrower's value of Kim`
       `Main: Borrower is Kim`
       `Setting borrower to —-`
       `Getting borrower's value of —-`
       `Main: Borrower is —-`

4-7
```
public string Title
{
  get { return title; }
}

public string Author
{
  get { return author; }
}
```

4-8   Yes; without knowing the method names, the programmer does not know how to make the object perform its behavior.

4-9   No; the actual implementation of how the methods work is not something that the programmer needs to know. You took advantage of this in previous chapters to call methods on C# objects, like calling `IndexOf` on a `string` object without knowing how `IndexOf` is written.

4-10   Methods declared with the `public` modifier are known in all methods of the class and in every block where an object of the type is constructed or is specified as a parameter.

4-11   Methods and fields declared with the `private` modifier can be accessed only inside the same class. They are known in every part of the class.

4-12   `Chris borrows 'Early Bird'`
       `Chris returns 'Early Bird'`
       `Kim borrows 'Night Hawk'`
       `Kim returns 'Night Hawk'`

4-13   `'Early Bird', by Joist, borrowed by —-`
       `'Early Bird', by Joist, borrowed by Kim`

```
4-14   public class PiggyBank
       {
         private double amount;

         public PiggyBank(double initialAmount)
         {
           amount = initialAmount;
         }

         public void AddPennies(int pennies)
         {
           amount = amount + (pennies * 0.01);
         }

         public void AddNickels(int nickels)
         {
           amount = amount + (nickels * 0.05);
         }

         public void AddDimes(int dimes)
         {
           amount = amount + (dimes * 0.10);
         }

         public double TotalMoney
         {
           get
           {
             return amount;
           }
         }
       }
```

4-15   `public static readonly int DaysInLeapYear = 366;`

4-16   `public static readonly double MaxGPA = 4.0;`

4-17   A `DaysInLeapYear` constant might find itself in a `DateTime` or `Calendar` class. A `MaxGPA` constant probably belongs in a `Student` or `School` class.

4-18   `public static readonly string NON_BORROWER_CODE = "-";`

4-19   The constructor and `ReturnBook`.

4-20
```
       public static double SumAll(double d1, double d2, double d3)
       {
         return d1 + d2 + d3;
       }
```

4-21
```
       public static int Max3(int i1, int i2, int i3)
       {
         return Math.Max(i1, Math.Max(i2, i3));
       }
```

4-22   a, b, c, d, e, and j are legal. The rest are illegal because they are not in object context.

4-23   Yes. This is why it is a good idea to design a class so carefully that it rarely, if ever, needs to be changed.

4-24   Yes; that might be reasonable. Applying interest to an account is related to the function of a `BankAccount` object, so adding `ApplyInterest` to `BankAccount` might be sensible.

4-25   No. That would not be high cohesion. The message is not related to a `BankAccount`.

5-1   (a) `true`
        (b) `true`
        (c) `true`
        (d) `true`

5-2   (a) `true`   (e) `true`
        (b) `false`   (f) `true`
        (c) `false`   (g) `false`
        (d) `true`   (h) `true`

5-3   `Less`
        `Same`

5-4   (a) `dubious`
        `failing`

        (b) `dubious`

5-5   ```
        if (option == 1)
           Console.WriteLine("Your name");
        if (option == 0)
           Console.WriteLine("Your School");
        ```

5-6     At line 29 of the CD class, insert the following code: `if (unitsSold >= 0)`

5-7     `Tune-up due in 0 miles`

5-8     (a) 38.0           (c) 43.0
        (b) 40.0           (d) 44.5

5-9     (a) `true`
           `after if/else`
        (b) `zero or pos`
        (c) `x is low`

5-10    (a) `true`          (e) `true`
        (b) `false`         (f) `false`
        (c) `true`          (g) `false`
        (d) `false`         (h) `true`

5-11    `((score >= 1) && (score <= 10))`

5-12    `((test > 100) || (score < 0))`

5-13    There will be no output; the test expression (`GPA == 4.0`) is false.

5-14    `anInt % 5 == 0`

5-15    (a) `addRecord`
        (b) `deleteRecord`
        (c)
        `R > M`
        `R >= D`
        ```

5-16   1/1/2000 12:00:00 AM compared to 1/1/2000 12:00:00 AM is: 0

       1/1/2000 12:00:00 AM is earlier

5-17   42 is divisible by 2

       42 is divisible by 3

       42 is divisible by 6

       42 is divisible by 7

5-18
```
int num1 = 8;
int num2 = 3;
int num3 = 12;

if (num1 < num2 && num1 < num3)
  Console.WriteLine(num1);
else if (num2 < num1 && num2 < num3)
  Console.WriteLine(num2);
else
  Console.WriteLine(num3);
```

or (without selection),

```
int smallest = Math.Min(num1, Math.Min(num2, num3));
Console.WriteLine(smallest);
```

5-19   (a) AAA   (b) Neither

5-20   BBB

5-21   Invalid

5-22
```
switch(choice)
{
  case "music":
    Console.WriteLine("Jazz");
    break;
  case "food":
    Console.WriteLine("Tacos");
    break;
  case "teacher":
    Console.WriteLine("Blaire");
    break;
  default:
    Console.WriteLine("Invalid choice");
    break;
}
```

6-1   (a)   (b)

(a)	(b)
1	4
2	3
3	2
4	1
5	0

6-2   (a)
```
int i = 2;
while (i >= 0)
  Console.WriteLine(i);
```

(b)
```
string message = "a";
while (message.Length <= 3)
{
  Console.WriteLine(message);
  message += "a";
}
```

(c)
```
int i = 1;
while (i <= 8)
{
  Console.WriteLine(i);
  i = i * 2;
}
```

(d)
```
int i = 2;
while (i <= 8)
{
  Console.WriteLine(i);
  i = i * i;    // or Math.Pow(i, 2)
}
```

6-3
```
int sum = 0;
Console.Write("Enter number to sum or a negative number to quit: ");
int input = int.Parse(Console.ReadLine());
while (input >= 0)
{
  sum += input ; // Accumulate inputs, only not negative
  Console.Write("Enter number to sum or a negative number to quit: ");
  input = int.Parse(Console.ReadLine());
  // If negative, the loop test fails and input is not added
}
Console.WriteLine("Sum: {0}", sum);
```

6-4
```
int newInt;
int oldInt;
Console.WriteLine("Enter numbers until two differ by more than 100: ");
newInt = int.Parse(Console.ReadLine());
oldInt = newInt;
while (Math.abs(oldInt - newInt) <= 100.0)
{
```

```
    oldInt = newInt;
    newInt = int.Parse(Console.ReadLine());
}
Console.WriteLine("Last two numbers were {0} and {1}", oldInt,
newInt);
```

6-5

(a) 1   2   3

(b) 2   4   6   8   10

(c) There is no output due the semicolon to the right of the loop test. C# gives the warning "Possible mistaken null statement", but if you ignore the warning, the expression counter > 0 remains true. The compute evaluates this expression virtually forever. Terminate with Ctrl-C.

6-6   (a) 20   (d) Infinite

(b) 0   (e) Infinite

(c) 5   (f) 10

6-7   (a) Increment the loop counting variable j

(b) Remove the ; from the right of the loop test

(c) Put all statements in a block: { }

6-8   No, the update step happens at the end of the loop iteration. The init statement happens first, and only once.

6-9   No, you can use increments of any amount, including negative increments (decrements).

6-10 No, consider for (int j = 1; j < n; j++) { /*do nothing*/ } when n == 0.

6-11 If the update step does not increment j. Or if inside the loop, j is decremented as much as it is incremented. Here are two examples. The example on the left contains a subtle, but common, mistake. The example on the right contains a rare mistake. However, it was presented here to show what happens if the loop-counting variable (named j here) gets messed up.

```
for (int j = 1; j < n; j + 1)
{ // j + 1 does not change j
  // j remains the same: 1
}
for (int j = 1; j < n; j++)
{
   j--;   // Now it'll never end
}
```

6-12 (a) 1 2 3 4

(b) 1 2 3 4 5

(c) -3 -1 1 3

(d) 0 1 2 3 4

(e) 5 4 3 2 1

(f) before   after

6-13
```
for (int j = 1; j <= 100; j++)
{
   Console.WriteLine(j);
}
```

6-14
```
for (int k = 10; k >= 1; k—)
{
    Console.WriteLine(k);
}
```

6-15   Range is 6. lowest never changes from 0. 6 - 0 is 6. The algorithm is currently flawed.

6-16   Range is 30 (this is correct)
```
highest        -999    -5  8        22      22      22
lowest          999    -5 -5        -5      -7      -7
```

6-17   Range is 5 (this is correct).
```
highest        -999    5   5         5       5       5
lowest          999    999 4         3       2       1
```

6-18   Range = -993 (this is obviously incorrect).
```
highest        -999    1   2         3       4       5
lowest          999    999 999     999     999     999
```

6-19   (b) When the input is entered in ascending order.

6-20   Get rid of the else. Then when the inputs are in ascending order, the check for lowest is never made. Another more elegant solution is to initialize highest and lowest to the first input, as shown in the previous range implementation.

```
int aTemp = int.Parse(Console.ReadLine());
int highest = aTemp    // The first input can be viewed as
int lowest = aTemp;    // both highest AND lowest; it is the only one!
// Now process n-1 inputs by starting j at 2 rather than 1
for (int j = 2; j <= n; j++)
{
    aTemp = int.Parse(Console.ReadLine());
    // ...
```

6-21   (a) 46.333333333333336 (46.3 will do) (b)   70.0

6-22   Do you see how (a) does not accumulate 70.0? Instead, it accumulates -1 (60 + 80 + -1) / 3 is 46.3.

6-23   Zero iterations, the loop-test fails before the repeat part.

6-24   Input another number as the last statement in the loop.

6-25   (a) 1 2 3   (b)
```
                                abcdef
                                bcdef
                                cdef
                                def
                                ef
                                f
```

6-26
```
Random rand = new Random();
do
{
    randomNumber = rand.Next();
    Console.WriteLine(randomNumber);
}
while (randomNumber % 6 != 0);
```

6-27
```
int number;
do
{
   Console.Write("Enter a number in the range of 1 through 10: ");
   number = int.Parse(Console.ReadLine());
}
while (number < 1 || number > 10);
```

6-28 (a) olleH

(b) aabbccddeeff

6-29
```
string myName = "amanda banana ranna";
foreach (char ch in myName)
{
   if (ch >= 'a' && ch <= 'z')
   {
      int letterNum = ch - 'a' + 1;
      Console.WriteLine("{0} is letter {1} in the alphabet",
         ch, letterNum);
   }
}
```

6-30 (a) A for loop, since n is known.

(b) A for loop, since n is known.

(c) An indeterminate loop, that terminates when the sentinel is read.

(d) An indeterminate that terminates when a valid input is read.

6-31 (a) Both j and n

(b) Both n and inc

7-1 100

7-2 0

7-3 99

7-4 0

7-5 `x[0] = 78;`

7-6
```
int n = 100;
for (int j = 0; j < n; j++)
{
    x[j] = n - j;     // When j is 0, n - j is 100
}
```

7-7
```
for (int j = 0; j < n; j++)
{
    Console.WriteLine(x[j]);
}
```

7-8 An exception is thrown and the program terminates

7-9
```
0    9
1    8
2    7
3    6
4    5
```

7-10   Jody $0.00
        Rachael $111.11
        Troy $222.22
        Neha $333.33
        Jim $444.44

7-11   ```
        for (int j = 0; j < 5; j++)
        {
           if (tinyBank[j].Balance > 150.00)
              Console.WriteLine(tinyBank[j].ToString());
        }
        ```

7-12    2 2 6 6 10 10 14 14

7-13    t
        d
        d
        l

7-14    ABE
        BEV
        CY
        DEB

7-15    current length of x: 3
        11
        22
        33
        current length of x: 6
        11
        22
        33
        current length of x: 2
        11
        22
        An unhandled exception of type 'System.IndexOutOfRangeException'

7-16

```
using System;

public class RestaurantBill
{
  public static double TAX_RATE = 0.06;
  private double[] item;
  private double sum;
  private int numberOfItems;

  public RestaurantBill()
  {
    item = new double[20]; // Prediction: never more than 20 items
    sum = 0.0;
    numberOfItems = 0;
  }
```
```

```
public void Add(double anItem)
{
  item[numberOfItems] = anItem;
  sum+= anItem;
  numberOfItems++;
}

override public String ToString()
{
  String result = "===Restaurant Bill===\n";
  for (int index = 0; index < numberOfItems; index++)
    result += String.Format("{0}) {1:F2} {2}",
                             index+1, item[index], "\n");

  double tax = sum * 0.06;
  result += String.Format("Tax: {0:C} {1}", tax, "\n");
  result += String.Format("Total: {0:C} {1}", (sum + tax), "\n");

  return result;
}
}
```

7-17 (a) "SUSIE"
(b) "MIKEY"
(c) null, the default string value
(d) my_friends[10] is not part of the array. This generates an
IndexOutOfBoundsException.
(e) null. The find method is not yet working—it always returns null.
(f) null

7-18 The program terminates with IndexOutOfRangeException when the array index get to 10. There is nothing to stop the loop from incrementing index to more than the number of meaningful elements.

7-19 1

7-20 4

7-21 n

7-22 0 Short circuit Boolean evaluation causes the loop test to become false before any comparisons are made

7-23
```
Size = 3
Elements = [One $21.00, Two $2.00, Three $2.99]
Size = 1
```

7-24 The message results in false and the collection is not changed.

7-25 The message results in false and the collection is not changed.

7-26 The message results in false and the collection is not changed.

7-27

```
AccountList accounts = new AccountList();
accounts.Add(new BankAccount("Marty", 100.00));
accounts.RemoveAccountWithID("Marty");
```

7-28   No, not in this collection class (maintaining order require a different remove algorithm

7-29   Advantage: Runs much faster, completing in fewer steps than a sequential search.
        Possible disadvantage: Harder to write the code for it correctly!

7-30   1,024; 512; 256; 128; 64; 32; 16; 8; 4; 2; 1 == 11

7-31   When first becomes greater than last.

7-32   Change the comparison from less than to greater than.
```
if (searchString.compareTo(str[mid]) > 0)
  last = mid - 1;
else
        first= mid + 1;  // ...
```

7-33   Ascending

7-34   The first element is swapped with itself.

7-35
```
int largest = x[0];
for( int j = 0; j < n; j++ )
if( x[j] > largest )
        largest = x[j];
```

7-36   Yes, as do all C# arrays.

7-37   12

7-38   0 through 2

7-39   0 through 3

7-40
```
for (int row = 0;  row < a.GetLength(0);  row++)
{
  for (int col = 0;  col < a.GetLength(1);  col++)
  {
    a[row, col] = 999;
  }
        }
```

7-41
```
for (row = 0;  row < a.GetLength(0); row++)
{
  for (col = 0; col < a.GetLength(1); col++)
  {
      Console.Write("{0,8}", a[row, col]);
  }
  Console.WriteLine();
        }
```

7-42   `double[,] sales = new double[10, 12];`

7-43   `double[,] sales = new double[12, 10];`

7-44   row

7-45   column

7-46
```
int sum = 0;
for (int r = 0; r < rows; r++)
{
```

```
        for (int c = 0; c < cols; c++)
          sum += t[r, c];
      }
      System.out.println("Sum = {0}", sum );
7-47  for (int r = 0; r < rows; r++)
      {
        int largest = t[r, 0];
        for (int c = 1; c < cols; c++)
        {
          if (t[r, c] > largest)
            largest = t[r, c];
        }
        Console.WriteLine("Largest in row {0} = {1}", r, largest);
      }
```

8-1 Streams can read data from files, network connections, the web, or straight from memory.

8-2 Peek returns -1 when a stream reader has no more data to read.

8-3 If Peek returned -1 initially before any data was even read, you could assume that the file was empty. (Note that an empty file is not the same thing as a non(e)xistent file; an empty file does exist but is 0 bytes long and has no contents!)

8-4 (a) Absolute: @"C:\Programs\Test\MyCode.cs", Relative: "MyCode.cs"

(b) Absolute: @"C:\Programs\Test\input\debug\data.txt", Relative: "debug\data.txt"

(c) Absolute: @"D:\WINNT\SYSTEM32\MSHTML.DLL", Relative: N/A

8-5
```
using System;
using System.IO;

class FirstLetter
{
  static void Main()
  {
    StreamReader reader = new StreamReader("input.dat");
    String message = "";
    while (reader.Peek() != -1)
    {
      String line = reader.ReadLine();
      message += line[0];
    }
    reader.Close();
    Console.WriteLine("Message: {0}", message);
  }
}
```

8-6 (a) 8 tokens: "Marty" "$12.50" "|" "Kate" "$50.00" "|" "Julie" "$20.56"

(b) 3 tokens: "Marty $12.50 " " Kate $50.00 " " Julie $20.56"

(c) 10 tokens: "Marty" "$12.50" "" "" "Kate" "$50.00" "" "" "Julie" "$20.56"

(d) 9 tokens: "Marty " "12" "50 " " Kate " "50" "00 " " Julie " "20" "56"

8-7
```
using System;
using System.IO;

class WriteFilesToScreen
{
  static void Main(String[] args)
  {
    foreach (String filename in args)
    {
      StreamReader reader = new StreamReader(filename);
      while (reader.Peek() != -1)
        Console.WriteLine(reader.ReadLine());
      reader.Close();
    }
  }
}
```

8-8
```
using System;

class WriteTree
{
  static void Main(String[] args)
  {
    String filename = args[0];
    String[] arr = filename.Split('\\');

    Console.WriteLine(arr[0]);
    String spacer = "";
    for (int index = 1; index < arr.Length; index++)
    {
      Console.WriteLine("{0}|", spacer);
      Console.WriteLine("{0}+-{1}", spacer, arr[index]);
      spacer += "   ";
    }
  }
}
```

8-9 Append a \n character to get around the lack of a WriteLine method; use string.Format to use a formatted string.

8-10 Make sure to call Close on the writer to finish the writing.

8-11
```
using System;
using System.IO;

class WriteReverse
{
  static void Main(String[] args)
  {
    StreamReader reader = new StreamReader(args[0]);
    StreamWriter writer = new StreamWriter(args[1]);
```

```
      while (reader.Peek() != -1)
      {
        String line = reader.ReadLine();
        String revLine = "";

        foreach (char c in line.ToCharArray())
          revLine = c + revLine;

        writer.Write(revLine + "\n");
      }
      writer.Close();
    }
  }
```

8-12 (a) DivideByZeroException

(b) FormatException (if user does not type a valid number), DivideByZeroException (if user types 0)

(c) NullReferenceException

(d) FileNotFoundException

8-13 using System;

```
class HandleArrayIndices
{
  static void Main()
  {
    String[] names = new String[] {"Jane", null, "Mary"};
    Console.Write("Index? ");

    try
    {
      int index = int.Parse(Console.ReadLine());
      Console.WriteLine(names[index].ToUpper());
    }
    catch (IndexOutOfRangeException)
    {
      Console.WriteLine("Index out of range");
    }
  }
}
```

8-14
```
bool validNumber = false;
double number = 0.0;
do
{
  Console.Write("Enter a number: ");
  try
  {
    number = double.Parse(Console.ReadLine());
    validNumber = true;
  }
```

```
      catch (FormatException)
      {
        Console.WriteLine("Invalid number, try again");
      }
    }
    while (!validNumber);

    Console.WriteLine("Valid number: {0}", number);
```

8-15
```
public static void TryIt(BankAccount arg)
{
  if (arg == null)
    throw new ArgumentException("The argument is null!");
  else
    Console.WriteLine(arg);
}
```

8-16
```
public bool Deposit(double amount)
{
  bool result = true;

  if (amount <= 0.00)
    throw new ArgumentException("Invalid amount");
  else
    balance = balance + amount;

  return result;
}

public bool Withdraw(double amount)
{
  bool result = true;

  if (amount > this.Balance || amount <= 0.00)
    throw new ArgumentException("Invalid amount");
  else
    balance = balance - amount;

  return result;
}
```

8-17 The high score list could be represented as an object, such as a `HighScoreList` object, then this object could be serialized to disk and deserialized between executions of the program.

8-18
```
DateTime dt1 = new DateTime(1981, 5, 8);
DateTime dt2 = new DateTime(1979, 9, 19);

FileStream stream = new FileStream("dates.dat", FileMode.Create);
BinaryFormatter formatter = new BinaryFormatter();
formatter.Serialize(stream, dt1);
formatter.Serialize(stream, dt2);
```

8-19
```
FileStream stream = new FileStream("dates.dat", FileMode.Open);
BinaryFormatter formatter = new BinaryFormatter();
DateTime dt1 = (DateTime)formatter.Deserialize(stream);
DateTime dt2 = (DateTime)formatter.Deserialize(stream);
```

9-1   1

9-2   3

9-3

9-4   10 | 8 | 6 | 4 | 2 |

9-5   2 | 4 | 6 | 8 | 10 |

9-6
```
public static void Backward(int high, int low)
{
   if (high >= low)
   {
      Console.Write("{0} ", high);
      Backward(high - 1, low);
   }
}
```

9-7   -3

9-8   1 + f(-1) = 1 + -1 = 0

9-9   3 + f(1) = 3 + 1 + f(-1) = 3 + 1 + -1 = 3

9-10   7 + f(5) = 7 + f(5) = 7 + 8 = 15

9-11   For all values >= 0, you would get infinite recursion.

9-12   true

9-13   false

9-14   +abc+

abc

a-b-c

abc

9-15
```
public static void PrintReverse(Object[] array, int last)
{
   if (last >= 0)
   {
      Console.Write("{0} ", array[last]);
      PrintReverse(array, last - 1);
   }
}
```

9-16
```
public static void PrintForward(Object[] array, int last)
{
   if (last >= 0)
   {
      PrintForward(array, last - 1);
      Console.Write("{0} ", array[last]);
   }
}
```

10-1   `MessageBox.Show(DateTime.Now.ToString());`

10-2   namespaces: `System.Windows.Forms`

classes: `Form, Application`

10-3
```
Button button = new Button();
button.Text = "Click me!";

Form window = new Form();        // Construct a Form object
window.Text = "My first GUI!";   // Set form properties
window.Controls.Add(button);     // add button to form
Application.Run(window);         // Show Form on screen
```

10-4   `DockStyle.Fill`

10-5
```
Button bt = new Button();
bt.Text = "Hello!";
bt.Left = 25;
bt.Top = 40;
bt.Width = 80;
bt.Height = 32;
myForm.Controls.Add(bt);
```

10-6
```
public void ShowRandomNumber(object o, EventArgs args)
{
   Random rand = new Random();
   MessageBox.Show(string.Format("{0}", rand.Next(10) + 1);
}
```

10-7   `okButton.Click += new EventHandler(ShowRandomNumber);`

10-8   (a) CheckBox   (b) RadioButton   (c) RadioButton   (d) CheckBox

10-9
```
public void MyHandler(object o, EventArgs args)
{
   if (myCheckBox.Checked)
      myForm.BackColor = Color.Red;
}

   . . .

myCheckBox.CheckedChanged += new EventHandler(MyHandler);
```

10-10   There are ten controls (counting the form itself) and four types of controls: `Form`, `Button`, `Label`, and `TextBox`.

10-11   A new label would need to be added to the form, and the text of this label would be set to the same string that is currently in the message box. Each time a transaction was made on an account, the label would need to be updated to reflect this.

Index

Symbols

Operators

    !=, 223

    %, 42, 43, 79

    &&, 241

    *, 44

    +, 118, 119, 120, 121, 133, 223

    ++ 46, 283

    -, 43

    --, 45, 46

    /, 42, 43, 47

    <, 402

    >, 402, 403

    ||, 242, 252

A

.NET, 21, 25, 28, 67, 79, 95, 96, 112, 154, 245, 458, 466, 469

abstract, 29

abstraction, 150, 151, 154, 168, 201

accessor method, 182

AccountList class, 380, 381, 382–383, 387–390, 430–431

address, 95, 115, 131, 145, 146, 202, 238, 492, 551–553

algorithm, 1, 7, 8, 9, 10, 13, 15, 16, 277, 302, 372, 376

algorithm walkthrough, 10, 399

algorithmic pattern, 8, 9, 16, 64, 226, 231, 248, 290, 292

alternative action, 8, 231–234, 261, 263

analysis, 1, 2, 3, 4

AnArrayOfAccounts, 354

anchor, 543

AnchorStyles, 537, 543, 544, 546

argument, 96, 102, 362–366, 370, 377, 382, 386

ArgumentException, 456, 458, 464, 465

ArithmeticException, 456

array, 341–344

    array element, 42, 343–359, 363–364, 371–372, 374–375, 377, 385, 388, 391, 393, 397–399, 402–403, 405, 407, 417, 419, 423, 427–428, 432, 463

    array initializer, 359, 360

    array processing, 351, 352, 370, 380, 404, 409, 428, 429

    column-by-column processing, 408

    row-by-row processing, 408, 415

ArrayList, 380

as keyword, 29

B

BankAccount, 96, 157, 212, 341, 343–344, 353, 354–355, 357–358, 360, 362

    Deposit method, 96, 98, 102–103

BankTeller, 560

base, 486–488, 490, 491, 496–497

base case, 483, 486–488, 490–491, 496, 497–505, 507–511, 516, 518, 521, 525–526

behavior, 34, 40, 45, 47, 66, 98, 115, 164, 179, 182,